THE SOCIOLOGY OF EDUCATION a sourcebook

edited by ROBERT R. BELL
and
HOLGER R. STUB

both of Temple University

Revised Edition · 1968

THE DORSEY PRESS   Homewood, Illinois
IRWIN-DORSEY LIMITED   Nobleton, Ontario

Revised Edition

First Printing, June, 1968

Library of Congress Catalog Card No. 68–23349

Printed in the United States of America

Preface

The academic discipline which studies the social nature of education both as an institution and as an integral part of the total society is the sociology of education. In comparison with other institutional subdivisions of sociology, the interest and research in this field has lagged. However, since the first edition of this sourcebook was published, the scope and content of research and writing in the sociology of education has greatly increased. The availability and pertinence of much of this recent work has allowed us to do a very substantial revision. Over two thirds of the articles in this volume were not published in the first edition. Moreover, a new section on *Higher Education* has been added. Most of the selections used are journal articles, but there are also some excerpts taken from books. Not all of the articles were written by professionally trained sociologists, but the different contributions are of a sociological nature and offer some insights into the social institution of education in the United States.

In the organization of the sourcebook we have stayed away from a common procedure found in many books of readings—the use of a large number of articles, usually condensed. Our assumption is that if an article warranted inclusion it should be presented in its entirety so that the student could see the nature and logic of it as a total piece of work.

An introduction for each of the sections was written with the aim of providing a broad and easily understood background for the readings that follow. We have refrained from the common practice of predigesting the articles for the student. The intent is that the articles can and should stand on their own with the student needing only a general introduction to the subject matter.

The sourcebook is divided into six sections. Part I: *Education and Social Change.* In this section we are concerned with the changing nature of education in American society, characterized by rapid social change. Part II: *Nonformal Aspects of Learning.* Here we direct the student to the many aspects of learning that are not a part of the formal educational system. Part III: *Social Class.* Attention is directed to the interrelationships between social stratification and formal education. Part IV: *The School as a Social System.* Here we bring in some of the formal and informal aspects of the school as a system of social relationships. Part V: *The Teacher.* In this section we look at the occupation of teacher as seen from within the profession, the school, and the community at large. Part VI: *Higher Education.* This final section is devoted to some of the sociological aspects of the structure of higher education.

The topic subdivision and the articles are an arbitrary choice of what is considered to be important in the sociology of education. There are many other important topics and articles not included in this book. We do not presume that our judgment will be shared by all others in the field. The choices were made on the basis of our own reading knowledge and experience in teaching courses in the sociology of education.

It is hoped that this book will meet some of the needs of sociology of education courses taught in many colleges and universities. This sourcebook may also be of value to a variety of different education courses that have, in part, a sociological orientation—for example, educational sociology and social foundations of education. The sourcebook was designed to be used either as a textbook, with the instructor supplementing other material, or in conjunction with a textbook of the instructor's choice.

We fully acknowledge our great debt to the authors of the articles that constitute most of the material presented. In addition, we wish to express our gratitude to our many friends and colleagues who have contributed, both formally and informally, to this project. Finally we are grateful to our wives, Phyllis L. Bell and Elin H. Stub, for their aid and forbearance.

Temple University   Holger R. Stub
Philadelphia, Pennsylvania   Robert R. Bell
May, 1968

Table of contents

Introduction   1

PART I
SOCIAL CHANGE AND EDUCATION   3

1. Two Problems in American Public Education, *Martin Trow*   8
2. The High School's Role in Adolescent Status Transition,
   John I. Kitsuse and Aaron V. Cicourel 44
3. Some Effects of Parochial School Education in America,
   Peter H. Rossi and Alice S. Rossi 53

PART II
NONFORMAL ASPECTS OF LEARNING 79

4. Socialization, *Harry M. Johnson* 83
5. Lower Class Negro Mothers' Aspirations for Their Children,
   Robert R. Bell 105
6. The Education of Organization Man, *William H. Whyte, Jr.* 115

PART III
SOCIAL CLASS 125

7. Education, Social Mobility, and Social Change in Four So-
   cieties, *Robert J. Havighurst* 129
8. Local Social Structure and Educational Selection, *Natalie
   Rogoff* 145
9. Social-Class Variations in the Teacher-Pupil Relationship,
   Howard S. Becker 155
10. Education and Status Ascription, *E. Digby Baltzell* 167

PART IV
THE SCHOOL AS A SOCIAL SYSTEM 183

11. The School as a Social Environment, *Edgar Z. Friedenberg* 186
12. The School Class as a Social System: Some of Its Functions
    in American Society, *Talcott Parsons* 199

13. Sponsored and Contest Mobility and the School System, *Ralph H. Turner* 219

14. Bureaucracy and Teachers' Sense of Power, *Gerald H. Moeller* 236

15. The Professional Prestige of Classroom Teachers: A Consequence of Organizational and Community Status, *Holger R. Stub* 251

PART V
THE TEACHER 269

16. The Teacher, *Alma S. Wittlin* 273

17. The Role of the Teacher in the Social Structure of the High School, *C. Wayne Gordon* 288

18. The Teacher in the Authority System of the Public School, *Howard S. Becker* 298

19. Docility, or Giving Teacher What She Wants, *Jules Henry* 310

20. Sociological Aspects of Professional Salaries in Education, *Edward Gross* 319

PART VI
HIGHER EDUCATION 329

21. A Social Theory of Intellectual Development, *Christian Bay* 333

22. The "Cooling-Out" Function in Higher Education, *Burton R. Clark* 362

23. Student Culture and Academic Effort, *Everett C. Hughes, Howard S. Becker, and Blanche Geer* 372

INDEXES

Author Index 389

Subject Index 395

Introduction

The sociology of education may be defined as a scientific analysis of a specific social institution. The word sociology denotes a body of theory and method that may be applied to the organization and behavior of any subdivision or institution of society. Sociology therefore refers to the particular scientific approach being used. Education refers to the particular subdivision or institution of society that is to be studied. Education is an institutional abstraction taken from society in the same manner that the family, politics, religion, etc. are selected by the sociologist for specific study. Therefore, education refers to the particular institution being studied.

The abstracting of an institution of society for purposes of study does not imply that it is a socially autonomous unit. For the sociologist there is a constant attempt to recognize the interrelationships of the institution being studied with the rest of society. For example, education is greatly affected by a number of social influences—by other institutions such as the family, by social and population changes, and by shifts and changes in the social psychological makeup of the overall American society. It is therefore imperative that the sociologist studying the field of education constantly relate to other elements of society.

The sociologist perceives the institution of education in a broader sense than has traditionally been the case with educators. The educator often places the major emphasis on the formal and structured aspects of education. In contrast, the sociologist defines education to include the formal and informal as well as the structured and unstructured elements. Generally speaking, the sociologist sees education as being almost synonymous with socialization. This means that the sociologist is interested in more than just the formal school system and what goes on within it. His attention is directed at the child in the home during the preschool years. Here the initial and most crucial learning takes place in an educational atmosphere that is usually pedagogically informal, unplanned, and often nonoriented. The sociologist is concerned with how such nonschool associations as the peer group affect the functioning of the child in the formal educational structure. He further recognizes and studies how such broad social influences as social class may be crucial elements in determining the attitudes that youngsters carry with them into the school system. All of the complex and interrelated elements of a highly dynamic society are of interest to the sociologist in studying American education. He must constantly be aware of the reciprocal nature between formal education and the rest of society. For example, to what extent does formal education affect, and how is it affected by, social change?

1

There has been a sociological interest in education for a number of years, but only recently has it been treated as an important subdivision of sociology.[1] The reasons for the limited interest on the part of sociologists are complicated. Few sociologists would deny the importance of education as an intrinsic part of society, but, nevertheless, there has been a resistance to entering this as a field of sociological specialty.[2] One of the reasons for this resistance has been the suspicion of, and even lack of intellectual respect for, education and educators. This may have been due in part to the academic insecurity of sociologists themselves. It may also represent, for sociologists, intellectual snobbishness and the need to feel superior to some academic group. Like the resistance to the study of the homosexual, because of the assumed danger of being labeled one, the sociologist may be resistant to the study of education because he is afraid of being labeled an educator. There is some evidence that the sociologist's resistance to the study of education is breaking down and that he is and will be making an increasingly greater contribution to the understanding of this important area of society.[3] This will continue to happen as long as there is the realization that merit, or lack of it, goes with the theory and method of scientific approach, rather than being inherent in the subject matter analyzed.

A part of the void left by sociology in failing to study education has been filled by educational sociology. Under the heading of educational sociology there has been some work of a definite sociological nature, but most of it falls into a wide variety of areas that have little or nothing to do with academic sociology. Educational sociologists have dealt with a wide spectrum of subjects ranging from specific curriculum planning to the creation of broad educational value systems. While this work may be of value and interest to the educator, it is not sociology. It would seem axiomatic that if there is to be development within a sociological framework of theory and method, it must be done by people with the special training of that field. It therefore follows that the sociology of education is the logical vehicle for a sociological contribution to an understanding of education, and that more sociologically trained persons are needed to work in this area. This can be argued not only for the scientific contribution to the understanding of education but also for the need the sociologist has of it to give him a better understanding of the total society in which he is basically interested.

---

[1] For a good historical discussion see Neal Gross, "The Sociology of Education," in Robert K. Merton and others, *Sociology Today* (New York: Basic Books, Inc., 1960), pp. 128–52.

[2] Gross, *op. cit.,* pp. 128–31.

[3] *Ibid.,* p. 129.

PART I

Education and

social change

American society can be characterized as highly dynamic. The amount and degree of change over the past hundred years has been very great. No one can reasonably predict if, or when, a slowdown in social change may take place. As one of the major institutions, education has been vitally affected by the dynamism of American society. The nature and scope of education in modern industrial societies has changed considerably in the recent past and may change even more rapidly in the near future. Some of the important changes and their effect on education will be discussed.

POPULATION CHANGE

The raw material of society is its population. The number and kinds of people comprising a society are of critical importance in determining the nature of the society and the educational institution that becomes a part of it. The basic elements of population change are birth, death, and migration. Some of the major population changes that have occurred in the United States during the past 100 years are: (1) an increase in the older population, due largely to social and scientific factors that have increased longevity; (2) a greater percentage of the population being female, because of increasingly greater life expectancy for women than for men; (3) a birth rate that decreased until the 1930's and then reversed itself for the next 30 years; (4) a decrease in the death rate, particularly in regard to infant mortality; and (5) large-scale migration from Europe, and in recent years an internal migration resulting in major population shifts within the

United States. These, plus other population factors, are both directly and indirectly related to changes in education.

An aging population places an increasing percentage of the population in the adult years and leads to a proportionately larger adult work force. Add to this the increasing number of women who have entered and are entering the adult work force, and it can be seen that young people are no longer occupationally needed to the extent they once were. Still another factor has been the extensive educational preparation for a larger number of occupations. It is sometimes difficult to determine whether the main function of extended formal education in regard to occupations is, from the point of view of societies' needs, preparatory or restraining.

There are some important relationships between the birth rate and broad socioeconomic factors. For example, birth rates go down during depressions and war and up during periods of prosperity and peace. These population factors have a direct influence on education in contemporary American society. The post–World War II birth rate boom has been high, creating an expanding youth base in the American population. This has led to a concern over educational facilities—though the concern has not always been strong enough to prod the American people into providing adequate educational facilities. The great increase of children due to the post–World War II birth increase created problems in elementary and secondary education, and is at present affecting the colleges and universities. An increasing population problem is particularly acute on the college level not only because of the numerically increasing youth population, but also because of the increasing percentage in the younger age groups going to college.[1]

Still another population factor since the end of World War II has been the ever-increasing suburban movement and the rapid emergence of a new type of housing community. Many of the new housing developments have special age characteristics. Often the bulk of the population is either infants or children and young to middle-aged adults. This creates an increasing need for more schools, but the community tax base is often limited because the income of parents has not reached its potential growth and because of limited industrial tax dollars due to an overbalance of residential land use.

Not quite as readily observed as population influence on education is the influence of education on population. A significant influence on the decreasing birth rate of the American population has been the awareness and application of greater rational control of fertility, which for most of man's history was assumed to be beyond rational control. Both the number and spacing of children has been greatly influenced by the increased education of the American society.[2] In general, the higher the education, the greater the willingness and ability to exert

---

[1] Robert J. Havighurst and Bernice L. Neugarten, *Society and Education* (Boston: Allyn and Bacon, Inc., 1957), p. 258.

[2] Arnold M. Rose, *Sociology* (New York: Alfred A. Knopf, 1956), p. 379.

control over family size. This tendency has been somewhat altered by the relatively high birth rate of the more highly educated strata of the population since 1946. But this may, to a great degree, be the result of high economic prosperity, and it may be predicted that any future depression will bring about a lowering of the birth rate in this group.

Education is also related to life expectancy.[3] In general, the higher the education, the greater the life expectancy. This is in part due to the less dangerous physical occupations that the more educated male enters. Even more important is the positive attitude in regard to preventive medical care. The better educated person frequently has a rational awareness of basic health needs and follows precautions that often insure better health and greater life expectancy. The school system, with its middle-class value stress, is committed to a program of encouraging and contributing to high health standards.

EXTENSION OF EDUCATION

Over the years the amount of time spent in formal education has shown a constant increase. For example, at age 17, in 1900, 6.4 percent had graduated from high school, but by 1964 the figure had increased to 76.3 percent.[4] Years of formal education have been added at both ends of the educational process, starting at an earlier age and extending to later years. This has not been an arbitrary decision made by professional educators but rather the result of broad demands made by society for more and different types of formal education.

High school graduation is rapidly becoming the norm for the American population and a college education increasingly common. Some of the social factors leading to this have been: (1) the need for more specialized and extensive education (or at least the assumption that this is needed); (2) the social emancipation of the female; (3) the extension of formal education to meet professional requirements; (4) an increasingly technological society with its related demands, and (5) the influence of the G.I. Bill. These were influences often initially external to education, but because of the interrelativeness of elements of society, they have had a great impact on formal education in the United States. Many of the past social demands have led to drastically changed college curriculums, determined often as a result of pragmatic needs. This can be illustrated by the steady decrease of the proportion of college students in the traditional liberal arts areas and the increase in such specialized divisions as engineering and business. Expansion and changing stresses on subject matter have characterized the upper levels of formal education.[5]

At the lower end of formal education the school has started to reach the child

---

[3] Jessie Bernard, *Social Problems at Midcentury* (New York: Dryden Press, 1957), p. 58.

[4] U.S. Bureau of the Census, *Statistical Abstract of the United States: 1967* (88th ed.; Washington, D.C.: U.S. Government Printing Office, 1967).

[5] Havighurst and Neugarten, *op. cit.,* pp. 251-57.

at younger ages. First was the advent of the kindergarten and later the nursery and even prenursery school. In many middle-class families a child may enter formal education, at least part-time, at age three or four. The earlier formal education of the child has been based to some degree on sound educational theory, but other factors have also been influential. For example, the increased number of women in the work force often leads to the lower levels of education providing "baby-sitting" facilities. Or it may be the desire of many parents to provide their children with an adequate peer environment because of the belief that this type of relationship is of great importance during the early years of childhood. For many parents and educators the early years of formal education are organized around the belief in extended social contacts with peers for a good personality development.

In recent years there has also been a great expansion in what might be called quasi-formal educational areas. I will mention only a few that would fall into this broad category. This can be illustrated at the upper end of education by the recent development of industrial "finishing schools" where the male graduate from college is prepared for his occupational specialty by the industrial organization he joins. There are also many structured lecture and discussion groups referred to as educational, covering a vast variety of interests and making a strong appeal to many middle-class people. Even many of the traditional play areas of children have taken on formalized educational overtones. For example, the organized structure of Little League baseball has replaced the unstructured sandlot variety of 30 years ago.

INCREASED EDUCATION OF WOMEN

There are still many illustrations of discrimination against the female in the work force, but over the years her position has constantly improved.[6] A woman can now enter many occupations closed to her in the past. But increased educational and occupational opportunities for women have not replaced their strong desire for and interest in marriage. It is significant that while American women have greater equality with men than ever before, they are nevertheless marrying at a very high rate.[7] The present-day pattern is to combine marriage and occupation, especially during the early and later years of marriage.[8]

The motivations for acquiring a formal education are often different for the male than for the female. Education for most men is the means of achieving occupational preparation that will lead to their adult work career. But for most women formal education is an end in itself, with a limited relationship to an occupational future. As a result, many colleges are today partially functioning

---

[6] Harry M. Johnson, *Sociology: A Systematic Introduction* (New York: Harcourt, Brace & Co., 1960), p. 237.

[7] Francis E. Merrill, *Courtship and Marriage* (New York: Henry Holt & Co., 1959), p. 3.

[8] *Ibid.*, pp. 241–43.

as matrimonial agencies, as finding a husband is the most important motive for many coeds. Many college girls select a curriculum that is not too demanding, that they enjoy, and that may offer some occupational security for the far distant future. Increasingly a favorite "premarriage major" for college girls is elementary education.

Many young, educated middle-class women are entering marriage and filling the roles of mother and wife in a very different way than did their mothers. An important factor in the changing role of mother and wife has been the increased formal education for the young women. There seems to be an attempt on the part of many well-educated mothers to "professionalize" their roles—that is, to relate their extended formal education to the role demands and fulfillment of marriage. They often have a general interest in school activities because they are both formally educated and as mothers have a strong interest in the education of their children. In recent years there has been a rapid increase in specialized types of education that the middle-class mother sees as important to the proper growth of her children. Piano and dancing lessons are illustrations. The mothers also often feel that they should actively participate in the many adult-supervised activities for children. This allows the mothers to partially apply their educational training and gives them at least some feeling of intellectual fulfillment.

There are other important social changes that will be discussed in later sections—for example, the importance of changes in the family and the changes in the overall learning process. The concept of social change is basic to sociological analysis because an understanding of contemporary society must be seen within a dynamic context. While formal education has to some extent been self-determined, to a greater extent it has been changed as a result of being a part of a highly changing society.

1. Two problems in American public education*

MARTIN TROW

TWO CONCEPTIONS OF EDUCATIONAL OPPORTUNITY

Social problems are social phenomena—patterns of behavior or belief or attitude—that some people who can make their voices heard think ought to be changed. Moreover, those who define a phenomenon as a "problem" usually see it as morally wrong, not merely as a technical difficulty in achieving some desired end. Thus a social problem changes not only with the prevalence or objective consequences of the social pattern so defined, but also with the size and importance of the groups concerned about it, and with the moral force of their condemnation of or concern with it. For example, the denial of civil rights to Negroes is a major social problem today in a way it was not 30 years ago, though the objective conditions of Southern Negroes were certainly worse then than today. On the other hand, "big city political machines" constitute less of a social problem today than during the first decade of this century, though there is no evidence of less civic corruption now than then. Problems become problems when they are authoritatively defined as problems; the objective conditions themselves, their prevalence and consequences, are only one, though an important one, of the elements entering into such a definition.

In American education, the central problems today are the education of the culturally deprived and the academic preparation of those going on to higher education. The first centers on the elementary school, the second on the high school. Most of the issues that are discussed and debated—the preparation and credentialing of teachers, the organization and content of the curriculum, the location of schools and the composition of their student bodies, and so forth—derive from one or the other of these concerns. Though they address themselves to what appear to be diametrically different kinds of students—the most and the least academically able—nevertheless both problems are generated at least in part by the same forces in American society and American education. Both reflect

---

*From: Howard S. Becker (ed.), *Social Problems: A Modern Approach* (New York: John Wiley & Sons, 1966), pp. 76–117.

8

the increased importance of formal education in our society. Both of them acquired their present urgency after World War II with the growth of mass higher education, broad changes in the occupational structure, and the revolution in the status of Negroes. Although the education of the urban slum child and the college preparatory student was certainly not worse after World War II than in the preceding decades, these other forces and developments outside education changed people's conceptions of the functions of schools, and thus also their notions of what constitutes an adequate or successful education, both for slum children and for those headed for college.

In both cases demands for reform arose outside the schools themselves. Pressure to strengthen the academic side of secondary education grew after World War II as the rapid expansion of college enrollments began to transform what had been for 50 years a system providing chiefly terminal secondary education into what was increasingly a system of college preparatory education. This development, in turn, created a growing body of parents concerned with their children's preparation for (and admission to) college. And these parents were (and are) the "attentive audience" for the growing numbers of academic men who mounted a sharp criticism of the quality of American secondary education.[1]

For the lower-class urban child, the demands came from Negro civil rights organizations and their growing numbers of white supporters. Perhaps most important, governmental agencies on the city and national level in the past decade have become increasingly concerned with the large numbers of poorly educated slum youth who are unemployed and in our economy unemployable, and who therefore constitute a danger to public order and a burden on local welfare agencies. These same governmental agencies are also sensitive to increasing political pressures to deal with this problem. In addition, the problem of school performance of Northern urban slum children assumed greater urgency with the increasingly widespread demands of Negro groups for the abolition or reduction of *de facto* school segregation. Quite apart from the merits of any specific proposal to change the racial ratios of urban schools, such demands force people both inside and outside of schools to consider the comparative school performance of white middle-class children and Negro lower-class children. And when the performance of Negro slum children is compared with that of white children in the same city, rather than with one another or with Negro schools in the South, the very wide discrepancies are seen as wrong, as a violation of new and stronger conceptions of equality of opportunity, as a condition which we must do something about, as indeed, a social problem.

Attacks on the problem of the secondary education of college preparatory students have centered almost exclusively on the school curriculum; teacher training; and new modes of instruction, such as programmed learning, designed to circumvent existing limitations of teachers and curricula. The education of

---

[1]See M. A. Trow, "The Second Transformation of American Secondary Education," *International Journal of Comparative Sociology*, 2, 2 (September 1961), pp. 144–66.

the culturally deprived has called forth a more varied set of proposals reflecting the wider range of factors thought to be involved in their poor academic performance and high dropout rates. The difference in the character of the attack on the two problems lies in the assessment of their social and psychological sources. For the college preparatory student, it is assumed, the question is not of his motivation; he would not be planning to attend college if he were not motivated in some degree to meet the requirements of the educational system. Nor is the question raised of the adequacy of his experience or his present environment; these are assumed to be sufficiently beneficent or supportive to allow him to be knocking on the doors of a college. By contrast, the difficulties of the culturally deprived child are seen as having manifold sources—in early socialization, family attitudes, peer group influences, class and racial segregation, teacher attitudes, inadequate or inappropriate counseling—as well as in the curriculum itself. Moreover, college-bound youngsters typically come from families that are more or less successful in managing their own lives and those of their children; the only "welfare" agency they are usually served by is the school system, and it is to the school system alone that reformers look in seeking ways of strengthening the intellectual and academic preparation of college-bound youngsters. By contrast, the parents of culturally deprived youth are typically, and almost by definition, unsuccessful in their efforts to steer their own lives, or to gain even a modest share of the available material goods, or economic, familial, or emotional stability and security. They are, typically, the objects of attention by many agencies engaged in social welfare, and the discussions of the plight of their children naturally turn to the assistance that all these and additional projected agencies, as well as the school, can offer.

Although the sources of their difficulties in school lie in race, class, and family, and their effects on early experience, almost all the discussion of the education of the slum children is directed toward improving their academic performance, reducing the numbers who drop out before graduation from high school, and increasing the numbers who qualify for better jobs or higher education. This may appear a narrow criterion of success; certainly there are other important qualities of mind or spirit that those concerned with this problem want to enhance. "The fullest capacity to fulfill one's own talents and abilities" is one way to describe the broader aim that appears to give proper recognition to a wider range of qualities than is defined by performance in school. And yet it is the criterion of school performance against which the suggested reforms and innovations are always assessed. This is in part because school performance is more easily assessed than are the more subtle human qualities of spontaneity, emotional maturity, freedom and creativity in work and in relations with others. But it is also because in our society intellectual and emotional growth usually reflect themselves in satisfactory school performance, and even more because our society makes it extremely difficult for these other qualities to emerge *unless* the individual has done at least moderately well in school. There are certainly many happy and productive people in our society whose school careers were not marked by any high academic distinction. Yet, at the extremes, and it is the extremes we are discussing here, a career of repeated failure in school and early dropout from school is an extremely poor foundation for a happy and productive adult life.

We may think of potential talents as the biological and genetic endowments of people, their inherent and latent capacities for acquiring and using knowledge and skills in the service of themselves and others. Realized talent is the capacity actually to do these things. In contemporary America, potential talents are not often realized unless they are developed and certified through formal education, and increasingly, through higher education. However intellectually well endowed a child may be by nature, he is not likely to show evidence of his talents without the training and opportunities that schooling affords. Potential talent that is not cultivated and certified in schools is rarely evidenced; and this is increasingly true as formal education becomes to an ever greater extent the prerequisite for occupations and other adult roles in which many of these talents can be evidenced. When high potential intelligence is not developed and certified in the schools, it is usually aborted or frustrated. Thus the realization of talent is, at least in its early phases, in large part a matter of achievement in schools. And the social forces that work for or against the realization of talent are very much the same forces that work for or against achievement in school.

The discussions of the culturally deprived and the academically ambitious both center on what they learn in school; in the former, the question is mainly of their capacities for learning as affected by forces both inside and outside the school; in the latter, the question centers on how their assumed capacities are focused and developed by their teachers and the curriculum. But the two sets of problems differ in another important respect, that is, in the conceptions of equality of opportunity that provide the moral force in their definition. With the culturally deprived, there is increasingly applied a "radical" conception of equality of opportunity, whereas in the demands for the reform and extension of college preparatory work, we see applied an older "liberal" conception of equality of opportunity.[2]

The "weaker" conception—the traditional liberal view of equality of opportunity—would reduce or remove all external handicaps of birth or poverty which interfere with the translation of intelligence into academic achievement and thus into social, political, or economic leadership. In this view, intelligence is largely genetically given and substantially fixed; the demand is that intelligent children of humble birth be given access to preparatory schools and universities if they can show they are able. It is this conception of equality which was the driving force behind the Education Act of 1944 in Britain, which for the first time

---

[2] See Anthony Crosland, *The Conservative Enemy* (London: Jonathan Cape, 1962), pp. 169–74. Crosland refers to these as "strong" and "weak" conceptions of equality of opportunity. Considering the enormous consequences of the "weak" conception and of its continuing strength and relevance to many educational problems, it seems preferable to use a term which stresses its roots in the liberal conception of society open to talent and self-help.

provided free secondary school places for all youth, as well as free places in the preparatory grammar schools for the academically able youth. It is also the conception that lies behind the stipends (or scholarships) awarded to nearly all students admitted to British universities, so that poor but able students will not be prevented from attending a university.

The radical conception of equality of opportunity sees intelligence as itself in large part achieved, and calls for equalizing the opportunities for gaining intelligence. This demand is also more radical in its implications, since it holds that intelligence has been determined to a large degree before the child ordinarily begins to attend school.[3] The policy implications of this doctrine are active measures to help the family with the intellectual growth of children and additional measures to supplement the family's efforts through what might be called "compensatory socialization." This conception thus leads to a commitment by public authorities to help the child acquire intelligence despite the family's indifference or even active opposition.

A growing part of the political and educational leadership in the United States is increasingly committed to the radical conception of equality of opportunity. (This was a central though obscured issue in the presidential election of 1964.) This marks a profound shift in the dominant conceptions of equality in America and in the public policies necessary to achieve that equality. It certainly was not Jefferson's conception of educational opportunity when he proposed to "sift the rubbish heap" for the few ablest youth of humble origins whom the state should aid in gaining secondary and higher education. It was not even the conception of equality of educational opportunity that underlay the establishment of the common school in America, or that led to the natural extension of that policy in the creation of a free universal and comprehensive system of secondary education between the Civil War and World War II. The comprehensive public high school and the growth of the junior college and of mass higher education today can be seen as the fullest expression of the liberal conception of equality of educational opportunity. They are based on the recognition that the more advanced the *nonselective* education that is provided, the more attenuated are the handicaps of humble birth for educational achievement. Thus the free comprehensive secondary school, like the relatively unselective junior colleges and state colleges today, give more and more time for native talents to demonstrate themselves and to qualify for still further education. This liberal conception recognizes that the poor but able child does start with handicaps; his family is less able to pay for his schooling or for the kinds of social and cultural experience which would enable him to compete successfully in the school against children from wealthier homes. It is assumed that if public schooling is free, easily accessible, and prolonged, these handicaps of birth become attenuated the longer the child remains in school.

---

[3] This view is finding increasing support in psychological research. See Benjamin S. Bloom, *Stability and Change in Human Characteristics* (New York: John Wiley & Sons, 1964).

But the assumptions on which these institutions have been built are only valid if the deficiency in the home is financial and cultural,[4] and not motivational or emotional. When these conditions are met or approximated—when, that is, ambition and intelligence are randomly distributed in the population—the poor but able and ambitious boy may need more time to translate his talents into achievement, using the school, the free public library, and so forth. But the society and the schools need do no more (and this is considerable) than to provide him with the time and the opportunities; his talents will reveal themselves even in the face of a culturally alien or impoverished home, indeed, even despite indifferent teaching and an obsolete curriculum.

Of course, the assumptions of the liberal concept of equality were never wholly or even substantially met in the United States; the poverty of the Irish, Italian, Polish, and Russian immigrants of the post–Civil War decades was a poverty not only of money but also of the resources for gaining intelligence. But those assumptions were close enough to being true, and the conditions of the immigrants close enough to the intellectual conditions and resources of native white Americans, so that the schools could be seen as providing opportunities for acquiring education and demonstrating intelligence, despite the handicaps of wealth, ethnic origin, or class.

There were in the writings of Dewey and his followers some hints of the stronger conception of equality of opportunity that is only now becoming dominant. They perceived that the urban slums did not provide children of the new immigrants with the intellectual and motivational resources that they remembered or imputed to the older small town and rural America. Many of their specific suggestions were aimed at generating in the school qualities of mind and interest that we could no longer assume were being created in the home or by the larger society. But these subtle and imaginative efforts to develop the intellectual and moral resources of slum children were not widely accepted by American public education. The elements of the Progressive doctrine which were accepted (often in debased and vulgarized form) were increased emphasis on the useful aspects of curriculum and de-emphasis of the traditional curriculum which, it was argued, was irrelevant to the great mass of students and beyond the attainments of most.[5] This selective adoption of Progressive teaching was also guided by a peculiar interpretation of the liberal conception of equality of educational opportunity, and led to an effort to reduce inequalities by bringing the content of public education within the reach of all. Broadly speaking, the stronger and earlier the emphasis on competitive academic achievement in the schools, the greater the weight of the home environment in academic achieve-

---

[4] "Cultural" in the sense of exposure to books, art, music, etc., rather than in the anthropologist's sense.

[5] See Lawrence A. Cremin, *The Transformation of the School* (New York: Alfred A. Knopf, 1961), and Richard Hofstadter, *Anti-Intellectualism in American Life* (New York: Alfred A. Knopf, 1963), pp. 299–390.

ment. Conversely, watering down the curriculum and reducing the element of academic achievement serve to reduce the initial competitive advantage of birth and home environment; and there was a broad if uneven movement of American education in that direction between the two world wars. By not teaching too much in high school, final educational placement could be further delayed, and relatively unselective colleges and universities provided to give still another chance to children who start with an initial disadvantage to realize their potential talents. Our system of comprehensive high schools, "open-door" colleges, extension courses, and adult education means that these chances are not closed at age eleven, sixteen, eighteen, or even later for those who possess some motivation to "improve themselves."

Although a renewed emphasis on academic work over the past decade has increased the competitive tone, and to some extent selective "tracking," in the schools, the rapid expansion of American higher education has prevented this tendency from increasing the competitive advantage of birth or breeding. Rather, by extending formal schooling for more people still longer, its net effect is probably to reduce those advantages still further. At the same time, it makes the penalties for not having gained much schooling more severe.

The increasingly widespread acceptance of the radical concept of equality of opportunity is closely related to the growing recognition of the lower-class urban Negro as a major social problem after World War II. Their rapidly growing numbers, the Negro "revolution" and the demands that it makes for better education in the North as well as the South, coupled with the growing body of evidence of the wide gap in the educational performance of white and Negro children in Northern cities—a gap which increases the longer they remain in school—have been a severe shock to the liberal conception of equality of educational opportunity and to the belief in the unreformed public school as the chief vehicle for the assimilation and mobility of new groups entering the society at the bottom. The system of public education has earned considerable respect for having apparently coped so well with the mass immigrations of the late nineteenth and early twentieth centuries. In the Northern cities the lower-class Negro immigrants from the South were the system's first highly visible failure (apart from Soviet successes in rocketry for which it was unfairly blamed).

We are now coming to recognize that the persistent effects of slavery, discrimination, degradation, and exploitation result in handicaps to lower-class Negro children more profound than, and in some ways qualitatively different from, those of the children of European immigrant groups.[6] The growing recognition of these facts, together with the traditional American view of education as a central instrument for the achievement of social ends, leads directly to the acceptance of the radical conception of its role in the provision of equality of opportunity, a commitment which requires the school to see itself not merely as

---

[6] See Stanley M. Elkins, *Slavery* (Chicago: University of Chicago Press, 1959).

the arena where talent *realizes* and then *reveals* itself, but as the place where indeed for some children talent will have to be *created* and *nurtured* against strong counterforces in the child, his home, the community, and the larger society. This stronger conception is by no means universally accepted as the guiding principle of public education, either in the general population or by all teachers and educators. It is more widely held where the problems of the Negro slum child are felt most acutely—that is, in the large Northern cities—and by educators and social scientists most aware of the inadequacies of the traditional role of the school in meeting the special problems and disabilities of the Negro slum child. The uneven acceptance of the new role of the school by different professional and lay groups is the source of both social and political problems, and of conflicts within and around education itself.

A basic difference between the liberal and the radical concepts of equality of educational opportunity is the demands they make on the school for the success of the student. Under the liberal concept, responsibility for the student's success or failure is placed largely on his own shoulders; although the quality of the school and the teachers is thought to have some bearing on the matter, the primary cause of success or failure in school is seen to be the student's own moral and intellectual resources. Under the radical concept the student's success or, more commonly, failure is seen as the failure of the school or teacher, a failure to create in the child the moral and intellectual resources that lead to academic success. This view of the matter, of course, makes much more severe demands on the educational system and underlies the new stronger calls for educational reforms and the search for ways to intervene effectively in the socialization of the child. The pressure for new modes of intervention arises, then, out of the application of the strong concept of educational opportunity to schools attended by "groups whose characteristics are those of poor ability, scanty knowledge, and low levels of motivation, at levels of deficiency far below those 'normally' encountered in dealing with the 'standard' American school population."[7]

Rossi suggests that "For the practitioner (in education) the answer to how to intervene in order to reduce the spread of differences in the general population is given largely through an understanding of the same mechanisms in which the social scientist has a more academic interest. Without understanding processes through which lower-class persons and Negroes maintain their characteristic differences from others it is not possible to make inroads into the problem."[8] Although this statement is broadly true, there are some important differences between the academic explanations of these differences and the practitioners' prescriptions for dealing with them. The social scientist's explanation of these differences necessarily puts heavy weight on historical and institutional forces—

---

[7]Peter Rossi, "The Challenge of Group Differences" (Chicago: National Opinion Research Center, mimeographed, 1964), p. 10.

[8]*Ibid.,* pp. 10–11.

including the nature and consequences of American slavery for the slaves and their descendants, the long-range effects of discrimination and prejudice, changes in the economy and the occupational structure, and so forth—which the schools can do nothing about. Conversely, the practitioners and those social scientists directly concerned with their problems are likely to focus in much more detail on the aspects of education that they can manipulate.

Without minimizing the importance of the fuller understanding of Negro and lower-class disabilities being gained by historians and students of American society, it may be useful to look briefly at some characteristics of the slum schools and culturally deprived children that can be linked to the trouble these children have in school and that might be modified. I can point here to only a fragment of a broader discussion of the problem of poor and ill-educated youth, much of which centers on the question of what can be done outside the school. This includes some of the work on juvenile delinquency and youth unemployment; indeed, much of the federal poverty program is oriented to the problems of school dropouts through measures for their support and training outside the school system.

Within the slum school, increasing attention has been given to the teachers it recruits and retains, and to their conceptions and stereotypes of the students they teach. These attitudes shape the expectations teachers hold of their students and the climate of the classroom. We see in these discussions the subtle interplay between the child's own intellectual and emotional handicaps, the culture of the slum school, and academic achievement. These discussions are informed by the "radical" conception of equality and lead to new diagnoses and new prescriptions.

THE SLUM SCHOOL AND THE CULTURE OF DEFEAT

The quality of instruction in the slum schools is obviously affected by the quality and character of the teachers. By and large, slum schools cannot attract or hold the more able and experienced teachers. With some notable exceptions whose numbers may now be growing, slum schools are staffed by new teachers who, because of lack of tenure and seniority, have to accept the least attractive posts, and by older teachers who have settled more or less comfortably into undemanding if not pleasant roles. As Becker notes, slum schools are for a variety of reasons less attractive to teachers than are middle-class schools; "it is typically the schools handling children of subordinate groups which are least desired, and teachers' careers tend to be structured in terms of movement away from such schools."[9] He continues:

> Such a pattern of movement means that the less desirable schools, those teachers want to avoid, get something less than an equal share of teaching

---

[9] Howard S. Becker, "Schools and Systems of Stratification," in A. H. Halsey, J. Floud, and C. A. Anderson, eds., *Education, Economy, and Society* (New York: Free Press of Glencoe, Inc., 1961), p. 99.

talent. At the least, it typically means that they do not get the experienced teachers, for experience is almost always a ticket to a better job, whether through the workings of a seniority system or through the greater bargaining power it provides in bidding for jobs. In Chicago, many lower-class Negro schools are staffed almost entirely by teachers fresh from training school, the only ones who cannot choose their assignments; as soon as they build up enough seniority to move, they go, to be replaced by a new batch of beginners. More generally, it is probably true that, whatever the qualities a school system wishes to reward in its teachers, those qualities can be effectively rewarded only by assignment to the more desired schools, so that disadvantaged groups, who require the most skilled and experienced teachers, get the opposite and something less than an equal chance to an education.[10]

Another author notes that "thirty-four out of a hundred teachers appointed to the borough of Manhattan do not accept appointment to the schools to which they have been assigned. Some selected schools have much higher rates."[11]

The teachers' conception of the slum school as unattractive and depressing rather than challenging has been reinforced by school administrators who have used assignment to these schools as a form of punishment for teachers. "It is no secret that in many cities across the country, the depressed areas have been the 'Siberia' of the local school system, and those who for a variety of reasons were to be disciplined were sent to these undesirable schools."[12]

The high turnover of teachers drains the slum schools of much teacher talent, experience, and vitality. Among those who remain, along with a dedicated minority, are many teachers whose conception of their job works against the education of their pupils. A study of teachers in ten public schools located in depressed areas of a large Northern city found that "while there were some outstanding exceptions . . . the overwhelming majority of these teachers and their supervisors rejected these children and looked upon them as inherently inferior. For most, the teachers indicated that they considered these children to be incapable of profiting from a normal curriculum. The children were seen as intellectually inferior and therefore not capable of learning."[13]

There is widespread agreement that, as Carl Marburger puts it, "teacher expectations have surprising impact on pupil-achievement."

[10]*Ibid.,* p. 100.

[11]Vernon F. Haubrich, "Teachers for Big-City Schools," in A. Harry Passow, ed., *Education in Depressed Areas* (New York: Teachers College Bureau of Publications, 1963), pp. 246–47. This difficulty of recruitment and high turnover in lower class or slum schools is common in many countries. In some countries it takes the form of reluctance to leave the cities and teach in the poorer and isolated rural areas, and as an eagerness to return to the cities when the chance arises. See, for example, Ministry of Education, *Half Our Future* (London: HMSO, 1963), pp. 22–23 and 245–49.

[12]Mel Ravitz, "The Role of the School in the Urban Setting," in Passow, ed., *op. cit.,* p. 19.

[13]Kenneth B. Clark, "Educational Stimulation of Racially Disadvantaged Children," in Passow, ed., *op. cit.,* p. 148.

The teacher who expects achievement, who has hope for the educability of his pupils, indeed conveys this through every nuance and subtlety of his behavior. The teacher who conveys hopelessness for the educability of his children usually does so without ever really verbalising such an attitude—at least, in front of his pupils . . . Certainly the expectations of the teacher for his pupils can determine, particularly in depressed-urban-area schools, the school survival or non-survival of the youth.[14]

If there is agreement on the importance of teacher expectations for pupil achievement, there is equally wide agreement that such expectations are commonly lacking. Many observers have identified the attitudes and stereotypes of teachers in slum schools as a major factor in the poor academic performance of children in those schools. As one observer notes,

> Not infrequently teachers, counselors, principals assigned to the depressed-area school have been people without any real concern for these children and with the common stereotype of them as children of low ability. As a result of this low estimate of potential, the self-fulfilling prophecy went into effect. The children were not encouraged to learn very much; the teacher expended little energy on anything but maintaining order and bemoaning her lot; as a consequence, the children fulfilled the low expectation, which in turn reinforced the original assumption to prove the teacher was right.[15]

The view of slum children as mostly incapable of learning held by many of their teachers is a stereotype charged as often with pity as with hostility. But it is no less crippling in its effects on the teacher's behavior and ultimately on the child. As Frank Riessman observes,

> Another subtle form of discrimination is patronisation in all its guises . . . The specific forms of patronisation are manifold; the tendency to talk down to the deprived child—to speak his language, to imitate his slang and speech inflection; the assumption that these children are lacking in intellectual curiosity and conceptual ability; the lowering of academic standards, and the failure to set high goals for the deprived; the too-quick taking for granted that they are not interested in learning.[16]

Many forces shape the attitudes and stereotypes that teachers hold about slum children. Their own social origins, typically lower-middle or upper working class, do not equip them to view with understanding or tolerance the lower-class norms and culture of the slum. Moreover, even if a beginning teacher in a slum school does not have these attitudes, he often finds them the dominant attitudes among the experienced teachers whom he may look to for guidance. One com-

---

[14] Carl L. Marburger, "Consideration for Educational Planning," in Passow, ed., *op. cit.,* p. 306.

[15] Mel Ravitz, in Passow, ed., *op. cit.,* pp. 19–20.

[16] Frank Riessman, *The Culturally Deprived Child* (New York: Harper & Bros., 1962), p. 22.

mentator suggests that it is probably just as well that the beginning teacher is immediately assigned a full teaching load and therefore "rarely sees his colleagues except for a brief nod in the corridors or for a few minutes of casual conversation in the cafeteria."

Even if there were time to confer seriously with his fellows it would probably be more debilitating than useful. In many lower-class schools, freer access to experienced teachers would simply shorten the time required for the beginner to water down his courses and to resign himself to drastically lowered aspirations of what youngsters can reasonably be expected to learn. The great majority of experienced slum school teachers seem to have grown wearily pessimistic and to have concluded that personal sanity requires coming to terms with the limitations of "reality."[17]

Shaeffer is describing what might be called "the culture of defeat," a set of attitudes shared by veteran teachers in slum schools, reinforced by bitter daily experience and serving to rationalize and justify classroom routines which they have evolved for dealing with (and surviving in) an unrewarding and difficult environment. Whether the new teacher encounters these attitudes immediately or in the course of time, they cannot but have great influence on how he or she views the task; they are, after all, the settled sentiments and approved practices of those whose survival in the slum school is itself the strongest testimony to success. And new teachers with higher goals than simple survival may find the older teacher not merely discouraging but actively hostile. Successful teaching in a slum school can be seen and felt as a distinct threat by an older group who have made their accommodations to its problems in other ways.

Reference to the culture of defeat in the slum schools should not obscure the real and discouraging difficulties encountered in teaching in them, nor should we ignore the devoted teachers who continue to struggle against those difficulties. But in many schools the teachers who have not surrendered to those difficulties are rare or isolated, and a beginning teacher with hopes as well as fears finds little support among his older colleagues for his plans and ideas. It would be difficult in any circumstances to sustain those hopes without support from one's peers; in the conditions of a slum school it is often close to impossible.

The improvement of teaching in the slum schools calls not only for changes in the curriculum, in teaching methods, and in materials, but also for an attack on the culture of defeat, and for the development of support for a teacher's own higher expectations of herself as well as of her pupils. Thus the director of a school improvement project in Detroit observes that "the involvement of an almost total staff, including administration, would seem then to be essential for innovation in curriculum, and for modification of behavior to insure truly effective teaching."[18] And he speaks of the necessity to reinforce continually the

---

[17] Robert J. Shaeffer, "The Recruitment and Training of Schoolmen," paper read at the Conference on Quality and Equality in Education, Princeton, N.J., December 1964.

[18] Carl L. Marburger, in Passow, ed., *op. cit.,* p. 307.

teachers' enthusiasm and hope for the educability of children in lower-class schools. One way to do that is to provide additional personnel and resources; another, proposed by Haubrich in describing the Hunter project, is for a teacher training institution to "adopt" one or more lower-class schools, and gradually increase the proportions of its trainees among the school personnel, with the school or department of education itself providing the continuing professional and psychological support for the students it places in its "adopted" schools.[19]

The attitudes of teachers toward lower-class pupils, and especially toward Negro children, are reinforced by the widespread use of IQ tests as measures of "inherent" intelligence. As Ravitz observes,

> We now recognize that it is no longer sufficient to rely on traditional IQ tests as measures of innate intelligence, learning ability, or creativity. Much evidence suggests not only that the test itself is the product of middle-class attitudes and values, but that many children who take such tests are wholly unfamiliar with both the materials of paper and pencil and the language patterns used. We are beginning to suspect that if some youngsters who do poorly on IQ tests were to function in their familiar environment, we might well see their performances improve. Finally, we are slowly coming to appreciate that the real damage of the IQ test is its subtle influence on the mind of the teacher. Teachers, often unconsciously, expect the level of performance from the child that his IQ test indicated, a practice which, taking into account the weaknesses and inadequacies of these tests, really doesn't give some children half a chance to succeed. Paradoxically, the teacher herself may be the greatest impediment to the child's successful learning experience.[20]

The uncritical use of IQ tests reinforces the widespread stereotype of lower-class children as unable to learn much by presenting what is really a measure of "achieved" intelligence as a measure of latent or potential intelligence. The test results thus justify lower levels of expectation and lower standards of instruction by providing other convenient explanations for the student's low level of performance.

IQ tests have been criticized in two different ways—first, as "unfair" to the lower-class child since they test skills and knowledge he is not likely to have by virtue of his class or ethnically conditioned culture and experience.[21] The other criticism is more fundamental; the modes of thought, not merely the bits of knowledge and vocabulary, tested by IQ tests are themselves affected by the child's cultural background and by how he has been taught in school.[22] Vernon

---

[19] Vernon F. Haubrich, in Passow, ed., *op. cit.,* pp. 248 ff.

[20] Mel Ravitz, in Passow, ed., *op. cit.,* pp. 15–16.

[21] See K. Eells *et al., Intelligence and Cultural Differences* (Chicago: University of Chicago Press, 1951).

[22] See P. E. Vernon, *Intelligence and Attainment Tests* (London: University of London Press, 1960), and his "Pool of Ability," *Sociological Review Monograph No. 7,* University of Keele, October 1963, pp. 45–59.

asserts that "the provision of higher education is not so much dependent on, as capable itself of raising the IQ." He cites "Husén in Sweden and Lorge in America who have, in effect, followed up children who were of the same IQ level at the presecondary stage and found that those who obtained a full secondary and university education scored adult IQ's averaging some twelve points higher than those who left school at the earliest opportunity and obtained no further education."[23]

Verbal skills are a prerequisite for academic success; they can be gained through education, as Vernon and others observe, but in turn they also heavily condition the success of formal instruction. Children who are "linguistically deprived" on arrival in school do not learn to read easily and begin very early a career of relative but progressive academic failure. Intelligence tests, such as the one designed by Davis and Eells, which try to reduce the influence of class (or more accurately, of the cultural and intellectual climate of the home) on test performance must minimize the effects of verbal skills. But these authors, although denying the relation of verbal skills to "pure" or "potential" intelligence, do not deny the relation of the class-influenced verbal skills that "ordinary" IQ tests measure to later academic performance. Therefore, if we sidestep what is probably a sterile quest for a way to measure "pure" or potential intelligence, we may find it more profitable to consider the ways in which early experience affects the resources of language that a child brings to school.

In a series of papers, Basil Bernstein, an English social psychologist, has explored the culture and socialization patterns of English working-class families that lead to a relative impoverishment of the language of their children in ways that have marked consequences for their formal education.[24] Bernstein's studies of English working-class children have relevance for American lower-class children as well, though the patterns and problems he points to take somewhat different and more extreme forms among some of our minority ethnic and racial groups. He shows that in English working-class families the language by which parents communicate with their children is much less differentiated, personal, and qualified than it is in middle-class families, but the role of nonverbal communication is greater ("shut up" versus "will you kindly be quieter"). The working-class child is the object of short commands and simple statements directed largely to specific objects and familiar events. There is less emphasis on the relation of immediate action to distant consequences, and thus less concern with the logical and rational connections between means and ends. Where in the working-class home things simply *are,* in the middle-class home "objects in the present are not taken as given, but become centers of inquiry and starting points for relationships."[25] The result is to intensify the child's curiosity and reward his explorations. By contrast, in the working-class home "sustained curi-

---

[23] *Ibid.,* p. 48.

[24] Basil Bernstein, "Some Sociological Determinants of Perception: An Inquiry into Subcultural Differences," *British Journal of Sociology,* 1, 2 (June 1958), pp. 159–74.

[25] *Ibid.,* p. 165.

osity is not fostered or rewarded, as answers to questions rarely lead beyond the object or further than a simple statement about the object."[26] Correlatively, the absence in the language patterns of a relatively long time perspective organized in rational cause-effect terms makes more difficult the postponement of present pleasure for future gratification.

The poverty of language, the blunted curiosity, and the tendency to subordinate future to present gratification are familiar problems to all who have worked with or studied lower-class children. These characteristics of lower-class children are very heavy handicaps to them in school; as the Ausubels note, "Since schools place great emphasis on the learning of abstract relationships, and on the abstract use of language, lower-class children, on the average, experience much greater difficulty than middle-class children in mastering the curriculum."[27]

Many of the difficulties of lower-class children, including their language problems, can be traced to their attenuated relationships with their parents and other adults. Speaking of a group of first- and fifth-grade lower-class children, both white and Negro, Suzanne Keller is struck by how little attention is typically paid to them:

> There is clearly a lack of sustained interaction with adult members of their families. . . . Only about one-half, for example, regularly eat one meal with one or both parents, the rest either eat alone or with brothers and sisters only. This robs them of one of the important socializing and intellectually stimulating experiences of childhood. . . . Participation and interaction with significant others in an organized way helps shape the personality and sensitizes the participants to each other's needs and inclinations. Organized conversation helps shape the development of verbal facility and subtlety and determines a whole set of complex attitudes and feelings about the use of language. The family meal also serves as an acculturating agency, for, in their interaction, the members teach each other and develop a way of seeing themselves and the world in which they live.[28]

Keller sees the climate of indifference in the lower-class child's home as only one, though perhaps the central, element in a pattern of constricted experience and monotonous repetition of activities, dominated by television and by play with other children. "This constriction of experience and the poverty of the spirit it engenders may account for the below-normal IQ scores of this group of poor children by the time of the fifth grade . . . confirming countless other studies that have shown a similar scholastic and verbal inferiority for children from underprivileged environments."[29] It is noteworthy that the average IQs of

---

[26] *Ibid.,* p. 169.

[27] David P. Ausubel and Pearl Ausubel, "Ego Development Among Segregated Negro Children," in Passow, ed., *op. cit.,* p. 114.

[28] Suzanne Keller, "The Social World of the Urban Slum Child: Some Early Findings," *American Journal of Orthopsychiatry,* 33, 5 (October 1963), pp. 823–31.

[29] *Ibid.,* p. 829.

the group Keller studied were not merely low but also declined by some seven points between first and fifth grade.[30]

The social and psychological forces that handicap lower-class Negro children are generally found in extreme forms and with additional handicaps special to their condition. The Ausubels, who reviewed a large body of literature on the problem, point to a number of factors that inhibit the realization of potential talents of Negro youth.[31] Among these are (1) the high rates of family instability among Negroes, and the frequent absence of a father in the home; (2) the low self-esteem, flowing from the inferior caste status of Negroes, which, with confused feelings of hatred, both for themselves and others, is a major handicap to successful school performance; and (3) the greater and earlier freedom from parental supervision which Negro youth have in common with most lower-class whites and which makes for a precocious independence from the family, while greatly increasing the socializing influence of the peer group whose values are usually opposed to those of the school.

Behind these patterns of Negro American life lies the destructive effect of what may well have been the most degrading form of slavery in history, followed by a century which did little to modify and much to perpetuate the political, economic, and social subordination of the descendants of the slaves. Where early efforts were made to counter the results of slavery and subordination, their effects are clearly visible. Horace Mann Bond, after documenting the almost total absence of Negroes among winners and runners-up in the National Merit Scholarship contests, links this to the paucity of Negroes among the educated professional groups which supply a hugely disproportionate number of the National Merit Scholars. He then raises the interesting question of the social origins of those Negro Americans who have demonstrated high academic talent by earning a doctoral degree.

---

[30] The relative and often absolute deterioration of both achievement and measured intelligence of lower-class children during the years they are in school is gaining additional confirmation in many studies and situations. For example, a study done in England during the 1950s reports that, "At 11 years the average test scores made by children in the four social classes differ more widely than they did at eight. The two middle-class groups come closer together and move further away from the manual working-classes; this shows itself in intelligence tests as well as tests of school achievement" [J. W. B. Douglas, *The Home and the School* (London: MacGibbon and Kee, 1963), p. 46]. The combined and progressive effects of social origins and the social class composition of the school, both in primary and secondary schools, is shown in the Robbins Report, *Higher Education*, Appendix I (London: HMSO, Cmnd. 2154-I, 1963), pp. 46–50.

See also Patricia Sexton, *Education and Income* (New York: Viking Press, 1961), pp. 25–28; Allen H. Barton and David E. Wilder, "Research and Practice in the Teaching of Reading; A Progress Report," in Matthew B. Miles, ed., *Innovation in Education* (New York: Teachers College Bureau of Publications, 1964), p. 386, Table 10; and Martin Deutsch, "The Disadvantaged Child and the Learning Process," in Passow, ed., *op. cit.*, p. 165.

[31] See also Martin Deutsch and Bert Brown, "Social Influences in Negro-White Intelligence Differences," *Journal of Social Issues*, 20, 2 (1964), pp. 24–35; and the studies cited by Thomas F. Pettigrew, "Negro-American Personality; Why Isn't More Known," *Journal of Social Issues*, 20, 2 (1964), pp. 4–23.

When the childhood residences of the parents and grandparents of my doctoral sample are located on a map, they cluster in certain localities; and these localities are likely to coincide with what had been the locations, immediately after the Civil War, of mission schools founded by Northern missionary societies, and principally staffed by the inimitable Yankee schoolmarms, gently bred women, either from New England itself, or from New England families transplanted to the Western Reserve.

These women were available to teach former slaves because of the humanitarian zeal of the times; but also, because they represented, in their generation, a surplus of their class, when so many of the marriageable males had been killed in the War, or were adventuring far out on the Western frontier. For whatever reason, their availability and their devotion stand out unmistakeably on a spot-map of an emerging Negro intellectual elite, almost a century after they began their unsung labors among the Freedmen.

Among the lessons to be drawn from their work is that teachers in the best intellectual tradition may have a tremendous effect upon the most deprived of populations. The emancipation of women has now long since made other occupations perhaps too strong a competitor for modern prototypes of these inimitable carriers of academic and moral culture.[32]

Bond's findings are not only a very powerful rebuttal of assumptions about the inherent intellectual limitations of Negro children, a corrosive and self-defeating stereotype that persists, as we have seen, even among educators in our own time. But his observations and the historical experience of other ethnic groups which entered American society with at least some of the characteristics of Negro Americans suggest that the transformation of ethnic subcultures necessary for full participation in American society on equal terms may take several generations.

But in the changed moral and political climate of the United States, Negroes will not be satisfied with the prolonged gestation of talent in isolated communities that Bond describes. What is now demanded is more even than a very rapid extension of full social, political, and economic rights and opportunities for all Negroes, a demand flowing from the liberal conception of equality of opportunity for individuals. The more radical demand, flowing from the radical conception of equality of opportunity, is for interventions by the society to ensure that Negroes rapidly and as a *group* show distributions of achievement in all areas of life comparable to those of other groups in the population. The basis for this demand is that it is only equivalence of group distributions of performance that provides sure evidence of genuine equality of opportunity. These new and stronger claims (new in the sense that the older immigrant groups appealed to the liberal conception of equality and to individual achievement

---

[32] Horace Mann Bond, *The Search for Talent* (Cambridge, Mass.: Harvard University Press, 1959), p. 56.

rather than group distributions)[33] are made at a time when the concentration of great numbers of poor Negroes in the urban slum ghettos provides a very difficult environment for the compensatory socialization and education that is required. In addition, rapid transformation of the occupational structure is destroying the kinds of unskilled work on which immigrant families established a stable pattern of life, enabling children to develop their abilities and aspirations for more education and better occupations than their parents. Furthermore, the rapid development of mass higher education is increasingly making college attendance a mark of respectability as well as a prerequisite for a decent standard of living, at the same time that it draws out of the public schools the kinds of teachers Bond describes. Today the rate of social and economic change is much faster than it was a hundred years ago; the question is whether the efforts we are now making to transform social and educational conditions that stunt and deform the abilities of so many Negro (and other culturally deprived) children can have equally rapid effects.

THE "PROBLEM" OF AMERICAN SECONDARY EDUCATION: SOURCES AND RESPONSES

As I have suggested, current thought on the educational problems of slum children reflects an increasing application of a radical conception of equality of opportunity with its strong stimulus to the study (and manipulation) of the social sources of intelligence. By contrast, the critical discussions over the past decade of the academic quality of our schools, especially high schools, reflect the continuing power of the older, liberal conception of equality of opportunity. American mass higher education is the natural extension of this liberal conception of equality of educational opportunity. And a secondary system geared to the preparation of students for higher education, that is, a system much more concerned than our high schools have been with the quality of college preparatory work, is a corollary of the extension of higher education to a majority of college-age youth.

It may be useful to raise the question of why the quality of academic work in the schools came to be seen as an especially acute problem in the mid-1950s, as a problem calling for major educational reforms and innovations. It may also be useful to look at one of the forms the response to this "new" problem has taken: the widespread and rapid growth of interest in new technical and organizational forms of instruction. Finally, we want to consider very briefly how this specific response to the problem has been conditioned; first, by the way the educational problem has been defined; second, by the nature of American public

---

[33] Of course the older immigrant groups looked after the welfare of the group, through self-help societies, political pressure, and the like. But they did not claim group advancement as a right to be guaranteed by governmental agencies.

schools and their personnel; and third, by the values of the society in which it is put forward.[34]

The national discussion that has gone on in recent years about the quality of American public education is conventionally linked to the shock of the Soviet success in space exploration and rocketry, marked by its first successful satellite in 1956. Behind this, of course, lies the Cold War competition, a competition which generates worry about our pool of technically trained manpower and the relative merits of the Soviet and American school systems. But pressures for higher standards in American education would have developed even if the Soviets had not challenged us widely on scientific and military fronts. The more basic sources of the new emphasis on the content of public education lie elsewhere.[35]

They lie first in the character and development of American secondary education. In the 50 years between 1880 and 1930, the numbers of students in public high schools in the United States roughly doubled every decade, rising from 110,000 to nearly 4.5 million. The new secondary education that emerged during those years was shaped both by the enormous increase in the numbers of students and by their social characteristics. Many of the new students were in school unwillingly, in obedience to the new or more stringent state compulsory education laws; many came from poor, culturally impoverished homes and had modest vocational goals; many were the sons and daughters of recent immigrants and seemed to observers greatly in need of "Americanization." These new students posed new problems for secondary education; these problems, and the answers which they engendered, transformed public secondary education, its philosophy, and its curriculum.

The creation of a system of mass secondary education could not simply be the extension of the old elite secondary system; it was different in function (terminal rather than preparatory) and in organization (publicly rather than privately controlled). Moreover, it needed its own curriculum and its own teacher-training programs and institutions because the sheer number of secondary teachers required by mass secondary education was far beyond the capacities of the traditional colleges to supply.[36] In the old academies the principals and masters were college products and often went on to teach in the colleges; there was no sharp break between the academies and the colleges, since they taught similar subjects to the same kind of students. This was no longer possible with the new terminal public high school; the students were different and the curriculum was not, by and large, preparation for college. New departments of education and

---

[34] Much of the following is drawn from my essay on "American Education and the New Modes of Instruction" in Bruce J. Biddle and Peter H. Rossi, eds., *The Impact of New Communication Media on Education,* Chicago (Aldine Publishing Co., 1966).

[35] See Trow, "The Second Transformation of American Secondary Education," *op. cit.*

[36] The number of public high school teachers increased from about 20,000 in 1900 to over 200,000 in 1930. U.S. Office of Education, *Biennial Survey of Education, 1928–1930, Bulletin,* 20, 2 (1931), pp. 8–222.

state teachers colleges began to train the staffs of these new high schools.[37] These centers of professional education were not identified with the older, elite traditions of higher education, but created their own traditions of education for life, for citizenship, for useful tasks, the traditions, that is, of the mass democratic terminal secondary system that came to full flower between 1910 and 1940.[38]

Since the end of World War II, American higher education has been undergoing a very rapid expansion which in many ways resembles the growth of mass secondary education in the first half of the century. As recently as 1940 our colleges and universities enrolled only about 1.3 million students, who comprised about 15 percent of the college-age population, the eighteen- to twenty-one-year-olds. (The same proportion of the high school age group—the fourteen- to seventeen-year-olds—were enrolled in high school in 1910.) By 1965 the number earning credits in our colleges and universities was over five million. This fourfold increase resulted largely from rising rates of enrollment, since the college-age population was almost exactly as large in 1940 as in 1960. The difference is that whereas the college enrollments in 1940 comprised about 15 percent of the age group, in 1964 that figure was over 40 percent and increasing at an average of more than one percent a year.[39]

The growth in numbers will be even faster in the decades to come because, in addition to rising enrollment rates, the rise in birthrates after World War II is even now greatly increasing the pool of college-age youngsters. College enrollments in 1970, projected from present trends, will be over seven million.[40]

The growth of college going is transforming what has, for 60 years or more, been predominantly a system of mass terminal education into one that is increasingly asked to prepare large numbers, and even majorities, of students for college work. By 1962 well over half of all high school graduates went directly to some form of higher education, and in some parts of the country the proportion was

---

[37] On the upgrading of normal schools to the status of four-year state teachers colleges and the establishment of departments of education in other colleges and universities in the decades before 1920, see Benjamin W. Frazier, "History of the Professional Education of Teachers in the United States," and E. S. Evenden *et al.,* "Summary and Interpretations," U.S. Office of Education, *National Survey of Education Bulletin 1933,* 10, 5 and 6 (1935).

[38] During the first half of the present century, while many liberal arts colleges turned their backs on the problems of teacher education, legal requirements for certification were established in nearly all states. . . . While the liberal arts colleges were preoccupied with other things, while they ignored the problems of teacher education, a like-minded group of school administrators and other professional educators came to agreement among themselves on the necessity for professional preparation for teachers and transmitted their convictions into law. It was during this period that the educators became imbued with a new philosophy of education, one far removed from the academic traditions of the liberal arts colleges." Paul Woodring, *New Directions in Teacher Education* (New York: Fund for the Advancement of Education, 1957), p. 23. See also Merle L. Borrowman, *The Liberal and Technical in Teacher Education* (New York: Teachers College Bureau of Publications, 1956).

[39] American Council on Education, *Fact Book on Higher Education* (Washington, D.C., n.d.), p. 233.

[40] *Ibid.*

much higher.[41] Thus transformation is being imposed on the secondary schools by forces external to it.

In the course of this transformation the high schools find themselves confronted not only with a different kind of student but also with a different kind of parent. During the formative years of the mass terminal secondary system in the United States, the teachers and educators who were building the system were dealing by and large with parents who themselves had gone no further than grade school. These people, many of them immigrants or of rural origin, whose children were going no further than high school, had neither the competence nor the motivation to be greatly concerned with the high school curriculum. And the debates about secondary education were carried on largely over the heads of these parents, among the professionals themselves (and between the educators and sections of the academic community). But increasingly, secondary school people are dealing with educated parents of preparatory students, parents who possess both the competence and the direct motivation to be concerned with the character of their children's secondary education. As recently as 1940 three American adults in five had never been to high school, and only one in four had completed high school.[42] By 1960 three in five had been to high school, and over 40 percent were high school graduates.[43] By 1970 over 50 percent will be high school graduates, and by 1980 it is estimated that figure will reach 60 percent.[44] Parents who themselves have been through high school, many of them through some years of college as well, feel themselves more competent to pass judgment on the secondary education of their children and are less likely to accept on faith the professional recommendations of school administrators, educators, and counselors. It is this rapidly growing group of educated parents whose children are going on to college that provides both the audience and the support for the academic critics of the secondary school and its curriculum. There is every reason to believe that parental interest will grow as competition among their children for the better colleges heightens.

The increased numbers of students going on to college, the resulting heightened interest among academic men in primary and especially secondary education, the increasing concern with scientific and technological manpower as an element in national power and economic growth, the large and growing numbers of educationally competent parents—all of these and other forces have since World War II created pressures for the improvement of the quality of education. The responses to these pressures over the past decade have taken two distinct

---

[41] *Ibid.*, p. 253.

[42] See Donald J. Bogue, *The Population of the United States* (Glencoe, Ill.: The Free Press, 1959), Table 13–8, p. 343.

[43] Between 1940 and 1962 the average educational level of the whole American adult population rose from 8.7 to 11.9 years of schooling completed. See U.S. Bureau of the Census, *Current Population Reports,* Series P-20, Nos. 99 and 121 (1959), p. 5. See also Denis F. Johnston, "Educational Attainment of Workers, March, 1962," *Monthly Labor View,* Special Labor Force Report 30, May 1963.

[44] Bogue, *op. cit.,* Table 26–11, p. 779.

forms. One of these has been a variety of efforts to improve American education by working through the classroom teacher. Among these efforts has been the work, largely undertaken by college and university professors, to reshape the school curriculum, first in the sciences, and increasingly in foreign languages, English, and the social sciences, through the preparation of new syllabi, texts, and other teaching materials. All these efforts have been aimed at introducing new knowledge and conceptions into the classroom and bringing what is taught there closer to the academic disciplines as they are taught in colleges and universities. Along with these reforms in curriculum have gone efforts and proposals to strengthen the academic preparation of teachers, to ensure that they have been educated in what they teach and that they teach only what they know. Some states have revised credential requirements so that most new teachers must have a subject matter major. New and wider opportunities have been provided for older teachers to continue their education at National Science Foundation Summer Institutes. Working in the same direction, proposals have been made to reform teacher training to emphasize academic work and supervised teaching. Some schools and departments of education have tried to recruit better teachers by raising admissions requirements.[45] Not all these efforts can be attributed to the widespread concern about education that developed after World War II, but certainly the new climate of criticism has reinforced and accelerated these efforts. What they all have in common is that they are addressed to the education and training of the teachers.

The other major response to the pressures for strengthening the academic side of American education has been the enormous interest in and development of new technical and organizational forms of instruction, notably classroom television, teaching machines, and team teaching. They represent attempts to strengthen education not primarily through the teachers but, to a considerable extent, independently of them. These efforts are a product of the disparity between what it is widely felt needed to be done and the possibilities of doing it quickly by improving the performance of 1.5 million classroom teachers.

Efforts to raise the quality of education by strengthening the school curriculum and teacher training—that is, by raising the quality of the teacher's performance in the classroom—are agonizingly slow to take effect. They are slow partly because the enormous institutional complex, represented by the schools, departments of education, credential requirements, and the like, has great inertia and powers of resistance to innovation. The men and women who staff the teacher-training programs and lead the state departments of education and the state and

---

[45] On the reforms of the curriculum, see the essays in *The School Review,* 70, 1 (Spring 1962). Proposals and current projects looking toward the improvement of teacher education can be found in James D. Koerner, *The Miseducation of American Teachers* (Boston: Houghton Mifflin, 1963); James B. Conant, *The Education of American Teachers* (New York: McGraw-Hill, 1963); and Paul Woodring, *New Directions in Teacher Education, op. cit.* On programs of inservice education, keyed to curriculum reforms, see "Secondary School Curricular Areas," *The Bulletin of the National Association of Secondary School Principals,* 47, 286 (November 1963).

national educational associations are, by and large, the people (or students of the people) who with great dedication and devotion created the system of mass terminal secondary education, and who hold with almost religious fervor the values associated with terminal education, the values of education for life and for useful work that characterized American secondary education for 50 years or more. Many of them are less than enthusiastic about the new emphasis on academic performance and the changes it is bringing to the curriculum and to instructional methods. Commenting on a National Education Association report on new approaches to instruction, Fred Hechinger observes that:

> The startling fact—as one looks over the list of innovations covered by the report—is that few, if any, of the experiments were begun by public school educators or, having been started, welcomed by the rank and file. Team teaching, TV and the use of non-professional teacher aides appear to have sprung from Ford Foundation research; the mathematics reform movement was initiated by the Carnegie Corporation, the physics, chemistry and biology curriculum reform was born at the universities, and not predominantly at their schools of education.[46]

But over and above the inertia and resistances of teachers and educators, efforts to upgrade the curriculum and the education of teachers are slow to take effect because the academic qualifications and abilities of teachers are relatively low compared with other professional and college-educated groups.

Many high school teachers of academic subjects are inadequately prepared in the subjects they teach. A study conducted by the National Council of Teachers of English of over 7000 high school English teachers, whose average experience was nine years, reports that "only 50.5 percent had majored in English. One-third majored in a field with no relationship to English. Two-thirds rated themselves as poorly prepared to teach composition and oral skills, 90 percent said they were poorly prepared to teach reading, and almost 50 percent said they were poorly prepared to teach literature."[47] A national study of junior and senior high school science and mathematics teachers sponsored by the National Science Foundation in 1960 and 1961 concludes that "a teacher who has less than eighteen semester hours of college work in a science does not have a substantial education in it, and we have seen that two-thirds of the physics classes, a third of the chemistry classes, and more than a fifth of the biology classes and upper level mathematics classes (and over half of the junior high mathematics classes) are taught by such teachers."[48] The proportion of teachers with inade-

---

[46] See *New York Times* (Western Edition), October 16, 1963. One study done in Ohio in the early 1950s found that "teachers were more likely to resist significant curriculum change than either administrators, students, or parents." Cited in Ronald Urick and Jack R. Frymier, "Personalities, Teachers, and Curriculum Change," *Educational Leadership*, 21, 2 (November, 1963), p. 108.

[47] See *New York Times* (Western Edition), December 30, 1963.

[48] See *Secondary School Science and Mathematics Teachers: Characteristics and Teaching Loads* (National Science Foundation, Washington, D.C., 1963), p. 11.

quate preparation in these subjects is even higher than the proportion of classes taught by them.[49] A study by the U.S. Office of Education in three states in the late 1950s showed that 39 percent of the teachers in the study who were teaching one or more courses in high school mathematics had not studied the calculus or a more advanced course in mathematics, and 7 percent had studied no college mathematics at all.[50] At about the same time, 35 percent of California students in mathematics classes were being taught by teachers who had neither a major nor a minor in mathematics.[51]

With respect to abilities, the pattern of negative selection to teaching below the college level has been abundantly documented. The extensive studies done with national samples by the Educational Testing Service and others show that students who major in education score lowest on comprehensive tests of verbal and mathematical competence as compared with majors in almost every other field.[52] In a review of some sixteen studies of the ability of teacher education students, extending from 1928 to 1958, and in many different populations, North found without a single reversal that teacher education students were in general less able academically than other college students.[53] The negative selection to teaching is even more marked for men than for women, and this has special significance for college preparatory work in the high schools, where men comprise about half of all teachers.[54] Moreover, among those who go into education, there is a further negative selection of those remaining in classroom teaching. A follow-up study done in 1955 by Thorndike and Hagen of 10,000 Air Force cadets who had taken comprehensive aptitude tests during World War II shows that of all those who went into public school teaching after the war, "those who were academically more capable and talented tended to drop

[49] *Ibid.*, p. 8.

[50] See K. E. Brown and E. S. Obourne, *Qualifications and Teaching Loads of Mathematics and Science Teachers in Maryland, New Jersey, and Virginia*, Office of Education, Circular 575 (1959), Tables 20 and 22, p. 46.

[51] See J. A. Kershaw and Roland M. McKean, *Teacher Shortages and Salary Schedules* (New York: McGraw-Hill, 1962), Table 13, p. 91.

[52] See Henry Chauncy, "The Use of the Selective Service College Qualification Test on the Deferment of College Students," *Science*, 116, 3001 (July 4, 1952), p. 75; Dael Wolfe and Toby Oxtoby, "Distribution of Ability of Students Specializing in Different Fields," *Science*, 116, 3013 (September 26, 1952), pp. 311–14; and Dael Wolfe, *America's Resources of Specialized Talent* (New York: Harper & Bros., 1954), pp. 189–208.

[53] Robert D. North, "The Teacher Education Student: How Does He Compare Academically with Other College Students?" in NEA, National Commission on Teacher Education and Profession Standards, *The Education of Teachers: New Perspectives* (Washington, D.C.: 1958).

[54] North, reporting on the results of the 1956 College Qualification Test, which was administered to more than 24,000 freshmen in 37 colleges and universities across the country, notes that: "Norms for college freshmen in programs leading to the degree in education are given for a group of 274 men and 583 women. Comparison of these norms reveals that in the education group about 80 per cent of the men and about 60 per cent of the women had scores below average on the general norms. In contrast, only about 40 per cent of the freshmen in programs leading to the B.A. degree ranked in the lower half of the general norms" (*ibid.*, p. 283).

out of teaching and that those who remained as classroom teachers in the elementary and secondary schools were the less capable members of the original group." [55] Both the men who remained in education as administrators and those who had left education completely showed more ability on the Air Force tests of reading comprehension, arithmetic reasoning, and mathematics than did those who stayed in the classrooms.

The lower incomes of teachers, as compared with the incomes of school administrators, of men who leave education, and of most other occupations requiring a comparable amount of education, account for much of this unfortunate pattern of recruitment and retention of male teachers. Moreover, the relatively low status of teaching below the college level, which is both a cause and a consequence of the low salaries, also helps to explain why teaching attracts and holds too few of the most able men. And although teachers' salaries are rising, it is unlikely that the gross differentials in pay and prestige between high school teachers and other occupations requiring a college education are likely to be significantly narrowed in the near future. [56] On the contrary, there is reason to fear they may be widened. The continued extension of opportunities for higher education to able students, through public and private scholarships, the expansion of public higher education, and the like are offering to able young high school students a wider range of educational and occupational alternatives, many of which carry greater prestige and higher income than does teaching.

In the past a career in teaching was often the only intellectual occupation (aside from the ministry) open to serious young boys from farms and small towns; and the local normal schools or state teachers colleges were often the only educational avenues of mobility open to such boys. Able young men and women with academic interests are more likely to be drawn to schoolteaching when their opportunities are limited by poor or immigrant or rural backgrounds, by scarce employment, or by the difficulties or expense of getting a higher education in other than a teacher training institution. The able students whose horizons and aspirations were formerly bound by a local normal school now have wider opportunities and higher aspirations. This, together with the continued growth of the "intellectual occupations," is almost certain to make the competition for able men keener in the years to come. [57] Our society's demands

---

[55] R. L. Thorndike and Elizabeth Hagen, "Men Teachers and Ex-Teachers: Some Attitudes and Traits," *Teachers College Record,* 62, 4 (January 1961), p. 311.

[56] Over the six years between 1955–1956 and 1961–1962, the average salaries of all public school teachers, principals, and supervisors rose by 37 percent. But during the same period the salaries of college teachers in all ranks rose by about as much, and in most categories of institutions by more. From data in *Fact Book on Higher Education, op. cit.,* pp. 105, 106, 239.

[57] Between 1940 and 1950, "professional, technical and kindred workers," which is the census category for the occupations that require at least some part of a college education, rose from 7.5 percent of the labor force to almost 12 percent. In the decade 1950–1960 that category grew by 48 percent while the whole labor force was growing by only a little over 10 percent. It is estimated that the category is increasing during the 1960s by an additional 40 percent, from about 7.2 million to about 10.4 million. Stella P. Manor, "Geographic

for scientists, engineers, and technically trained people of all kinds appear insatiable, and the rewards for such work are usually considerably more generous than they are for schoolteaching. Of even greater importance, the very rapid expansion of higher education currently underway, and the enormous demands for college teachers that it creates, constitutes perhaps the strongest set of competitive opportunities for young men and women who want to teach. Junior colleges, in particular, draw a substantial proportion of their faculties directly from the high schools, and they get the more academically oriented teachers at that. The continued expansion of the colleges and junior colleges cannot help but impoverish the teaching staffs of high schools.

Substantial increases in pay for public school teachers may ameliorate, but are not likely to reverse, the pattern of recruitment of academically less able men to high school teaching. Thus, no matter how teacher education and secondary school curricula are reformed to strengthen the college preparatory function of the high schools, a substantial part of the actual teaching itself will be carried on by relatively poorly paid, low-status, and academically less able people. This may not have mattered so much when secondary education was largely terminal—at least it can be argued that qualities other than academic ability, for example, a deep interest in young people and skills in working with them, are more important for teachers of students whose interests are not academic or intellectual.[58] But this claim can hardly be made for teachers of college-bound youngsters whose success in college will rest very heavily on the knowledge and intellectual habits they acquire in secondary school.

Consider the lot of the high school teacher today, as described by Francis Keppel, then Commissioner of Education:

> In many cases, his salary and social status are still only slightly above those of an office worker. The public tends to consider him neither a scholar nor a man of affairs, but a compromise between the two who could probably succeed at neither. His working day, while theoretically short, is packed with teaching assignments, corridor patrol, or lunchroom supervision. His chances for advancement, either in rank or salary, are limited and usually require him to leave the classroom, where he is badly needed, to enter administration, which also has a shortage of qualified men.
>
> He has little academic stature compared even to the lowliest college instructor. His contacts with the main stream of American intellectual life are limited, if not non-existent. If he is conscientious, he may spend many after-hours correcting papers or preparing for future classes. More often,

---

Changes in U.S. Employment from 1950 to 1960," *Monthly Labor Review,* 86, 1 (January 1963), Table 4; U.S. Bureau of the Census, *Historical Statistics of the United States: Colonial Times to 1957* (Washington, D.C., 1960), p. 74, Table D72–122; *Fact Book on Higher Education, op. cit.,* p. 146.

[58] Although many critics argue that it is precisely the weaker students who need the most serious attention to academic subjects in secondary school. See the publications of the Council for Basic Education.

he will find that he has to pump gasoline at a filling station. During the summer, he frequently has to work at a non-teaching job rather than take additional studies that he can afford only by starving his family. The university courses he does take are likely to be chosen for their accessibility and economy (or for their effect on the salary schedule) rather than for their contribution to his knowledge in his teaching field. When he looks at the years ahead, he often sees a future of mediocrity and stagnation rather than one of achievement and challenge. The contrast to many other walks of life is all too evident. . . . Under these circumstances it is little wonder that the high schools have not attracted their proper share of able young men and women with a commitment to teaching. It is not surprising, either, that many new teachers come to their jobs with inadequate preparation either in academic knowledge or professional skill. Nor should we marvel that a discouragingly large proportion of the 67,000 who begin high school teaching each year soon leave it for greener fields.[59]

It is significant that this description is part of an article in which Keppel recommended programs which offer the master of arts in teaching to a relatively small number of very able students in elite colleges and universities, such as Harvard, Oberlin, and Reed. The graduates of the program, Keppel reports, seem to be "on the way to well-paid and responsible positions that make education an attractive career for the able and dedicated candidate."[60] It is clear that Keppel saw these programs as a way of recruiting considerably larger numbers of students from the strong selective undergraduate colleges which in the past had not "provided their fair share of potential teachers."[61] Much the same concern with improving the quality of education by recruiting relatively small numbers of highly able teachers who could occupy posts of special responsibility and reward lay behind Keppel's early interest in team teaching. He believed team teaching could offer genuinely able recruits (such as the products of the master of arts in teaching programs) a "career"—a hierarchical series of steps in teaching—comparable to that offered by other professions. As Keppel put it, "if the schools were organized in teaching teams, I could go to Amherst and say, 'You will start as an intern, and you can work up to Master Teacher—at a salary, I'd hope, of ten to twelve thousand dollars a year.' We have a million and a quarter teachers. I'm prepared to believe that the American people will pay ten to twelve thousand a year to two hundred thousand—but not to a million and a quarter."[62]

---

[59] Francis Keppel, "Masters of Arts in Teaching," in Paul Woodring and John Scanlon, eds., *American Education Today* (New York: McGraw-Hill, 1963), pp. 146–47. Mr. Keppel's predecessor as U.S. Commissioner of Education shares these concerns: "It is a national tragedy that the generality of our teachers are not fully qualified to assume the burden of responsibility that we must place upon them in the future. Many are lacking the native talent demanded by the art of teaching. Others in large numbers are inadequately prepared by general education or education in their teaching specialties." Sterling M. McMurrin, "A Crisis of Conscience," in Woodring and Scanlon, eds., *op. cit.*, p. 22.

[60] Keppel, *op. cit.*, p. 253.

[61] *Ibid.*, p. 248.

[62] Quoted in Martin Mayer, *The Schools* (New York: Harper & Bros., 1961), p. 388.

In a sense, all the new modes of instruction I have been discussing—programmed learning, classroom television, and team teaching—are efforts to use to best advantage the elite of talented and well-educated teachers that Keppel wants to recruit or identify. These innovations all involve the creation of a hierarchy of skill and reward among teachers, coupled with a division of labor and function aimed at increasing the educational impact of the minority of the ablest teachers—the most talented, energetic, committed, and academically well-grounded.

Stiles and Chandler make the connection between the new modes of instruction and the development of a hierarchy among teachers explicit:

> Urban schools in the future will offer multiple opportunities for professional service, specialization, and advancement. Although it is to be expected that guild organizations will exert persistent pressures to prevent the professionalization of teaching services in city systems, it is highly probable that differentiations will be developed in the quality and utilization of teaching competence that will permit outstanding teachers to be rewarded for professional competence and contributions. Examples of such recognition of quality teaching are already available in television teachers, instructional team leaders, and specialist teachers in some school systems. In the future, it is likely that the uniform scale salaries that educational guilds defend so vigorously will apply only to the lowest echelon of teaching. Others who prove their professional competence will be able to advance within the function of teaching to higher assignments that carry greater professional responsibility and greater financial rewards.[63]

Stiles and Chandler do not distinguish among the several new approaches to instruction by the elite groups they create within teaching; they refer rather casually to rewarding outstanding teachers who can "prove their professional competence." But teaching machines and classroom television differ from team teaching in this respect, which may partly account for the relatively easy acceptance of television and teaching machines by the schools, as compared with the spotty and slow progress of team teaching.[64] Teaching machines and television have built into them fairly clear technical skill criteria for differentiating among teachers. Moreover, the elite teachers, the programmers and television teachers, are rarely the classroom teacher's colleagues and do their work outside the teacher's own school. The "differentiation" between elite and ordinary teachers arising out of programming and television develops in the *occupation,* but typically not within any given *school.* By contrast, team teaching brings these

---

[63] Lindley J. Stiles and B. J. Chandler, "Urban Schools for the Future," in B. J. Chandler, Lindley J. Stiles, and John I. Kitsuse, *Education in Urban Society* (New York: Dodd, Mead, 1962), p. 260. See also Judson T. Shaplin, "Team Teaching," in Woodring and Scanlon, eds., *op. cit.,* pp. 214–15.

[64] The acceptance of television and teaching machines is also due in part to the vulnerability of school administrators to external demands for greater efficiency and higher productivity in education. See Raymond E. Callahan, *Education and the Cult of Efficiency* (Chicago: University of Chicago Press, 1962).

distinctions into the school, where the selection of the master teacher or team leader runs into all the difficulties involved in assessing the processes of classroom teaching. Teachers and their guild organizations are traditionally highly suspicious of efforts to differentiate among them on the basis of their abilities as teachers. We can see this attitude in the enormous resistance teachers put up to schemes for merit pay and the tendency to link pay differentials to criteria other than the invidious distinctions between better and poorer teachers—most commonly to seniority and credit hours in schools of education.[65]

All three of the new modes of instruction distinguish between elite and ordinary teachers, but compared with the visible technical skills of the machine programmer or television teacher, the distinction within a team of teachers is likely to be felt as illegitimate, invidious, and arbitrary, for the basis of the distinction is not a technical skill but merely somebody's judgment of how able one teacher is in relation to his peers. And it is not surprising that in some schools where team teaching has been introduced, the hierarchical principle has been successfully resisted; the teams, after a period of floundering, have "organized themselves as groups of subject-matter specialists or in patterns as close as possible to those prevailing in the self-contained classroom."[66]

THE IMPACT OF NEW MODES OF INSTRUCTION ON THE CLASSROOM AND PROFESSION

The impact of the new forms of instruction will be conditioned by the characteristics of the craft on which they impinge.[67] Among these characteristics are three of special importance: the indeterminacy of the teacher's product, the relatively low visibility of the teaching process, and the limited control teachers have over their working conditions.

The new forms of instruction modify, in their different ways, each of these characteristics of the teacher's job. They affect what teachers do, how they are related to one another, what rewards they can gain from their work, and ultimately, the kinds of people who will be recruited and retained in the classroom. Indeed, it is likely that an important source of the support for these new forms of instruction lies in their potential for reshaping the nature of instruction more directly and more drastically than is possible through the traditional efforts to improve the quality of the teachers themselves or their training.

---

[65] An NEA study done in 1960 showed that between 1938–1939 and 1958–1959, the proportion of large school districts studied having a merit pay plan in operation had fallen from 20.4 percent to 6.2 percent. Of the districts that had tried such a plan but had dropped it, a third reported that they had done so because of the difficulties of evaluating teachers, another third because the plans had created dissension among teachers. "Why Few School Systems Use Merit Ratings," *NEA Research Bulletin,* 39, 2 (May 1961), pp. 61–62.

[66] Mayer, *op. cit.,* p. 390.

[67] For a number of these ideas I am indebted to a penetrating essay by Dan C. Lortie, "Craftsman, Professional, Bureaucrat," Interpretation Project, AACTE Studies Committee (mimeographed, n.d.).

We generally recognize that it is extremely difficult to assess the effectiveness of the classroom teacher. Teaching aims to transmit bodies of knowledge, develop habits of logical inquiry and critical reflection, contribute to the child's psychological well-being, cultivate social responsibility and "good citizenship," encourage enduring interests—the list can be extended almost indefinitely. Many of these desired results are difficult if not impossible to measure; moreover, the teacher's impact is difficult to distinguish from all the other influences on the moral and intellectual development of the child. And finally, a teacher's most important effects on students may not be visible, and thus assignable, in the short run, but may bear fruit long after the student has left his classroom.

Coupled with the indeterminacy of his effectiveness is the relatively low visibility of his efforts. The teacher in his classroom is insulated both from the general public and from his fellow teachers and administrators. As Lortie notes, "The witnesses of a teacher's mastery of the processes of teaching are primarily legal minors whose testimony and judgment are somewhat suspect."[68] The process of teaching is invisible in another sense, in that it is obscured by all the other forces affecting learning. Even when we observe a teacher at work, the responsiveness or apathy of his students can rarely, with any confidence, be attributed to the teacher.

Nevertheless, teachers, like other craftsmen, seek and find rewards in their work. The societal rewards, in pay and prestige, are typically felt to be deficient. Moreover, as teachers recognize, these rewards cannot be closely linked to their effectiveness as teachers, in large part because of the indeterminacy of the product and the difficulties of assigning credit for success. Lortie's research leads him to suggest that, in their search for rewards in their work, teachers substitute "proximate, somewhat accessible goals for the ultimate goals stressed in the rhetoric of educational philosophy."

> The individual teacher works out his own definition of his desired product and monitors his performance in terms of that production definition. Since this process is undertaken individually (and largely without official sanction), it leads to a diversity of product definitions among teachers. One teacher will get his rewards of craft pride from seeing that his classes obtain a high average score on college board examinations where another will influence youngsters to choose teaching as a career.[69]

Although for some the rewards of raising the intellectual capacities, or academic performance, or career aspirations of their students will be central, for many their chief rewards lie in their ability to relate to students as persons. For these "their pleasure at indications that their students like and enjoy them, and the affective response they obtain"[70] is the chief pleasure they find in teaching, when their own dispositions, training, and the characteristics of their students

---

[68]*Ibid.,* pp. 9–10.

[69]*Ibid.,* p. 4.

[70]*Ibid.,* p. 20.

all work to reduce the rewards from the intellectual and academic content of the teaching itself.

The indeterminacy of the product and the invisibility of the process of teaching both increase the importance of the personal characteristics of teachers for the goals they set for themselves and the rewards they seek in the classroom. Insofar as these definitions of success are private, they are highly variable, affected very greatly by a teacher's temperament, intellectual ability and training, and history of intellectual success or failure. Many teachers have not themselves been liberally educated, nor have they enjoyed or done well in their academic careers. Such people are not likely to find their chief rewards in the intellectual growth of their students or to see their students' academic achievements as a major goal and an important criterion of their own success as teachers.[71] Nor, until recently, have such criteria been strongly urged and supported by school administrators and boards.

One function of educational philosophies is to shape and justify the product definitions of teachers. But the absence of any consensus among educational philosophers about the aims and priorities of education has diminished their influence on what the teachers themselves take to be important. Vulgarized versions of progressivism certainly helped to demolish the authority of the classical tradition but gave little support to the notion that the distinctive function of the schools is intellectual training.[72] Rather, these versions of "progressivism," most notably the life adjustment movement, tended to justify the private product definitions of teachers, especially those that minimized the importance of academic achievement.[73]

Underlying the widespread criticism of American education over the past decade is a mistrust of the private product definitions of teachers and of the educational philosophies, formal and implicit, which legitimate them. The new modes of instruction, reflecting this mistrust, insert themselves directly into the classroom and take the definition of the product out of the hands of the teachers (and to some extent out of the hands of professional educators), centralizing it and making it more visible.

Programmed learning, for example, focuses the student's attention on a body of material to be learned. A student attending to a program of instruction is not at that moment engaged in "interpersonal relations with the teacher," or in a group discussion whose character and direction are far more vulnerable to the teacher's notions of success and to his private search for gratification in his work. Insofar as the programs themselves are written by subject matter experts, their product definitions are introduced more directly and forcefully into the classroom than has heretofore been possible. (To an important extent, programmed instruction not only substitutes one set of definitions of success for

---

[71] See Edgar Z. Friedenberg, "The Gifted Student and His Enemies," *Commentary*, 33, 5 (May 1962), pp. 410–19.

[72] See Cremin, *op. cit.*

[73] See Hofstadter, *op. cit.*, pp. 299–390.

whatever set the teacher may have held, but by directing the teacher's as well as the student's attention to the program, may in fact modify the teacher's conceptions of desired outcomes, and thus his sources of intrinsic gratification in his work.)

Similarly with televised courses; television makes the teaching process widely visible,[74] and the televised teachers themselves more likely to be subject matter specialists, with aims closer to those of their counterparts in the colleges. It is true, as Lortie notes, that television could conceivably become an instrument of the individual teacher who uses it very much as teachers use films today, to supplement the teacher's own instruction and demonstration. But this, in his view, is unlikely:

> The high costs involved in equipment and technical personnel, however, make it more probable that television facilities and transmission will be centralized at the school system level or in larger units of cooperating systems. Under such circumstances, television will become a central office function and it is also likely that with time, it will lead to a specialized role of television instructor. Such television becomes an instrument for projecting the teaching of one teacher into many classrooms.[75]

The televised teacher is far from representative of teachers as a group, and is much closer in temperament, talent, and training to the models projected by the critics of contemporary education. He is more likely to have the grasp of the subject demanded by the curriculum reform groups, a sense of the structure of the discipline called for by Bruner, and the creativity and imagination in presentation admired by Mayer. Unworried by discipline problems, with time and resources for scholarly preparation unknown to the classroom teacher, and debarred from the rewards flowing from personal relationships with the students, the televised teacher, more nearly than the great majority of classroom teachers, can meet the demands for intellectual challenge and academic achievement that accompany the growth of mass higher education and the concomitant transformation of secondary education.[76] And similarly, the master teacher or team

---

[74] One observer has expressed concern precisely about the increased visibility of teaching by television, which he sees as inhibiting the presentation of controversial or original material. For this and other criticisms of televised teaching, see Richard Franko Goldman, "The Little-Read Schoolhouse," *Columbia University Forum,* 4, 1 (Winter 1961).

[75] Lortie, *op. cit.,* p. 23.

[76] However, some observers have doubts about the extent to which watching a master teacher on television will help the classroom teacher's own teaching effectiveness: "The television teacher often pitches his presentation above the level of the classroom teacher's competence, showing the latter at a disadvantage and exposing him or her to student questions that he cannot answer. This kind of embarrassment doesn't necessarily motivate improvement; rather it increases tensions and the fear of threat to the classroom teacher's authority. Resistance rather than learning may derive from this experience; the dynamics of the individual situation are not taken into account in the more optimistic predictions" [John Fritz, as reported by Lester Asheim, "A Survey of Informed Opinion on Television's Future Place in Education," *Educational Television: The Next Ten Years* (Stanford, Calif.: Institute for Communication Research, 1962), p. 27]. But we have very little knowledge of the effects of television on the classroom teachers, or how they deal with the problems which the master teachers on television create for them.

leader, at least in theory, will be a subject matter specialist, abreast of advanced work in his discipline.[77]

These new approaches to instruction are, each in its own way, a response to the pressures for upgrading the quality of American education in the face of the very considerable difficulties of raising the quality of performance of the great mass of American teachers. In addressing themselves to the technology and organization of production, rather than to the level of skill or effort of the individual workers, they represent a measure of rationalization of production which involves, at least to some degree, the transformation of a labor-intensive craft into a capital-intensive industry.[78] And in this respect these innovations represent the application to education of a characteristically American tendency to circumvent shortages of labor or skill by the more efficient utilization of what labor or skill is available.[79]

The "technological revolution" in education involves forces working both to raise and to lower the status of teachers. Where teaching remains a craft, where the skills, training, and abilities of classroom teachers are strengthened and cultivated more intensively, and where teachers are in control of the new technology of instruction, teaching will assume more of the characteristics of a profession and the teacher's activities will be governed more by professional norms, rules, and his own discretion than by orders from above. By contrast, where the new media come to play a major role in instruction, where they supplant rather than come under the authority of the classroom teacher, the teacher will have less and less the characteristics of a professional. In the short run this seems likely to be the more common tendency in elementary and high schools.

The more centralized and extensive the planning of instruction through the new media, the more important will be the planning and administrative staffs in city, county, and state departments of education. These staff people already rank higher in status and salary than classroom teachers. The gap will be widened, and these central staffs will come to include more people directly involved in teaching (as television or master teachers) or in developing instructional materials (programmers). But in addition to the widening of status differentials, the rationalization of instruction will centralize power as well. The classroom teacher now has relatively narrow discretion in the shaping of the curriculum and the choice of materials. The new media, if governed from above, will further narrow

---

[77] See Shaplin, *op. cit.*, pp. 211–17.

[78] An English economist, commenting on the use of teaching machines and television in American schools, observes: "In these and other experiments a complex procedure of replacing labour by machines to subdivide the teachers' tasks is proceeding just as it did in Adam Smith's pin factory. The unpleasantness of individual experiments to those of us more accustomed to the easier, more slipshod labour-intensive methods of ordinary education should not blind us to the historical trend which is inevitable in a society where capital is more abundant (relatively) than skills" [John Vaizey, *The Economics of Education* (London: Faber and Faber, 1962), p. 80].

[79] On the relation of scarcities of labor and skill to technological innovations in nineteenth-century America, see H. J. Habakkuk, *American and British Technology in the Nineteenth Century* (Cambridge: Cambridge University Press, 1962).

the scope of his discretion. By reducing the calls on him for other than routine skills and custodial functions, the new media will lower the status of the non-elite teacher.

In any event, the consequences of these innovations will certainly be greater than their intended effects on the quality of instruction. They are likely to affect the structure of the teaching profession, replacing a unitary status by a hierarchy of profession and status; they may affect the rewards of teaching by reducing the scope for private "product definitions" and by standardizing criteria of success; and ultimately they will affect the patterns of teacher recruitment by establishing within education different tracks for different groups and strata.

SUMMARY AND CONCLUSION

In this essay I have discussed, more illustratively than exhaustively, two broad "problems" faced by American education. One of these is the education of culturally deprived children; the other is the academic preparation of the growing numbers of students headed for colleges and universities. These problems have both similarities and differences.

In both cases the emergence of the problem was not associated with a worsening of the education of the groups in question; the education of culturally deprived and college-bound children was no worse (and almost certainly better) in 1955 than in 1925 or 1935.

In both cases the emergence of the problem was associated with changes in what was expected of the schools by large or influential groups outside the schools. The slum school, over the past decade, has come to be seen as the institution through which society can attempt to reduce in the children of slum dwellers the damage, emotional and intellectual, resulting from poverty and deprivations of many kinds in their homes. At the same time the high schools have come to be seen as preparatory schools for college, rather than as the termination of formal education.

The changes in the demands made on the schools reflected changes in the larger society which also created the attentive audiences for the critics who defined the problems and pressed the demands. The new demands on the slum school were part of a major change in the position of Negro Americans and were made by civil rights organizations, parents' organizations, and social scientists professionally interested in the social psychology of learning. These demands found support among public officials who were responsive both to the political pressures involved and to the social dangers posed by large numbers of school dropouts, for whom the economy was providing fewer and fewer jobs, who were creating major problems for police and welfare agencies, and whose potentialities for violence and crime constituted a major danger to urban life.

The new demands in academic education were voiced by the growing body of parents of college-bound children, by academic men increasingly aware of the inadequate preparation of many college students, by scientists concerned with the gulf between their subjects as taught in the colleges and as taught in the schools, and by public officials concerned with the quality of education and its bearing on national strength and our resources of skilled manpower in the context of a global competition with the Soviet Union.

The two conceptions of equality of opportunity which provided the moral force behind the new demands on the schools are different. For the culturally deprived, a radical conception demanded that the schools devise ways of strengthening the child's cognitive, intellectual, and motivational resources for dealing with formal schooling. For the college-bound student, the older liberal conception of equality of educational opportunity demanded that schools respond to the growth of higher education by improving the quality and content of their academic curriculum.

Action to meet the two defined problems, initiated to a considerable extent outside the educational profession, has been conditioned by the nature of the schools and their teaching and administrative staffs. The "culture of defeat" noted by so many observers as an obstacle to the education of the slum child has been especially difficult to modify. Other efforts are made to circumvent existing school routines and attitudes by extending and improving preschool education for slum children and by training ancillary and specialized personnel able to develop forms of education that supplement the ordinary curriculum and are designed to improve the child's chances of coping with the regular schoolwork.

In the problem of the high school and its academic program, the response has taken two forms: efforts to improve the skills and knowledge of the teachers themselves, and other efforts to improve teaching through measures relatively independent of the teachers' own abilities or limitations. Of these latter efforts, the technological innovations in instruction have met with less resistance in the schools than have such innovations as team teaching which modify the status and authority relations among teachers and administrators.

The progressive and meliorist values of American society, coupled with its rapid rate of social change, tend sooner or later to convert almost all aspects of national life into "problems," at least as defined by some. A "problem" implies reform, or change, and places established institutions and customary procedures in question. In education, demands for reform are made on the institutions of education and on their professional personnel. The clash between the forces for educational change and the relatively conservative educational institutions results in a very large number of educational innovations, such as the ones which attempt to circumvent the school and the teacher by reaching the child either before he enters school, outside of school, after he drops out of school, or directly through technical or organizational devices, during regular school hours. These efforts, and parallel efforts to reform the educational practices of the schools and teachers themselves, can be understood as attacks on the two problems under discussion. Their "solutions" will surely be marked by new educational problems, defined by new groups and audiences, reflecting other changes in the society and calling for further changes in the forms and functions of American education. Just as the educational philosophies, institutions, and practices which were the responses of yesterday's problems are themselves part of our current difficulties, so our present solutions will be seen as sources of the educational problems of the future.

2. The high school's role in adolescent status transition*

JOHN I. KITSUSE and AARON V. CICOUREL

The so-called "youth problem," together with the emerging "problem of the aged," are relatively recent by-products of industrial urban society. These two age groups combined represent almost 40 per cent of the total population in the United States.[1] In spite of their impressive numbers, they remain virtually unassimilated within the status organization of American society. Legally, socially, economically, and politically, their presence has been accommodated in a variety of ways. Yet culturally, neither youth nor the aged has been accorded a defined and recognized status within the society.

It is sociologically as well as culturally significant that as between these two age groups, one standing at the threshold and the other near the end of social competence, public interest and concern is largely focused on the youth problem. Politicians, public figures, educators, jurists frequently call attention to "youth offenders"; high-ranking military officials express concern about the "soft recruit" and often blame current educational philosophies and practices; social scientists research and analyze the "youth culture"; intellectuals express their analyses of youth problems through popular journals some of which devote entire special issues to "youth in America"; the channels of the mass media are filled with advice and caution for parents of youth.

What are the reasons for such intense interest and concern about the present youth population? Of course, the "young generation" as a subject of discussion and controversy is not novel. Adults have always been the jealous guardians of tradition and the critical arbiters of the young to whom social customs and controls must be relinquished. It is, however, precisely the confusion that surrounds the question of the content and validity of the tradition transmitted, and the relation of the young to it, that underlies the controversial spirit of the contemporary debate concerning the young.

---

*Reprinted by permission of Dodd, Mead & Company from *Education in Urban Society* by B. J. Chandler, Lindley J. Stiles, and John I. Kitsuse. Copyright © by Dodd, Mead & Company, Inc.
[1]United States Department of Commerce, *Statistical Abstract of the United States* (Washington, D.C.: U.S. Government Printing Office, 1961), p. 26.

SOCIALIZATION AND PLACEMENT OF ADOLESCENTS

Social continuity in human society requires that the young be prepared for and ultimately given a place in organized adult life. The degree to which the process of socialization and placement becomes a problem, as Margaret Mead has pointed out, is related to the social and cultural organization of particular societies.[2] The kind of society in which the transition of the young to adulthood is not considered a problem period, however, is fast disappearing under the impact of modern civilization, particularly in urban environments. Government, scientific, literary, and journalistic reports suggest that the industrialization of societies throughout the world characteristically produces, among other attendant problems, many that are related to youth. The behavioral manifestations of such problems may vary from society to society, but a common basis of all relates to the socialization and placement of the young in adult society.

In societies characterized by rapid social and cultural change, tradition provides few adult models for the young. The validity and relevance of the existing models are problematic, both as guides for adolescent conduct and as projections of the roles young people are expected to assume as adults. In such situations, the preparation of youth lacks the orientation of a clearly and confidently envisaged image of the society in which they are expected to take their place. Indeed, the fact that city parents rear their children under conditions of rapid social and cultural change is the crux of urban youth problems.

Social experience, like technical knowledge, acquires a dysfunctional burden of obsolescence. In consequence, urban youth, many of whom come from families who are recent migrants from rural areas, find themselves expected to adapt to the deteriorating or nonfunctioning social codes familiar to their parents. At the same time, they confront rapidly changing demands and temptations that the realities of growing metropolitan complexes present. Difference between the obsolete social experience of parents and the dynamic demands of a new and industrialized culture operate to compound the age-old conflict between parents and their adolescent sons and daughters.

Kingsley Davis has suggested that an invariant factor in parent-youth conflict is the decelerating rate of socialization as individuals grow older.[3] He has observed that the rate of socialization among adolescents is increasing rapidly while that of parents is in a period of deceleration. Thus, adolescents are not only much more exposed to social and cultural changes, but are also more responsive and adaptive to them than are their parents. It is true, of course, that parents possess a greater residue of experience. Such a legacy, which is always in process of becoming obsolete, becomes vulnerable in a rapidly changing society, being easily discredited by youth as inappropriate to the times. As a consequence, the voice of parents may lack confidence, or else it may become belligerently defi-

---

[2] Margaret Mead, *Coming of Age in Samoa* (New York: William Morrow & Co., 1928).
[3] Kingsley Davis, "The Sociology of Parent-Youth Conflicts," *American Sociological Review*, 1940, 5:523–34.

ant, in dealing with the young. Thus, parent-youth conflicts express problems of socialization as well as reflect the difficulties of social control.

The continual changes in forms and fashions of adolescent behavior present specific issues of contention for each generation of parents and youth. The intergenerational controversies are both public and private, with every man serving as an "expert," or at least a commentator on the scene. Adolescents, it is often charged, are indolent, wild, and undisciplined, concerned only with having a good time; they run with the crowd, pursuing every fad and fashion. The frequently uninhibited and bizarre quality of adolescent activities is interpreted as an indication of the degree to which adolescents are sociologically as well as psychologically "inaccessible" to the traditional agents of socialization.

The cogency and relevance of the myriad problems discussed by analysts of adolescence in contemporary society are not to be denied. Those who are confronted daily with responsibilities, official as well as personal, *vis-à-vis* adolescents, will attest to the reality of the phenomena described. It should be noted, however, that the "social problems" approach to the study of adolescence, or any other social phenomenon, tends to emphasize the breakdown of social controls and the degree of *anomie* which exists within the society. Attention is deflected from changes in various institutional areas of society which may represent emergent forms of integration and control of the problem in question. In American society, where the orientation to social change and control is characteristically rationalistic, the examination of institutional changes is particularly relevant.

In the following discussion, therefore, we shall consider some recent developments in one of the traditional institutions of socialization, namely, the school system. More specifically, we shall consider how the organizational activities of the high school order and control the adolescent status transition, and in turn how they generate a range of adolescent "types," "problems," and methods of treatment and control.

THE HIGH SCHOOL—HIGHWAY TO ADULTHOOD

Ruth Benedict, in a discussion of rites that mark the passage of individuals to adult status,[4] suggests that what we need to know about such rites is: What is identified in different cultures with the beginning of adulthood and what are their methods of admitting novitiates to the new status? In American society, the legal and political maturity of the individual is acknowledged when he reaches the age of twenty-one, but the acknowledgement of complete social competence is generally withheld until the individual becomes a full-time member of the labor force. Only then is he considered to have divested himself of his dependence upon parental support and to have acquired full adult social status.

The strategic and singular importance of the individual's occupation for his

---

[4] Ruth Benedict, "Continuities and Discontinuities of Cultural Conditioning," *Psychiatry* (May, 1939), pp. 161–67.

status, in American as well as other modern societies, has been documented by a large body of research.[5] The relevance of such findings to the present discussion is that one of the major social products of the adolescent status transition is the distribution of individuals within the occupational structure of society. In technologically advanced industrial societies, the degree of formal educational training determines largely the individual's placement in the occupational structure, and thus his social status.

The recent trend for students of lower-middle-class and working-class backgrounds to hold expectations for going to college represents one index of the degree to which college training is recognized as essential for access to occupational opportunities. Further evidence is found in the competition among college-bound youth for admission to prestige institutions of higher learning particularly, and to all colleges and universities as enrollment mushrooms beyond institutional capacities. Such developments emphasize, anew, the role secondary schools in the United States play in controlling and regulating access to higher education. We may ask, therefore, how the adolescent's status within the high school is related to policies and practices of the organization, and how that status affects the progress and outcome of his transition to adult society.

Compulsory education laws, which in most states prescribe school attendance until age sixteen, insure that each generation of youth will pass through the school system during its formative years. Thus, this institution plays a major role in determining the status of youth, in both school and community. Not only does the school shape the development of young people, it is the only agency that systematically assesses, records, and reports the progress adolescents make toward adulthood. Inasmuch as adolescents are excluded from equal participation in the social, economic, and political activities of the larger society, the school provides the only highway by which young people may make the journey to adulthood. As such, the school, particularly the high school, represents the only formally defined link between adolescent status and projected adult careers.

The importance of the high school as the major force in determining the status transitions of adolescents is increasing, particularly in urban situations in which youth are denied the traditional alternate route of work. For six or more hours a day, city boys and girls are socially and ecologically isolated in school where their performance and behavior are evaluated by teachers and school officials, by either implicitly or explicitly defined standards. In addition, school regulations and responsibilities typically control the time and activities of adolescents to a considerable degree during out-of-school hours. Those who characterize contemporary high school teenagers as indolent, carefree, and irresponsible creatures—not subject to the rigors of chores and helping with the family farm or business as were their predecessors of a generation or so past—underestimate the significance of this fact. Not only do the day-to-day school assignments impose limitations upon the time and energies of young people, but also the

---

[5]For a representative sample of this literature, see Reinhard Bendix and Seymour Lipset, eds., *Class, Status, and Power* (Glencoe, Ill.: Free Press, 1953).

school maintains a system of rewards and sanctions that influence adolescent behavior and hold undeniable consequences for postschool status.

As a consequence of compulsory attendance regulations, the school with which the adolescent and, consequently, his family are affiliated becomes one of the first institutions to which reports of misconduct are referred. The school, for example, is the agency to which police, shopkeepers, civic organizations, welfare agencies, and parents report on pupil behavior. In this strategic position as a coordinating agency between the activities of the family, peer groups, and various community institutions, the school frequently serves as a "clearing house" which receives and releases information concerning adolescents from and to other agencies including college admissions offices and prospective employers.[6] For this reason, if for no other, the organizational activities of the school are of more than incidental concern to adolescents, as even a limited number of interviews with students will reveal.

The range of the school's influence and authority has established it as the dominant institution in the control and socialization of students. The shift in the center of socialization from family to school dramatizes the degree to which the former has been eclipsed as the major matrix of adolescent experience and activities. The significance of this change, however, is not fully comprehended by the common summary statement that responsibility and authority have been delegated to the school. Implicit in the transfer to the school of the function of socialization is the judgment that the family is inadequate to the task of socializing the young in a complex urban society. Such a judgment relegates parents to the status of laymen in a world of specialists, a position which has made them the audience of every self-styled "expert" on matters pertaining to the control and socialization of their own children.

Traditionally, the authority and responsibility legally delegated to the schools have been interpreted as a mandate to "educate the young" in the broadest sense of that phrase. Accordingly, the school has undertaken the tasks of preparing its charges to become "responsible citizens," and "well-rounded personalities" as well as intellectually disciplined persons. The allocation of time and resources among these institutional tasks has long been the center of controversies concerning the legitimacy and effectiveness of educational policies and practices. In recent years, for example, the schools' emphasis upon the personal, emotional, and social development of students has been the target of criticism on the grounds that intellectual development is being neglected.

---

[6] In his introduction to Edgar Z. Friedenberg's *The Vanishing Adolescent* (Boston: Beacon Press, 1958, p. xii), David Riesman comments: "One new technique . . . has sprung up almost without anyone noticing: it is the dossier, the personnel folder which increasingly contains information on adjustment as well as on academic standing and the more obvious breaches of discipline." The author states that high school students are already quite aware of the threat by a teacher or guidance official that "this will go on your record," and is furious that the school has allowed itself to become, not only a sorting station for academic aptitude, but a monitor for conduct and personality as well; he feels that this contaminates whatever confidential relations might develop between students and staff.

THE TREND TOWARD BUREAUCRATIC METHODS

The so-called "crisis in education" precipitated by Soviet advances in education, science, and technology has intensified the criticism of school-organized and -sponsored group activities that are directed toward the development of "social skills." Such attitudes, it is claimed, result in the neglect and waste of "talent." The ensuing debate has launched a "search for talent" within high schools and sharpened the focus of organizational efforts to raise the academic achievement of students. The search for talent has led to the development and application of "scientific" techniques to identify talented students as well as bureaucratic methods to develop systematically the talent so identified.

The search for talent

American high schools, particularly those in college-oriented, middle-class urban areas, have employed educational specialists, revised curricula, instituted new teaching methods, and modified their organizational structures to implement their search for talent.[7] The cumulative academic records of each cohort of freshmen are reviewed and evaluated; the comments and recommendations of their teachers are examined; their past difficulties, personal and academic, are noted. A variety of aptitude and intelligence tests are administered to differentiate the exceptionally talented from those with lesser mental ability. Their performance is systematically analyzed to assess the degree to which the students' course grades are commensurate with their tested abilities.

The use of psychological tests and measures of "achievement" by schools to identify talented students has produced a population of youth who are described by school personnel as "academic problems." If test scores are interpreted to be measures of the student's innate ability, if course grades are considered a reliable measure of the development of that ability, and, further, if it is assumed that a given level of ability is correlated with a given level of coursework performance, i.e., course grades, then it follows that any discrepancy between test scores and course grades may be considered a consequence of an over- or under-utilization of ability. Thus, the use of the correlation between test scores and course grades as a measure of the development of talent produces, first of all, a distribution of students who are classified as "under-achievers," "over-achievers," and "normal-achievers."

Identification, classification, and treatment of academic problems

The identification of "academic problems" presents the school with the organizational task of reducing the "ability-achievement" discrepancy. In a bureau-

---

[7] The discussion and analysis of some consequences of the "search for talent" in contemporary high schools are based on our study of an American high school which is widely regarded as among the best institutions in the nation.

cratic system such as the metropolitan comprehensive high school, a classification system explicitly contains procedural rules for processing persons or "cases" so classified. The logical implications of the "academic" classification of students is that, with the exception of the "normal-achiever," its use identifies "problems" for the school system, problems that may not be recognized or acknowledged by the students who are conceived to "have" them by the school personnel. "Under-achievers" and "over-achievers" present organizational problems in that they represent the under- and over-utilization and development of "talent." So conceived, the organizational problem becomes one of *inducing* or *reducing* the motivation of students to develop their talent. The effectiveness of the organizational methods used to meet this problem is measured by the degree to which the discrepancy between ability and achievement is minimized.

The conception of the discrepancy between test scores and course-work performance as a problem of motivation has important consequences for the organizational activities of the high school and the processing of students within it. The school is confronted with the task not only of identifying and developing the talent, but also of motivating it. Thus, the motivational interpretation of "academic problems" has paved the way for remedial methods that are couched primarily in social and psychological, rather than educational, terms.

In the organizational effort to raise the achievement level of its students, the counseling and guidance service has assumed a particularly significant role. Counselors, as specialists in the diagnosis, interpretation, and treatment of "adolescent problems," have been assigned the responsibility of monitoring the student's academic progress. They counsel him on the various difficulties he encounters in meeting the level of achievement expected of him by school personnel, as well as by his parents, his peers, and himself. Through their professional training, counselors have been alerted to motivational factors which affect academic achievement — "emotional immaturity," rebellion against authority, family conflicts, and other difficulties.

The terms in which the diagnosis is phrased suggest the nature of the remedy. If "academic problems" are conceived by counselors to be products of "over-" or "under-" motivation, and if the sources of motivation are social and psychological in nature, then "academic problems" may be viewed as symptoms of personal problems. Thus, the failure of a "high-ability" student to achieve in the classroom may be interpreted by the counselor as an indication of his "resistance to authority" rather than simply a consequence of his failure to do the assigned homework. The motivational problem is conceived to lie "beneath" his failure to do the assigned work. On the other hand, the "over-achiever," who is somewhat of an anomaly in the "search for talent," is "driven" by parental pressure and so strongly motivated that he stands in danger of social and psychological "maladjustment."

The relevance of the motivational interpretation of "academic problems" for the organization and control of the adolescent status transition is that students who are conceived to "have" such problems become the objects of an organizational effort to "solve" them. The student is summoned by the counselor and encouraged to discuss his "difficulty": "Is anything bothering you?" "How is everything at home?" "Do you get along all right with your friends?" In the case of an "over-achiever," for example, the counselor may decide that although his course grades indicate that "he can do the work," the student is too "nervous and anxious" to be placed in the "highly competitive" honors courses. The counselors may also confer with the teachers of the classes to which the student is assigned in order to inform them of the student's "situation." Special attention may be given to "integrating" the student in group activities to facilitate a more "healthy adjustment" to his peer group. The student's parents may be advised of his "difficulties" and requested to confer with the counselor and teachers to "work out a program for him at home."

The coordination of organizational actions with reference to the treatment of "academic problems" may foreclose alternative interpretations of the so-called problem, sharply reduce the alternative ways for the student to relate himself to it, and impose an identity upon him. Such solicitous treatment may be sufficiently rewarding to the student to lead him to accept the status imposed upon him, and he may more than fulfill the counselor's prophecy.

THE NEED FOR PSYCHOSOCIAL MORATORIUMS FOR YOUTH

In a discussion of the social psychological corollary of the adolescent status transition, Erik H. Erikson observes that as individuals approach the status of adulthood, societies provide psychosocial moratoriums in varying forms and duration, i.e., a period that institutionally sanctions "a delay of adult commitments, and yet not only a delay . . . a period that is characterized by a selective permissiveness on the part of society and of provocative playfulness on the part of youth; and yet also a period of deep (if often transitory) commitment on the part of youth, and ceremonial acceptance of commitment on the part of society."[8]

If contemporary adolescence is a period of mindless fun and games, the demands of future adulthood are progressively intruding upon the adolescing of youth and foreshortening the psychosocial moratorium. In the less psychologistic era of the past, an adolescent was allowed a period of erratic confusions, self-doubt, and despair as a normal manifestation of his transition to adulthood. Such an adolescent, as Edgar Z. Friedenberg has observed, is vanishing from the American scene. The contemporary schools have developed and legitimized a system by which a wide range of information—medical, psychological, personal, and social, as well as academic—about students may be obtained, interpreted, and recorded. School personnel, according to David Riesman, are able to ". . . find out more about youngsters than previous generations of teachers had time for, cared about, or knew about it." The increasingly organized efforts to use such

---

[8] Erik H. Erikson, "The Problem of Identity," mimeographed, 1956, p. 16; see also *Childhood and Society* (New York: W. W. Norton & Co., 1950), chap. 7.

information to guide, counsel, and solicitously "adjust" the adolescent into adulthood may impose an identity upon him by organizing the expectations of teachers, parents, and others in their interactions with him as an adolescent "with problems."

In this regard, the following statement by Friedenberg deserves thoughtful consideration by all who propose or seek a "solution" to the "youth problem":

> Adolescence is not simply a physical process; there is more to it than sexual maturation. It is also—and primarily—a social process, whose fundamental task is clear and stable self-identification. . . . This process may be frustrated and emptied of meaning in a society which, like our own, is hostile to clarity and vividness. Our culture impedes the clear definition of any faithful self-image—indeed, of any clear image whatsoever. We do not break images; there are few iconoclasts among us. Instead, we blur and soften them. The resulting pliability gives life in our society its familiar, plastic texture. It also makes adolescence more difficult, more dangerous, and more troublesome to the adolescent and to society itself. And it makes adolescence rarer. Few youngsters really dare to go through with it; they merely undergo puberty and simulate maturity.[9]

If the "highly developed" comprehensive urban high school which we have described is, in fact, a model of the high schools of the future, it is pertinent to consider the consequences of the continuous flow of each generation of adolescents through this organizationally controlled system for the socialization of adolescents. Our analysis, in contrast to the widely held view of adolescent socialization as institutionally unorganized and uncontrolled, suggests that it is becoming increasingly bureaucratized by the activities of the high school. The products of such a system of control may prove to be a more rigidly conformist population of adults than those of the much maligned adolescent peer groups.

---

[9] Friedenberg, *op. cit.,* p. 2.

3. Some effects of parochial
school education in America*

PETER H. ROSSI and ALICE S. ROSSI

INTRODUCTION

The most popular conception of American material well-being sees the great wealth of this country primarily as being poured into the hectic consumption of a glittering variety of chrome-trimmed conveniences and high-calorie foods. While there is some truth in this conception, as there is in any stereotype, the high national income manifests itself in a number of ways. Quite impressive are the numbers of voluntarily supported religious and educational institutions, privately financed community services, and private public health organizations. America's better universities (and some of its worse) exist on private bounty, past and present, despite the fact that state governments provide inexpensive and generally good higher education in state universities.

Americans also maintain what is undoubtedly the largest privately financed elementary school system: the denominational schools of the Roman Catholic Church. On a smaller scale, other denominations, notably the Evangelical Lutheran Church (the Missouri Synod), also maintain private elementary schools. At present some six and a half million pupils are enrolled in the denominational schools in this country, constituting approximately fifteen per cent of the total elementary school population.[1] Of these six and a half million, approximately 85 per cent, or five and a half million, are enrolled in the parochial schools of the Roman Catholic Church.

Privately financed denominational elementary schools paralleling an excellent state financed system can be found in other countries, e.g., France, but the unique characteristic of the American denominational schools is their attempt to provide education on a mass basis. In France, for example, Church schools primarily serve the upper classes. In contrast, our parochial schools recruit their pupils from all levels of society. These are not schools for the elite and primarily

*From *Harvard Educational Review,* Vol. XXVII, No. 3 (Summer, 1957), pp. 168–99. By permission of authors and *Harvard Educational Review.*

[1]*Health, Education, and Welfare Trends,* U.S. Department of Health, Education, and Welfare (Washington, D.C.: U.S. Government Printing Office, 1960).

supported by high tuition rates, but a privately financed school system designed to serve the mass of Catholics who, by virtue of their origins in Europe and the recency of arrival in this country, can be found spread throughout our class system with heavy concentrations in the lower strata of American society.

How this unique institution arose and what functions it serves at present constitute the central concerns of this paper. While our attention will center almost exclusively on the Roman Catholic schools, we shall also refer to others at various points. Specifically, this paper will attempt to provide answers to three major questions:

1. How and why did the extensive parochial school system arise in the United States?
2. What is the present-day institutional patterning of the Roman Catholic schools?
3. What are the consequences of the parochial school system for the individual Catholic, his church, the social groups of which he may be a part, and the larger community?

The treatment of the first two questions will be light in favor of a heavy consideration of the last question. In answering the last question, the paper will draw upon sociological studies, with much of the data to be presented not having been previously published.

THE HISTORICAL ROOTS OF THE PAROCHIAL SCHOOLS IN AMERICA[2]

At the time of the adoption of the Federal Constitution, nine of the American states had established churches, with several denominations represented. Perhaps only the little state of Rhode Island had complete religious liberty as we conceive of it today. When supported as a state enterprise or as an arm of local government, the schools of the time were denominational in character, upholding in instruction the doctrines of a particular church. Some of today's great secular universities were then primarily denominational seminaries: Harvard was a state-supported Congregational seminary. For some decades after Independence, this condition persisted, for the First Amendment prohibited the Federal Government from establishing a national church, but did not prevent individual states from giving special recognition to particular denominations.

The state churches of the 18th century did not last long into the 19th. Immigration and schisms in established denominations brought about a proliferation of sects, so that by 1840 the separation of church and state had taken place in every state within the Union.

During the same period, interest was growing in public education. Public

[2] Up-to-date comprehensive histories of denominational schooling in this country are apparently still to be written. The material in this section rests heavily on more general works, specifically Theodore Roemer, *The Catholic Church in the U.S.* (St. Louis: B. Herder, 1950) and Walter H. Beck, *Lutheran Elementary Schools in the U.S.* (St. Louis: Concordia Press, 1939).

school systems were being established and controversies arose over what were to be the religious teachings to be taught within them. In state after state, the solution to the diversity of denominations was to make the new schools "non-sectarian."

As the public schools extended their coverage and became increasingly "non-sectarian," they came under fire from the more orthodox denominations whose religious leaders felt that a secular education would weaken the faith of children. Several denominations began to consider the advisability of setting up parochial schools. In the 1840's, the Presbyterian Church urged its congregations to set up schools for children between the ages of five and twelve. The Presbyterian experiment was at best feeble and by 1870 this denomination had given up its attempt. The various Lutheran denominations, which since their arrival in this country had maintained denominational schools, renewed their emphasis on the importance of church schools. In 1846, the Evangelical Lutheran Church (Missouri Synod) was established in this country. From its inception, the Missouri Synod emphasized denominational schooling and today operates the largest parochial school system among the Protestant denominations.

It was also during this period that the Roman Catholic Church began to grow to the stature of a major denomination. Heavy Irish immigration to the Eastern seaboard cities plus the arrival of many from the German Catholic states swelled the ranks of the Church. To the Church leaders of the time, the "non-sectarian" public schools, where the King James version of the Bible was used, were "Protestant" schools. Early in this period the bishops of the Church urged each parish to establish a denominational school. But it was not until the Third Plenary Council of the hierarchy, held in Baltimore in 1884, that the Church made it obligatory for each parish to set up its school and for each Catholic to send his children to the parochial schools. Catholic parochial schools—state-supported, if possible, privately financed, if necessary—were seen as the answer to the felt need for the religious education of Catholic youth.

Of the several 19th-century attempts to set up mass denominational school systems in the United States, only the German Lutheran and the Roman Catholic efforts were successful and survive to this day. From the attempts of the other denominations only a few secondary schools have survived, but these are primarily serving an elite clientele.

It is crucial for understanding the contemporary functioning of parochial schools to consider what were the factors which made for the success of the Roman Catholic and the German Lutheran denominational schools. There are several salient features of the two successful parochial school systems which are probably among the most important reasons for their success. To begin with, in both cases, more than denominational purity was at stake. In each case very self-conscious ethnic groups were identified with each denomination: the Irish and Germans in the case of the Roman Catholics, and the Germans alone in the case of the Lutheran Church. In each case the church was a major point of identification in the old country, and the strength of identification was augmented by experience in the new land. Both the Irish and the Lutherans had had some experience in maintaining their church under unfavorable conditions, the Ortho-dox Lutherans against a reformed state church in Germany and the Irish against the established church of England. The Irish particularly had developed the institutional devices for maintaining their church in a hostile environment and had also evolved customs favoring heavy financial support of church activities. In addition, each group brought with it an experienced religious cadre, and when established in this country quickly set up organizations for the recruitment and training of future cadres.

In the case of the Lutheran schools, their ethnic character was quite obvious. These were German language schools in which, at the least, religious subjects were taught in that language. German was the liturgical language of the Missouri Synod up to only a few decades ago and the church leaders even today are primarily from German ethnic stock. It should be noted that the success of the Lutheran schools was greatest in rural areas and small towns of the Midwest, where many Germans had settled. Even as late as 1947 a majority of the Lu-theran schools were one- or two-room rural schools. Although the amount of instruction conducted in German has decreased considerably since the anti-German hysteria of World War I, it seems likely that these schools played an important part in keeping German as the most widely-spoken foreign language in American households: in 1940, of the fourteen million Americans who spoke a foreign language as their "mother tongue," over three and a quarter million spoke German, more than twice as many as spoke the next most popular lan-guage, Italian.[3]

While the rural isolation of the German Lutherans helped them to maintain a viable denominational school system, the urban Irish Catholic schools derived a similar strength from their position on the bottom of the urban heap. The anti-Catholic movements of the 19th century helped to maintain the strong attachment of the Irish to the Roman Catholic Church. The German Catholics benefited from very much the same geographical isolation as the Lutherans.

Undoubtedly these two denominations were aided in the struggle to maintain their parochial schools by their ideologies of non-compromise with their environ-ments. Both the Roman Catholic Church and the Missouri Synod were militant and dogmatic bodies whose leaders insisted that their churches alone were truly Christian.

Thus, the successful denominational schools were those which were identified with particular ethnic groups and were run by religious organizations which either already had or quickly developed the institutions for maintaining and recruiting a cadre of teaching personnel. In more recent times, the success of the French Canadian immigrants in establishing and maintaining an extensive foreign-language parochial school system provides another illustration of the importance

---

[3] Department of Commerce, *16th Census of the U.S., 1940* (Washington, D.C.: U.S. Government Printing Office). (More recent censuses did not obtain information on lan-guages spoken.)

of this pattern. As we shall see later on, these historical origins have left their mark on the Roman Catholic schools of today.

Although these are factors which apparently make for initial success in establishing a successful denominational school system, they are not as well suited to the maintenance of such systems over long periods of time, given the processes of assimilation which all ethnic groups in America sooner or later apparently undergo. As the period of initial entry into this country recedes into the past, the attachment of each group to its national origins tends to be dissipated and the continued success of a denominational school system may perhaps be best assured by calling upon other types of motivation. The denominational schools, compared to the public schools, must provide as much or more aid to the aspirations of the emerging middle classes and at the same time lose some of their ethnic stamp. In this connection we may note the heavier emphasis during the past two decades in both Roman Catholic and Missouri Synod schools on higher educational standards and a corresponding decline of instruction in foreign languages. At present the Roman Catholic schools are more than holding their own, but the evidence seems to point to a considerable decline in the popularity of the German Lutheran schools.

THE CONTEMPORARY ROMAN CATHOLIC PAROCHIAL SCHOOLS

Doctrinal basis and organizational structure

The doctrinal basis of the Roman Catholic parochial schools stems from the Third Plenary Council of the American hierarchy held in Baltimore in 1884, and has been reiterated a number of times. The Council declared that it was morally binding on every Catholic to see to it that his children had proper religious training. The vehicle for such training was the parochial school, or if such schools were not available, provision in some other fashion for such training. In order to provide for proper training, each parish was ordered to set up denominational schools within two years and to make provisions for the religious instruction of those children who could not be accommodated in parochial schools. In this pronouncement the hierarchy set the pattern of mass education under parochial jurisdiction.

The goal of a school in every parish and every Catholic child in a parochial school is still far from fulfillment today. (See Table 1, p. 59.) Slightly more than half of the parishes in the United States at present support parochial schools and about the same proportion of Catholics have attended them. It should be noted here that statistics on school attendance in private schools are notoriously unreliable and the proportions quoted here are subject to a large and unknown error.

With few exceptions, the Catholic elementary schools of today are financed

and administered by individual parishes. The parish pastor undertaking to organize a school has full responsibility for raising the necessary capital, obtaining
teaching personnel from one of the teaching orders, and for providing operating
funds. A diocese may often undertake to provide building funds to be repaid on
easy terms. A diocesan superintendent of schools, whose powers are primarily
administrative and advisory, provides some degree of uniformity in curriculum
and standards. He may also have direct control over diocesan high schools;
few parishes are large or rich enough to support the more expensive secondary
education.

The Plenary Council of 1884 urged the establishment of free parochial
schools. Today, however, most parochial schools charge tuition fees. Compared
to those charged in secular private schools, these fees are nominal—estimated to
be about $25 per year per pupil in the Chicago area—and are usually waived for
pupils in need. The major part of school expenses is raised from voluntary contributions from the total congregation. Compared to public or secular private
schools, the *per capita* cost of parochial schooling must be considerably less,
since wages paid to the Sisters and Brothers are nominal. In fact, mass denominational schooling is a tribute to the dedication of the members of the teaching
orders.

The teaching personnel of the typical parochial school are provided to the
parish by a religious community. The parish undertakes to furnish housing,
subsistence, and a nominal wage. When it is not possible to obtain enough Sisters
from a religious community, lay persons may be employed to round out the full
complement, a practice that has become more common recently during postwar
expansion of the parochial school system.

The curriculum of the parochial school must, of course, conform to whatever
standards individual states set up. Catholic textbooks contain obvious differences
from those in use in public schools, stressing Church doctrine where applicable.
The more or less standard curriculum of American schools is further heavily supplemented by instruction in both doctrine and ritual.

Catholic secondary schools are most frequently organized on a diocesan level.
The curriculum is primarily college preparatory, few schools offering the comparatively more expensive training in either commerce or the manual arts. Greater
stress is placed on the provision of secondary education for girls than for boys.

Because statistics on school attendance in the United States are so poor, it is
hard to judge what have been the long-term trends in the number of children
educated in parochial schools. Certainly, as one may see in Table 1, the number
of parochial schools has grown considerably since 1900, even though the proportion of parishes supporting schools has remained fairly constant. What fragmentary statistics exist on school attendance indicate a different trend: parochial
schools are educating a larger proportion of the total population in school today
than in 1920. One thing is certain: the growth of parochial schools and numbers
of pupils in absolute terms demonstrate the viability of this institution.

TABLE 1
Number of Roman Catholic Parishes and Parishes
with Schools: 1900–1959*

Year*	Number of Parishes	Parishes with Schools	Proportion with Schools	Proportion Elementary School Children in Non-Public Schools
1900	6,127	3,812	63%	7.6%
1930	12,475	7,387	59%	9.8%
1938	13,132	7,597	58%	10.2%
1952	15,164	8,493	56%	13.2%
1959	16,753	9,814	58%	14.8%

*Sources: The figures in the first two columns for the years 1900 and 1930 were taken from Romer, *The Catholic Church in the U.S.A., 1950,* and for the years 1938 and 1954 from *The National Catholic Almanac,* 1941, 1955 and 1960. Data in the last column were obtained from *Health, Education and Welfare Trends* (Washington, D.C.: U.S. Government Printing Office, 1960).

The social context of the parochial schools

In order to obtain a more intimate understanding of the contemporary functioning of parochial schools, we shall now turn to a number of sociological studies[4] of various Catholic populations. Our tactic will be to compare Catholics who are products of the parochial schools with Catholics who have attended public schools. In some instances, it will be possible to compare Catholic parents who have sent their children to the two school systems. It must be borne in mind that these data are fragmentary. The researches which will be cited were not designed primarily for the purposes to which we shall put them. In addition,

---

[4]The data cited are derived from four main sources as cited below:
1. The "Bay City Study," conducted at the Graduate School of Education at Harvard University by J. Leiper Freeman, James Shipton and the authors. "Bay City" is the pseudonym given to a small industrial city in Massachusetts where the project carried out a series of interrelated studies on opinion formation and decision making on local issues.
2. The Arlington-Somerville Study: This study of 41 Catholic families with children of school age is reported in Barnard Portis, "An Empirical Analysis of Catholics' Choices Between Public and Parochial Elementary Schools" (unpublished Bachelor's Honors Thesis, Harvard University; Department of Social Relations, 1956).
3. The New Haven High School Study. Conducted by Professor Fred L. Strodtbeck and reported in David C. McClelland *et al.* (eds.), *Talent and Society* (Princeton, N.J.: Van Nostrand, 1958). The data appearing in this paper were prepared from the basic data kindly made available to the authors by Mr. Strodtbeck, whose generosity in allowing access to his data is gratefully acknowledged.
4. The Diocese of St. Augustine Study. Based on an extensive census of all Catholics in the diocese of St. Augustine, an area covering almost the entire state of Florida, in which more than 50,000 persons were interviewed. All tables shown here were recomputed from data presented in Father George A. Kelly, *Catholics and the Practice of the Faith* (Washington, D.C.: Catholic University Press, 1946).

they cover but a small proportion of the total Catholic population in the United States, the New England area being heavily favored. A note of warning: the interpretation of these findings is fraught with ambiguity. A difference in some quality between parochial and public school Catholics may be a consequence of the difference in educational experience or it may merely reflect differences in family backgrounds between Catholics who send their children to parochial schools and those who send their offspring to the public schools.

Although it is virtually impossible to fix with any great exactness the proportion of Catholics who have either attended parochial schools or who have enrolled their children therein, it is probable that this proportion for the United States is around fifty per cent. Parochial schools are available in only three out of every five parishes, and the capacity of the schools is ordinarily below the maximum needs of the parishioners. Attendance at parochial school is not an alternative which is either open to all Catholics or of which advantage is taken by all. Data from studies in "Bay City," Massachusetts, and the Diocese of St. Augustine, Florida, yield respective estimates that fifty-seven per cent and fifty-five per cent of the adult populations concerned have attended parochial schools. (See Table 2.)

TABLE 2
Type of School Attended by Sex

A. *Diocese of St. Augustine, Florida**			
Married Adult Catholics	*Men*	*Women*	*Total*
Proportion who have attended parochial schools . . .	55%	58%	57%
100% = ...	[7,045]	[8,757]	[15,802]

B. *"Bay City," Massachusetts**			
Catholics Aged 20 and Over	*Men*	*Women*	*Total*
Proportion attended parochial schools	49%	58%	55%
100% = ...	[236]	[270]	[506]

*Sources: A., Kelly, p. 43; B., unpublished data from the Bay City Project.

Given the fact that not all Catholics attend parochial schools what are the major differences between those who do and those who don't?

First of all, there is a slight tendency for parents to favor parochial schooling for their female as compared with their male children. Table 2 indicates that both in Massachusetts and Florida, adult female Catholics are more likely to have attended parochial schools. This sex difference, however, is not very large.

Evidence on the class level of families sending their children to parochial school is somewhat equivocal. In industrial "Bay City," it appears to be the "blue collar" families who prefer parochial schools; Strodtbeck's study of the

New Haven high schools shows an even stronger tendency for the class difference to show a "white collar" parochial school preference; Kelly's study of Florida indicates that parochial school attendance increases with greater educational attainment. (See Table 3.)

In short, the preponderance of evidence indicates that parochial school attendance is associated with higher occupational status;[5] the contradictory data from "Bay City," as we shall see, are partly explained by that community's ethnic composition. There are two fairly obvious explanations for this general tendency. To begin with, upper-status groups in America have been found to be generally more "religious" in their behavior—to belong to church organizations and to attend church services more frequently. Secondly, sending their children to parochial school may be felt as a financial burden to lower-income families. Although the average tuition fee may be small, lower-income families with a number of children of school age may find even this charge more than they can afford.

However, economic differences within the Catholic group also reflect ethnic origins. The earlier immigrants have risen higher in the occupational scale than later arrivals. In Table 4, it can be seen that ethnic group differences in parochial school attendance considerably overshadow those between the "white collar" and "blue collar" occupational levels, as shown in Table 3. In "Bay City," where a large contingent of French Canadians maintains a French-language parochial school, it is they who are most partial to the parochial schools. In this community, the French Canadians, being the most recent immigrants, are on the bottom of the occupational ladder. The Italians, whose parish has only started its parochial school within the last decade, show the smallest attendance level at parochial schools. Ranking behind the French but considerably ahead of the Italians are the Irish, whose parochial schools date from 1880.

Note that in "Bay City," parents in every ethnic group are more likely to send their children to parochial schools than to have attended themselves. This generational difference is particularly striking for the Italians. In the parents' generation only twelve per cent attended parochial school, whereas fifty per cent of the parents are presently sending their children to such schools. The increase in parochial school attendance over the generations probably reflects the growth of parochial school facilities in the community.

In Portis' study of Arlington and Somerville, we have only the Irish and Italians to compare. Here we find that the former are strikingly more likely to send their children to the parochial schools. It should be noted that in the two neighborhoods studied by Portis, the parishes were "American," headed by pastors of Irish ancestry. In the eyes of the Italians in these neighborhoods, the churches were "Irish." Indeed, for Italian immigrants on the Eastern seaboard, the "American" church often appears to be heavily Irish.

In New Haven the same ethnic pattern is repeated. The Irish are the most

---

[5] Fichter's study of a South Bend, Indiana parish also shows the same tendency. Joseph H. Fichter, S.J., *Parochial School* (Notre Dame, Ind.: University of Notre Dame Press, 1958), p. 384.

likely to send their sons to Catholic high schools, followed by the Italians, and trailed by the Poles.

TABLE 3
Socio-Economic Status and Attendance at Parochial Schools

A. "Bay City," Massachusetts*

Adult Catholics	"White Collar" Occupations	"Blue Collar" Occupations
Proportion who have attended parochial schools	44%	50%
100% = ...	[143]	[342]
Proportion who have sent their children to parochial schools	56%	69%
100% = ...	[74]†	[165]†

B. Arlington-Somerville, Massachusetts*

Catholic Families with Oldest Child between 6 and 10	"White Collar"	"Blue Collar"
Proportion who have sent their children to parochial schools	55%	29%
100% = ...	[20]	[21]

C. New Haven, Connecticut*

Catholic Boys in First Three Years of High School	"White Collar"	"Blue Collar"
Proportion attending Catholic high schools	49%	26%
100% = ...	[267]	[518]

D. Diocese of St. Augustine, Florida*

All Married Catholics in Diocese	Educational Attainment				
	Less than 8 Years	8 Years	9-11 Years	12 Years	More than 12 Years
Proportion who have attended parochial schools	49%	53%	57%	59%	66%
100% = ...	[1,464]	[3,740]	[2,725]	[6,564]	[1,861]

*Sources: A., the "Bay City" Project; B., Portis, Table 2.12; C., Strodtbeck, unpublished data; D., Kelly, p. 43.
†Only parents of children who have reached school age.

In the data of Table 4, an overall pattern can be discerned: except where non-Irish ethnic groups have set up their own parochial schools in connection with their national parishes, it has been the Irish Catholics who have been most faithful to the church doctrine concerning school attendance. The parochial schools have been attractive to each ethnic group when they have been identified as ethnic in character, with the "American" or English-language parish in New England being identified as primarily Irish.

A measure of the extent to which parochial school attendance represents

TABLE 4
Ethnic Background and Attendance at Parochial Schools*

A. *"Bay City," Massachusetts †*

Catholics Aged 20 or Over	Irish	Italians	French Canadian	Unclassifiable and Other Catholics
Proportion who have attended parochial schools	57%	12%	72%	41%
100% = ...	[99]	[61]	[230]	[103]
Proportion who have sent children to parochial schools	63%	50%	74%	52%
100% = ...	[38]	[28]	[123]	[50]

B. *Arlington-Somerville, Massachusetts †*

Catholic Families with Oldest Child between 6 and 10	Irish	Italian
Proportion sending children to parochial schools	74%	14%
100% = ...	[19]	[22]

C. *New Haven, Connecticut †*

Catholic Boys in First 3 Years of High School	Irish	Italian	Poles	Other
Proportion sending children to Catholic high schools	45%	31%	19%	34%
100% = ...	[158]	[354]	[75]	[203]

*In the "Bay City" study, ethnic background was determined by classifying persons according to the country of origin of the most closely related foreign-born ancestor. When this information was lacking, respondent was classified according to his surname. A similar procedure was employed by Strodtbeck. Undoubtedly, many of the unclassifiable respondents are of Irish origin, whose families have been in this country for more generations than our short genealogies would detect and whose names are not detectably Irish.

†Sources: A., the "Bay City" Project; B., Portis, Table 2.4; C., Strodtbeck, unpublished data.

attachment to an ethnic group can be ascertained from Table 5. Those parents who felt that it was *"not* important to keep some of the ties and customs of the land your people came from" were the most likely to deviate from the school attendance practice of their ethnic group, i.e., Italians sending their children to the parochial schools or Irish sending their children to public schools.

A somewhat different approach to the determiners of parochial school attendance is afforded by Strodtbeck's study of New Haven high school students. Because the major purpose of his study was to investigate factors involved in mobility aspirations, his data allow a contrast between parochial and public school students according to the degree to which each group is mobility-oriented.

TABLE 5

Importance of Ethnic Ties and Conformity to School Attendance Practices of Ethnic Group: Arlington-Somerville, Massachusetts*

	Importance of Ethnic Ties and Customs	
School Attendance	*Important*	*Unimportant*
Deviates from ethnic group practice	0%	31%
Conforms to ethnic group practice	100%	69%
100% = ...	[14]	[26]

*Source: Portis, Table 2.5.

Table 6 presents the responses of the two groups of students to a series of questions designed to measure the extent to which they are willing to break away from their families and in addition to strive for occupational success. Since the achievement of mobility involves both dimensions, these questions measure to some extent aspirations for mobility. Because such desires are usually conditioned by the class levels of the students' families, fathers' occupations are held constant in the table.

TABLE 6

Attachment to Family and Achievement Orientation among Public and Parochial High School Students: New Haven, Connecticut*

	Type of School Attended	
	Public High School	*Catholic High School*
A. Attachment to Family		
Proportion agreeing to ". . . when teenagers get married their main loyalty belongs to their [parents]."	49%	38%
Proportion agreeing to "Nothing in life is worth the sacrifice of moving away from your parents."	33%	25%
Proportion agreeing to "To me a family means a large family of parents, their children and grandchildren, the uncles, aunts, cousins and inlaws."	55%	42%
B. Occupational Achievement		
Proportion disagreeing to "The best kind of job is a secure not too difficult job with enough pay to afford a nice car and eventually my own home."	27%	39%
Proportion disagreeing to ". . . success is already in the cards, so a man might just as well accept it and not fight against it."	27%	39%
100% = ...	[522]	[268]

*Source: Strodtbeck, unpublished data.

Although the differences between parochial and public high school students are not very large, they do tell a consistent story: the parochial student, whether from a "white collar" or a "blue collar" background, is less attached to his family group and more oriented toward the prevalent middle-class norms of occupational success. If these data are to be taken as indicative of Catholic secondary schools in general, it would appear that the more mobility-conscious Catholics are to be found within such schools. Perhaps by virtue of their curriculum or teaching methods, the Catholic high schools serve as better mobility channels for Catholics than the public schools.

In summary, the data reviewed so far have emphasized the role played by ethnicity in attendance at parochial schools.[6] The differences in school attendance among ethnic groups have by and large been greater than other contrasts, either of occupational class or sex. Attendance at parochial schools appears to be primarily a manifestation of attachment to an ethnic group. In communities where each ethnic group has its "own" parochial school, attendance will be high in every such group. Where only "American" parishes are established in a community, it is the Irish Catholics who are most partial to the parochial schools, reflecting the extent to which this ethnic group has dominated the Catholic Church in America. It should be remembered that these findings apply primarily to the New England area. Perhaps in other areas, where other ethnic groups have played dominant roles, e.g., the Germans in Wisconsin, the dominant group exhibits the same behavior as the Irish in New England.

The "effects" of parochial school attendance on the individual Catholic

In this section, the analysis enters a more difficult area, attempting to provide answers to the question, "What effect does parochial schooling have upon the individual Catholic's attachment to and his attitudes toward his social environment: his church, ethnic group, and community?" The analysis will pursue the same strategy as before—parochial school Catholics will be compared with persons who have attended the public schools. As before, when we find differences between the two groups, it will not be possible to tell whether these are differences which antecede school attendance or which are consequences of differences in schooling. However, we shall be on safer ground when it is found that the two groups are alike. In such cases we can be reasonably sure that the type of schooling experienced by the individuals had no effect on the particular characteristic being studied.

---

[6]Fichter's *(op. cit.)* study of a South Bend, Indiana parish found no differences among persons of different ethnic background in sending their children to parochial school and indeed some difficulty in determining the ethnic background of parents to begin with, since more than seventy per cent had come from mixed ethnic background. Fichter describes his parish as the "parish of the future" in which the national origins of American Catholics have become so dilute as to no longer have any meaning for present day behavior.

In evaluating the data of this section, it must be borne in mind that large differences cannot be expected between adults who have had different types of schooling. For most of the adults studied, their school days are long past, and the effects of this experience can be expected to have diminished with time as subsequent experiences diluted the residue of earlier events.

"Effects" on Religious Behavior and Attachment to the Church.   Perhaps the most obvious place to look for the effects of parochial schooling is in the area of religious behavior. The manifest purpose of the schools is to preserve Catholics in the faith of their fathers. A good part of the curriculum is given over to the teaching of ritual behavior and the doctrinal tenets of the Church. According to the studies we have surveyed, the parochial schools are apparently successful in achieving their purpose, although this success is not outstanding.

The data of Table 7 indicate that parochial school education does predispose one to be more observant of certain types of ritual duties. Thus parochial school attenders are more likely to perform their Easter duties—receive Holy Communion during the Lenten season—but the differences between men and women

TABLE 7
Religious Observances and Types of Schooling,
Diocese of St. Augustine, Florida*

A. Religion of Spouse and Validity of Marriages	Married Catholic Males	
Type of Marriage	Attended Public Schools	Attended Parochial Schools
Proportion married to Catholic spouses	81%	84%
Proportion validly married	85%	89%
100% = ...	[2,768]	[2,503]

	Married Catholic Females	
Type of Marriage	Attended Public Schools	Attended Parochial Schools
Proportion married to Catholic spouses	67%	71%
Proportion validly married	88%	89%
100% = ...	[3,012]	[3,298]

	Married Men		Married Women	
	Attended		Attended	
B. Observance of Easter Duties	Public Schools	Parochial Schools	Public Schools	Parochial Schools
Proportion receiving Holy Communion during Lent.	63%	74%	72%	81%
100% = ...	[2,699]	[2,456]	[2,939]	[3,300]

*Sources: A., Kelly, pp. 128–29; B., Kelly, p. 126.

overshadow those between persons with different types of schooling. In contrast, the effect of parochial school education on patterns of marriage is considerably less. Parochial school graduates are slightly more likely to marry Catholics and to contract valid marriages (i.e., marriages solemnized by Catholic clergy). Again this difference is considerably overshadowed by differences between the sexes. Among the Florida Catholics, females are much more likely than males to marry outside their religious group, perhaps indicating greater chances for women to marry up the social ladder. [7]

All told, the data from Kelly's study of Florida Catholics do not indicate that parochial schooling is a very effective means of preserving the faith. Parochial school graduates are more observant of their religious ritual duties, but this difference in their favor is not very large, being overshadowed by both sex and educational differences.

"Effects" on Attachment to Ethnic Groups.   Since it was one of our main conclusions in the last section that attendance at parochial schools was a function of ethnic group attachment, it is particularly unfortunate that the studies available have so little direct evidence on how attendance aids in preserving this ethnic attachment.

An earlier table (Table 5) showed that those who considered ethnic ties important were unlikely to deviate from their ethnic group's pattern of school attendance. Apparently whether an individual attends such a school or not depends on the custom in his ethnic group and on his parents' attachment to this group. Now we shall consider how experience with parochial schooling aids the French Canadians to retain their language as a household tongue. The data pertain to the French Canadians in "Bay City," Massachusetts, where it will be recalled that a parochial school gives at least part of its instruction in French.

Although it is not possible to make statements on the basis of the data of Table 8, one thing is fairly certain, that the persistence of French as a household tongue is intimately associated with the French parochial school, and the greater a family's experience with this schooling, the more likely it is that French is spoken in the home. The parochial school, then, may play a crucial role in maintenance of this ethnic group over time.

Attachment to Catholic Leaders as a Reference Group. [8]   How effective are parochial schools in welding the Catholic group together into a cohesive aggregate? Because these institutions function to reinforce the individual pupil's sense of identity with his denomination, it might be anticipated that this experience

---

[7] Father Schnepp's study of an unnamed South Eastern seaboard city parish during the late 30's showed a stronger preservative effect of parochial school education. Gerald J. Schnepp, *Leakage from a Catholic Parish* (Washington, D.C.: Catholic University Press, 1942), pp. 106-11.

[8] Data in this section have been more fully analyzed in Alice S. Rossi, "Determinants of Reliance on Religious Leaders as Reference Groups" (unpublished memorandum of the Bay City Research Project) and James M. Shipton, "Reference Groups in the Formation of Public Opinion" (unpublished Ph.D. dissertation, Harvard University, Department of Social Relations, 1955).

would also carry with it a heightened readiness to "think and act like a Catholic" in a variety of situations. Parochial school Catholics would therefore be more likely influenced by what their religious leaders have to say on a number of non-religious issues. In more technical terms the Church leaders might serve as a reference group to whom the individual looks for advice and guidance. Indeed, if we are correct in our interpretation of the meaning of parochial school attendance as a manifestation of group attachments, we should expect that religious

TABLE 8
The Use of French as a Household Language among
French Canadians: "Bay City," Massachusetts*

Types of Schooling Experience	Proportion Speaking French in the Home	100% =
Parents and children attended public schools	40%	[78]
Mixed public and parochial experience	58%	[26]
Parent with public school, children with parochial	71%	[24]
Parent with parochial, children with public	71%	[24]
Parents and children attended parochial schools	86%	[107]

*Source: "Bay City Project," unpublished data.

leaders will be an important reference group for Catholics who have attended the church schools.

We turn to the "Bay City" Study for empirical evidence. The major focus of this study was on the processes of opinion formation and change in a local election. The persons interviewed were asked to designate to which groups of leaders they would look for advice and guidance in making up their minds on local issues. A list of twenty-four such potential reference groups, including labor leaders, social classes, and so on, was presented to each person and he was asked to select his reference groups from among the list. Included in the list were the categories "Catholic leaders" and "Protestant leaders." We have taken a respondent's choice of a category as an indication that he would be willing to pay at least some attention to the statements of this group on the issues in question. This provides a measure of the respondents' *potential* reference groups, in the sense that we have measured only willingness to pay attention, not whether they in fact have ever done so.

Another question, asked in connection with other queries on a recent local election, was whether or not the same reference groups had *in fact* been "helpful" to the respondents in making up their minds on the candidates and issues in the election. The answers to this last question yielded a measure on the *actual* reference groups of the persons interviewed.

Highlights of the analysis of religious reference groups are given in Table 9. Parochial school Catholics are the most likely to cite religious leaders as both potential and actual reference groups. Catholic leaders apparently have a ready audience within their religious group for any attempts to wield mass influence. Furthermore, it can be seen also that all of the Catholics are more likely to be influenced by their religious leaders than are the Protestants. This religious dif-

TABLE 9
Catholic Leaders as Reference Groups, Ethnicity, and Types
of Schooling, "Bay City," Massachusetts

A. *Religious Leaders as Potential Reference Groups on School Issues*	Parochial School Catholics	Public School Catholics	Public School Protestants
Proportion citing religious leaders as			
reference groups	53%	34%	22%
100% = ...	[321]	[166]	[251]

B. *Religious Leaders as Actual Reference Groups in School Board and Mayoralty Elections**	Parochial School	Public School
Proportion citing Catholic leaders as having been helpful in:		
School board election	24%	18%
Mayoralty and council election	16%	12%
100% = ...	[193]	[193]

C. *Religious Leaders as Potential Reference Groups and Ethnicity*	*Proportion Citing Catholic Leaders as Reference Groups on School Issues*		
Respondent Attended:	*Irish*	*Italian*	*French*
Public schools	29%	32%	47%
100% = ...	[51]	[56]	[66]
Parochial schools	49%	55%	51%
100% = ...	[59]	[11]	[174]

*Only those Catholics who *voted* in the election are included in this table.

ference may well reflect the different role definitions of the clergy in the two groups.

If the second part of Table 9 is compared with the first part, it can be discerned that the Catholic leaders have a stronger position as *potential* than as *actual* reference groups. Furthermore, the leadership of the Catholic clergy is acknowledged more frequently in school elections than in the election for mayor and city council. This last finding indicates either that school issues are viewed as more within the realm of legitimate concerns of the clergy or that the clergy were more active in one rather than the other contest.

Finally, in the third part of this table, it can be seen that the effect of parochial schooling holds up within each of the three ethnic groups. Note that the least willing to accept leadership from the clergy are the public school Irish, perhaps reflecting the greater educational attainment of this group. Among the parochial school Catholics, ethnic background makes very little difference in the designation of Catholic leaders as reference groups.

Participation in and Interest in Community Affairs.   Parochial schooling apparently is related to both the individual Catholic's attachment to his religious leaders and to the cohesion of the Catholic group. We shall now raise the question of whether this internal cohesion is bought at the price of weakening ties to the larger society. In other words, is the strength of the in-group accompanied by a withdrawal of interest in and support of community institutions? Many of the critics of denominational schools have advanced this weakening of the community as one of the most serious consequences of parochial schools.

For some empirical evidence on this question, we turn again to the "Bay City" research. Most of the data contained in Table 10 indicate that the type of

TABLE 10
Catholic Interest in and Attachment to the Community and Its
Institutions, "Bay City," Massachusetts

	Parochial School	*Public School*
A. *Attachment to the Community*		
Proportion strongly attached to the community*	80%	76%
100% = ...	[193]	[193]
B. *Interest in Local Politics*		
Proportion with high interest in local politics†	28%	29%
100% = ...	[220]	[207]
C. *Interest in Public School Affairs*		
Proportion with high interest in school affairs‡	22%	35%
100% = ...	[220]	[217]

*Answers to a series of questions concerning willingness to migrate from the community.
†Answers to a series of questions on readership of political news in local newspaper, attention paid to events in City Council, self-rating of interest in local elections, etc.
‡Answers to a series of questions similar to those in B, above.

schooling experienced by Catholics of the community has only a small effect on the individual's relationship to his community. Parochial school Catholics are about as interested in local politics and as attached to the community as public school Catholics. However, the type of school attended does have an effect on the amount of interest shown in school affairs. Public school Catholics are more concerned with the issues that may arise concerning the public schools.

The lower interest of parochial school Catholics in the affairs of public schools should not be interpreted as a withdrawal of attention. Rather, as can be seen in Table 11, parochial school Catholics are no less interested in the public schools than other persons who do not have children who have attended the local public school system. In other words, the group with the highest interest in school issues consists of those who are currently sending their children to the public schools. Those who have no children or whose children were sent to schools in other communities show as low an interest in the local system as parents who are sending or have sent children to the parochial schools.

All told, the evidence we have brought to bear from the "Bay City" study points to very little effect of parochial schooling on the individual Catholic's

TABLE 11

Interest in School Affairs According to Relationship to Local
Public Schools, "Bay City," Massachusetts*

Current Relationship to "Bay City" Schools	*Proportion with High Interest in School Affairs*	
		100% =
Currently with children in the local public schools	51%	[179]
Currently with children in local parochial schools	28%	[104]
Children attended local public schools in past	22%	[102]
Children attended local parochial schools in past	23%	[34]
Childless or sent children to schools in other communities† . .	21%	[397]

*Adults, aged 20 or over.
†Essentially no difference between being childless or having sent children to school in other communities.

relationship to his local community. Compared to other Catholics of similar occupational level or educational attainment, the products of the Church schools show little difference in their attachment to the community and their interest in local politics. Even the parochial school Catholics' interest in the affairs of the local public schools does not differ significantly from that of other citizens whose children are not currently in the local schools.

Attitudes toward Community Institutions and Public Issues. Although there does not seem to be a great difference between the two types of schooling in their effects on the *amount* of involvement in community affairs, there may still be some effect on specific *attitudes* toward community institutions and public issues. Both sides of a controversy may be equally involved and yet be divided sharply in the direction of policy to be taken on the issues in question. Thus public school Catholics may feel quite differently from the products of parochial schools about the quality of the public schools or in their political loyalties. Table 12 compares the two groups of Catholics with each other and with the Protestants in "Bay City."

Only small and inconsistent differences can be discerned between parochial and public school Catholics in their attitudes toward either "Bay City's" public school system or its school committee. Nor can it be said that the Catholics as a group differ radically from the Protestants on this score. If anything, there is a slight tendency for the parochial school Catholics to have a higher opinion of the local public schools than the Protestants.

Nor are there any appreciable or consistent differences in agreement to a number of stereotyped statements about the public schools. Even on the charge that public schools change children away from the ideas of their parents, we cannot find that parochial school Catholics differ consistently from either other Catholics or from Protestants.

When the relationships between church and state are in question, however, major and consistent differences appear between the two religious groups and within the Catholic contingent. Parochial school Catholics are the most favorable to state aid for Church schools and to released time for religious instruction. Protestants stand at the opposite extreme, while public school Catholics occupy a position in between.

In short, only when religion itself enters as a direct issue can we discern the Catholic's school experience as affecting his attitudes toward public schools. Perhaps we see here the consequence of the reference group phenomena discussed in an earlier section of this paper.

The voting records of the three groups in a local school board election present something of a paradox. (Table 12.) From close observation of the course of the

TABLE 12
Attitudes toward Local Institutions and on Public Issues
"Bay City," Massachusetts

	Catholics		
Adults Aged 20 and Over	*Parochial*	*Public*	*Protestants*
Per cent rating local school board "very good" 25%		19%	21%
100% – .... [281]		[158]	[241]
Per cent rating local public schools as "very good" ... 13%		17%	10%
100% = ... [281]		[165]	[254]
Per cent agreeing that "public schools change children away from their parents' ideas" 17%		12%	17%
100% = ... [223]		[242]	[208]
Per cent agreeing that "public schools are not teaching the fundamentals as well today" 37%		37%	46%
100% = ... [254]		[157]	[236]
Per cent agreeing that "all schools, including church schools, should get financial aid from the state" ... 90%		68%	43%
100% = ... [328]		[170]	[240]
Per cent agreeing that "public schools should give time off for religious teaching" 86%		48%	44%
100% = ... [324]		[168]	[255]
Average percentage vote for Republican candidates in school board election 52%		57%	80%
100% = ... [301]		[147]	[215]
Average percentage vote for Democratic candidates in school board election 41%		45%	15%
100% = ... [216]		[124]	[185]

election, one could not observe any overt reference to religious issues. Yet the data indicate that voters were divided primarily along religious lines, the Protestants clearly preferring Republican candidates and the Catholics showing a relative preference for Democratic candidates. Parochial school Catholics gave the Republican candidates the smallest percentages, although they were not consistently the strongest supporters of Democratic candidates.

Although primary attention in this paper is being paid to the Catholics, it is of some interest to note that it is the Protestants who behaved with the highest degree of partisanship in the school board elections. The degree of support given by this group to the two parties is considerably greater than the difference in vote given by the Catholics. In other words, the Protestants were more heavily Republican than the Catholics were Democratic. In these results we are presented with another paradox: although the Protestants were less likely to acknowledge religious leaders as potential and actual reference groups in school elections, their behavior was much more determined by their religious membership than the Catholics. Perhaps the solidarity of the Protestants is not a product of their churches and clergy acting as leaders, but stems from more informally organized group processes. This phenomenon may also reflect the greater stake which the Protestant group may have felt in this particular election.

Table 13 contains data on more general political and social orientations. In their preferences for one rather than another political party, the parochial and

TABLE 13
General Political Attitudes, "Bay City," Massachusetts

Catholic Adults, Aged 20 or Over	*Parochial*	*Public*
Proportion Democratic in local politics.	69%	68%
100% = ...	[210]	[209]
Proportion high in Economic Liberalism Scale*	36%	25%
100% = ...	[220]	[210]
Proportion "pro-labor" on attitudes toward labor scale	61%	57%
100% = ...	[206]	[193]

*The Economic Liberalism Scale contains questions on government ownership of public utilities, extension of social security, government health insurance, etc. A high score on this scale indicates a generally favorable response to measures of the New Deal–Fair Deal variety.

public school Catholics cannot be distinguished from each other. However, differences can be discerned in attitudes toward labor organizations and toward the social welfare activities of the New Deal–Fair Deal variety. On both counts the parochial school Catholics are slightly more "liberal," expressing greater approval of labor unions and of social welfare legislation. It is hard to interpret what these results signify. Without knowing more about the attitudinal atmospheres in either the public or parochial schools, it would be hazardous to impute these differences to the content of the instruction in either one or the other school system. Perhaps we are again dealing here with concealed ethnic differences which further analysis may yet uncover.

Some Conclusions Concerning Effects.   Out of the welter of data presented in the preceding pages, only two clear patterns emerge. First of all, it is apparent that the parochial school Catholic is more closely identified with his Church than the public school Catholic. Although he is only slightly more likely to conform to Church requirements concerning ritual obligations, he has a high regard for his religious leaders as guides in public affairs when the welfare of his church is at stake. The Church and its leadership are for him a significant reference group, and he is a staunch supporter of the Church on such matters as state aid for Church schools.

Secondly, we could find no evidence that parochial schools tend to alienate individual Catholics from their communities. Parochial school Catholics were as involved in community affairs as anyone else of comparable occupational position. Furthermore, the choice of parochial school education is apparently not so much a rejection of the public schools as a choice of something qualitatively different. It would appear that an improvement in the quality of the public schools would not materially affect their attractiveness to Catholics, for the greater pull of Church schools is based on religious qualities which the public schools have deliberately avoided.

SOME CONCLUSIONS

From the body of materials presented in this paper, two main conclusions can be drawn concerning the parochial schools of the American Roman Catholic Church:

First, there is apparently an intimate connection between the cultural backgrounds of American Catholics and their success in establishing and maintaining a mass educational enterprise. Early in the history of the Catholic Church in America the parochial schools became a symbol of the integrity of the Church and the attachment of the immigrant ethnic groups to their national backgrounds and to the Church. The parochial schools furthermore served as an important institutional device for maintaining group attachment over time. Even today the parochial schools still play very much the same role, particularly for the Irish and French Canadians in the New England states.

Secondly, despite the historical origins of these schools and their present importance in the life of certain ethnic groups, we were unable to find strong evidence that parochial school Catholics were very different from other Catholics. The influence of the school is shown most dramatically in areas where the Church has traditionally taken a strong stand, e.g., on support for religious education, or on the performance of ritual duties. In other areas of life the parochial school Catholic is only marginally differentiated from other Catholics. It would appear that solidarity of the Catholic group or of the ethnic groups within the Catholic fold maintains itself primarily through other more informal means. In this sense, the parochial schools do not appear to be the main mechanism by which Catholics maintain themselves as a distinct grouping among the American people.

These conclusions are not given without some modifying qualifications discussed below. Furthermore, they raise almost as many points as they settle concerning the nature of the Catholic Church and its parochial schools in America.

The most important qualification that must be placed upon these conclusions is that they apply primarily to New England where the major part of our data have been obtained. In that part of our country, Catholic-Protestant relations have long been poor, with both sides all too quick to see the slights in the actions of the other. Nineteenth-century New England was scarcely a hospitable place in which to settle for the Irish Catholic immigrant, and when the Catholics became a majority in the twentieth century they did not lose this opportunity to redress an unfavorable balance of wrongs. Where Catholic-Protestant relations do not have as long a history of suspicion and rivalry the Church may not be so central to the self-conceptions of the Catholic group, and the social-psychological meaning of parochial schools, as we have shown it to be in this article, may be somewhat different. Indeed, Fichter's recent study of a parochial school in South Bend, Indiana, indicates that this may be the case in places where ethnic identities have lost their fervor and the mixing has gone on longer in the American pot. In South Bend, Catholics apparently feel themselves merely another Christian denomination rather than the embattled and beleaguered underdogs in a well-established caste system.

A second qualification stems from the nature of the data which we have been able to assemble. We have viewed the Church and the parochial schools through the eyes of the ordinary parishioner, but the Roman Catholic Church is much more than a body of believers. It is also composed of a cadre of clergy and an organization which are not lacking in experience in this world of power and politicking. We have seen how parishioners use and are affected by parochial schools, but we have not seen how the existence itself of such a school system affects the cadre of the Church and the institutions of the local community.

In this last connection, several hypotheses may be advanced. First of all, there is no doubt that the parochial schools represent useful recruiting grounds for the clergy and the religious orders. Teaching sisters and priests scan the student body carefully for signs of vocations, and the measure of a good parochial school is often not how many achieve success in the secular world but how many take the vows of poverty and chastity.

The participation of the Roman Catholic Church in the job of educating our youth imparts more legitimacy to their concern with education in general. In towns and cities throughout the land where parochial schools educate a goodly proportion of the young, the public system is sensitive to what the Church hierarchy thinks and says about education in general. For some public school educators, the very existence of a parallel mass education appears as a threat. The parochial elementary schools of the Roman Catholic Church have the explicit aim of enrolling about 8,000,000 out of the 33,000,000 children of elementary school age. In cities where the Catholics form the majority, the kind of financial and political support for good public school education may often seem in jeopardy by that fact alone. If, in addition, the public school educator is someone to whom the Roman Catholic Church is a distasteful, medieval anachronism, the success of the Church in maintaining its schools may seem to have been bought at the price of a lowering in quality of public education in general.

In the data which we have presented in this article, there seems some substantiation for this conclusion. We noted that the parent who has sent his children to the parochial school manifested a low degree of concern for public school. The parochial school parent pays little attention to the affairs of the school board or to public controversies which arise over school issues. In addition, when we consider that he must support parochial schools by voluntary contributions, his interest in the public schools may consist primarily of a concern for the tax rate rather than with the quality of public school education.

Furthermore, there is some evidence that the politics of school elections become transformed. In Massachusetts, so the experienced politicians say, a place on the school board is often the first step in a promising political career. This may certainly be one of the hazards of being the school official in a community where there is a well developed parochial school system. If school board elections become means to other ends, then they can also be easily transformed into battlegrounds for demagogues, with irresponsible demands being voiced for lowered school taxes. There is no doubt that the school systems in the metropolitan areas of New England were once the most advanced in the country. Their decline has often been attributed to the factors we have suggested above.

There is yet another way in which the existence of a parochial school system affects the public schools. In a city like "Bay City," Massachusetts, where about sixty per cent of the population is Catholic, with an even larger proportion in the lower middle classes from which public school teachers are recruited, the personnel of the public school system is largely Catholic and largely educated in the parochial school system. In "Bay City," Protestants concerned with the public school often pointed to the composition of the teaching personnel as affecting strongly the kind of education given. We, of course, cannot evaluate this claim from our data.

Finally, we must consider the effect of the withdrawal of a significant portion of the potential student population into the parochial schools. Strodtbeck's study of the New Haven high schools indicates that it is the Catholic with a higher IQ and higher motivation who goes to parochial school. Under these conditions, the public schools may become dumping grounds for the less gifted and "problem" Catholic children. This has actually occurred in the French Canadian neighborhood of "Bay City" where the public school contains a handful of Protestant children and the problem children whom the French Canadian parochial school either would not accept or expelled. Among the general population, and more significantly among the teachers in "Bay City," this school is reputed to be the worst in the system. This effect may become all the more serious as the Catholic group rises in occupational and class status and is replaced on the lower levels by other groups. In some neighborhoods in our large metropolitan areas, the public schools have as their constituencies children from the two extremes of the class system, those from the fairly high non-Catholic groups and those from the lowest rungs of the occupational ladder. This phenomenon helps to explain the recent spurt in popularity of private non-denominational schools as, for example, those in Cambridge, Massachusetts and in the University of Chicago neighborhood.

In this article we have tried to show how it is possible to employ the techniques developed in the empirical branches of social science to cast some light on important issues on the contemporary American scene. The controversies surrounding public education and its alternatives need more material than we have been able to assemble here. These data are fragments, but they can be augmented by studies which are wider in scope and cover in greater depth some of the more important topics such as the power position of the Catholic Church in America.

PART II

Nonformal

aspects of

learning[1]

The socialization of the individual can be used as a broad category to include all learning of both a formal and informal nature. "The child learns from his parents, from other relatives, from friends of his parents, from teachers, from older siblings (both brothers and sisters), from playmates, and in fact from nearly everyone with whom he comes into contact."[2] The interrelationships of formal and informal learning are in many situations very complex.[3] One may predispose or contradict the other and lead to difficult problems of relating the many parts into a meaningful and understandable whole. There follow several important areas of informal or nonformal learning as related to the formal learning situation.

FAMILY LEARNING

The impact and vast importance of the family in the learning and social development of the child is due to the family's getting the child first and during the most formative years. Preschool children learn within a family setting that

---

[1] Nonformal learning is used to refer to learning in a variety of settings other than the traditional formal educational institution; i.e., the elementary, secondary, and college level.

[2] Arnold M. Rose, *Sociology* (New York: Alfred A. Knopf, 1956), p. 32.

[3] *Cf.* Harry M. Johnson, *Sociology: A Systematic Introduction* (New York: Harcourt, Brace & World, Inc., 1960), pp. 280–81.

has an informal and emotional climate. Most family learning is not consciously or deliberately presented to the child because it occurs without the parents or siblings being consciously aware that they are teachers. In those areas where learning is conscious and deliberate, it is often of a hit-or-miss nature; for example, the teaching of such basic functions as eating and toilet habits is not usually determined within a preconceived and predetermined pedagogical framework but rather emerges from the long-accumulated attitudes and emotions of the parents. The more educated parent is often the exception in that he may rear his children from the "book," though there may be anxiety as to whether or not it is the right "book." The high emotional setting is, of course, due to the basic closeness of the parent-child relationship. This can be illustrated by the expression of the father as he disciplines his child that "this hurts me more than you." For many fathers there is pain because psychologically and emotionally they are torn between love for the child and the desire to protect him, and, at the same time, the feeling that they must on occasion withhold their love or punish the child if he is to learn.

EDUCATIONAL VALUES

The initial and often most basic values of the individual in regard to formal education are acquired in the family. How the growing adolescent views school and its personal implications for him is often a reflection of the values that he acquires at home. This is true in regard to the young person's identification with values of education as well as action patterns he will pursue in school. If the parents indicate that school is unimportant and that leaving school and getting a job is more important, the young person may find it difficult to accept the contrary values of formal education. Of course, many parents rear their children with the assumption that education is valuable and assume that the child will grow up and go to college. Along with, or in contrast to, the family values are those of the peer group. The family and the peer group attitudes often have a great influence on how a student will perform in school. One study indicates that, while native ability is the important factor in regard to academic success during the first few years of school, social class and related values soon take over and strongly influence the school work of the student.[4] Studies also indicate that those students who succeed in school despite negative educational values in their social environment usually have strong motivations or important encouragement.[5]

PEER GROUP INFLUENCE

Associations with peer groups affect the behavior of most human beings at all ages of life. But for the child and adolescent, the peer group often has excep-

[4] Joseph A. Kahl, *The American Class Structure* (New York: Rinehart & Co., Inc., 1957), pp. 283–84.
[5] *Ibid.*, pp. 287–88.

tionally strong influences. For the young preschool child, playmates often function in a crucial way in providing the child with basic conditions for the emergence of his social self. The play group often provides the first social setting in which the child makes a shift from an essentially ego-centered world to one more socially oriented. The young child learns in this setting to relate his personal needs and wants to those of other children.

Age-sex typing as transitional stages are created primarily within a peer group setting. The child has provided for him models of his future role behavior as filled by older children. As he grows older he constantly must learn the changing sets of rights and obligations that go with different age roles. The youngster growing up is highly conscious of his present age role and of those behind him as well as those ahead of him. For example, the eight-year-old is told to quit acting like a six-year-old, the implication being that the past age-role behavior is no longer appropriate. Also indicated is that there are many things he is not allowed to do because he is too young, and he must wait until he is older. Because future age-role rights often are ones desired, youngsters often feel the important time is not the present, but the future.

The child must learn early the values of the peer group and their importance if he is to gain group acceptance. In some instances the values may be in conflict with those of the parents or the more extended adult community. The traits that make a boy a good son are not always the ones that give him prestige in the peer group. The situation may be further complicated because the school usually reflects middle-class adult attitudes. This means that many times the youngster is confronted with three sets of values, and while in many situations they may be compatible and complementary, such is not always the case. The potential value conflict may be illustrated by values associated with academic success in the school where the family, peer group, and school may be presenting different and even contradictory values to the youngster.

The play group of the youngster can also be basic in the learning of the structure and function of group interaction and behavior. From other children will be learned a number of social factors: the relationship of various social roles, as leader and follower; how rules and group control are developed and maintained (to some extent this is being lost because of the increase in adult supervision of many child play activities); how to relate to others to achieve group ends; and so forth. The extent and degree of learning that occurs during these years may set the pattern for many of the future group activities of the individual.

MASS MEDIA INFLUENCES

It is difficult to calculate the amount of learning that occurs through the various media of mass communication. The learning impact of movies, comic books, and particularly television is without question very great. Since the late 1940's, television has created a world of sight and sound never before experienced by man in his home. Children growing up in this period have experienced the world in a very different way from the childhood world of their parents. Growing up to singing commercials rather than rhymes is a sign of our times. The impact of the newer mass media has been dramatized by Marshall McLuhan. He has characterized the new developments as creating a "classroom without walls," and asserts that "these new mass media threaten, instead of merely reinforce, the procedures of this traditional classroom."[6]

Of considerable importance are the values that children acquire from television that may influence both present and future behavior: for example, attitudes in regard to morality and ethics; or distorted television images of various roles in the family and how the family functions. How these images are presented is determined by standards of commercial appeal and not by rational educational theory. It is too early to adequately assess the influence this kind of learning will have on children when they reach their adult years. But mass communication, particularly television, is unquestionably a tremendous force in the informal learning of the contemporary American child.

---

[6] Marshall McLuhan, "Classrooms Without Walls," in Edmund Carpenter and Marshall McLuhan, *Explorations in Communication* (Boston: Beacon Press, 1960), pp. 1–3.

4. Socialization*

HARRY M. JOHNSON

At birth the human infant is unable to take part in any human society. What its mental life is like we cannot know directly, but we do know that it has no interest in regulating its bowel movements, no sense of propriety about revealing various parts of its body—indeed, no conception of its body as something distinct from other objects, or of its fingers and toes as distinct parts of its body. It has no conception of a "self" of its own, with wishes that may or may not be opposed to the wishes of other people. It is thus unable to distinguish between its own presumably vague inner life and the "reality" of objects independently existing; it has no idea that such a distinction is possible. Consequently, ideas of property rights, regulation of "aggressive" impulses, and logical reasoning are as foreign to the newborn infant as they are to sunflowers.

Yet not so foreign: for somehow human infants develop into more or less adequate members of human societies. As we shall see, this development is largely a process of learning. "Socialization" is learning that enables the learner to perform social roles. Thus, not all learning is socialization, since presumably some learning is irrelevant to the motivation and ability necessary for participation in social systems.

Culture is what is learned in socialization. The extent to which seemingly inborn attitudes are cultural—and therefore learned—is not always appreciated. In a recent work on socialization in a collective farm *(kibbutz)*, Spiro[1] maintains that the *kibbutz* emphasis on collective property requires that the child be weaned away from his "natural" adherence to the institution of private property. Actually, however, private property has no more (or less) basis in original nature than collective property has. It is true that young children vigorously object to having "their" things taken away from them. But private property also involves recognizing other people's property rights, and this young children do no more readily than they recognize or understand collective property.

In this chapter, however, we are mainly concerned with the *process* by which individuals acquire the already existing culture of groups they come into. In

*From Harry M. Johnson, *Sociology: A Systematic Introduction* (New York: Harcourt, Brace & World, Inc., 1960), pp. 110–31.
[1] M. E. Spiro and A. G. Spiro, *Children of the Kibbutz* (Cambridge, Mass.: Harvard University Press, 1958), pp. 375–76.

83

many ways, this process is similar in all societies, but we shall pay some attention to differences as well as to similarities.

PRELIMINARY OBSERVATIONS

Biological potentialities

Although we shall say little about the biological characteristics of the human
species, we must assume, of course, that human learning depends upon them.
For example, the large size of the human brain as compared with the brains of
other species is necessary for man's capacity to form and retain concepts and to
develop speech. Man's upright posture, made possible by the structure of his
body, frees the arms and hands for "manipulation" of tools. Prehensile hands
and opposable thumbs are important for the same reason.[2]

Plasticity of the infant

Within fairly broad limits, the same human infant is capable of growing into
different kinds of adult. His potentialities cannot all be realized. His adult personality, formed in one society, will be more or less unfitted for participation in
many others. He is *capable* of learning how to write a sestina, but of course he
may never have the chance. If reared in the Masai tribe of Africa, he will eat
nothing but meat, drink milk and blood, and grasp wild lions by the tail and
hang on while his companions come in for the kill. There is a trustworthy
account of an Australian aborigine who had had no chance to learn his tribal
language; instead, he had been trained to speak English, which he did with a
perfect Irish brogue, like that of his teachers.[3]

The biological potentialities do not develop automatically. Socialization must
be distinguished from that growing up and gradual changing of the organism
which we call maturation, and which is inevitable provided that the organism
survives without serious physical injury.

> The process [of learning] is *not* merely one of unfolding. Botanists tell
> us, for example, that microscopic examination of the tulip bulb reveals a
> blossom in miniature which, under proper culture, is merely elevated, en-
> larged, and colored until it assumes the familiar form of the spring flower.
> The development of social behavior is not of this sort; there is no minia-
> ture social response already present and waiting to be unfolded. There is
> nothing, to begin with, but biological imperatives and biological capacities.
> In being irritated, in responding, and in learning, the organism literally
> changes itself. It is necessary to say "changes itself" because it is only
> through *responding* that the changes occur. It is also true that it is

---

[2] J. Huxley, "The Uniqueness of Man," *Yale Review,* Vol. 28, No. 3 (March, 1939), pp.
473-500.

[3] J. S. Slotkin, *Personality Development* (New York: Harper & Bros., 1952), pp. 172-74.

"changed by" the environment, because without external stimuli the infant could not make the responses by which he changes himself.[4]

As this quotation implies, all learning involves some change in the organism—perhaps in the cells of the brain or in the paths by which nerves are activated. This aspect of learning is largely ignored in the present account, but if we keep it in mind we shall realize that the human infant, although plastic, is not infinitely so; his biological nature has limitations as well as potentialities. No amount of training will give him the qualities for which the springbok, the bloodhound, or the elephant is famous. Whether he grows up to be a Masai warrior or a Buddhist monk, he will still be first of all a human being.[5]

Timing

Maturation could not produce fully human adults without socialization. But socialization and maturation proceed together in the early years of the life cycle, and attempts to teach will have varying effects depending upon the point reached in the maturation of the pupil. "Timing is important. It is foolish to expect successful bowel training before the neuro-muscular system is sufficiently matured to control the sphincters, or to expect the child to be quiet before he is capable of sustained inhibition."[6]

What is learned early influences later learning in two ways. First, some learning depends upon prior mastery of other skills. For example, it would be impossible to learn the calculus without the ability to speak or read. Secondly, some early learning makes it *difficult* for some other learning to occur. This is particularly true of learned fears. Since fear often leads to avoidance of what is feared, the child may never allow himself the opportunity to test reality adequately and learn to make realistic discriminations. (We must remember that not all learning is "good.")

Social patterning of socialization

Since the infant at birth is largely helpless, he is dependent upon adults for his survival and for training. Moreover, the process by which adults train him is not left to their unguided ingenuity. On the contrary, ways of training children are part of the culture of every society, and the task is performed by occupants of definite roles. The family in particular is organized in such a way as to make socialization possible.

---

[4] T. Newcomb, *Social Psychology* (New York: Dryden Press, 1950), p. 51.

[5] In one sense, to be human is to be socialized. So-called "feral children" (brought up in relative isolation from human beings) do not become human in this sense. For example, they do not learn how to talk until after they have been trained by socialized human beings. For brief accounts of feral children, see K. Davis, *Human Society* (New York: Macmillan Co., 1949), pp. 204–8 and Newcomb, *op. cit.*, p. 49.

[6] R. W. White, *The Abnormal Personality: A Textbook* (New York: Ronald Press Co., 1948), p. 117.

INTERNALIZED OBJECTS

Before attempting to describe the process by which an infant becomes an adult, we must have some understanding of the contrast between the infant's organism and the adult's personality. We cannot speak of the infant's "personality" because the newborn infant does not have a personality in a strict sense. A personality, in one aspect, is a complex inner system "representing" the outer world. It depends upon a consciousness of self as against this outer world of objects, animate and inanimate. The adult's inner construction of the outer world will not be accurate in all details; yet even a psychotic's personality reflects, however imperfectly, some of the features of objective reality. But for the newborn infant there is no objective reality: no space, no time, no causality. The mother's breast, a bottle, a rattle are not things in themselves, existing independently of the infant's own existence; to him they are somewhat capricious comings and goings of sensory images, images not perceived as images of things nor distinguished, presumably, from the acts of sucking, seeing, hearing, touching. That is to say, at first the infant does not distinguish between his own perceiving and the things perceived. Having as yet no self-consciousness, he acts as if the whole world impinging upon him were part of himself.[7]

According to Piaget,[8] the infant goes through six stages before he convinces himself that there are external objects with an existence of their own. In the first stage, reflexes such as sucking "produce" sensations of a breast and a nipple; there is no evidence that the infant "thinks" of these sensations as anything other than his own act of sucking. In the second stage, simple motor habits, such as looking from a certain perspective, "produce" sensations or incipient perceptions; but the infant seems to think that his act of looking sometimes produces and sometimes does not produce the desired images: he will not search for them if they disappear. In the third stage, which appears sometime during the third to the sixth month, the infant grasps what he sees, if it is within reach. He is beginning to coordinate the information obtained through different senses: sight, hearing, touch, and perhaps smell. But during the fifth month, if an object is dropped directly in front of him, he will make no effort to follow it with his eyes; he continues to look hopefully at the spot from which it was dropped, or his attention lapses. If he is hungry and he is given a bottle with the wrong end toward him, he will not turn the bottle around so that he can put the nipple into his mouth. (He has not yet "constructed" the bottle.) During the fourth stage (ninth to tenth month), he learns to search for an object that he has seen an adult put under a cloth; he will remove the cloth. But he is not yet able to take account of a sequence of changes of position: if he twice discovers a toy parrot under cloth A and then before his eyes it is placed under cloth B, he will continue to look for it under cloth A. During the fifth stage (twelfth to eighteenth

---

[7] J. Piaget, *The Construction of Reality in the Child,* trans., M. Cook (New York: Basic Books, Inc., 1954), esp. chap. 1.

[8] *Ibid.,* chap. 1.

month), the child learns to take account of changes of position, but still imperfectly. During the sixth stage (fifteenth to nineteenth month), he apparently "constructs" the object so that he can imagine its existence when it is invisible and can find it readily although its position has been changed several times. We may say that the child now has the ability to have "internalized objects" corresponding, to some extent, to the external objects as they are perceived by adults.[9]

What is an internalized object? On the physiological level, it may be conceived as a group of cell assemblies in the brain, a set of "traces" left by experience. Psychologically, it has two aspects. First, it is a "cognitive map" of an external object (or class of objects).[10] The object itself is "external" in the sense that it has a socially agreed-upon objective existence; it is not a figment of the imagination. The term "cognitive map" is appropriate. Like an ordinary map, the internalized object is a *symbol* of something else. As a map of Paris "represents" the various buildings and streets of the city, so the internalized object represents the external object (which of course may be a person or a thing, or a class of persons or things). Looking at the map of a city, one may go in imagination from place to place within that city; the parts of the city are represented in a way analogous to the way in which they are related in reality. So with the internalized object. One may "predict" with varying degrees of confidence and accuracy, according to the nature of the external object and the extent of one's experience with it, what one will find if one goes around the object, speaks to it under varying circumstances, touches it, manipulates it in certain ways, and so on. These "predictions" are made possible by the internalized object.[11]

In its first aspect, then, an internalized object

. . . is a series or a system of "If A then B" propositions, hence the [internalized] object seems to be a set of implications.

. . . an automobile is a thing which, (i) if you turn on the keys and step on the starter, gives out an engine noise, (ii) if you then engage the gears, gives a postural feeling of accelerating motion, (iii) if you then turn the wheel, gives visual and postural feelings of left or right turning, (iv) if you stand in its path when it is moving, gives you an injury, (v) if it gives an

---

[9] Piaget is here interested in the stages by which the child develops the *concept* of external objects—the general idea that there are such things as external objects. He is not in this chapter interested in the process by which *particular* objects or classes of objects come to be internalized, each with its personal meaning in the motivational system of the developing personality. Because Piaget conducted his ingenious experiments with a small number of subjects (his own children), the specified ages at which the several stages are reached must be regarded as rough approximations for children in general. A larger number of subjects might show a wider range of variation.

[10] The term "cognitive map" is used by Edward C. Tolman in several publications. See, for example, "A Psychological Model," Part III of Talcott Parsons and E. A. Shils (eds.), *Toward a General Theory of Action* (Cambridge, Mass.: Harvard University Press, 1951).

[11] The present description of internalized objects is largely based upon J. Olds, *The Growth and Structure of Motives: Psychological Studies in the Theory of Action* (Glencoe, Ill.: Free Press, 1955), esp. chap. 5. His analysis deals with many complex problems for which we have no space.

auto-standing-still-nearby type of configuration, and if you approach and touch, you get a cold, smooth, metallic sensation, and so forth.[12]

In addition to the cognitive aspect of an internalized object, there is a motivational aspect. The internalized object is never an emotionally neutral concept. Even in its latent state (that is, when the external object is not being thought of, remembered, wished for, perceived, or enjoyed), the internalized object, as a system of cell assemblies, carries a potential of motivational energy, a set of positive and negative charges, so to speak. When the necessary cell assemblies are activated (that is, when the external object is thought of or perceived in some one of its possible conditions), the cell assemblies are capable of mobilizing a certain amount of energy from the organism. Moreover, this energy has a certain direction of flow; it motivates the subject to "approach" or "avoid" the external object, to seek to change the aspect of the external object that is contemplated or presented, or otherwise to influence the relation between the subject and the external object. In short, the internalized object is more than a cognitive map; it is charged with "meaning" in the emotional life of the personality; it is related, through the deposits of "traces" of experience, to other internalized objects within the same personality; and the whole system of internalized objects is related to the "world" of persons and things outside the personality. If the subject thinks of Jones, whom he admires and whose approval he would like to have, and if his cognitive map of Jones has in it a "region" showing Jones disapproving of the subject, then this "region" of the internalized object will mobilize a certain amount of energy directed toward changing Jones's attitude, so that the subject may enjoy a slightly different internalized object—one with a "region" showing Jones approving of the subject.[13]

It will be obvious from what has been said that an internalized object "representing" another person is far more than a stored image of that person's physical appearance. Of course, the physical appearance of the external object, as seen from varying distances and perspectives, may well constitute a certain part of the cognitive map.[14]

Internalized objects are built up gradually in the course of interaction with the environment. This is obvious when the internalized object is a "social object" (a person), but it is no less true when the object is nonsocial. The coordinated sensory powers of the organism must accommodate themselves to the objective properties of the object; these properties interact, so to speak, with the organism. We shall return to this point below, when we consider in greater detail the

---

[12] Olds, *op. cit.,* pp. 207–8.

[13] This example is paraphrased freely from Olds *(ibid.)*.

[14] Cooley had the complex internalized object in mind when he wrote: "Thus the face of a friend has power over us in much the same way as the sight of a favorite book, of the flag of one's country, or the refrain of an old song; it starts a train of thought, lifts the curtain from an intimate experience. And his presence does not consist in the pressure of his flesh upon a neighboring chair, but in the thoughts clustering about some symbol of him, whether the latter be his tangible person or something else." C. H. Cooley, *Human Nature and the Social Order* (New York: Charles Scribner's Sons, 1902), p. 82.

process of internalizing objects. Note, however, that experience of the world ("interaction" with it) may be indirect as well as direct. A person may have an internalized object representing Jones even if he has never seen Jones but has only heard or read about him. Many sources of information contribute to the internalized object.[15]

The self

As we have noted, the infant at birth has no self-consciousness. But at the same time that he is building up internalized objects corresponding to other people and to things, he is also building up a concept of himself as an object. The "self" might be regarded as the internalized object representing one's own personality. Thus it includes one's own conception of one's abilities and characteristics, an evaluation of these aspects of one's personality, and certain feelings of pride, shame, and self-respect, any one of which can be activated under certain circumstances. The construction of the self and the construction of other internalized objects obviously go on together; if one's own being has not been distinguished as a separate entity, one cannot distinguish other beings or things as separate entities.

Many writers have emphasized that the self arises in interaction with the social and nonsocial environment. The social environment, of course, is especially important. The baby cries, and mother responds with milk or cuddling or a fresh diaper—with something good. If the mother continues to respond with care and love, the baby will eventually learn to distinguish between the state of affairs when the mother is present and the state of affairs when the mother is absent. The mother will be "internalized" as an object system. Primitive symbolic communication will be established. For example, the baby's crying will come to mean "I want mother." The mother's behavior will eventually come to mean to him "Mother is pleased with me, Mother loves me." Here we have the beginning of a self. ("I am lovable. I can influence Mother.")

The formation of the self thus involves "taking the role of the other"—seeing oneself, in imagination, as an object seen by someone else.[16] The child, putting himself in the place of another, not only forms a concept of himself but also evaluates that concept, invests it with feeling and worth. To a considerable ex-

---

[15] "Now suppose . . . that I take up Froude's 'Caesar,' and presently find myself, under the guidance of that skillful writer, imagining a hero whose body long ago turned to clay. He is alive in my thought: there is perhaps some notion of his visible presence, and along with this the awakening of sentiments of audacity, magnanimity, and the like, that glow with intense life, consume my energy, make me resolve to be like Caesar in some respect, and cause me to see right and wrong and other great questions as I conceive he would have seen them." *Ibid.,* p. 99.

[16] "Taking the role of the other" is analyzed at great length in G. H. Mead, *Mind, Self, and Society: From the Standpoint of a Social Behaviorist,* ed. with introduction, C. W. Morris (Chicago: University of Chicago Press, 1934), Part III. By an extension of the meaning of "role," Mead also speaks of taking the role of things: in manipulating nonsocial objects, one builds up expectations of the way in which they will "respond" in various situations—of the "role" they will play.

tent, then, the self is, in Cooley's phrase,[17] "looking-glass self"—a reflection of the attitudes and evaluations of others. Needless to say, one's interpretation of the behavior of others is subject to error: the self must be revised as new evidence comes in, or as one actively "tests reality" to find out how others feel. The term "looking-glass self," although undoubtedly appropriate, can be misunderstood. There is no implication that one's conception of one's own being changes radically every time one confronts a new person (as a looking glass shows a new image if a new person confronts it). The deposits of experience build up a more and more definite and stable self, just as they build up more and more definite and stable "representors" for all the other external objects besides one's own personality. (One's own personality, of course, has certain characteristics regardless of one's conception of it; in this sense, it is an "external" object.)

The self develops gradually. The "egocentricity" of the young child is due, paradoxically, to his uncertain grasp of the fact that he is a distinct being, located in a certain way relative to others. A child may reveal some ability to "take the role" of another, but for a long time he will be far from able to match adults in this respect. A child who can tell his own right hand from his left may not be able to tell someone else's right hand from the left. Adults often think that children are lying when in fact children are for a long time unable to distinguish between fiction, possibility, and observed reality (socially agreed-upon reality).[18]

Roles

From a sociological point of view, social roles are among the most important "objects" that are internalized in the course of socialization. Later sections of this chapter will be concerned mainly with the social conditions in which the child learns the roles of himself and others. For the present we must notice that an internalized role is a little different from the role itself. In this respect, internalized roles are similar to all other internalized objects. The role itself is composed of norms, . . . As an "establishment" in the personality, however, a role, like any other internalized object, is invested with *personal* meaning. Its character is determined in part by the place it has in that personality—its place among the other internalized roles, persons, and things. The motivation it commands in a particular personality will not be quite the same as the motivation similar establishments command in other personalities. For example, the role of boy in a particular society is part of the culture of that society, but the role object internalized in any particular boy is a particular variant of the cultural role, and it contains more than culture. In the same way, the internalized object "representing" the city I live in bears a close relation at many points to the actual city and, moreover, is similar in many ways to the corresponding object internalized

---

[17]Cooley, *op. cit.*, pp. 151 ff.

[18] J. Piaget, *Judgement and Reasoning in the Child* (New York: Harcourt, Brace & World, Inc., 1928), chap. 5.

in any other inhabitant fairly familiar with the city; and yet "my" city is also intensely personal and in some ways different from the "cities" of my fellow residents.

CONDITIONS OF LEARNING

If all our experience leaves "traces" in the brain and hence in the personality, then in a sense "learning" is going on all the time. For good or bad, "cognitive maps" are being constructed or confirmed, motives are being strengthened or weakened, and action patterns are becoming more (or less) habitual. This is a neutral sense of "learning." In this sense, as far as socialization is concerned, some learning is regarded as "good" or "successful," and some learning is regarded as "bad" or "unsuccessful." Socialization, being learning that contributes to one's ability to perform social roles, is learning with a particular direction and quality; from the point of view of some particular social system, it is desirable and desired learning. It is therefore appropriate to ask under what conditions "successful" learning takes place. We shall distinguish three conditions.

Discrimination

Successful learning of new behavior patterns, or successful internalization of new objects, requires that the person being socialized be able to distinguish between the new objects and behavior patterns and the ones with which he is already familiar. The socializing agent must present him with "cues" that will enable him to perceive the new object as something different from those that he has encountered hitherto. All students of learning recognize that there is a kind of inertia in the personality such that we tend to class new objects with old ones unless we are struck by differences great enough to arouse "testing" activity. Even then, the testing activity is designed to find out to what extent we can safely assimilate this new object to categories already established. A child who has been treated well by adults will tend to trust new adults he encounters, provided that they do not act in ways too strange. In general, if we are to react appropriately, we have to know what we are reacting to; we have to be able to define the situation correctly, for often the same manner of behaving is appropriate in some situations but inappropriate in others.

Reward and punishment

We have already noted that internalized objects are always vested with some degree of latent or active motivational energy, and that this energy guides action in patterned ways. We can hardly speak of objects in the external world without suggesting behavior patterns appropriate in relation to them. If the socializing agent wishes a child to control his bowel movements, for example, he must first make it clear to the child in what situations it is "all right" to release and in what situations it is not. Placing the child on a pot will probably be the distinguishing cue in our society. But the socializing agent must also reward the child for "correct" performances and either withhold reward or punish for "incorrect" performances. Reward and punishment are said to "reinforce" the desired behavior pattern. Reward and punishment need not come in tangible form; a smile may be more effective than a piece of candy.

The effectiveness of reinforcement increases (1) the more often the "correct" behavior is rewarded, (2) the more consistently it is rewarded, (3) the greater difference there is between the satisfaction resulting from the correct behavior and the satisfaction (or dissatisfaction) resulting from incorrect behavior in the same situation, and (4) the sooner the reward comes after the correct behavior.[19]

The theory of reinforcement, which is based on numerous experiments, holds that both reward and punishment are effective in training. Some societies, however, depend more on one than on the other. The question arises whether reward and punishment are equally effective, or whether one is always better than the other, or whether some combination is best.

There is no doubt that reward can be quite effective and that it is less likely than punishment to produce undesirable side effects in the personality. In one study,[20] nursery-school children were given some training in putting on and taking off their wraps, and they were praised for correct performances. A control group was given no training and no praise. At a later point, the members of the experimental group refused help more often than the members of the control group. In another study,[21] twenty-nine boys aged eight to ten were given the Thematic Apperception Test. This is a standard "projective" test, in which the subject is asked to tell a story for each of a series of ambiguous pictures; the stories reveal the relative prominence of different trends in the personality of the subject. The stories of the twenty-nine boys showed that the boys differed in their concern for achievement according to the training they had received. Those with the greatest interest in achieving had been most rewarded for their achievements in the past. Moreover, although these boys had been subject to more restrictions than the others tested, they had also been rewarded more for accepting restrictions. The mothers of the boys most interested in achievement had also made "demands" for achievement earlier than the other mothers. The same study contained other evidence that the rewarded boys were more interested in achieving than the other boys were.

Before considering the effects of punishment, we should be careful to make a distinction between punishment and the imposition of frustrations. The expe-

---

[19] These statements about learning are not phrased with technical rigor. For an authoritative, more thorough, and more technical summary, see Olds, *op. cit.*, chaps. 2, 3. Olds gives a brief summary on pp. 76–78.

[20] E. Fales, "Genesis of Level of Aspiration in Children from One and One-half to Three Years of Age" (unpublished manuscript, 1937, reported in *Child*, 1954).

[21] M. R. Winterbottom, "The Relation of Childhood Training in Independence to Achievement Motivation" (unpublished dissertation, University of Michigan, 1953, reported in *Child*, 1954).

rience of frustration is necessary for learning to take place, even if the frustration is only relative: reward will not have the desired effect unless incorrect responses are *not* rewarded—in other words, unless the subject is rewarded for some responses and frustrated for others. Punishment, properly speaking, is some painful action that symbolizes the socializing agent's attitude of disapproval (as reward symbolizes his attitude of approval). There are at least two dangers in punishment. Both seem to lie in *excessive* punishment relative to some standard of justice, or relative to the level of tolerance for pain in the subject being trained.

The first danger is that punishment will produce hatred for the socializing agent and will either make the subject less sensitive to his disapproval or give the subject a motive for frustrating the socializing agent by disobeying in retaliation. The motive of frustrating the socializing agent can become stronger than the motive of avoiding punishment.

Another danger in punishment is that the subject will "overlearn." He may develop so much anxiety in the behavior field in which he has been punished that he will be inhibited in "normal" and desirable behavior patterns. There is some evidence, for example, that punishment for "aggressive" behavior may produce anxiety about normal self-expression.[22] The precise effect of "excessive" punishment, as of any other experience, depends upon the subject's prior experience and the personality structure that has been developed. It also depends upon the nature of the punishment, what it is being administered for, what the punishment agent's motives are, and the general nature of the relationship between the punishing agent and the person being punished. It has been surmised that this second danger has perhaps led some societies to depend much more on reward than on punishment. Examples are the Comanche Indians[23] and the Eskimos. The avoidance of punishment in socialization in these societies is no doubt functional, for the conditions of life are so exacting that the ability to act autonomously, swiftly, and courageously is virtually necessary for survival.

Nevertheless, good reasons have been advanced for not eschewing punishment altogether in socialization. Some acts are dangerous, and it is not always possible or convenient to provide an environment in which the child will not be able to hurt himself. Better to train by punishing than to let the child take risks that he is not able to appreciate. Further, it is perhaps desirable to make a child sensitive to disapproval early, so that in later life he can be guided by hints of disapproval from others. Mild expressions of disapproval are among the most common means by which adults "control" one another's incipient tendencies to social deviation.[24]

---

[22] I. L. Child, "Socialization," in Gardner Lindzey (ed.), *Handbook of Social Psychology* (Reading, Mass.: Addison-Wesley Publishing Co., Inc., 1954), Vol. 2, chap. 18, p. 671.

[23] A. Kardiner with the collaboration of R. Linton, Cora DuBois, and J. West, *The Psychological Frontiers of Society* (New York: Columbia University Press, 1945), chaps. 3, 4.

[24] O. H. Mowrer, "Discipline and Mental Health," *Harvard Educational Review* (Oct., 1947), Vol. 17, pp. 465–67. Mowrer gives other reasons, but it is not clear that he distin-

Control of the effects of frustration

A third condition for learning is control of the effects of frustration. The feeling of frustration is the unpleasant response that one has to being thwarted in some activity, deprived of something one has been enjoying, refused something one wishes to have. Obviously, a great deal of frustration occurs in socialization. Frustration is likely to be especially severe during the early years, since the young child cannot understand the "reasons" for others' frustrating him, and since he has not yet learned how to cope well with his own feelings. The thwarting, depriving, refusing, and demanding by socializing agents must often seem arbitrary at best, and at worst, as we shall see, unjust. In any case, frustration tends to produce aggressive feelings and possibly indignation. If the frustrating agent—for example, the mother—is also loved, then the child may develop anxiety as well: anxiety lest the mother withdraw her love and care. From the point of view of the socializing agent, the danger in these feelings of aggression, indignation, and anxiety is that they make the child unable or unwilling to give his attention to the "task" of learning; he may not be able to make the discriminations necessary; he may develop a strong motive to thwart the socializing agent by refusing to cooperate. It is necessary, therefore, for the socializing agent to do something to counteract the effects of frustration, to reassure the child, to reward him whenever he does what is required. Here we see a good example of the fact that socialization takes place in social interaction.

In the "growth gradients" that Gesell and Ilg have published, showing at what age certain kinds of activity are "normally" manifested by middle-class American children, we can see evidence that frustration is common. We read, concerning the two-and-a-half-year-old child (who is trying to cope with new "demands" being made upon him): "Crying from temper. Stormy. . . . Whining." In the growth gradient for assertion and anger, we read: "Tantrums: extremely aggressive whole-body response. Caused chiefly by mother. . . . Anger chiefly aroused by interference with his physical activity or with his possessions." For the average child at five and a half, we read: "Abrupt onset of temper tantrums, with loud angry crying. . . . Some moodiness, whining, expression of resentment." Under "assertion and anger," we find: "Temper tantrums. Slams doors. Strikes parents or other children." [25]

In addition to such overt behavior, the dreams characteristic of five-and-a-half-year-old children also show anxiety: "Dream of things in their beds. Waken and go to mother's bed. . . . Wild animals (wolves, bears, foxes, snakes) chase or bite the child." [26] Children whose mothers punish them for aggressive acts may

---

guishes properly between punishment and the imposition of frustration. (Making a child go to school, for example, is not punishing him, and one might argue that it is better to reward him for going than to punish him for not going.)

[25] A. Gesell and F. L. Ilg, *The Child from Five to Ten* (New York: Harper & Bros., 1946), pp. 292–94.

[26] *Ibid.*, p. 306.

become inhibited in expressing aggression directly, but they may reveal more aggressive fantasies in their doll play than other children.[27]

The amount of frustration the child must undergo in socialization varies considerably from one society to another. In one of the best relevant investigations,[28] ethnographic reports on seventy-five primitive societies were analyzed in order to provide a statistical test of certain hypotheses.[29] The societies were rated with respect to degree of severity in the socialization of children. Five areas of training were rated: nursing and weaning, toilet training, sexual training, training for independence, and training with respect to aggressive behavior. Great variation was found, for example, in the age of weaning. The most indulgent society was the Chenchu tribe of India, who do not wean their children before the age of five or six. Middle-class Americans wean children at a little over half a year. Of fifty-two primitive societies for which the evidence on weaning was adequate, only one was more "severe" than ours.[30]

Training with regard to aggressive behavior varies from that of the Siriono (South American Indians), who are most permissive, to that of the Harney Valley Paiute (North American Indians), of whom it is written: "If siblings fight among themselves, the older ones are whipped. If a child strikes his parents, they hit him back."[31] Of thirty-one primitive societies for which the data were adequate for rating, only seven were thought to treat aggressive behavior more severely than the American middle class. Indeed, for all five "areas" of training, with respect to indulgence or severity in the early weeks and months, the average rating of the American middle class was the same as that of the two most severe primitive societies. In a contest between the forty-eight societies for which the data were considered adequate, the American middle class would be tied for second place in severity of socialization—that is, in imposition of frustration. Yet the United States may not be the most severe of modern Western societies. From a description of child training in a village in southeastern France,[32] one gets the impression that in many ways the average French child experiences more frustration than the average American child.

In general, however, Whiting and Child found that all societies impose frustration, and that most societies are relatively severe in some areas of training and relatively indulgent in others.

We may conclude for indulgence and severity, and with less certainty

---

[27] E. Hollenberg, and M. Sperry, "Some Antecedents of Aggression and Effects of Frustration in Doll Play," *Personality*, Vol. 1, 1951.

[28] J. W. M. Whiting and I. L. Child, *Child Training and Personality: A Cross-Cultural Study* (New Haven, Conn.: Yale University Press, 1953).

[29] The hypotheses tested have only peripheral relevance to the present chapter.

[30] American practices were rated according to the same system that was used for primitive societies. The evidence for the United States was found in two works by A. Davis and R. J. Havighurst, "Social Class and Color Differences in Child Rearing," Vol. 11, *American Sociological Review;* and *Father of the Man* (Boston: Houghton Mifflin Co., 1947).

[31] B. B. Whiting, *Paiute Sorcery,* Viking Fund Publications in Anthropology, No. 15, 1950, p. 68.

[32] L. Wylie, *Village in the Vaucluse* (Cambridge, Mass.: Harvard University Press, 1957).

for age, that the practices of a society for one system of behavior are almost entirely independent of its practices with respect to other systems of behavior.[33]

STAGES OF SOCIALIZATION

One of the most obvious things about socialization is that the socializing agent does not try to teach everything at once. He (or she) concentrates on one task or on a few tasks at a time. Moreover, the process of accomplishing any one of the aims of socialization is gradual. Especially during the early stages of life (infancy and childhood), socialization takes place within a "simplified" social world; that is, the social system in which the infant or child is being trained is much less complex than the society as a whole. This simplification makes it possible for the child to attend to relatively few things at a time. Thus he has a better opportunity to make the necessary discriminations, to cope with his negative reactions due to frustration, to establish new learning more firmly, to integrate new learning with old, and to reorganize his inner world slowly. He is not allowed to be overwhelmed with social stimuli. Gradually the social system within which socialization is going on is broadened to include more objects to be discriminated and internalized.[34]

Since socialization is learning to participate in social roles, the most important objects to be internalized are the social roles themselves. But, . . . in order to perform any social role adequately, one must "know" the other social roles in the same social system. In the terms of the present chapter, the child must internalize the roles he will be expected to perform himself and also the roles of the other persons with whom he will interact. As the self grows concomitantly with other internalized social objects, so one's own roles grow in one's personality concomitantly with other roles. In fact, the internalization of roles is almost the same thing as the growth of personality, and those internalized roles with which one "identifies" (makes one's *own* roles) are at least the main focus of one's "self." At each stage of socialization, therefore, the child internalizes a *system* of roles, not just one role.

We shall describe briefly four stages of socialization from infancy to adulthood. The names given to the stages have become fixed in usage, and they are fairly appropriate although far from adequately descriptive. They are (1) the oral stage, (2) the anal stage, (3) the oedipal stage and latency, and (4) adolescence. (The third stage is sometimes regarded as two stages, but, as we shall see, the logical symmetry of the whole division into stages—which in any case is only a rough indication of the sequence of events in actual life—requires that the oedipal stage and the latency period be treated as substages of one main stage.)

In all these stages, but especially in the first three, the family is the main

---

[33] Whiting and Child, *op. cit.,* p. 117.
[34] This whole section is based largely on Talcott Parsons and Robert F. Bales, *Family, Socialization and Interaction Process* (Glencoe, Ill.: Free Press, 1955).

socializing group. Therefore, we must consider the structure of the family as it bears on socialization. The family varies in composition from one society to another, but the nuclear family is universal (except for the Nayars of India).[35] For our purpose, we shall ignore the variation in particular families and concentrate on the *institutional* structure of the nuclear family. There are four roles: husband-father, wife-mother, son-brother, and daughter-sister. In detail, these roles also vary from one society to another, but again there are all-but-universal features. One such feature is obvious: the division according to generation is also a division according to relative power to control interaction; father and mother are able to control son and daughter more than son and daughter are able to control parents. Another "universal" feature has to do with the division according to sex.

Zelditch[36] examined ethnographic reports on a sample of fifty-six societies to test the hypotheses (1) that in all nuclear families "instrumental" leadership is differentiated by role from "expressive" leadership, and (2) that in all nuclear families the instrumental leader is institutionally the father and the expressive leader is the mother.

> Ego . . . [is] considered *instrumental* leader of the nuclear family if the ethnographer's report offers statements of the form:
> 1. Ego is boss-manager of the farm, leader of the hunt, etc. Ego is the final court of appeals, final judge and executor of punishment, discipline, and control over the children of the family.
>
> Ego . . . [is] considered *expressive* leader of the nuclear family if the ethnographer's report offers statements of the form:
> 2. Ego is the mediator, conciliator, of the family; ego soothes over disputes, resolves hostilities in the family. Ego is affectionate, solicitous, warm, emotional to the children of the family; ego is the "comforter," the "consoler," is relatively indulgent, relatively unpunishing.[37]

Of the fifty-six societies, forty-six made a role differentiation for instrumental and expressive leadership. Careful study of the ten negative cases, however, throws considerable doubt on the ethnographers' reports, or at least on the conclusion that the cases should be regarded as inconsistent with the first hypothesis.

What about the second hypothesis? Of the fifty-six societies, forty-eight clearly made the husband-father the instrumental leader and eight did not. But here again the "negative" evidence was far from conclusive. (For example, some of the "negative" cases are societies in which the wife's brother is the provider for her children. As far as the *nuclear family* is concerned, however, there is no case in which there is clear evidence that the wife herself has "instrumental" superiority over the husband, and no case in which the husband clearly has

---

[35] Nayars of India discussed in H. M. Johnson, *Sociology* (New York: Harcourt, Brace & World, Inc., 1960), chap. 6.

[36] M. Zelditch, Jr., "Role Differentiation in the Nuclear Family: A Comparative Study," in Parsons and Bales, *op. cit.*

[37] Zelditch used four other "designation rules" for classifying his cases, but the two quoted give the basic meaning of "instrumental" and "expressive." *Ibid.,* p. 318.

"expressive" superiority over the wife. We are speaking, of course, of the institutionalized roles; "bossy" women probably exist in every society as deviants.) In experimental work with small task-oriented groups of the same sex, Bales and Slater[38] had found a definite tendency for instrumental and expressive leadership to be separated. They also found, however, that the task leader and the "best-liked" leader often formed a coalition, and they pointed out that the stability of the family, as of their experimental groups, probably depends on such a coalition. The investigation by Zelditch checked and supported their analysis.

As for the younger generation, there is a universal tendency (no one will dispute) for the son's role to be more like the father's and for the daughter's role to be more like the mother's. We have been speaking of the four roles in their developed form; as we shall see, the child does not internalize any of these roles *in this form* until he is fairly well along in the third stage.

The first stage

In the womb the fetus is presumably warm and comfortable. At birth the infant faces his first crisis: he must breathe, he must exert himself to be fed, he is susceptible to cold, wet, and other discomforts; he cries a good deal. The essential goal of the first stage of socialization is to establish oral dependency. The infant builds up fairly definite expectations about feeding time, and he learns to signal his pressing needs for care. During this stage, the infant is not involved in the family as a whole. He is involved only in the subsystem consisting of him and his mother. For the other members of the family, as Parsons says, the baby is little more than a "possession." If the father or anyone else shares with the mother the task of caring for the baby, no role differentiation is involved: that person will also be performing the role of "mother" (in its simplest form at this "oral" stage).

What does the infant internalize? He is so passive relative to the "mother" that it is questionable whether he internalizes two roles at all. This is the stage of what Freud called "primary identification." In the personality of the infant, by the time oral dependency has been established, his own role and that of the mother (or other provider of care) are probably not clearly distinguished. Mother and infant are "merged."

Some control over the hunger drive has been established, and the infant has been sensitized to the diffusely "erotic" pleasure of bodily contact with the mother.

The second stage

The time at which the second stage of socialization begins varies depending upon the society, the social class, and the particular family. In the American

[38] R. F. Bales and D. E. Slater, "Role Differentiation in Small Decision-Making Groups," in Parsons and Bales, *op. cit.,* chap. 5.

middle class it probably begins soon after the first year and is completed during the third year. The "anal" crisis, with which the stage begins, is caused by the imposition of new "demands," notably the demand for the child to take over some degree of care for himself. Toilet training is the main focus of *new* concern. During this stage, the child internalizes two roles—his own and that of his mother, now clearly separate. The child not only receives *care;* he also receives *love,* and gives love in return. Psychoanalysts have pointed out that to the child in this stage the feces are a gift, a symbol of the child's love for his mother. On the other hand, withholding feces or releasing at the "wrong" time is an expression of aggression (defiance). The positive sanction for correct performances is the mother's love. In the more "severe" societies, punishment is also used to discourage incorrect performances; but in all societies the child is enabled to discriminate between correct and incorrect, first by cues given by the socializing agent, and secondly by being rewarded for correct performance and not rewarded for incorrect.

In this second stage we see clearly the importance of a general fact about all socialization: the socializing agent always has a dual role. During this "anal" stage, for example, the mother participates, first, in the limited social system consisting of her interaction with the child; secondly, she participates in the family as a whole. In the subsystem she is the instrumental leader *relative to the child,* for she is still chiefly responsible for meeting his specific needs. The child's contribution to the system is mainly expressive: he helps to integrate the system by cooperating and giving love; he is still too young and dependent to contribute very much to task accomplishment.

The dual role of the socializing agent is important for several reasons. The task of the socializing agent, after all, is to train the child so that he will ultimately be able to participate in a more complex social system; obviously the socializing agent has to know the roles and common values of that larger system.

Secondly, socialization is an unpleasant task, to some extent, for the socializing agent as well as for the child. The mother does not enjoy seeing her child suffer through the process of weaning, toilet training, and the like. No doubt she can console herself (as the child cannot) with thoughts of the final accomplishment; but probably she is "forced," to some extent, by pressure from the larger social system of which she is a member. Her husband may feel sooner than she (probably too soon, as Gesell says) that it's about time his son were doing more for himself and whining less often. This pressure from the larger system is, of course, only one of the cues for the mother that she had better be getting along with her task.

The counterpart of this pressure is resistance on the part of the mother. Her dual role enables her to protect the child to some extent from the excessive pressure of the other members of the family. Thus the mother "represents" the larger social system in relation to the smaller, and the smaller in relation to the larger. Viewed in another way, her dual representative role is an aspect of her "expressive" leadership in the whole family as a social system.

Finally, at the same time that the mother (as socializing agent) is mediating between the subsystem and the larger system—now yielding, now resisting—she is also supported by that larger system. Her husband especially (in the "normal" case we are using for the framework of analysis) will understand the strain she is undergoing, will relieve her of some other burdens (for example, by spending more time with the other children), and will back her up when she must be firm with the child being socialized.[39]

The third stage

The third stage (in the American middle class) extends from about the fourth year to puberty (the age of twelve or thirteen: the age varies somewhat, and puberty is merely a rough dividing line). The "oedipal crisis" occurs typically during the fourth and fifth years, and the so-called "latency" period follows.

In the course of the third stage, the child becomes a member of the family as a whole. He must internalize all four roles of the family, and he must above all identify himself with the social role ascribed to him on the basis of his biological sex. We shall discuss below what "identification" means.

The "Oedipus complex," as Freud named it, is the feeling of jealousy the boy is believed to have toward his father on account of their rivalry for the mother; and the boy's feelings are believed to be sexual. For the girl, the "Electra complex" is the corresponding set of feelings: she is believed to be in love with her father and therefore jealous of her mother.

It is perhaps desirable to distinguish between sexual and erotic feelings, even though the two are closely related. In our own society at least (not necessarily in all others), the child of four, five, or six does not necessarily have a clear understanding of the fact that there are two sexes; he may have observed the anatomical differences between boys and girls, but he probably has no appreciation of their sexual function. His mother is not yet female in the sexual sense, nor his father male. Therefore the child at first is incapable of "sexual" feelings in a narrow sense. Yet there is no doubt that the child, and probably the infant, has a diffuse erotic attachment to his mother. He not only loves her in the sense that he wants to please her and would be desolate if she were taken away from him; he also derives bodily pleasure from contact with her.[40] Indeed, this aspect of the child's attachment to his mother is important for socialization, since the mother can use bodily contact as a reward for "correct" performances on the child's part. The erotic attachment, moreover, is mutual. The danger that it might go "too far" (thus disrupting the family and making it difficult for the mother to keep love conditional upon the child's correct role performance) is prevented by the incest taboo, which restrains mother and child both.

---

[39] The dual role of the socializing agent is discussed by Parsons and Bales, *op. cit.* and also by T. Parsons and J. Olds, "The Mechanisms of Personality Functioning with Special Reference to Socialization," in Parsons and Bales, *op. cit.,* chap. 4.

[40] See e.g., White, *op. cit.,* pp. 120–21.

The boy's feeling of chagrin at having to share his mother with siblings and father, and his jealousy, are quite understandable whether the boy has "sexual" feelings for his mother or not. The same is true of the girl, who is equally disturbed, at first, at having her "exclusive" relation with the *mother* disturbed. In the following remarks, Gesell and Ilg are not distinguishing between boys and girls:

> Fathers also come in for their share of a 5-year-old's affection. The father, however, is rarely the preferred parent. . . . In the insecurity of the middle of the night [the child] wants his mother most of all. If, however, the mother is sick, some Fives who have been slow to build up a relationship with their fathers will now accept them.[41]

The child at six is also chiefly concerned with his (or her) mother, although the mother as socializing agent, making and enforcing demands, is also the main target of aggression:

> Although Six is often described as being "embroiled with" his mother, he is actually extremely ambivalent in regard to her. He may say "I love you" at one minute and "I hate you, I wish you were dead" at the next. He is most loving with his mother, yet most of his tantrums are directed against her.[42]

When the proper stage of socialization has been reached, many social pressures are brought to bear on the child to identify with the appropriate sex. Boys begin to be rewarded for behavior appropriate to boys (according to the culture), and girls are rewarded for acting like girls. More and more, the toys given to boys are different from those given to their sisters. Fairly striking anatomical differences make the correct identification easy; yet the correct identification is largely an achievement of socialization. Moreover, despite social pressures, some children fail to identify with the correct sex for them, and others, as we shall see, make an ambivalent identification.

When the boy has successfully identified with his father with regard to sex role, it is understandable that he should be particularly jealous of his father. And when the girl has successfully identified with her mother, it is equally understandable that she should be jealous of her mother. Special interest in the opposite sex is not inborn; nor is interest in the opposite sex the cause of identification with one's own sex. On the contrary, identification with one's own sex is the cause of one's interest in the opposite sex. Failure to make the correct identification is a cause of homosexuality.[43]

Following the turmoil caused by the "intrusion" of the father and possibly of siblings into the "romance" of mother and child, the child must settle down to mastering many new demands for independence. He has to go to school. He joins

---

[41] Gesell and Ilg, *op. cit.,* pp. 80–81.

[42] *Ibid.,* p. 118.

[43] O. H. Mowrer, *Learning Theory and Personality Dynamics: Selected Papers* (New York: Ronald Press Co., 1950), chap. 21, esp. pp. 605 ff.

groups of playmates ("peer groups," as they are called). In many situations he must learn to get along without the immediate guidance and support of his family. In our society, this period is one in which interest in the opposite sex (particularly for boys) tends to be suppressed to some extent in favor of devotion to the problems of mastering skills. Boys are no doubt struggling with the task of being *boys,* hence of being unlike the mother and sisters; their rejection of girls, after a certain point, is probably a reaction-formation—a repression of "girlish" dependency needs and a somewhat ill-assured assertion of masculinity. In this period, interest in the opposite sex is relatively "latent" (hidden, inactive). However, the latency period, so called, seems to have no physiological basis and is not found in all societies.[44]

The Meanings of "Identification." The term "identification" has been used in different ways.[45] We shall use it to mean either of two closely related things: (1) One is said to identify with a social *role* if one not only internalizes the role but adopts it as one's own, striving to attain the necessary skills and to conform with the role norms. (2) One is said to identify with a social *group* if one internalizes the role system of the group and considers oneself a member of it. Identification in the first sense links a boy with his father and brothers, for example, but not with his mother. Identification in the second sense links a boy with his family, including both parents and all siblings. No new principles of learning are involved in the process of identification. The three basic conditions of all learning are of course necessary: cues for discrimination, relative deprivation (reward for correct performance, no reward for incorrect performance), and control of reactions to frustration.

According to the definition we adopt, the boy makes three identifications during the third stage of socialization. First, he identifies with his father and brothers (sex-role identification); secondly, he identifies with all his siblings (role of child in the family); and finally, he identifies with the whole family as a member. (The last identification can hardly be made firm until the child has considerable experience with nonmembers of his family; school and peer group thus help him to identify with his family.) In this third stage, identification does not affect only the roles identified with. Identification with the sex role, for example, obviously requires a change in the internalized objects "representing" mother, father, and siblings of each sex. Up to this point, the difference between father and mother has not been clearly a *role* difference. Now the father appears clearly as the "instrumental" leader of the family, while the mother, who has hitherto been the instrumental leader in her relation with the child, now appears to him clearly as the "expressive" leader of the family.

The selective character of identification should be emphasized. In "identifying" with his father, a boy does not *become* his father (even in imagination); he

---

[44] White, *op. cit.,* p. 121.

[45] For an excellent analysis of the ways in which Sigmund and Anna Freud used it, see Mowrer, *op. cit.,* chap. 21. In the text, however, we follow Parsons and Bales, *op. cit.,* pp. 91–94.

wants to be *like* his father (and his older male siblings) in sex *role*. Moreover, the "sex role" at this point is far from being the same thing as the adult's "sexual role"; in his emphasis on generally masculine qualities, including interest in "instrumental" activities, the boy can successfully identify with his father at this stage even though the boy may still have a hazy idea of the nature of sexual intercourse.

The selective character of identification helps us to see how the mother can also help the boy to make the proper sex identification. Being a socialized adult, the mother has already internalized both the female and the male role, and she is able to reward the boy selectively for choosing the right one for him.

Nevertheless, the father is especially important in helping the boy to make the necessary discriminations, for the father can serve as a direct model in certain ways. Probably in every society the father helps his son by showing him how to do things. For example, of a father in Wogeo (New Guinea) we read:

> . . . when Marigum was making a new canoe he allowed his youngest son, Sabwakai, to take an adze and chip at the dugout. On my inquiring whether the boy did not impede his progress, the father agreed that he would be able to work much faster alone. "But if I send the child away," he added, "how can I expect him to know anything? This time he was in the way, but I'm showing him, and when we have to make another canoe he'll be really useful." [46]

The Eskimo father makes small bows and arrows and carves toy animals for his son to play with, and the father shows the boy how to shoot; as the boy gets older, the father makes larger bows and eventually lets the boy try his skill on small game. In Bali, where the boy begins to learn how to dance before he can walk, the father stands behind him, holding him up, and guides the boy's arms and hands in the traditional movements. [47] In general, of course, once the boy has learned the goal of being like men, he will tend to imitate men, especially his father.

Identification with one's sex role may or may not be complete or "whole-hearted." The likelihood of successful identification is greater (1) if the main model for a boy's sex role (the father) shows affection for the boy; (2) if the boy's acquaintance with the role model is intimate and prolonged; (3) if other important persons (notably the mother) encourage the boy to take his father as a model (in which case the boy will be doubly rewarded: first by the father and then by the mother); and (4) if the role model treats the boy's mother well (for then the boy, who presumably loves his mother, will *want* to be like him). Obviously, the reverse of any of these conditions will tend to have the opposite effect. For example, if the boy's mother has contempt for her husband, the boy

---

[46] H. I. Hogbin, "A New Guinea Childhood: From Weaning till the Eighth Year in Wogeo," *Oceania*, Vol. 16 (1946), p. 152.

[47] G. Bateson, and M. Mead, "Balinese Character: A Photographic Analysis," Special Publications of the New York Academy of Sciences, Vol. 2, Dec. 7, 1942, pp. 14, 86–87.

will be in conflict about the goal of becoming a man, lest he become "contempt-ible," like his father.[48]

The fourth stage

In general, adolescence, which begins roughly at puberty, is the stage during which the young boy or girl is ordinarily more and more "emancipated" from parental control. The "crisis" of the period is precisely the strain produced by much greater demands for independence. At the same time, in the middle class of our own society at least, the adolescent is still controlled to some extent by his parents in many activities in which he might like greater freedom. This is especially true, perhaps, of sexual activity. The physiological changes that ac-company adolescence would not in themselves produce problems if full sexual activity were permitted, but since it is not, these changes, in our own society, may intensify the ambivalence with which the adolescent approaches adult-hood—impatient of restriction, desiring independence, yet fearing freedom at the same time.

In our society, the goal of adulthood is considered to be attained when a person can support himself or herself entirely independently of the parental family. Full adulthood also implies the ability to form a family of one's own. Here an explicit distinction should perhaps be made between the ability to do so and the decision to do so; on the one hand, certain persons marry and become parents without being very well prepared, and, on the other hand, there are others who would be competent in marriage and parenthood and who possess the necessary skills to approach the opposite sex successfully but who deliber-ately decide not to marry.

Whether adolescence is a period of great strain depends upon the cultural definition of adult roles. There seems to be considerable variation from one society to another in the ease or difficulty with which the transition is typically accomplished. Adolescence is probably unusually difficult in our society be-cause the adult-to-be is required to make important decisions more or less on his own. In many other societies the choice of a marriage partner is made by elders within conventional rules. The other great life-decision, for men especially, is the choice of an occupation. Here again, in our society the burden of choice is placed largely on the individual himself.

---

[48] On variables affecting the success or failure of sex identification, see S. M. Stoke, "An Inquiry into the Concept of Identification," *Journal of General Psychology*, Vol. 76, 1950, and Mowrer, *op. cit.*, chap. 21. Both articles contain excellent descriptions of cases.

5. Lower class Negro mothers' aspirations for their children[*]

ROBERT R. BELL

Social values are primarily transmitted to the growing child through the major social agencies of the family, the school, and the peer group. When those three agencies are in basic agreement as to values they tend to reinforce one another and thereby minimize personal or social conflict for the individual in the socialization process. However, there are two general ways in which the transmission of social values may lead to conflict: first, if the agencies of society transmit values that are in conflict with one another; second, even when the values of the various agencies are in essential agreement the realities of the social milieu may make the achievement of internalized values difficult or impossible for the individual.

There has been in the past some disagreement among social scientists as to the relationship between general American values and social class. One view has been that major American values are a part of the total American society, regardless of social class level, and therefore shared by almost all Americans. The opposite view has been that many American values are unshared and often vary by social class.[1] Because the focus of this paper centers on some lower class values the above disagreements are conceptually important. A useful approach for resolving this disagreement has been suggested by Hyman Rodman through his concept of "the lower class value stretch." Rodman writes, "by the value stretch I mean that the lower class person, without abandoning the general values of the society, develops an alternative set of values. The result is that the members of the lower class, in many areas, have a wider range of values than others within the society. They share the general values of the society with members of other classes, but

[*] Revision of a paper read at the annual meeting of the Eastern Sociological Society, April, 1964. We wish to acknowledge partial support for this study by a Ford Foundation grant administered through the Philadelphia Council for Community Advancement. We also extend our thanks to those teachers and administrators in the four elementary schools who cooperated in helping make this study possible.

Reprinted from *Social Forces*, Vol. 43, No. 4, May, 1965, pp. 493–500; by permission of the University of North Carolina Press.

[1] For a comprehensive discussion of these points of view, see Hyman Rodman, "The Lower Class Value Stretch," *Social Forces* (December 1963), pp. 205–15.

in addition they have stretched these values, or developed alternative values, which help them to adjust to their deprived circumstances."[2] Rodman goes on further to suggest that the result is "a stretched value system with a low degree of commitment to all the values within the range, including the dominant, middle class values."[3]

A related area of disagreement among sociologists has been whether or not values that tend to be peculiar to a social class level are essentially the same within both the dominant white and Negro social class systems. The general consensus of research findings offers support for the position that the class structures of the dominant white and Negro systems are basically the same, at least in reference to general values.[4] For example, in a recent study of Negroes in Philadelphia, Parker and Kleiner came to the conclusion that "Negroes in the higher status positions tend to have values more similar to those of the white middle class, stronger desires to associate with whites, more internalization of negative attitudes toward other Negroes, and relatively weaker ethnic identification, than individuals in lower status positions."[5]

Therefore, on the basis of the research findings and interpretations discussed above two assumptions are made about the Negro mothers to be discussed in this paper: first, that the Negro lower class, of which the mothers are a part, has a greater spread of values than does the Negro middle class; second, that the Negro lower class is similar to the white lower class in its acceptance of general social values. In this paper the interest centers around one category of values—the aspirations (i.e., ideal expectations) given by Negro mothers for their children's futures. In the lower class Negro family the mother has long been recognized as the most important adult figure—especially in reference to her children.[6] In our population the mother was the only common parent figure because no husband/father was present in 27 percent of the Negro families.

POPULATION STUDIED

On October 1, 1963, experimental nursery school classes started in four elementary school districts in Philadelphia. An attempt was made to acquire as random a group of nursery school pupils as possible from each of the four school districts. The four elementary schools had been asked to provide a list of children who would qualify by age for the nursery classes. During the spring of 1963 the schools had sent home with pupils requests to their mothers to send back

---

[2] *Ibid.,* p. 209.

[3] *Ibid.,* p. 209.

[4] See E. F. Frazier, *Black Bourgeoisie* (New York: Collier Books, 1962), p. 195, and August B. Hollingshead, and Fredrick C. Redlich, *Social Class and Mental Illness* (New York: John Wiley & Sons, 1958), p. 65.

[5] Seymour Parker and Robert J. Kleiner, "Status Position, Mobility, and Ethnic Identification of the Negro," manuscript copy, pp. 18–19.

[6] See Arnold Rose, *The Negro in America* (Boston: Beacon Press, 1956), p. 228 and George E. Simpson and J. Milton Yinger, *Racial and Cultural Minorities* (New York: Harper & Bros., 1958), pp. 518–23.

information on any children of pre-school age. It was decided to use the lists of mothers' replies from the four schools to draw nursery school pupils who qualified by age and who had at least one older sibling in kindergarten, first or second grade. However, the lists from the four schools were incomplete and often factually inaccurate. As a result it was only possible to contact and interview between 25 and 35 mothers in three of the four elementary school districts. Within each of those three elementary school areas the 15 children picked to enter the nursery classes were selected on a random basis. The mothers of nursery school children in the fourth school district were not included in this study because they were a racially and ethnically mixed group. Therefore, 90 of the mothers interviewed were those in three elementary school districts who had a child who qualified by age for the nursery school classes.

The range of mother interviews was expanded because the major focus of the study was on the lower class Negro woman's self-role image. This was done by acquiring a list of mothers and their home addresses who had a child in kindergarten and at least one other child in the same elementary school districts where the nursery class mothers were interviewed. From the kindergarten lists 65 percent of the mothers were interviewed. Five percent of the kindergarten mothers refused to be interviewed and another 30 percent could not be contacted after three attempts by the interviewers. The failure to contact and interview the 30 percent group was because many of them were working mothers, and this biased the population interviewed because of underrepresentation of working mothers.

The population to be discussed consists of 202 Negro mothers with a minimum of two children, one of whom was in nursery school or kindergarten, and who lived in three elementary school districts in Philadelphia. The three school districts are essentially alike and may be described as almost totally Negro and on the basis of demographic data classified as lower class.

The interviewing was done by three Negro female graduate students using a schedule consisting of 102 items. An initial interview schedule was pretested with 15 interviews and as a result of the pretest about 20 percent of the items used in the final questionnaire were added or modified. The final items included in the interview schedule were designed to get at various aspects of the Negro woman's self-role image; i.e., background data, her views of her marriage and her wife role, patterns and techniques of child rearing, her feelings about the schools and her expectations for her children when they reach their adult years.

ANALYSIS OF DATA

Hyman Rodman's concept of the lower class "value stretch" suggests that certain subgroups may fall at different points along a lower class continuum. Therefore, through the use of selected social variables an attempt was made to distinguish different lower class subgroups within the Negro mother population. It was hypothesized that *if* the selected Negro mother subgroups were in fact different from each other, they would show significant differences in: first, descriptive social class variables; and second, the aspirations they held for their children's futures. Therefore, the primary interest was to examine the Negro mother subgroups for any significant differences, with a secondary interest in whether or not the mother population can be established as falling into the Negro lower class.

In the analysis of the population four Negro mother subgroups were defined on the basis of their education and the number of their children. The use of education is supported by the conclusions of a number of researchers who have found education to be the best single index of Negro social class differences.[7] The size of family (number of children) has also been correlated with social class differences by researchers.[8] Therefore, amount of education and number of children provide a two-variable index for attempting to distinguish Negro social class differences. These two variables were used to divide the Negro mother population into the following four subgroups:

Group A: Low education (0 to 8 years) and a large number of children (7 or more), *low status*[9] mothers (N = 37).

Group B: Low education (0 to 8 years) and a small number of children (6 or fewer), *middle status* mothers (N = 43).

Group C: High education (9 or more years) and a large number of children (7 or more), *middle status* mothers (N = 29).

Group D: High education (9 or more years) and a small number of children (6 or fewer), *high status* mothers (N = 93).

Using the four subgroups as defined above it was possible to make a comparison of six different paired subgroups. Using 11 items related to the mother's aspirations for her children five of the six possible paired subgroup comparisons showed three or fewer significant differences.[10] In the sixth paired subgroup comparison, Group A: *low status* mothers and Group D: *high status* mothers, eight of the 11 aspiration items showed statistically significant differences.

In the discussion of data that follows the major focus is on the differences between the *low status* and *high status* mothers. If those two subgroups represent real social class differences then the data will show differences in several ways. First, the two mother subgroups will be different in reference to social

---

[7] See Frazier, *op. cit.,* p. 23; Joseph A. Kahl, *The American Class Structure* (New York: Rinehart & Co., 1957), pp. 236–37, 276–79; Rose, *op. cit.,* p. 281; and Simpson and Yinger, *op. cit.,* p. 686.

[8] See Ronald Freedman, Pascal K. Whelpton, and Arthur A. Campbell, *Family Planning, Sterility and Population Growth* (New York: McGraw-Hill Book Co., 1959), pp. 288–95; Paul H. Gebhard, Wardell B. Pomeroy, Clyde E. Martin, and Cornelia V. Christenson, *Pregnancy, Birth and Abortion* (New York: Harper & Bros., 1958), p. 154; Frank W. Notestein, "Class Differences in Fertility," in Reinhard Bendix and Seymour M. Lipset (eds.), *Class, Status and Power* (New York: Free Press of Glencoe, 1953), p. 276; and Leonard Reissman, *Class in American Society* (New York: Free Press of Glencoe, 1959), pp. 450–59; and Rose, *op. cit.,* p. 56.

[9] *Status* is used to describe different social class levels within the Negro lower class.

[10] Significant differences refer to chi-square tests with differences at least at the .05 level of confidence.

variables found to be meaningful in other studies as helping to distinguish social class differences. Second, the aspirations for their children will not only be different for the two Negro mother subgroups but the direction of difference will be logically and conceptually consistent. Third, if the *low status* and *high status* mother groups *do* represent social class extremes in the population studied the other two mother groups (Group B and Group C, *middle status* mothers) will fall between them in aspirations they give for their children.

Background Factors. Do the *low status* and *high status* mothers differ in social class variables other than education and number of children? Negroes born and reared in the south and migrating to the north have been found in studies to be overrepresented in the Negro lower class of northern cities.[11] In our population 65 percent of the *low status* mothers had been born and reared, until at least ten years of age, in the south as compared to 41 percent of the *high status* mothers.

Younger age at marriage and age when the first child is born have also been related to the lower class.[12] In our population 35 percent of the *low status* mothers had been married at 16 years of age or younger as compared to 12 percent of the *high status* mothers. In the *low status* mother group 56 percent had given birth to their first child at 18 years of age or younger as contrasted to 33 percent of the *high status* mothers.

Finally, crowded living conditions have been determined as a characteristic of the lower class.[13] A ratio of the number of rooms divided by the number of persons living in the housing unit was used in this study as a measurement of housing conditions; i.e., over-crowded defined as a room-to-person ratio of .9 or below. Eighty-two percent of the *low status* mothers and 50 percent of the *high status* mothers lived in housing units with a ratio of .9 or below.

The background variables of place of birth, age at marriage, age when first child born and living conditions were all statistically significant and in the predicted direction when comparing the two mother groups. When those differences are added to the differences of education and number of children the evidence contributes support to the contention that the *low status* and *high status* mothers represent different social class levels.

ASPIRATIONS FOR CHILDREN

Rodman has pointed out that in most aspiration studies the respondent "is asked to give a simple, single response and it is then impossible to tell exactly what the response means."[14] This suggests that not only should a number of different aspirational questions be used but they also should be examined for overall logical consistency. In the discussion that follows the aspirations given

[11] See Rose, *op. cit.,* pp. 64–67, 228; and Simpson and Yinger, *op. cit.,* p. 520.

[12] See Hollingshead and Redlich, *op. cit.,* p. 126; and Kahl, *op. cit.,* p. 212.

[13] See Rose, *op. cit.,* pp. 209–12, 313; and Simpson and Yinger, *op. cit.,* p. 490.

[14] Rodman, *op. cit.,* pp. 210–11.

by the Negro mothers for their children's futures are examined for internal consistency within the three response categories as well as to logical relationships between the three categories.

Education and Occupation.   In the first category the mothers were asked how many years of education they would like to see their son(s) get and also how many years for their daughter(s). For the sons there was a statistically significant difference between the educational aspirations given by the *low status* and *high status* mothers. In the *low status* mother group 44 percent wanted a college education for their sons as compared to 65 percent of the *high status* mother group. For daughters there was also a significant difference in the mothers' responses. Thirty-nine percent of the *low status* mothers and 61 percent of the *high status* mothers wanted a college education for their daughters. There were no differences by the sex of the child in either of the two mother groups in desired educational achievement for their children.

The mothers were also asked what kind of occupation they would like to see their son(s) and daughter(s) fill when they reached their adult years. The occupational responses given by the mothers were classified as "office and clerical," "skilled," "professional," and "don't know." In occupational aspirations for their sons the responses given by the *low status* and *high status* mothers showed no significant differences. They were equally apt to respond "professional" (47 percent), but the *low status* mothers were slightly higher in giving "skilled" occupations for their sons than were the *high status* mothers (21 percent vs. 12 percent). For the daughters there was a significant difference in one type of job aspiration given by the two mother groups. Thirty-eight percent of the *low status* mothers said "office or clerical" as the level of occupational aspiration they held for their daughters as contrasted to 21 percent of the *high status* mothers' responses for the same occupational grouping.

When the occupational choices are compared for sons and daughters the *low status* mother group shows no difference in the "professional" group, but there were significant differences in the combined groupings of "office, clerical and skilled" with occupations in that grouping suggested for 48 percent of their daughters and 25 percent of their sons. The *low status* mothers were less sure about their aspirations for their sons' occupations as illustrated by 29 percent responding "don't know" as compared to only 10 percent saying "don't know" for their daughters. In the *high status* mother group there were no significant differences in their occupational aspirations for sons and daughters. Our data suggest a lower level of educational and occupational aspirations by the *low status* mothers for both sons and daughters than was true for the *high status* mothers.

Marriage and Parenthood.   Educational and occupational items are the measures most commonly used to determine aspirational levels. Yet, other adult role expectations may also be important not only as independent measures but also because they may influence the achievement of educational and occupational goals. For example, if a mother holds high educational and occupational aspirations for her children and at the same time thinks they should marry young and have a large family, there is often, by implication, a contradiction in her aspirations. Therefore, one might expect that those mothers who have high educational and occupational aspirations for their children would also hold aspirations for them of older age at marriage and to have fewer children.

The mothers were asked what they thought would be the best ages for their children to marry. Best age given for son(s) showed significant differences between the two mother groups. Fifty percent of the *low status* mother group responded 21 years of age or under as compared to only 17 percent of the *high status* mothers; and in the older age range 37 percent of the *low status* mothers and 63 percent of the *high status* mothers answered that 24 years of age and older was the best age for a son to marry.

There were also significant differences between the two mother groups regarding the best age for daughters to marry. Thirty-five percent of the *low status* mothers and 7 percent of the *high status* mothers responded with 19 years of age or younger, and in the older age range 10 percent of the *low status* mothers and 27 percent of the *high status* mothers gave 24 years of age or older as the best age for a daughter to marry. As would be expected both the *low status* and *high status* mothers gave younger ages for the marriage of daughters than they did for sons.

The mothers were also asked what would be the best number of children for a son and daughter to have. There were significant differences in the number given by *low status* and *high status* mothers for their son(s). Sixty-one percent of the *low status* mothers and 41 percent of the *high status* mothers felt that two or fewer children were the best number for a son. At the other extreme 21 percent of the *low status* and 36 percent of the *high status* mothers suggested four or more children for their sons. The difference in ideal number of children for daughters given by the mothers was not statistically significant but the direction of difference was the same as that given for sons. Sixty percent of the *low status* and 50 percent of the *high status* mothers said two or fewer children and 19 percent of the *low status* and 33 percent of the *high status* mothers said four or more children. There were no differences as to ideal number of children for sons and daughters within either the *low status* or *high status* mother groups.

A question may be raised that if the *high status* mothers suggest a higher ideal number of children for both their sons and daughters than the *low status* mothers, doesn't that contradict their higher aspirational levels for their children? It is suggested that there may be no contradiction for several reasons. First, the range of ideal children suggested by the *high status* mothers is not greater than commonly found in studies of fertility ideals. Second, with the older age at marriage suggested by the mothers, the having of children generally would not occur until after the achievement of educational aspirations. Third, the smaller number of children suggested by the *low status* mothers was probably a reflection of their personal problems with their own large families, leading to the belief that if their children have smaller families they might escape some of the same problems.

The American Dream. The mothers' aspirations for their children in such areas as education, occupation, age at marriage and number of children were generally influenced by the realities of personal experience and interpretation. Yet, a part of the value system of aspirations for children also includes more abstract or less experimental values; i.e., what may be called "American dream" values. The already discussed aspirational values may be defined as essentially concrete and as Rodman points out, "the more concrete a value, the more differentiated a society may be with respect to it"; and further suggests that, "the more abstract a value, the more integrated a society may appear." [15] We would therefore expect the two mother groups to be less differentiated in their acceptance of more general or abstract American values than they were with the more concrete aspirational items.

While the mothers were asked specific questions in reference to educational aspirations for their children they were also asked a more general question about education. The mothers were asked what kind of education they thought a young man needed these days to be successful. On this item there were significant differences between the responses of *low status* and *high status* mother groups. Fifty percent of the *low status* mothers and 32 percent of the *high status* mothers said "high school" or "technical education" with the rest of the mothers in each group saying "college." This item as a general value is closely related to the more concrete item on educational aspirations for their sons. The number of years of schooling they would like to have their son(s) receive and the kind of education they think a young man needs to be successful are essentially the same. This would suggest that the general ideal held for educational success by each of the two mother groups was influenced by what each sees as the reality of the situation; i.e., what each mother group defines as the educational level they would like to see their sons achieve.

A second item focused on a more abstract value by asking the mother if she believed any young man with ability and hard work could hope to earn $10,000 a year. There were no differences between the *low status* and *high status* mothers in their responses to this question, with 72 percent of the *low status* mothers and 74 percent of the *high status* mothers answering "yes." For the *low status* mother group their high acceptance of that aspect of the "American dream" would suggest that on an abstract level they verbalize high aspirations although in the more concrete aspirational areas they do not.

A third item focused on one other aspect of the "American dream." The mothers were asked what they believed to be most important for a man to get ahead in his job: (1) hard work and ambition; (2) playing up to the boss; or, (3) to socialize with the boss. There were significant differences in the responses of the two mother groups with 69 percent of the *low status* and 95 percent of the *high status* mothers giving the traditional "American dream" response of "hard

---

[15] *Ibid.,* p. 210.

work and ambition." Even with the differences in responses between the two mother groups it is of interest that two-thirds of the *low status* mothers gave the traditional response.

The data on two of the items suggests there are differences between the *low status* and *high status* mothers in their acceptance of general "American dream" values. While there is a common acceptance of those values by the *low status* mother group it seems probable that for them the abstract values have minimal influence and are replaced by more concrete values to a greater degree than among *high status* mothers.

DISCUSSION

The data presented in this paper offers support for the hypothesis that it is possible to distinguish significantly different subgroups at relative points along the Negro lower class continuum. Support for the hypothesis was given by differences in variables that help distinguish social class levels as well as in the differences between the two mother subgroups in aspirations for their children.

It was suggested earlier in the paper that *if* the *low status* and *high status* Negro mother groups were representative of the social class extremes in our population, then the other two mother groups (*middle status:* Group B, low education and small family and Group C, high education and large family) should fall between in the aspirational responses for their children. When a comparison was made between the responses of the Group B and Group C mothers on the 11 aspirational items only one showed a significant difference. Because of the lack of difference between the Group B and Group C mothers the two groups were combined.

It was found that on all 11 aspirational items the combined BC (*middle status*) mother group fell between the *low status* and *high status* mothers. Furthermore, on only two of the 11 items were there significant differences between the combined BC mother group and *either* the *low status* or *high status* mothers.

While the two extreme groups used for comparison were designated as *low status* and *high status* groups it was assumed that the overall mother population studied would fall within the Negro lower class. While there are probably some exceptions within the *high status* mother group it is suggested that even for that group the greatest number are at least within the upper range of the Negro lower class. This suggestion is based on a comparison of the mother population to other studies of Negro social class. For example, the descriptions provided by other researchers of the Negro middle class are generally different from what was found in reference to even our *high status* mother group.[16]

More specifically it is possible to make a general comparison of our *high status* mothers with a population of Negroes in Philadelphia recently studied by Parker and Kleiner.[17] In their study they interviewed a random sample of Phila-

---

[16] See Frazier, *op. cit.,* chap. 9; and Simpson and Yinger, *op. cit.,* pp. 523–24.
[17] Parker and Kleiner, *op. cit.,* Table 1.

delphia Negroes between the ages of 20 and 60, and while they did not divide their sample into traditional social class levels (i.e., upper, middle and lower) they did rank them by status (social class) on a four-point scale, ranging from 1 (lowest) to 4 (highest). Their Group I and part of Group II corresponds to what is usually described as the Negro lower class. Parker and Kleiner asked their respondents two questions similar to two of the aspirational questions asked of the Negro mother population. They asked the respondent for educational *and* occupational aspirations in regard to a hypothetical son.

A comparison of the responses given only by the Group I (lowest) respondents in the Parker and Kleiner sample is made with the responses given by our *high status* mother group. In reference to educational aspirations 74 percent of the Group I respondents in the Parker and Kleiner sample said "college" as did 64 percent of the *high status* mother group. As to occupational aspirations 32 percent of the Parker and Kleiner Group I responded "unskilled, semi-skilled, skilled and clerical" as did 31 percent of the *high status* mother group.[18] Therefore, if the criteria used by Parker and Kleiner reliably place their Group I in the Negro lower class then by comparison our *high status* mothers can also be described as being in the Negro lower class.

CONCLUSIONS

It must be recognized that the aspirational values discussed in this paper were verbalized only by mothers. It is certainly possible that the mother's aspirations for her children may be altered through the influence of other family members, the school, peer groups or a variety of other social or personal forces. However, given the importance of the family, and especially the mother in the Negro lower class family, her values and aspirations in reference to her children are meaningful and influential for the children's future. It seems reasonable to assume that the closer the mother's aspirations for her children are to the lower end of the lower class value range the less likely are her children to be greatly influenced by other agencies and persons reflecting more middle class values. Therefore, the relative positions of Negro mothers in the lower class may be related to different aspirational values transmitted to their children, and may also contribute to a way of life which makes any alternative aspirational levels difficult for their children to internalize and possibly achieve.

The data in this paper provide some empirical support for Rodman's concept of the "lower class value stretch." The differences found between the Negro mother subgroups, at least in reference to aspirations, suggest a range of beliefs and values in the Negro lower class. Furthermore, the findings offer support for Rodman's suggestion that general social values have less exclusive force in the lower class and also indicate that the closer the mother is to the bottom of the lower class range the greater the deviation of her stated aspirations from those values.

---

[18] For this comparison the Negro mothers who responded "don't know" were eliminated.

6. The education of organization man*

WILLIAM H. WHYTE, JR.

To sharpen the fundamental differences, I am going to contrast two outstanding trainee programs. For an example of the first type, I am going to take the training program of the Vick Chemical Company as it was in the late thirties. There are several reasons for the choice. First, it has been one of the best-known programs in the whole personnel field. Second, though it has often been cited as a pioneer example of modern practice, it was in its fundamentals the essence of the Protestant Ethic and so undefiled by change that there was nothing in it which Henry Clews would take exception to. Third, I happen to have gone through it myself. If I grow unduly garrulous in these next pages, I bespeak the reader's indulgence; I have often pondered this odd experience, and since it furnishes so apt an illustration of certain principles of indoctrination, I would like to dwell on it at some length.

It was a school—the Vick School of Applied Merchandising, they called it. The idea, as it was presented to job-hunting seniors at the time, was that those who were chosen were not going off to a job, but to a postgraduate training institution set up by a farsighted management. In September, some thirty graduates would gather from different colleges to start a year's study in modern merchandising. There would be a spell of classroom work in New York, a continuing course in advertising, and, most important, eleven months of field study under the supervision of veteran students of merchandising and distribution. Theoretically, we should be charged a tuition, for though we understood we would do some work in connection with our studies, the company explained that its expenses far outweighed what incidental services we would perform. This notwithstanding, it was going to give us a salary of $75 a month and all traveling expenses. It would also, for reasons I was later to learn were substantial, give us an extra $25 a month to be held in escrow until the end of the course.

Let me now point out the first distinction between the Vick program and the more current type. It was not executive training or even junior-executive training. Vick's did argue that the program would help produce the leaders of tomor-

*From William H. Whyte, Jr., *The Organization Man* (New York: Simon and Schuster, Inc., 1956), pp. 124–38.

row, and prominent on the walls of the office was a framed picture of a captain at the wheel, with a statement by the president that the greatest duty of management was to bring along younger men. This notwithstanding, the question of whether or not any of us would one day be executives was considered a matter that could very easily be deferred. The training was directed almost entirely to the immediate job. The only exception was an International Correspondence Schools course in advertising, one of the main virtues of which, I always felt, was to keep us so occupied during the week ends that we wouldn't have time to think about our situation.

The formal schooling we got was of the briefest character. During our four weeks in New York, we learned of Richardson's discovery of VapoRub, spent a day watching the VapoRub being mixed, and went through a battery of tests the company was fooling around with to find the Vick's type. Most of the time we spent in memorizing list prices, sales spiels, counters to objections, and the prices and techniques of Plough, Inc., whose Penetro line was one of Vick's most troublesome competitors. There was no talk about the social responsibilities of business or the broad view that I can remember, and I'm quite sure the phrase *human relations* never came up at all.

What management philosophy we did get was brief and to the point. Shortly before we were to set out from New York, the president, Mr. H. S. Richardson, took us up to the Cloud Club atop the Chrysler Building. The symbolism did not escape us. As we looked from this executive eyrie down on the skyscraper spires below, Golconda stretched out before us. One day, we gathered, some of us would be coming back up again—and not as temporary guests either. Some would not. The race would be to the swiftest.

Over coffee Mr. Richardson drove home to us the kind of philosophy that would get us back up. He posed a hypothetical problem. Suppose, he said, that you are a manufacturer and for years a small firm has been making paper cartons for your product. He has specialized so much to service you, as a matter of fact, that that's all he does make. He is utterly dependent on your business. For years the relationship has continued to be eminently satisfactory to both parties. But then one day another man walks in and says he will make the boxes for you cheaper. What do you do?

He bade each one of us in turn to answer.

But *how much* cheaper? we asked. How much time could we give the old supplier to match the new bid? Mr. Richardson became impatient. There was only one decision. Either you were a businessman or you were not a businessman. The new man, obviously, should get the contract. Mr. Richardson, who had strong views on the necessity of holding to the old American virtues, advised us emphatically against letting sentimentality obscure fundamentals. Business was survival of the fittest, he indicated, and we would soon learn the fact.

He was as good as his word. The Vick curriculum was just that—survival of the fittest. In the newer type of programs, companies will indeed fire incompetents, but a man joins with the idea that the company intends to keep him, and this is the company's wish also. The Vick School, however, was frankly based on the principle of elimination. It wouldn't make any difference how wonderful all of us might turn out to be; of the thirty-eight who sat there in the Cloud Club, the rules of the game dictated that only six or seven of us would be asked to stay with Vick. The rest would graduate to make way for the next batch of students.

Another difference between Vick's approach and that now more characteristic became very evident as soon as we arrived in the field. While the work, as the company said, was educational, it was in no sense make-work. Within a few days of our session at the Cloud Club, we were dispatched to the hinterland—in my case, the hill country of eastern Kentucky. Each of us was given a panel delivery truck, a full supply of signs, a ladder, a stock of samples, and an order pad. After several days under the eye of a senior salesman, we were each assigned a string of counties and left to shift for ourselves.

The merchandising was nothing if not applied. To take a typical day of any one of us, we would rise at 6:00 or 6:30 in some bleak boarding house or run-down hotel and after a greasy breakfast set off to squeeze in some advertising practice before the first call. This consisted of bostitching a quota of large fiber signs on barns and clamping smaller metal ones to telephone poles and trees by hog rings. By eight, we would have arrived at a general store for our exercise in merchandising. Our assignment was to persuade the dealer to take a year's supply all at once, or, preferably, more than a year's supply, so that he would have no money or shelf space left for other brands. After the sale, or nosale, we would turn to market research and note down the amount sold him by "chiseling" competitors (i.e., competitors; there was no acknowledgment on our report blanks of any other kind).

Next we did some sampling work: "Tilt your head back, Mr. Jones," we would suddenly say to the dealer. For a brief second he would obey and we would quickly shoot a whopping dropperful of Vatronol up his nose. His eyes smarting from the sting, the dealer would smile with simple pleasure. Turning to the loungers by the stove, he would tell them to let the drummer fella give them some of that stuff. After the messy job was done, we plastered the place with cardboard signs, and left. Then, some more signposting in barnyards, and ten or twelve miles of mud road to the next call. So, on through the day, the routine was repeated until at length, long after dark, we would get back to our lodgings in time for dinner—and two hours' work on our report forms.

The acquisition of a proper frame of mind toward all this was a slow process. The faded yellow second sheets of our daily report book tell the story. At first, utter demoralization. Day after day, the number of calls would be a skimpy eight or nine, and the number of sales sometimes zero. But it was never our fault. In the large space left for explanations, we would affect a cheerful humor—

the gay adventurer in the provinces—but this pathetic bravado could not mask a recurrent note of despair. [1]

To all these bids for sympathy, the home office was adamantine. The weekly letter written to each trainee would start with some perfunctory remarks that it was too bad about the clutch breaking down, the cut knee, and so on. But this spurious sympathy did not conceal a strong preoccupation with results, and lest we miss the point we were told of comrades who would no longer be with us. We too are sorry about those absent dealers, the office would say. Perhaps if you got up earlier in the morning?

As the office sensed quite correctly from my daily reports, I was growing sorry for myself. I used to read timetables at night, and often in the evening I would somehow find myself by the C & O tracks when the George Washington swept by, its steamy windows a reminder of civilization left behind. I was also sorry for many of the storekeepers, most of whom existed on a precarious credit relationship with wholesalers, and as a consequence I sold them very little of anything.

The company sent its head training supervisor to see if anything could be salvaged. After several days with me, this old veteran of the road told me he knew what was the matter. It wasn't so much my routine, wretched as this was. It was my state of mind. "Fella," he told me, "you will never sell anybody anything until you learn one simple thing. The man on the other side of the counter is the *enemy*."

It was a gladiators' school we were in. Selling may be no less competitive now, but in the Vick program, strife was honored far more openly than today's climate would permit. Combat was the ideal—combat with the dealer, combat with the "chiseling competitors," and combat with each other. There was some talk about "the team," but it was highly abstract. Our success depended entirely on beating our fellow students, and while we got along when we met for occasional sales meetings the camaraderie was quite extracurricular.

Slowly, as our sales-to-calls ratios crept up, we gained in rapacity. Somewhere along the line, by accident or skill, each of us finally manipulated a person into doing what we wanted him to do. Innocence was lost, and by the end of six months, with the pack down to about twenty-three men, we were fairly ravening for the home stretch back to the Cloud Club. At this point, the company took us off general store and grocery work and turned us loose in the rich drugstore territory.

The advice of the old salesman now became invaluable. While he had a dis-

---

[1] I quote some entries from my own daily report forms: "They use 'dry' creek beds for roads in this country. 'Dry!' Ha! Ha! . . . Sorry about making only four calls today, but I had to go over to Ervine to pick up a drop shipment of ¾ tins and my clutch broke down. . . . Everybody's on WPA in this country. Met only one dealer who sold more than a couple dozen VR a year. Ah, well, it's all in the game! . . . Bostitched my left thumb to a barn this morning and couldn't pick up my first call until after lunch. . . . The local brick plant here is shut down and nobody's buying anything. . . . Five, count 'em, *five* absent dealers in a row. . . . Sorry about the $20.85 but the clutch broke down again. . . ."

taste for any kind of dealer, with druggists he was implacably combative. He was one of the most decent and kindly men I have ever met, but when he gave us pep talks about this enemy ahead of us, he spoke with great intensity. Some druggists were good enough fellows, he told us (i.e., successful ones who bought big deals), but the tough ones were a mean, servile crew; they would insult you, keep you waiting while they pretended to fill prescriptions, lie to you about their inventory, whine at anything less than a 300 per cent markup, and switch their customers to chiseling competitors.

The old salesman would bring us together in batches for several days of demonstration. It was a tremendous experience for us, for though he seemed outwardly a phlegmatic man, we knew him for the artist he was. Outside the store he was jumpy and sometimes perspired, but once inside, he was composed to the point of apparent boredom. He rarely smiled, almost never opened with a joke. His demeanor seemed to say, I am a busy man and you are damned lucky I have stopped by your miserable store. Sometimes, if the druggist was unusually insolent, he would blow cigar smoke at his face. "Can't sell it if you don't have it," he would say contemptuously, and then, rather pleased with himself, glance back at us, loitering in the wings, to see if we had marked that.

Only old pros like himself could get away with that, he told us in the post-mortem sessions, but there were lots of little tricks we could pick up. As we gathered around him, like Fagin's brood, he would demonstrate how to watch for the victim's shoulders to relax before throwing the clincher; how to pick up the one-size jar of a competitive line that had an especially thick glass bottom and chuckle knowingly; how to feign suppressed worry that maybe the deal was too big for "the smaller druggist like yourself" to take; how to disarm the nervous druggist by fumbling and dropping a pencil. No mercy, he would tell us; give the devils no mercy.

We couldn't either. As the acid test of our gall the company now challenged us to see how many drugstores we could desecrate with "flange" signs. By all the standards of the trade this signposting should have been an impossible task. Almost every "chiseling competitor" would give the druggist at least five dollars to let him put up a sign; we could not offer the druggist a nickel. Our signs, furthermore, were not the usual cardboard kind the druggist could throw away after we had left. They were of metal, they were hideous, and they were to be screwed to the druggists' cherished oak cabinets.

The trick was in the timing. When we were in peak form the procedure went like this: Just after the druggist had signed the order, his shoulders would subside, and this would signal a fleeting period of mutual bonhomie. "New fella, aren't you?" the druggist was likely to say, relaxing. This was his mistake. As soon as we judged the good will to be at full flood, we would ask him if he had a ladder. (There was a ladder out in the car, but the fuss of fetching it would have broken the mood.) The druggist's train of thought would not at that moment connect the request with what was to follow, and he would good-naturedly dispatch someone to bring out a ladder. After another moment of chatter, we would make way for the waiting customer who would engage the druggist's attention. Then, forthrightly, we would slap the ladder up against a spot we had previously reconnoitered. "Just going to get this sign up for you," we would say, as if doing him the greatest favor in the world. He would nod absent-mindedly. Then up the ladder we would go; a few quick turns of the awl, place the bracket in position, and then, the automatic screw driver. Bang! bang! Down went the sign. (If the druggist had been unusually mean, we could break the thread of the screw for good measure.) Then down with the ladder, shift it over to the second spot, and up again.

About this time the druggist would start looking up a little unhappily, but the good will, while ebbing, was still enough to inhibit him from action. *He* felt sorry for us. Imagine that young man thinking those signs are good looking! Just as he would be about to mumble something about one sign being enough, we would hold up the second one. It had a picture on it of a woman squirting nose drops up her nostrils. We would leer fatuously at it. "Just going to lay this blonde on the top of the cabinet for you, Mr. Jones," we would say, winking. We were giants in those days.

I suppose I should be ashamed, but I must confess I'm really not, and to this day when I enter a drugstore I sometimes fancy the sound of the awl biting irretrievably into the druggist's limed oak. I think the reader will understand, of course, that I am not holding up the Vick School of Applied Merchandising as an ideal model, yet I must add, in all fairness to Vick, that most of us were grateful for the experience. When we get together periodically (we have an informal alumni association), we wallow in talk about how they really separated the men from the boys then, etc. It was truly an experience, and if we shudder to recall the things we did, we must admit that as a cram course in reality it was extraordinarily efficient.

The General Electric program to which I now turn was in full force in the thirties and is actually an older one than the Vick's program. Where the latter was a late flowering of a philosophy already in the descendant, however, GE's was a harbinger of things to come. Even today, it is still somewhat ahead of its time; at this moment there are not many corporation training programs which come near General Electric's, either in the size or elaborateness of facilities or, more importantly, in consistency of principles. Yet I believe that as we take up these principal features of the General Electric program, we will be seeing what in a decade or so hence may be the middle of the road.[2]

---

[2] Even Vick has moved considerably in this direction. The heroic years are over; now it is "The Vick Executive Development Program," and though there has been no basic shift in underlying philosophy (Mr. Richardson is still at the helm), Vick now offers many of the material features of the GE program. Security is reasonably guaranteed; no longer are trainees "graduated"— of the roughly one hundred seniors taken in each year, all but a handful can remain as permanent employees. They are exposed to many more aspects of management and they don't have to do things like putting up flange signs.

The most immediately apparent thing about the General Electric program is the fact that it *is* a school. While the plants serve as part of the campus, the company maintains a full-time staff of 250 instructors and an educational plant complete to such details as company-published textbooks, examinations, classrooms, and alumni publications. In direct operating costs alone the company spends over five million dollars annually—a budget larger than many a medium-sized college.

The program is highly centralized. To keep this plant running, GE's corps of recruiters each year delivers between 1,000 and 1,500 college graduates, mostly engineers, to the company's Schenectady headquarters. There the trainees enter what is for them a continuation of college life. Like fraternity brothers, they live together in boarding houses and attend classes in groups. For afterhours recreation, they have the privileges of the Edison Club where, along with other GE employees with college degrees, they can meet after classes to play golf, bridge, and enjoy a planned series of parties and dances. (GE employees who haven't gone to college are eligible to join if they have achieved a supervisory rating.)

The curriculum is arranged in much the same manner as a university's. The trainee enters under one of several courses, such as engineering and accounting. All these courses will have much in common, however, for the trainee's first eighteen months are regarded as the basic part of his training. At the end of this time he will then go on to a "major." If he has been in the manufacturing training course, for example, he can elect as a major factory operations, manufacturing engineering, production and purchasing, or plant engineering.

The work the trainee does during this training is not, like Vick's applied merchandising, considered an end in itself. From time to time the trainee will work at specific jobs, but these jobs, while not mere make-work, are outside the regular cost-accounted operations of the company. The company considers them vehicles for training, and it rotates students from one to another on a regular schedule.

The most noteworthy feature of the General Electric approach is the emphasis on the "professional" manager. As in all training programs, the bulk of the instruction is on specifics. Unlike most, however, there is considerable study in subjects that cut across every kind of job. Trainees study personnel philosophy, labor relations, law, and, most important, the managerial viewpoint. [3]

Only a minority of the trainees will ever become managers; in ten years 1,500 to 2,000 executive slots will open up, and this means that most of the thousands of young men trained during this time will never get further than middle management. Nevertheless, it is those future executive slots that the company is

---

[3] Among other things, the trainees take HOBSO. This is the course in How Our Business System Operates, originally developed by Du Pont to inoculate blue-collar employees against creeping socialism. Though GE has no reason to fear its trainees are ideologically unsound, it explains that the course will help them "detect any bad guidance they receive from union and political leaders, and even from educational and spiritual leaders."

thinking of, and it makes its concern plain to the trainee. On the report card form for trainees, there is a space for an evaluation as to whether the trainee is suited "for individual contribution" or whether, instead, he is suited "to manage the work of others." The company tells the trainees that it is perfectly all right for them to aim at "individual contribution," which is to say, a specialty. It would be a dull trainee, however, who did not pause before consigning himself to such a role. In one of GE's textbooks there is a picture of a man looking at two ladders. One leads up to a specialty, the other to general managing. The question before the young man, the textbook states, is: "Will I specialize in a particular field?"— or "Will I become broad-gauge, capable of effort in many fields?"

Who wants to be narrow-gauge? Trainees do not have to read too strenuously between the lines to see that one should aim to manage; as a matter of fact, they are predisposed to read a good bit more between the lines than many of their elders would like them to. Which brings us to an important point. In gauging the impact of the curriculum on the young man, his predispositions are as important as the weighting of the courses. Elders at General Electric can demonstrate that the actual amount of time devoted to the abstract arts of management is far less than the time devoted to specific skills. But the managerial part is what the trainees want to hear—and they want to hear it so much that one hour's exposure to the managerial view can be as four or five hours of something else in proportion to its effect on impressionable minds. Trainees are interested, to be sure, in how turbines are made, in the techniques of the accounting department and such, but they do not want to be *too* interested. It would make them unbalanced.

They regard specific work very much as many educators view "subject matter" courses: narrowing. As trainees play back the lesson, they see a distinction, sometimes a downright antithesis, between the qualities of the broad-gauge executive and the qualities that one must have to do a superlative piece of concrete work. Not work itself but the managing of other people's work is the skill that they aspire to. As they describe it, the manager is a man in charge of people getting along together, and his *expertise* is relatively independent of who or what is being managed. Or why.

Not surprisingly, the part of the curriculum for which they have the greatest affinity is the human-relations instruction. They are particularly enthusiastic about the "Effective Presentation" course worked up by the sales-training department. They can hardly be blamed. *"You can always get anybody to do what you wish,"* the textbook proclaims. To this end the students spend four months eagerly studying a battery of communication techniques and psychological principles which General Electric tells them will help them to be good managers. (Sample principle: "Never say anything controversial.")

There is nothing novel about teaching people how to manipulate other people, and GE's scientific psychological techniques bear a strong resemblance to the how-to-be-a-success precepts standard in the U.S. for decades. What is different about them is their justification. They are not presented on the grounds that they will help make people do what you want them to do so that you can make more money. GE trainees see it in much more eleemosynary terms. They do like the part about selling yourself to others so you can get ahead, for they think a lot about this. But they don't abide the thought of enemies on the other side of the counter; they see the manipulative skills as something that in the long run will make other people *happy*. When in years to come the trainees are charged with the destiny of subordinates—a possibility most take remarkably much for granted—they will be able to achieve a stable, well-adjusted work group. They won't drive subordinates, they explain. They will motivate them.

Trainees are also predisposed to emphasis on co-operation rather than competition, and this they get too. The emphasis is built into the structure of the school. For one thing, the student is given a high measure of security from the beginning, and while there may be promotion of the fittest there can be survival for all. There are exceptions, but one must be a very odd ball to be one. For the first two years the trainee is part of a system in which his salary raises will be automatic, and while later on he will be more on his own there will be no planned elimination as there was at Vick, nor an up-or-out policy such as the Navy's.

To get ahead, of course, one must compete—but not too much, and certainly not too obviously. While overt ambition is a bad posture for the ambitious anywhere, the GE system has especial sanctions for the rate-buster. The trainee is, first of all, a member of a group, and the group is entrusted to a surprising degree with the resolution of his future. How well, the company wants to know, does he fit in? His fellow trainees provide the answer, and in the "case study" group discussions the eager beaver or the deviant is quickly exposed. And brought to heel. Trainees speak frequently of the way close fraternity life atmosphere is valuable in ironing out some trainees' aberrant tendencies. It may be tough on him, they concede, but better now than later. In a few years the trainee will be released from this close association and the social character that he has perfected will be a fundamental necessity; he will be moving from one company branch to another, and he must be able to fit into the same kind of integrated social system.

The company officially recognizes the disciplining of the group. In its periodic rating of the man, the company frequently calls on his comrades to participate in the rating. If a man is liked especially well not only by his superiors but by his peers, he may be given the job of guiding about eight or ten of his fellow trainees. He is now a "sign-up," and if he keeps on maturing he may become a "head-of-tests," the seven "sign-ups" reporting to him. Since the opinions of one's peers are so integral to advancement, this system virtually insures that the overzealous or the "knocker" type of man will not get ahead—or, at the very least, that he will successfully remold himself to the managerial image.

The fact that the trainee must spend so much time thinking of what other people think of him does not oppress him. Quite the opposite, the constant surveillance is one of the things the average trainee talks about most enthusiastically. The rating system is highly standardized, he explains; it is the product of *many* people rather than one, and this denominator of judgments frees him from the harshness or caprice that might result from the traditional boss-employee relationship. He is also freed from being ignored; the system insures that other people must be thinking about him quite as much as he is thinking about them, and for this reason he won't get pigeonholed. At General Electric, as one trainee remarked, not only can't you get lost, you can't even hide.

Needless to say, ambition still pulses, and I am not trying to suggest that the General Electric man is any less set on the main chance than my Vick comrades. It is quite obvious, nevertheless, that he must pursue the main chance in a much more delicate fashion. To get ahead, he must co-operate with the others—but co-operate *better* than they do.

The rules of the game do permit a few lapses, but these lapses, characteristically, are the display of personality. Somewhere along the line the trainees must get themselves hired into a regular job, and to do this they must attract the attention of superiors. There is a tacit understanding among trainees that it is perfectly all right to make a bald play to get on a first name-basis with superiors that might do one some good. "As soon as you know your way around a new department you start telephoning," one trainee explains, tapping the intercommunication telephone directory. "Believe me, this little green book here is a man's best friend." The company encourages superiors to encourage this kind of contact. "I or anybody else," another trainee says, "can walk into a manager's office just as easily as we can each other's. By ten o'clock of the day I hit the New York office I was calling everybody by his first name."

PART III

Social class

One of the most important contributions to a broad understanding of human behavior made by sociologists has been their detailed study of social stratification. Many variables have been used to show variations in different social class levels, but three of the most important are education, occupation, and income. In general, the higher the formal education, the more prestigeful the occupation and the greater the income.[1] This means that for most males the decision as to formal educational achievement is a pivotal life decision that determines to a great extent their occupational future as well as having far-reaching effects for their families. We are here concerned with some of the relationships between education and social class, with a particular stress on how social class values may influence family and individual behavior in regard to formal education.

Social class mobility

For the newborn child social class is ascribed; he initially receives the class standing of his family. The receiving of class position from parents is more than just a description of childhood social class standing, for it is often a precondition of the child's future adult social class standing. Often the informal value system

---

[1] Joseph A. Kahl, *The American Class Structure* (New York: Rinehart & Co., 1957), p. 97.

that parents communicate to their children in regard to social class will greatly influence the child's future. A child may grow up without consciously being aware of how his future is being influenced by his membership in the social class level of his family. With education an important means of achieving social class mobility, the values of the parents, if negative to formal education, may lead the child to believe that formal education is unimportant. This may result in the child's adult class position being at the same general social class level as was his parents. Frequently in the lower classes there is a feeling of "inevitability" of class position with corresponding beliefs that the young person should make the best of the situation, rather than try to change it.[2] Education beyond that of the family class level may be seen as hopeless or a waste of time.

From the point of view of social change the concept of vertical social mobility is of great importance. In some situations the ascribed social class the child is born into may change because of his parents' mobility, but it is more often the case that vertical mobility is generational, with the child in his adult years achieving a higher social class level than that of his parents. There follows a brief discussion of formal education as related to each of the three general social classes: lower, middle, and upper.

Lower Class.   As mentioned, the values of parents in regard to formal education are of great importance. It can be said that the majority of children in the lower classes will remain there for their entire lives. There are a number of factors in the lower class environment that account for the limited amount of social mobility. One factor is that free education is not really free. While direct payment may not be required for attending public schools, there are the family costs of clothing and feeding the child while he is in school. This becomes particularly acute to the family when the youngster reaches the age when he can legally leave school and get a job. Keeping him in school means continued expense to the parents as well as the loss of his potential earning power.

Secondly, there are a limited number of adult models of success achieved through education available to the lower class child. Often the models of high success are not those that have achieved it through socially approved channels, but those that have been successful through illegal or semilegal methods. So the model of the successful educated individual is missing for many lower class youngsters. Thirdly, parental attitudes and childhood socialization that place a relatively low value on educational and intellectual activities are important factors. The 16-year-old boy leaving high school may know that he can find a job earning practically the same amount as his father. To do so would give the young man very great status in the eyes of his family and his peers and hence is the obvious choice when compared to going to school, which probably fails to appear either interesting or useful. He is unable to concern himself with the fact that 20 years later he may still be earning about the same income, because he has not learned to seriously consider the possibility of any other alternatives.

---

[2] *Ibid.*, p. 211.

Of course, a number of lower class children do achieve high levels of education and hence vertical social mobility. This is sometimes explained because their families "are in, but not of" the lower class. The family has lower class membership, but their reference group is the middle class. Therefore, the values for success communicated by the parents to their children are middle-class values. It is pointed out that successful mobility out of lower class origins is usually associated with family encouragement. There is also evidence that some lower class youngsters are socially mobile because of personality factors.[3] The strong personal desire to move socially upward and the push of wanting to escape lower class origins are often factors. In general, when this happens there must be some value system or identification which has greater impact and influence on the individual than the overall value system of the lower class of which he is a member.

Middle Class. It has been pointed out many times that the middle class is the social class level most highly mobility-oriented, and in this group education is increasingly used as a means of achieving higher social class standing. It must be remembered that, increasingly, education is seen primarily as a means of occupational preparation and that opportunities for success as presently defined in the United States are determined more and more within large business organizations, rather than through individual enterprise.

Many parents in the middle class are either insecure or unsatisfied with their own social class position and project their mobility ambitions to their children. Many high-school-educated parents in the lower middle class are extremely compulsive about their sons' growing up to be professionals, or their daughters' marrying professionals. The compulsiveness of the parental drive has implications ranging from parent-child conflict to the actual psychological breakdown of the unsuccessful child.

For many middle-class parents there is never the question of whether or not the children will be educated (go to college) but only the question of where and how the education will be financed. This often creates in the growing child the belief that extended education is his natural right. Many times this leads to positive attitudes on the part of the middle-class youngster about education and the methods of educational success. The middle-class parent is often in a financial position to make education as pleasant as possible because the child has the money and parental encouragement to enter into costly noneducational functions related to the school. But it must be stressed that often for both the parent and the child the attainment of formal education is not important in and of itself. Rather it is a means of qualifying for an occupation that will result in higher social prestige.

One often unanticipated consequence of successful social mobility through education is that the young adult finds himself in a world quite different from that of his parents. As a result of his educational achievement, he incorporates

---

[3] Jerome K. Myers and Bertan H. Roberts, *Family and Class Dynamics in Mental Health Illness* (New York: John Wiley & Sons, Inc., 1959), p. 60.

values, interests, and a way of life that leave him little in common with the social class milieu of his parents. Parents who encourage and implement success for their children may find that this has resulted in their children moving into a world of which they, the parents, are not a part; and as a result, they no longer can have meaningful contact with their offspring. So one consequence of mobility away from the family is that the young adult psychologically "can't go home again."

Upper Class.   On this social class level, education is not seen as a means of social mobility. However, it may be used by some as a means of solidifying social class position. In the upper class the stress is not on how much education one has achieved, but rather on where one received it. Higher education has only as a partial function the preparation of the individual for a specific occupation. The more important function is the broader social preparation that the proper education will give the young person for his ascribed social position.

Usually starting with nursery school, educational institutions are selected for the upper-class child according to the school's ability to indoctrinate the child with values defined as important by the parents in regard to their social class position. This means that usually the upper-class child has little or no contact with public education because he is sent to carefully selected private schools. Upper-class approved schools at all educational levels serve a somewhat different function than do middle-class schools. The schools provide a background of upper-class values to prepare the child for adult roles that are anticipated and can be trained for. This provides for the upper-class an extensive educational context that is impossible in the middle-class, where future adult roles cannot be accurately anticipated during childhood.

7. Education, social mobility, and social change in four societies*

ROBERT J. HAVIGHURST

One of the most important aspects of social change in modern times is the vertical social mobility connected with it. This movement up or down on a scale of socio-economic status is related to education. The three variables—social mobility, social change, and education—are related to each other in ways which this paper will discuss.

The interrelations of social mobility, social change, and education can be seen better if they are viewed comparatively in several societies which are in different stages of economic development. In this way one may avoid over-hasty generalizations and secure a broader sweep for such conclusions as can be drawn. Therefore we have used data from the United States of America, Brazil, England, and Australia. The data are not altogether adequate, but much is gained by using data as are available from several countries.

SOCIAL MOBILITY IN THE FOUR SOCIETIES

For the purpose of this paper we must define individual socio-economic mobility as mobility on a scale of occupational prestige. This procedure is not an ideal one, but it can be defended in modern urban-industrial societies, where work has a central position and a person is evaluated socially by the work he performs unless he is in the uppermost class. No doubt mobility on an occupational scale is more easily achieved than mobility on a more general social scale, and there is quantitatively more of it, in modern societies; but the correlation between occupational status and general status is so high that we can use mobility on an occupational scale as a good index of general social mobility.

The facts about individual social mobility in the four countries are summarized in Table 1, which tells what proportions of the present adult population have been stable, or upward or downward mobile during their lives—that is, how their social status at age 30 to 70 compares with that of their fathers when the latter were in the same age range.

The USA and Brazil show the greatest net upward mobility, while it appears

---

*From *International Review of Education,* Vol. 4 (1958), pp. 167–83.

that Great Britain and probably Australia have some net downward mobility during the present century.

These comparisons are crude, but they almost certainly show the relative differences between the four countries. They depend on studies made with different methods, but all using the same basic concept of socio-economic class, and using 4, 5, or 6 classes.

TABLE 1
Individual Social Mobility in the Four Societies.

	Crude Comparisons Percentages of Adults Who Have Been:		
Country	Stable	Upward Mobile	Downward Mobile
USA	55	33	12
England	40	27	33
Australia	45	20	35
Brazil (São Paulo) . . .	43	40	17

Note: These comparisons are highly tentative. The Australian and Brazilian data are based on a sample in only one urban area. The number of classes used in the analysis was 4 in Australia, 5 in the USA and England, and 6 in Brazil.

The British data are based on the best sample,[1] but are limited by the fact that social status was determined entirely on the basis of occupation, whereas the American data employed a broader socio-economic criterion. The American data are based on a sample of adults aged 40-70 in the metropolitan area of Kansas City.[2] While they represent only one (but a typical) area, there are other studies which agree with this one in reporting a net upward mobility of about 15 to 20 percent.[3] The Brazilian data are based on a sample of men in the city of São Paulo[4] and certainly over-estimate the degree of mobility for the country as a whole, since São Paulo is the center of industrial development. The Australian data are the least adequate, being taken from a study of the fathers of sixth grade children in a suburb of Melbourne of "mixed socio-economic classes."[5]

Group mobility

In addition to discussing *individual social mobility,* we shall consider *group mobility.* In this case a social group moves up or down on the socio-economic

[1] D. V. Glass *et al., Social Mobility in Britain* (London: Routledge & Kegan Paul, 1954).

[2] Robert J. Havighurst and Bernice L. Neugarten, *Society and Education* (Boston: Allyn and Bacon, 1957), chap. 2.

[3] National Opinion Research Center, "Jobs and Occupations: A Popular Evaluation," in Reinhard Bendix and Seymour M. Lipset (eds.), *Class, Status, and Power* (Glencoe, Ill.: Free Press, 1953).

[4] Bertram Hutchinson, "Social Mobility in the City of São Paulo," unpublished paper, 1957.

[5] O. A. Oeser and S. B. Hammond, *Social Structure and Personality in a City* (London: Routledge & Kegan Paul, 1954), p. 239.

scale. For instance, the urban working class has moved up on the socio-economic scale in all four countries. Possibly Australia has seen the greatest working-class gains, relative to the lower-middle class. Since 1900 the Australian working class has much improved its group status, through a government wage control board, and through a liberal system of family allowances (based on number of children) together with a fairly generous system of old-age benefits.

The British working class has also increased its relative status, compared with the middle class, mainly through a system of health service, insurance against unemployment and retirement and disability, and through an extensive program of free public secondary education. Most of Britain's increased productivity since 1900 has gone to raise the standard of living of the working class, after subtracting the cost of two disastrous World Wars.

Brazil's urban working class has seen a substantial increase of economic status since 1900, enough to put a big distance between it and the rural working class. Furthermore, the inflation since 1930 has hurt the middle classes more than the working class and thus has reduced the distance between them.

The American working class has been upward mobile as a group, perhaps as much as the Australian working class, and more than the working class of any of the other three countries if we consider only economic gains without making comparisons with the middle classes. This is evidenced by the increasing real income of the working-class group, and by its increasing possession of certain symbols of middle-class status, such as labor-saving devices in the home, vacation with pay, and secondary and higher education for the children.

Conditions which tend to produce net upward mobility

If we identify social status with occupational position, in order to study social mobility, we have to ask ourselves what conditions increase the number of positions of middle and upper status in a society; and, what conditions create vacancies in these positions that permit upward mobility.

There are two general conditions which make for a net upward mobility.

1. A shift in occupational distribution so as to increase the proportion of middle and higher status occupational positions. This could result from:

a. Change in technology of production which increases the proportion of more technical and highly-skilled and better-paid positions at the expense of semi-skilled and unskilled jobs. For instance, automation does this.

b. Change in type of industry from those with many unskilled jobs to those with more jobs requiring technical training. The change from agriculture to manufacturing industry usually does this; and so does a change from farming with human labor to farming with machinery.

c. Introduction of new industries which require a high proportion of technically-trained and well-paid workers.

d. Increase of industrial productivity with resultant increase in wages and salaries, which allows people to spend more of their income on services provided by professional people, thus increasing the proportion of such people.

e. Free or easy access to valuable natural resources, such as good land, gold, diamonds, oil, uranium. This creates people with wealth who take the status positions of owners of wealth.

2. Differential fertility, with upper and/or middle status people not reproducing their numbers. They leave gaps in the upper and middle classes which are filled from below, provided the society maintains or increases the number of its middle and higher status positions.

Conditions which promote balanced mobility, both upward and downward

Another set of conditions promote both upward and downward mobility—the relative amounts of the two being determined by the factors already mentioned They are:

1. Free and easy access to the kind of education that opens the way to middle and higher status occupations, combined with fairly rigorous standards. This condition tends to create an elite of talent rather than of birth.

2. Open competition for middle and higher status jobs, based on objective procedures for filling positions. Again, this condition tends to create an elite of talent rather than of birth.

3. Changing industrial procedures, creating new jobs and making old ones obsolete, thus preventing a man or his family from getting a vested interest in a particular position.

4. Upward group mobility of the lower classes, increasing their standard of living and thus enabling them to give advantages of better education and better health to their children, thus increasing their competitive ability.

SOCIAL CHANGE IN THE FOUR SOCIETIES

The basic proposition of this paper is that industrialization leads to social change which produces social mobility (group and/or individual) and that education may effect the pace of social change and the degree of social mobility.

Industrialization

Commencing with England in the beginning of the 19th century, the process of industrialization next became dominant in the USA, then Australia, and then Brazil. This involves a movement of population from rural areas to cities, a change in the occupational distribution of the population, a rise in economic productivity and in per capita income. England was mostly rural in the 18th century, but became urbanized in the 19th century. Agriculture was displaced as the principal occupation of the people with only 17 percent of the labor force in agriculture in 1871 and only 6 percent in 1931.

The United States followed the same course as Britain but about 50 years later. In the USA the proportion of the male labor force engaged in agriculture dropped from 65 to 13 percent in the century before 1950, while the proportion engaged in manufacturing and mining increased from 17 to 34 percent, the percentage in the professions increased from 2.5 to 6.3, and the percentage engaged in owning or managing a business increased from 4 to 13.

These social changes created and enlarged the "new middle class" of salaried and highly trained people — chemists, engineers, factory-managers, teachers, nurses, and office workers. Thus it was inevitable that there would be a movement of upward mobility into these new positions, unless the middle classes were producing many more than enough children to replace themselves.

Australia moved into a phase of industrialization during the present century, reducing her agricultural labor force to only 15 percent of the total. Output per worker in manufacturing and handicrafts in Australia was worth $3,600 in 1948, compared with $4,110 in the USA, $1,450 in Great Britain, and $520 in South America.[6]

Australia differs somewhat from the USA in that the proportion of manual workers' jobs in the labor force seems not to have declined in the present century. Oeser and Hammond[7] comment on this fact as follows:

> In the period 1900-48 there has been a clear decline in the relative proportion of the employer and self-employed class and a corresponding increase in the other levels, particularly in that of white-collar workers; for example, in factory employment in Australia since 1900 the proportion of owners has been halved while that of white-collar employees has practically doubled; this is owing to the greater centralization of industry going along with the increasing size of factory units. In factory employment the proportion of skilled and semi-skilled together has remained fairly constant at about 70 percent.

In England, also, the proportion of manual workers' positions in the labor force seems not to have declined since 1900.[8] This is an important fact, and goes far toward explaining why England and Australia probably do not have net upward mobility. Increasing productivity in these countries has taken place without a decrease of the proportion of manual workers, while in the USA there has been a substantial decrease in the proportion of manual workers.

Brazil's industrialization has only just commenced. As can be seen in the labor force data of Table 2, the agricultural labor force is still two-thirds of the total, and the proportion engaged in the tertiary occupations is less than half of what it is in the other three countries. Still, there has been a rapid trend toward indus-

---

[6] W. S. Woytinsky and E. S. Woytinsky, *World Population and Productivity* (New York: Twentieth Century Fund, 1953).

[7] Oeser and Hammond, *op. cit.*

[8] Glass *et al., op. cit.*

trialization and urbanization, especially since 1940. National production climbed at the rate of 6 percent a year from 1949 to 1955, while the population was increasing 2.5 percent a year. Brazilian agriculture and industry have a relatively

TABLE 2
Comparisons of Labor Force

	Primary		Secondary			Tertiary			
	% of Pop. in Labor Force	Agric. Min'g Frstry.	Mfg.	Con- struc- tion	Total	Com- merce	Transp. & Comm.	Ser- vices	Oth- ers
USA (1950) ...	39.8	13.8	28.2	6.2	51.8	18.5	7.0	23.7	2.6
Australia (1947) ...	42.2	17.0	27.1	7.3	48.6	15.1	8.0	18.0	7.5
Great Britain (1931) ...	43.0	12.1	40.0		48.0	15.8	6.9	24.4	0.9
Brazil (1950) ...	38.1	66.1	9.2	2.9	21.8	5.5	3.5	12.8	—

Source: United States Demographic Yearbook. 1955.

low level of productivity, which causes a low per capita income. Brazil is about at the place where the USA was in 1870, or Great Britain in 1840. The great changes for Brazil lie ahead.

Productivity and Income.   All of these countries have increased their productivity and therefore their per capita income as a result of industrialization. The USA is in the lead, as can be seen in Table 3. British per capita income multiplied about four-fold from 1870 to 1950, while that of the USA multiplied five-fold.

TABLE 3
Per Capita Income
(mean annual per capita income 1952–54, current prices)

United States of America $1,870
Australia   950
Great Britain   850
Brazil   230

Source: Statistical Report of the United Nations.

Note: Comparisons of this sort may be misleading, because no account is taken of differences in the cost of living in the several countries. Thus, if Britain had a lower cost of living than Australia, the per capita income in Britain would seem to be lower than its real value, as compared with Australia. The same criticism can be made of the comparisons of output per worker, made earlier. Colin Clark has made comparisons of "real income" per capita, using an "international unit," which still places the four countries in the same order, but reduces the differences between them.

Output per man-hour is higher in the USA and Australia than in England. Brazilian per capita income approximately doubled in the last ten years.

Natural Resources. The availability of natural resources has a great deal to do with national productivity. In this respect the USA and Australia have profited most during the past century, with cheap and fertile land, gold, oil, and then uranium. Englishmen exploited the natural resources of the Empire in the 19th century, by taking up cheap land in Canada, Australia, or South Africa, or by finding gold, diamonds, and exotic agricultural products. Brazil's exploitable natural resources are not fully known, but it seems that with oil, iron ore, and probably much undeveloped fertile land, there may be a considerable addition to Brazil's income from these sources in the future.

Differential birth-rates

The population growth of the four countries is shown in Table 4. England's period of rapid growth ended with the 19th century. The United States and

TABLE 4
Population Growth (millions)

Year	Country			
	USA	*Great Britain*	*Australia*	*Brazil*
1800	5	9.5	—	3
1850	23	20.0	0.43	7
1900	76	37.0	3.80	18
1940	132	46.0	7.00	42
1957	170	52.0	9.40	60

Australia probably have passed the peak of their growth rates but are still growing rapidly. Brazil's growth has been more rapid in the 20th than in the 19th century. All four countries show a differential birth-rate between the middle and the working classes. Britain probably has the greatest differential, but the USA has been quite similar to Britain during recent decades in this respect. In these two countries it has been some time since upper-middle and upper-class families have reproduced their numbers, and consequently they have left gaps in the social structure to be filled by children of working-class families. Some crude calculations made by the writer for the USA[9] indicate that the upward movement of youth from lower to higher status in order to make up for failure of the higher groups to reproduce themselves would create a net upward mobility of about 13 percent per generation, moving up one step on a five-step social class scale.

The failure of England to show a net upward mobility in spite of a differential

---

[9] Havighurst and Neugarten, *op. cit.*

birth-rate must be due to an actual decrease of middle and higher status positions in the past half-century.

Australia has a differential birth-rate, but a lesser one than that of the USA. At the same time, it appears that the proportion of upper-middle and upper-class positions in Australia may have decreased in the past half century.

Brazil certainly has a differential birth-rate, with differences between rural and urban people and between working-class and middle-class people.[10] On the other hand, this differential is partly neutralized by a differential infant mortality rate which reduces the relative numbers of working-class infants who survive. But infant mortality is declining rapidly, and may permit the differential birth-rate to become an effective force for upward mobility, provided the birth-rate of upper and middle-class people declines below the replacement level, as it has in other countries with the coming of urbanization and industrialization. At present the Brazilian upper and middle classes are reproducing themselves, though not with as much surplus as the lower classes are. Therefore, the differential birth-rate, though it exists, is not at present a source of upward mobility.

Social structure

The social structures of the four societies are basically similar, with a small upper class based on wealth acquired in the past, a growing middle class which can be divided into an upper-middle and a lower-middle segment, and a large working class which can also be divided into upper and lower segments, primarily depending on the possession of a trade or a technical skill and a steady job by the upper segment. Table 5 gives a rough estimate of the percentage distribution of the population in the five social classes. For England and the USA the estimates are fairly good.[11] For Australia the estimate is hardly more than an intelligent guess. For Brazil, the writer has worked out the distribution after studying data on occupational distribution, land ownership and income.[12] The relatively large middle classes of the USA and the relatively small middle classes of Brazil are the most important facts in the Table. This explains why the USA has had a net upward mobility in the past 50 years, and why Brazil may expect a net upward mobility for the next 50 years.

In the USA, the working classes have grown smaller and the middle classes larger since 1900. This is due mainly to the development of the tertiary occu-

---

[10]Alceu Vicente de Carvalho, "Alguns Aspectos da Natalidade No Brasil," *Revista Brasileira de Estatistica 15,* No. 59, July-September 1954, pp. 177-85.

[11]Glass *et al., op. cit.;* Havighurst and Neugarten, *op. cit.*

[12]See Instituto Brasileiro de Geografia e Estatistica, *Annuario Estatistico do Brasil, 1955* (Rio de Janeiro, 1955); *Conjuntura Social,* "Evolucão da Mao-de-Obra Brasileira," *Conjuntura Economica 10,* Nos. 7-9, July-August-September 1956, pp. 79-86, 49-56, 43-50; *Conjuntura Social,* "Tipos de Trabalhadores Rurais No Brasil," *Conjuntura Economica 10,* No. 12, December 1956, pp. 71-77; Américo Barbosa de Oliveira, "O Ensino, O Trabalho, A Populacão e A Renda," in Capes, Série *Estudos e Ensàios,* No. 1 (Rio de Janeiro: Ministério de Educacão e Cultura, December 1953); and Hutchinson, *op. cit.*

pations in a highly productive economy capable of supporting the people who perform the characteristic services of these occupations.

In Great Britain and Australia, the middle classes have not grown larger. They may actually have decreased in relative size in Great Britain, due to loss of middle class positions in the Empire's service as the Dominions filled more and more

TABLE 5
Comparative Data on Social Structure
(approximate percentages of the population in the various social classes)

Social Class	USA	Great Britain	Australia	Brazil
Upper	3	3	2	2
Upper middle	10	7	6	3
Lower middle	30	20	18	12
Upper lower	40	50	54	33
Lower lower	17	20	20	50

Note: These are very rough approximations, mainly because the social classes in the four countries are not strictly comparable. An attempt has been made to equate the other three countries as nearly as possible to the system of classes found in the USA.

of their higher status positions with their own natives. Furthermore, Britain's costly twentieth century wars have used up wealth which otherwise would have gone to maintain more people in hereditary upper and middle class statuses.

Brazil is in transition from an agricultural aristocracy to an industrial democracy. It seems certain that in Brazil the agricultural workers will decrease, the urban industrial workers will increase, and the tertiary occupations of commerce, transport and social services will increase. The middle classes might double in a generation, which would require a great deal of upward mobility. In addition, there certainly would be a great deal of mobility up from the agricultural lower-lower class to the urban upper-lower class.

The speed of social change in Brazil will depend on the relative strength of the two social structures which now exist—the aristocratic and rural social structure of the old Brazil and the incipient industrial democratic structure.

EDUCATION IN RELATION TO MOBILITY AND SOCIAL CHANGE

In discussing education in relation to social mobility, it is useful to distinguish between the *functional* and the *symbolic* values of education. Education has a functional value when it is used *directly* to accomplish a purpose. For example, when a person takes an engineering course and becomes an engineer, his education has had a functional value for him. Education has a *symbolic* value when it is used as a *symbol* of status. For example, when a person takes a doctor's degree in medicine and uses the degree as a symbol of status, but does not practice medicine, his education has a symbolic value. Or when an uneducated man earns a good deal of money in business and then sends his son to a selective private school before the son enters the family business, the son's education has a symbolic value.

Of all modern countries, the United States has gone the furthest in stressing the functional rather than the symbolic values of education, except perhaps the Soviet Union.

The great increase in American secondary school enrolment after 1900 came because parents thought their children could get better jobs through learning the skills and knowledge taught in school. In the United States there has been a great development of schools and courses of business administration in the universities, because boys and their parents believe that such courses will make successful business men. And the enormous technological development of the 20th century saw the multiplication of enrolments in schools of engineering, and of technical secondary school courses to train people directly for the new jobs in industry.

In Brazil, education of a functional type is beginning to be used consciously and explicitly as an instrument of social change to increase productivity. The use of functional education for economic and industrial development is an aspect of Brazilian government policy, as is indicated in the 1957 Annual Message to Congress of President Kubitschek, who called for a new type of education which would teach the farmers to use machines and thus to increase their productivity. At the same time he called for an expansion of the country's production of engineers and technicians. In effect President Kubitschek was asking Brazilians to give up their 19th century emphasis on the symbolic values of education in favor of a new kind of education with functional values. However, this change is only just beginning, and has not appreciably influenced the Brazilian secondary schools.

Great Britain and Australia have relied more on the symbolic values of education than has the USA. Secondary education has had a great symbolic value in the eyes of the English and Australians, though primary education has been recognized to possess functional values. Thus, after a man has had a primary education, he has been expected in England and Australia to learn "on the job," if he is a manual worker. If he is to go into business management, he has been expected to get a secondary education mainly for its symbolic value and then to learn "on the job."

Only since 1940 have Great Britain and Australia adopted a policy of using secondary education and higher education in a functional way for economic development of the society. Even as late as 1952, writing about "the Australian Way of Life," Mr. Frederic W. Eggleston could say, "The attitude of the ordinary Australian to education is not encouraging—so many people have succeeded in life without education, in politics, in business, and in the public service, that there is not the 'magic' in education that exists in some countries. It is not regarded as a step to wealth or to a higher social grade." [13]

---

[13] Frederic W. Eggleston, "The Australian Nation," in George Caiger (ed.), *The Australian Way of Life* (London: Wm. Heinemann, 1953), p. 17.

Education for mobility

A functional type of education serves both to promote individual upward mobility and group upward mobility, under certain conditions.

Individual Mobility. The major way in which education has fostered individual mobility is by training lower-status youth to take positions in the tertiary occupations and thus to enter the "new middle class." In the USA the new middle class has grown very rapidly. These people—engineers, chemists, accountants, teachers, nurses, etc., together with the older professions of law, medicine, and the clergy—increased from 6 percent of the labor force in 1870 to 25 percent in 1950. There were 7,000 engineers in 1870 and fifty times as many in 1950.

This group is now just beginning to grow rapidly in Brazil, and will require education to support its growth.

Individual upward mobility may be increased by a system of scholarship grants to poor but able youth, or by a system of free secondary and higher education. Table 6 shows the proportions of youth attending secondary school and university in the four countries, and gives some indication of the role of education in promoting upward mobility.

TABLE 6
Education of Youth in the Four Countries
(percentages of young people in primary and secondary school
and college, 1950–56)

	USA 1955	Great Britain 1950	Australia 1952	Brazil 1956
Primary school age 7–13	98	98	98	62 (7–11 incl.)
Secondary school age 14–17	81	38	60	12 (12–15 incl.) 4 (16–18 incl.)
University age 18–21	31	2.5	6	1.5 (19–22 incl.)

Enrolment figures from: UNESCO, *Current School Enrolment Statistics,* Jan. 1956; and James B. Conant, *Education and Liberty* (Cambridge, Mass.: Harvard University Press, 1953).

Obviously the USA has made greater use of education for this purpose than the other countries. Australia has made a considerable use of it, and is intensifying this at present by increasing the enrolments of secondary schools and by moving toward a more functional type of secondary and higher education. Great Britain has also extended free secondary education, and has changed the system to permit poor but able youth to get into the universities by means of a new "comprehensive" secondary school. Even though the number of university attendants in Great Britain is low, compared with the USA and Australia, the British system of government scholarships has made university attendance possible for many poor but able youth. Glass' study indicated that 26 percent of university graduates came from working class families during the past 30 or 40 years.[14]

In Brazil, Hutchinson's study of students at the University of São Paulo indicates that only 10 percent of entering students in 1954 were from working-class families. This indicates that Brazil is not yet using the universities to assist much individual mobility. The University of São Paulo probably draws more working-class students than most other Brazilian universities.

Table 7 shows how the social class origins of students in various types of higher institutions in the USA compare with Brazil and England.[15] It appears

TABLE 7
Social Status of University Students
(percentage distribution of students)

Social Status	São Paulo	University of Wisconsin, USA	USA in General	England (Graduates)
Upper	38	15	10	15
Upper middle	36	25	30	26
Lower middle	16	30	30	32
Upper working class	8	25	25	21
Lower working class	2	5	5	6

that there is a higher proportion of students of working class origin in American and British universities than in Brazil. Australia is more like Britain and the USA in this respect.

Group Mobility.   Education of a functional type is generally used by a government as a means of upward group mobility for the working classes. It serves to increase their productivity, and the additional income they obtain thereby is used by them to raise their socio-economic level.

Primary education was used for this purpose in Great Britain, the USA and Australia in the latter half of the 19th century, and is being used for the same purpose now in Brazil.

Secondary education has also been used for the purpose of group mobility since 1900 in the USA, and since World War II in England and Australia. Functional secondary education not only increases productivity and makes possible an increase of income for the working classes; it also increases the extent to which people may enjoy life, through reading, taking part in musical and artistic activities, travel, etc., and is therefore a mark of higher social status in itself.

---

[14] Glass *et al., op. cit.*

[15] Data on São Paulo students are from Hutchinson, *op. cit.;* on American university students, Havighurst and Neugarten, *op. cit.;* on English university graduates, Glass *et al., op. cit.*

Brazil has not yet made use of secondary education for group mobility.

CONCLUSIONS ABOUT MOBILITY AND EDUCATION

The purpose of this study was to find out how social mobility and education are related to each other in societies undergoing industrialization and urbanization. From the four societies we have studied, the following generalizations can be made.

A.   There is a great deal of social mobility in an industrial society.

There are two types of social mobility, individual upward or downward mobility and group upward or downward mobility.

Individual upward mobility is made possible in a society by:

1.   Technological development which increases productivity and changes the structure of the labor force so as to include higher proportions of middle class and of skilled worker positions.

2.   Differential fertility, with the higher classes failing to reproduce themselves.

3.   Individual talent and effort.

Group upward mobility is made possible by:

1.   Technological development which increases productivity.

2.   Distribution of the increased social income in such a manner that one or more groups get especially large shares.

3.   Use by the mobile group of its income to purchase the symbols of higher status (home furnishings, education for children, clothing, etc.).

B.   Education has tended to foster mobility.

Education affects all of these factors, directly or indirectly. Technological development depends upon the supply of technically trained people, while the improvement of technology requires research-trained people. Individual talent is developed by education, and children with potential talent are often motivated by education to develop their abilities. Indirectly, education probably affects differential fertility, by making it easier for the better educated people to get information on contraception. Education also affects the consumption habits of lower class people, teaching them about middle class values and middle class material possessions. Even the differential economic gains of the working class can be ascribed partly to the fact that through workers' education and through the extension of primary and secondary education, working-class people have learned how to organize and assert their interests.

But education is one factor among several which affect the degree of upward mobility, including natural resources, the nature of organization and administration of industry, religious and social beliefs concerning fertility and contraception, and politico-economic factors such as the ways in which national income is allocated, and immigration policy.

C. *Different countries make different uses of education in relation to social mobility.*

Brazil. Brazil is just at the beginning of industrialization and urbanization. While large sections of the country retain a rural and aristocratic social structure, the industrial areas exhibit a high individual upward mobility rate together with upward group mobility for the working class.

Education has been involved in this process to only a limited degree. Foreign technologists have been imported to assist the process of industrialization, which otherwise would have waited upon the development and expansion of technical education in Brazil.

At present, however, education is becoming important in the current phase of industrial development. Primary education is increasing the productivity of factory workers. Secondary and higher education are beginning to supply people for the new middle class positions created by developing technology. Enrolments in engineering and the physical sciences are increasing rapidly. Thus the individual talent and effort factor is being influenced by education more now than in the past.

Probably education will have more influence on group mobility in Brazil during the coming two or three decades. The question of how the national income shall be allocated among the several economic groups will be settled through political contests and through bargaining between capital and labor, with education assisting the working classes to formulate and argue their case more effectively.

The United States. The USA is past the middle of its evolution toward industrialization. At this point education is involved with all of the factors affecting social mobility. Technological development is tied closely to the training of technicians and managers. There may be further net upward mobility due to automation, but probably not much of it. Further increase of productivity will result in further upward group mobility for the working classes, but this will depend increasingly on their educational level. Individual mobility, both upward and downward, will be increased by the extension of educational opportunity to working-class youth through expanded scholarship aid.

Education will probably tend to decrease the amount of upward mobility through differential fertility, for the trend seems to be toward a roughly equal fertility rate among urban classes as the working classes get more education.

Great Britain. Great Britain is in a later phase of industrial development than the other countries. At this point education seems not to be productive of net upward mobility. Technological development is not increasing the productivity of the country at such a rapid rate as in the USA. Differential fertility is less than formerly, and less effective in producing mobility. But British education is becoming more functional at the secondary school and university levels, and therefore is likely to be more effective than formerly in promoting individual upward mobility through talent, together with an equal amount of downward mobility. If present political policies continue, most of the increased productivity of the country will go into group mobility of the working classes.

Australia. Australia is between the USA and Brazil in its stage of industrial evolution, but has adopted the English technology, which relies more on manual labor and less on mass production and automation than does the American technology. Consequently Australia has not had any increase of upward mobility due to technological change in the past 50 years. However, education is becoming more functional, and secondary and higher education are becoming more accessible to working-class youth, with the consequence that individual upward and downward mobility will be kept at a rather high level. In Australia, as in England, political policies will probably convert the increased productivity of the country into group mobility for the working class.

The future of social mobility in relation to education

It is foolhardy to predict the course of future productivity based upon technology, with atomic energy almost ready for use but with petroleum resources becoming depleted and other natural resources being used up in the more industrial countries. However, it seems reasonable to suppose that productivity may reach something of a plateau in the technologically mature nations, while it increases rapidly in the less industrialized countries. If this happens, social mobility due to technological development will be great in the less industrialized countries, as it is now in Brazil, and will tend to disappear in the more developed countries. What increase of productivity does take place in the more developed countries, such as Great Britain and the USA, will depend more and more on research and on the technical and managerial skills of the population—that is, upon their education.

Social mobility due to differential fertility is likely to decrease or disappear in the more industrialized countries, because differential fertility will decrease in size and importance. In this, education will play a part, both in reducing families of the working classes and in enlarging families of the middle classes. This process can already be seen in Sweden.

The upward group mobility of the working classes may reduce the social distance between the working classes and the middle classes. If the difference in income between manual and non-manual workers becomes less, then the main differences between classes will be non-economic, and the nature of these differences will be largely determined by the uses they make of their money and of their leisure time. These uses will be considerably affected by their education.

Finally, it appears that the evolution of a modern industrial society tends toward a reduction of net upward individual mobility or perhaps toward its disappearance; but at the same time, this evolution tends toward increasing the amount of balanced upward and downward individual mobility. In this type of society there is likely to be increased opportunity for people with talent and ambition to get the education they need for "better" positions and to achieve these positions while those with less talent and ambition will tend to be downward mobile.

The industrial and democratic society of the year 2000 will be even more open and fluid than the most highly industrialized societies today, so that education will be the main instrument for upward mobility, and lack of education or failure to do well in one's education will be the principal cause of downward mobility.

8. Local social structure and educational selection[*]

NATALIE ROGOFF

This paper is concerned with the way young people are allocated to positions in the social-class structure and the part played by education in the allocating process.

Numerous studies in America, Britain, and western Europe document the fact that youngsters who start life in a given social class vary in the class status they achieve as adults in proportion to the amount of formal schooling they obtain. The more education, the more advantaged the class status. Depending on the starting point, education facilitates either upward social mobility or the maintenance of a favored class position; lack of education brings on downward social mobility, or stability in a disadvantaged class position.

But what are we to make of these facts? Particularly, what is it that sets some youngsters on a path leading ultimately to graduation from college, while others never even complete their secondary education? As usually stated, the facts convey little of a sense of social process, of one thing occurring before another in an identifiable social location, or of one event or status affecting a later event or status through the advent of specific social mechanisms. It is possible that any one or any combination of at least three disparate sets of happenings might bring about the observed relationships. Each of the three, to be proposed here, emphasizes a different key process—one stemming from the effect of schools on individual differences in ability, another from the effect of individual family differences in motivation, and the third from differences in community and school environments. In each case, the social process has a specified mechanism operating in a specified context. That these are extremely divergent interpretations of the observed correlation should be evident by the following discussion of each.

First, schools, like all formal organizations, develop a system of rewards and punishments as one way of implementing their goals. The acquisition of skills and knowledge by students is clearly one of the goals of schools. It is certainly not improbable that students who demonstrate the greatest success in acquiring skills and knowledge should most frequently receive the rewards that schools

*Reprinted with the permission of The Macmillan Company, from *Education, Economy and Society* by A. H. Halsey, Jean Floud and C. Arnold Anderson, pp. 241–51. © The Free Press of Glencoe, Inc., 1961.

have at their disposal—promotion, high grades, prizes, and scholarships. Since the distribution of marked scholastic ability cuts across the social classes to at least some degree, the reward and punishment system of the schools would lead to a rearrangement of students with respect to their potential social achievement: the more able youngsters, motivated by scholastic rewards, would move further ahead in school, continue their education longer, and eventually move into more prestigeful occupational and social positions than the less able. Moreover, at the end of the school years, a certain amount of social mobility, upward and downward, could be attributed to the encouragement given by schools to the capable, no matter what their social origins, as well as to the discouragement given the less able of all social classes. The observed relationship between educational attainment and adult social-class position might, therefore, be due to the interaction between individual differences in ability and the reward systems of schools.

A second process that would lead to the observed results has its locus in the family, rather than the school, and hinges on attitudes rather than aptitude. Some families, valuing achievement, discipline, and social-economic success, encourage their children to do as well as possible in school; the youngster's ability, this interpretation runs, sets only the broadest of bounds on his school performance. More determining than ability is the family's attitude toward education—and the distribution of favorable attitudes toward education again cuts across the class structure to some degree. The education and, ultimately, the social-class achievement of youngsters represent family aspirations come true. Note that the school, in this process, plays essentially a passive role, or at least takes something of a secondary part. The school actually rewards, not necessarily those who merit it, but those who *want* to be rewarded, whether or not, in some abstract sense of equitable arrangements, they do merit it. The real locus of social mobility is the living room, not the classroom.

Finally, the possibility exists that educational attainment and adult class status are correlated because of processes arising from community and school structures. Because this idea is less familiar than the others and because the processes it highlights differ in certain formal ways from the others, it will be developed here at somewhat greater length. First, let it be granted that the various social classes are not randomly distributed among the diverse sizes and types of communities in the United States today. (We defer for the moment the evidence for this assertion.) It follows that each of the social classes will be more heavily concentrated in some kinds of community environments than in others, and that communities will vary in the predominant or average social-class affiliation of their residents. Such structural differences may set in motion both formal arrangements—such as school, library, and general cultural facilities in the community—and informal mechanisms, such as normative climates or modal levels of social aspiration, which are likely to affect *all* members of the community to some extent—parents and children, upper, middle, and working classes.

Many of the studies whose general findings are at issue here have, in fact, covered a wide variety of communities. By pooling the behavior of youngsters living in diverse communities, one of the sources of social mobility may be hidden from view, for it is possible that the formal arrangements and informal norms of the community set both a floor and a ceiling on the ultimate achievements in educational and social-class status of their young residents. For example, when we observe that youngsters from the more favored social origins end up on the average with greater educational attainment, we may in fact be observing the results of the greater concentration of such youngsters in communities that facilitate academic achievement through better schools and through prevailing climates of opinion that nurture and sustain high educational aspiration. Upward social mobility, under these conditions, would result for the lucky minority of working-class youngsters whose families live, by accident or design, in predominantly middle-class communities; and downward social mobility for the unlucky middle-class youngsters living in less favored environments; while stability of class position would be the typical outcome for the majority of youngsters living in towns, villages, or cities where their class status is not a deviant one.

One of the intriguing implications of this idea is that it proposes a continuing but ever-changing link between ecological processes that lead to spatial patterns of residence and work, on the one hand, and the processes through which persons are allocated to positions in the social-class structure, on the other. Socioeconomic position influences the type of community or neighborhood where families will live; their ecological status then affects the life chances of their children, some of whom will maintain the social-class status of the parents, while others will shift in status. Both individual and net shifts of class status in the second generation lead to further changes in ecological patterns, and so on, possibly until some kind of equilibrium is reached.

In sum, three variant interpretations have been offered for a recurrent empirical observation: that young people from given social origins vary in their educational attainment; such variations eventually leading to differences in the social-class status achieved in adulthood. Educational attainment thereby leads to upward or downward social mobility, or to maintenance of parental class status. In effect, the three interpretations can be ordered with respect to the importance they attach to events transpiring in the classroom itself. According to the first, the classroom is the central stage, for it is there that youngsters are rewarded or punished for their scholastic ability and performance, and it is the rewards and punishments they experience that lead to their academic and social attainments. According to the second interpretation, youngsters are carriers of aspirations and attitudes acquired from their families, and it is these states of mind that prevail, although they may be reinforced (unwittingly?) by the reward-and-punishment system of the school. The last interpretation calls attention to the community setting of both schools and families, and suggests that the ecological environment leads to formal and informal arrangements within and outside of the schools, affecting the educational attainment of residents.

None of these interpretations excludes the others. It is not necessary to demonstrate that only one of the social processes can be observed, the others being absent. Instead, a research design is called for that permits us to see whether all three are operative and, if possible, to gauge their relative significance. An empirical study with such a design is currently in process at the Bureau of Applied Social Research of Columbia University. We were fortunate enough to be given access to information gathered by the Educational Testing Service, concerning the college-going and career plans of over thirty-five thousand American high-school seniors, who constituted the entire senior class of 1955 of over five hundred public secondary schools. Concerning the schools, which provide a fairly representative sample of the twenty thousand-odd senior public high schools in the United States, information was collected, at the time of the field work, from their principals. This has now been supplemented by consulting national and state school directories, other published surveys, and census sources describing the towns and counties where the schools are located.

What kinds of information are needed to provide empirical tests of the ideas advanced here? We need to know something about the social origins of the youngsters, something about their future orientations, and their scholastic ability. Finally, we need to introduce some principle for classifying the communities where they attend high school. Specifically, here are the indicators to be used in attempting to compare the proposed types of social processes with the factual evidence. First, we shall see how youngsters who vary in scholastic ability—indicated by their performance on a twenty-item test devised especially for this study by the Educational Testing Service—compare with respect to their plans for going on to college. This will provide the evidence for seeing whether or not the reward-and-punishment system of the schools helps to channel the more capable youngsters into the route of higher education. Moreover, we shall simultaneously trace the effect of the youngster's social background on his college-going orientation. Several criteria have been used to classify the families of orientation of the high-school seniors: their fathers' occupational status, fathers' educational attainment, and the college experience of their older siblings. Combining these three properties of the families with the average college-going propensities of the high-school seniors who belonged to such family types permitted us to construct a set of ranked socio-educational classes, ranging from well-educated professional and managerial families, who clearly imbue their offspring with a desire to go to college, to poorly or uneducated unskilled manual and farm families who are far more indifferent to higher education as a desirable goal. Five such classes were finally discerned, each containing approximately 20 per cent of the thirty-five thousand high-school seniors, so that they may be referred to as the socio-educational status quintiles.

One further word about classifying the students according to their scholastic ability. At some of the high schools studied, the vast majority of seniors scored well above the mean, while at other schools, the bulk of the senior class did extremely poorly on the test. While this is in itself a significant result, it also has the following implication: if we were to classify individual seniors according to their absolute scholastic aptitude score, we should be comparing the behavior of youngsters who actually stood at just about all possible relative positions within their own school. Almost any given score represents the top, the middle, and the bottom relative position at one or more of the 518 high schools observed. Therefore, the scores were converted into school-specific quartiles for all those who were in a senior class of 15 or more. (This eliminates about 20 per cent of the schools, but less than 3 per cent of the 35,000 students.) Since we want to observe the effect of allocating rewards and punishments by school authorities, we clearly need to compare those who are at the top in their own school with those at the bottom, no matter what the absolute level of scholastic ability is at the school.

Finally, we have used the expressions "scholastic ability" and "scholastic performance" as though they were interchangeable, despite the fact that they are clearly disparate. Fortunately, the principals of about one hundred of the high schools were asked to check the school records of each of their seniors and indicate what his class standing was. The correlation between ability, as indicated by the short written test, and class standing, which summarizes the student's performance over a four-year period, is extremely high, although it does vary somewhat among the high schools. Table 1 presents the evidence—which we use as a justification for taking the student's performance on the aptitude test as a fairly good indicator of his behavior in the classroom.

TABLE 1
Class Standing and Scholastic Ability

Scholastic-Ability Quartile*	Per Cent Who Are in the Top Half of Their Senior Class, by Grade Average	No. of Cases
(Top) 4	75	1,558
3	56	1,614
2	40	1,689
(Bottom) 1	17	1,561

*Scores on the special aptitude test devised for this study were transformed into school-specific quartiles.

Scholastic ability plays a decisive role in students' plans to continue with their education. Some 61 per cent of all high-school seniors in the top quarter of their class planned to go to college; in successive quartiles, the proportion drops to 44 per cent, 33 per cent and 24 per cent. The preliminary evidence suggests that the high school in effect *does* allocate rewards and punishments in such a way as to encourage the competent and discourage the incompetent. At the same time, there is a marked tendency for students' further educational plans to be influenced by the socio-educational status of their families. Seventy-two per cent of those from professional or managerial families plan to attend college; the proportion decreases to 47 per cent, 35 per cent, 26 per cent, and finally 24 per cent through the succeeding socio-educational status categories. And, as many other studies have shown, the two social processes reinforce one another. The full picture is given in Table 2, where the proportions planning to attend college are shown at every level of scholastic ability and from each of the five types of social origins simultaneously. College-going propensities vary greatly among the twenty categories of high-school seniors: 83 per cent of the brightest youngsters from the most advantaged families plan to attend college, but only 16 per cent

TABLE 2

Per Cent of High-School Seniors Planning to Attend College,
According to Scholastic Ability (in Quartiles) and
Socio-Educational Status of the Family

Scholastic-Ability Quartile*	Family-Status Quintile					All Quintiles	No. of Cases
	(Top) 5	4	3	2	(Bottom) 1		
(Top) 4 ...	83	66	53	44	43	61	(8,647)
3 ...	70	53	37	29	29	44	(8,709)
2 ...	65	41	31	20	21	33	(8,696)
(Bottom) 1 ...	53	30	22	16	18	24	(8,509)
All quartiles	72	47	35	26	24	40	
No. of cases	(6,520)	(6,647)	(6,465)	(8,116)	(6,811)		(34,561)

Notes: Students are classified here according to their scholastic-aptitude quartile in their own high school. Family status position, however, is constant for all students coming from a given family background, no matter what the social composition of their high school.

The number of cases on which each of the percentages is based ranges from 963 to 2,505.

of the least competent children of skilled and semiskilled workers (category 2) are college-oriented. Both the school and the family play a part in determining who is to gain education beyond high school. Among previous studies, the relative importance of the two has varied greatly; Kahl's study in the suburbs of Boston[1] shows the family to be almost twice as influential as the school, while Sewell's Wisconsin data[2] suggest the school to be almost three times as important as the family; our own nation-wide sample falls squarely between the two, with each of the sources playing about an equal role.

So much, then, for the first two social processes leading to the observed correlation between educational attainment and social mobility or stability. What of the third? With the first two, it was clear, both from the logic of the argument and from the guidelines provided by past research, just what indicators to use in order to test the validity of our ideas. The third set of social processes are, we suggested, generated by conditions in the community, which affect the type of

[1] J. A. Kahl, "Education and Occupational Aspirations of 'Common Man' Boys," *Harvard Educational Review*, XXIII (1953), pp. 186–203.

[2] W. H. Sewell *et al.*, "Social Status and Educational and Occupational Aspiration," *American Sociological Review*, XXI (1956), pp. 203–11.

educational and cultural facilities the town can provide and which presumably also shape the average social and education aspiration level of the residents. But what types of indicators would most accurately portray such environmental states? This is clearly a major sociological problem and one to which we can make only a limited contribution. Furthermore, we have only begun to probe the data in this study for tentative leads and therefore offer the following evidence with the appropriate reservations.

We start with a principle of classifying communities that derives from a set of frequently used descriptive terms, employed by laymen, educators, social scientists, and just about everyone who has ever given a moment's thought to the varieties of educational experience: the size and type of community—village or small town, suburban or metropolitan—where the schools are located. The temptation is strong to clothe this idea in polysyllabic sociological garb, but in fact the impulse to use such a classification scheme arose from the fact that it is one of the very few environmental properties used frequently enough and over a long enough period of time to warrant a systematic empirical test.

Nine types of communities were discerned, varying in population size and in their relationship to a metropolitan area. Table 3 identifies the types and presents the salient results concerning the college-going propensities of youngsters attending high school in each environment. It is up to the reader to decide whether or not the results confirm his expectations. For example, who would have predicted that the college-going propensities of youngsters attending high school in the very largest cities is almost as low as that of youngsters residing in the smallest towns and villages and is surpassed by that of youngsters from the

TABLE 3
College-Planning Rates and Social Composition of High-School
Senior Classes in Diverse Community Contexts

Type of Community	Number of High Schools	Number of Seniors	Per Cent Planning to Attend College	Per Cent of Seniors in Each Family-Status Quintile (Top) 5	4	3	2	(Bottom) 1	Total
Small independent towns:									
Less than 2,500	270	6,991	33	9	17	12	20	42	100%
2,500–9,999	85	5,451	39	16	20	16	24	24	100%
10,000–49,999	42	5,591	48	21	20	19	24	16	100%
Suburbs:									
Less than 2,500	36	1,768	37	17	18	18	26	21	100%
2,500–9,999	15	1,085	46	30	18	19	23	10	100%
10,000–49,999	22	3,116	50	34	18	19	21	8	100%
Large towns and cities:									
50,000–99,999	10	2,176	45	22	20	22	23	13	100%
100,000–499,999 . . .	19	3,669	37	17	18	24	30	11	100%
500,000 or more	19	5,589	39	20	22	23	24	11	100%
All communities	518	35,436	40	19	19	19	23	20	100%

larger towns and, of course, the suburbs? College-going is apparently affected by the size and type of community where the decision to attend college is made—but hardly in a simple, linear fashion. One note of caution. We were able to observe only those young people who remained in school until the twelfth grade, and the tendency to stay in school that long varies among the diverse type of communities. The college-going proportions need to be corrected, therefore, by taking into account those youngsters who will not attend college because they have not completed a secondary education. Community educational-retention rates are positively correlated both with urbanization and with community wealth (median family income), and much more markedly with the latter than the former. Therefore, the wealthy suburbs should have their college-going proportions reduced the least, since most of their youngsters do stay in school through the twelfth grade, followed by the larger cities, and finally small towns and rural villages. This would keep the three main types of communities in the same rank order but would increase the gap between the smallest and largest places.

The second part of Table 3 describes the social composition of the student body attending high school in the various types of communities. Note the marked degree of social segregation implied by these distributions—the children of farmers (category 1) concentrated in the smallest villages and towns, the children of professionals and managers in the larger suburbs, and the children of industrial workers (category 2) most heavily concentrated in cities of 100,000–500,000. We cannot here mention more than a few of the major consequences of such ecological segregation.

One of the most interesting consequences concerns the scholastic aptitude of youngsters attending schools situated in diverse community contexts. Table 4 presents the trends, showing median aptitude scores of students coming from families of each of the five socio-educational status types and living in each type of community. Here, of course, we describe students according to their absolute scores on the aptitude test, since we want to evaluate the effect of the environment on scholastic ability. Test scores ranged from 0 to 20; the mean for all 35,000 seniors to whom it was given is 8.9; the standard deviation, 4.7.

Again, the suburbs stand out as most conducive to pronounced scholastic achievement. For convenience, an unweighted average aptitude score is given for all students attending schools in each community context. This enables us to see the effect that schools exert on their student's academic capacity, without that effect's being obscured by the advantages or disadvantages individual students enjoy by virtue of their family background. It appears that all students, whether in the majority or the minority in the school they attend, enjoy the blessings or pay the price their school affords. From those at the top to those at the bottom of the social-class hierarchy, all students attending large suburban schools emerge from their educational experience relatively better equipped in academic skills, while youngsters who attend school in small villages or large industrial cities emerge from their educational environments less adequately

TABLE 4
Scholastic Ability and College-Planning Rates, by
Social Origins and Community Context

A. Median Aptitude Scores

	Family-Status Quintile					Unweighted Mean of All Quintiles
Type of Community	(Top) 5	4	3	2	(Bottom) 1	
Small independent towns:						
Less than 2,500	11.1	9.2	8.3	7.7	6.9	8.7
2,500–9,999	11.6	9.7	8.6	8.1	7.4	9.1
10,000–49,999	12.7	10.1	9.0	9.1	7.3	9.6
Suburbs:						
Less than 2,500	11.9	9.8	9.0	8.2	7.2	9.2
2,500–9,999	*13.0+	10.8	9.4	8.2	7.2	10.0
10,000–49,999	13.0	11.3	10.5	9.9	8.5	10.6
Large towns and cities:						
50,000–99,999	12.0	8.8	8.0	7.1	*5.0–	8.0
100,000–499,999	11.8	9.5	8.4	7.7	7.0	8.9
500,000 or more	11.7	9.6	8.8	8.6	7.2	9.2

*Medians were computed from grouped data, using four score intervals. In these two cases, the medians fell in one of the extreme intervals, and interpolation was not carried out.

B. Per Cent Planning to Attend College

	Family-Status Quintile					Unweighted Mean of All Quintiles
Type of Community	(Top) 5	4	3	2	(Bottom) 1	
Small independent towns:						
Less than 2,500	66	45	35	25	25	39
2,500–9,999	73	50	33	25	27	42
10,000–49,999	78	55	42	32	32	48
Suburbs:						
Less than 2,500········	69	50	35	25	15	39
2,500–9,999	74	51	38	22	29	43
10,000–49,999	77	51	40	26	22	43
Large towns and cities:						
50,000–99,999	67	44	36	35	37	44
100,000–499,999	69	45	32	22	20	37
500,000 or more	64	46	31	28	24	39

prepared. Note how these trends account for some of the heterogeneity in scholastic aptitude *within* a given social class by the diversity in formal academic training received by the youngsters originating in that class.

The second part of Table 4 shows parallel trends for plans to attend college, according to young people's social origins and the type of community where they attend high school. On the face of it, small towns and suburbs appear to be at a par in producing college-oriented youngsters—but again, we should recall the difference between them in the school retention rates through the twelfth grade. After making the appropriate corrections, the suburbs will again rank first in productivity of college students.

The last word has hardly been said on the variety of ways young people may be affected by the community setting where they frame their career and educational goals. Quite the contrary—only after considerably more research effort has been expended will we be ready to make assertions with confidence on the whole matter of broad structural influences on individual behavior.

Specifically, when it comes to schools and social stratifications, the kind of analysis proposed here is carried out in the following spirit: heretofore, when sociologists have investigated the way education and social-class structure relate to one another, relatively scant attention has been accorded the fact that education is a long-term social process, occurring microscopically in the schoolroom and macroscopically in a definite and describable community context. Until now, the challenge of observing these processes has been evaded by the phrase: "Education is the high road to social mobility." No expression could more successfully divert us from the sociological point. The evasion has also directed sociologists to say that the heart of the matter is in the nuclear family, where all of the behavior and all of the attitudes and values are engendered that lead to scholastic achievement, and subsequent social-class achievement, by the members of each new generation. Nothing in our study belies the crucial role of the nuclear family, whose significance is so well recognized that we hardly feel the need to do any proselytizing in its behalf. But that this is all that counts in a bureaucratized, achievement-oriented society, where education is controlled by local communities each with its formally organized school system, is too much to believe. The more we turn in these other directions, the more we will learn about the social structure of our society.

9. Social-class variations in the teacher-pupil relationship*

HOWARD S. BECKER

The major problems of workers in the service occupations are likely to be a function of their relationship to their clients or customers, those for whom or on whom the occupational service is performed.[1] Members of such occupations typically have some image of the "ideal" client, and it is in terms of this fiction that they fashion their conceptions of how their work ought to be performed, and their actual work techniques. To the degree that actual clients approximate this ideal the worker will have no "client problem."

In a highly differentiated urban society, however, clients will vary greatly, and ordinarily only some fraction of the total of potential clients will be "good" ones. Workers tend to classify clients in terms of the way in which they vary from this ideal. The fact of client variation from the occupational ideal emphasizes the intimate relation of the institution in which work is carried on to its environing society. If that society does not prepare people to play their client roles in the manner desired by the occupation's members there will be conflicts, and problems for the workers in the performance of their work. One of the major factors affecting the production of suitable clients is the cultural diversity of various social classes in the society. The cultures of particular social-class groups may operate to produce clients who make the worker's position extremely difficult.

We deal here with this problem as it appears in the experience of the functionaries of a large urban educational institution, the Chicago public school system, discussing the way in which teachers in this system observe, classify and react to class-typed differences in the behavior of the children with whom they work. The material to be presented is thus relevant not only to problems of occupational organization but also to the problem of differences in the educational opportunities available to children of various social classes. Warner, Havig-

---

*From the *Journal of Educational Sociology*, 25 (April, 1952), 451–65.

[1] See Howard S. Becker, "The Professional Dance Musician and His Audience," *American Journal of Sociology*, 57 (September, 1951), 136–44, for further discussion of this point.

hurst, and Loeb,[2] and Hollingshead[3] have demonstrated the manner in which the schools tend to favor and select out children of the middle classes. Allison Davis has pointed to those factors in the class cultures involved which make lower-class children less and middle-class children more adaptable to the work and behavioral standards of the school.[4] This paper will contribute to knowledge in this area by analyzing the manner in which the public school teacher reacts to these cultural differences and, in so doing, perpetuates the discrimination of our educational system against the lower-class child.

The analysis is based on sixty interviews with teachers in the Chicago system.[5] The interviews were oriented around the general question of the problems of being a teacher and were not specifically directed toward discovering feelings about social-class differences among students. Since these differences created some of the teachers' most pressing problems they were continually brought up by the interviewees themselves. They typically distinguished three social-class groups with which they, as teachers, came in contact: (1) a bottom stratum, probably equivalent to the lower-lower and parts of the upper-lower class; (2) an upper stratum, probably equivalent to the upper-middle class; and (3) a middle stratum, probably equivalent to the lower-middle and parts of the upper-lower class. We will adopt the convention of referring to these groups as lower, upper and middle groups, but it should be understood that this terminology refers to the teachers' classification of students and not to the ordinary sociological description.

We will proceed by taking up the three problems that loomed largest in the teachers' discussion of adjustment to their students: (1) the problem of *teaching* itself, (2) the problem of *discipline,* and (3) the problem of the *moral acceptability* of the students. In each case the variation in the form of and adjustment to the problem by the characteristics of the children of the various class groups distinguished by teachers is discussed.

A basic problem in any occupation is that of performing one's given task successfully, and where this involves working with human beings their qualities are a major variable affecting the ease with which the work can be done. The teacher considers that she has done her job adequately when she has brought about an observable change in the children's skills and knowledge which she can attribute to her own efforts:

---

[2] W. Lloyd Warner, Robert J. Havighurst, and Martin B. Loeb, *Who Shall Be Educated?* (New York: Harper & Bros., 1944).

[3] August de B. Hollingshead, *Elmtown's Youth: The Impact of Social Class on Adolescents* (New York: John Wiley & Sons, Inc., 1949).

[4] Allison Davis, *Social-Class Influences upon Learning* (Cambridge, Mass.: Harvard University Press, 1950).

[5] The entire research has been reported in Howard S. Becker, "Role and Career Problems of the Chicago Public School Teacher," doctoral dissertation, University of Chicago, 1951.

Well, I would say that a teacher is successful when she is putting the material across to the children, when she is getting some response from them. I'll tell you something. Teaching is a very rewarding line of work, because you can see those children grow under your hands. You can see the difference in them after you've had them for five months. You can see where they've started and where they've got to. And it's all yours. It really is rewarding in that way, you can see results and know that it's your work that brought those results about.

She feels that she has a better chance of success in this area when her pupils are interested in attending and working hard in school, and are trained at home in such a way that they are bright and quick at school work. Her problems arise in teaching those groups who do not meet these specifications, for in these cases her teaching techniques, tailored to the "perfect" student, are inadequate to cope with the reality, and she is left with a feeling of having failed in performing her basic task.

Davis has described the orientations toward education in general, and school work in particular, of the lower and middle classes:

Thus, our educational system, which next to the family is the most effective agency in teaching good work habits to middle class people, is largely ineffective and unrealistic with underprivileged groups. Education fails to motivate such workers because our schools and our society both lack *real rewards* to offer underprivileged groups. Neither lower class children or adults will work hard in school or on the job just to please the teacher or boss. They are not going to learn to be ambitious, to be conscientious, and to study hard, as if school and work were a fine character-building game, which one plays just for the sake of playing. They can see, indeed, that those who work hard at school usually have families that already have the occupations, homes, and social acceptance that the school holds up as the rewards of education. The underprivileged workers can see also that the chances of their getting enough education to make their attainment of these rewards in the future at all probable is very slight. Since they can win the rewards of prestige and social acceptance in their own slum groups without much education, they do not take very seriously the motivation taught by the school.[6]

As these cultural differences produce variations from the image of the "ideal" student, teachers tend to use class terms in describing the children with whom they work.

Children of the lowest group, from slum areas, are characterized as the most difficult group to teach successfully, lacking in interest in school, learning ability, and outside training:

They don't have the right kind of study habits. They can't seem to apply themselves as well. Of course, it's not their fault; they aren't brought

---

[6] Allison Davis, "The Motivation of the Underprivileged Worker," in William F. Whyte (ed.), *Industry and Society* (New York: McGraw-Hill Book Co., Inc., 1947), p. 99.

up right. After all, the parents in a neighborhood like that really aren't interested. . . . But, as I say, those children don't learn very quickly. A great many of them don't seem to be really interested in getting an education. I don't think they are. It's hard to get anything done with children like that. They simply don't respond.

In definite contrast are the terms used to describe children of the upper groups:

In a neighborhood like this there's something about the children, you just feel like you're accomplishing so much more. You throw an idea out and you can see that it takes hold. The children know what you're talking about and they think about it. Then they come in with projects and pictures and additional information, and it just makes you feel good to see it. They go places and see things, and they know what you're talking about. For instance, you might be teaching social studies or geography. . . . You bring something up and a child says, "Oh, my parents took me to see that in a museum." You can just do more with material like that.

Ambivalent feelings are aroused by children of the middle group. While motivated to work hard in school they lack the proper out-of-school training:

Well, they're very nice here, very nice. They're not hard to handle. You see, they're taught respect in the home and they're respectful to the teacher. They want to work and do well. . . . Of course, they're not too brilliant. You know what I mean. But they are very nice children and very easy to work with.

In short, the differences between groups make it possible for the teacher to feel successful at her job only with the top group; with the other groups she feels, in greater or lesser measure, that she has failed.

These differences in ability to do school work, as perceived by teachers, have important consequences. They lead, in the first place, to differences in actual teaching techniques. A young high school teacher contrasted the techniques used in "slum" schools with those used in "better" schools:

At S—, there were a lot of guys who were just waiting till they were sixteen so they could get out of school. L—, everybody—well, a very large percentage, I'll say—was going on to secondary school, to college. That certainly made a difference in their classroom work. You had to teach differently at the different schools. For instance, at S—, if you had demonstrations in chemistry they had to be pretty flashy, lots of noise and smoke, before they'd get interested in it. That wasn't necessary at L—. Or at S— if you were having electricity or something like that you had to get the static electricity machine out and have them all stand around and hold hands so that they'd all get a little jolt.

Further, the teacher feels that where these differences are recognized by her superiors there will be a corresponding variation in the amount of work she is expected to accomplish. She expects that the amount of work and effort required of her will vary inversely with the social status of her pupils. This teacher compared schools from the extremes of the class range:

> So you have to be on your toes and keep up to where you're supposed to be in the course of study. Now, in a school like the D— [slum school] you're just not expected to complete all that work. It's almost impossible. For instance, in the second grade we're supposed to cover nine spelling words a week. Well, I can do that up here at the K— ["better" school], they can take nine new words a week. But the best class I ever had at the D— was only able to achieve six words a week and they had to work pretty hard to get that. So I never finished the year's work in spelling. I couldn't. And I really wasn't expected to.

One resultant of this situation—in which less is expected of those teachers whose students are more difficult to teach—is that the problem becomes more aggravated in each grade, as the gap between what the children should know and what they actually do know becomes wider and wider. A principal of such a school describes the degeneration there of the teaching problem into a struggle to get a few basic skills across, in a situation where this cumulative effect makes following the normal program of study impossible:

> The children come into our upper grades with very poor reading ability. That means that all the way through our school everybody is concentrating on reading. It's not like at a school like S— [middle group] where they have science and history and so on. At a school like that they figure that from first to fourth you learn to read and from fifth to eighth you read to learn. You use your reading to learn other material. Well, these children don't reach that second stage while they're with us. We have to plug along getting them to learn to read. Our teachers are pretty well satisfied if the children can read and do simple number work when they leave here. You'll find that they don't think very much of subjects like science, and so on. They haven't got any time for that. They're just trying to get these basic things over. . . . That's why our school is different from one like the S—.

Such consequences of teachers' differential reaction to various class groups obviously operate to further perpetuate those class-cultural characteristics to which they object in the first place.

II

Discipline is the second of the teacher's major problems with her students. Willard Waller pointed to its basis when he wrote that "Teacher and pupil confront each other in the school with an original conflict of desires, and however much that conflict may be reduced in amount, or however much it may be hidden, it still remains."[7] We must recognize that conflict, either actual or potential, is ever present in the teacher-pupil relationship, the teacher attempting

---

[7] Willard Waller, *Sociology of Teaching* (New York: John Wiley & Sons, Inc., 1932), p. 197.

to maintain her control against the children's efforts to break it.[8] This conflict is felt even with those children who present least difficulty; a teacher who considered her pupils models of good behavior nevertheless said:

> But there's that tension all the time. Between you and the students. It's hard on your nerves. Teaching is fun, if you enjoy your subject, but it's the discipline that keeps your nerves on edge, you know what I mean? There's always that tension. Sometimes people say, "Oh, you teach school. That's an easy job, just sitting around all day long." They don't know what it's really like. It's hard on your nerves.

The teacher is tense because she fears that she will lose control, which she tends to define in terms of some line beyond which she will not allow the children to go. Wherever she may draw this line (and there is considerable variation), the teacher feels that she has a "discipline" problem when the children attempt to push beyond it. The form and intensity of this problem are felt to vary from one social-class group to another, as might be expected from Davis' description of class emphases on aggression:

> In general, middle-class aggression is taught to adolescents in the form of social and economic skills which will enable them to compete effectively at that level. . . . In lower-class families, physical aggression is as much a normal, socially approved and socially inculcated type of behavior as it is in frontier communities.[9]

These differences in child training are matched by variation in the teachers' reactions.

Children in "slum" schools are considered most difficult to control, being given to unrestrained behavior and physical violence. The interviews are filled with descriptions of such difficulties. Miriam Wagenschein, in a parallel study of the beginning school teacher, gave this summary of the experiences of these younger teachers in lower-class schools:

> The reports which these teachers give of what *can be* done by a group of children are nothing short of amazing. A young white teacher walked into her new classroom and was greeted with the comment, "Another damn white one." Another was "rushed" at her desk by the entire class when she tried to be extremely strict with them. Teachers report having been bitten, tripped, and pushed on the stairs. Another gave an account of a second grader throwing a milk bottle at the teacher and of a first grader having such a temper tantrum that it took the principal and two policemen to get him out of the room. In another school, following a fight on the playground, the principal took thirty-two razor blades from children in a first grade room. Some teachers indicated fear that they might be attacked

---

[8] Although all service occupations tend to have such problems of control over their clients, the problem is undoubtedly aggravated in situations like the school where those upon whom the service is being performed are not there of their own volition, but rather because of the wishes of some other group (the parents, in this case).

[9] Allison Davis, *Social-Class Influence upon Learning, op. cit.*, pp. 34–35.

by irate persons in the neighborhoods in which they teach. Other teachers report that their pupils carry long pieces of glass and have been known to threaten other pupils with them, while others jab each other with hypodermic needles. One boy got angry with his teacher and knocked in the fender of her car.[10]

In these schools a major part of the teacher's time must be devoted to discipline; as one said: "It's just a question of keeping them in line." This emphasis on discipline detracts from the school's primary function of teaching, thus discriminating, in terms of available educational opportunity, against the children of these schools.

Children of the middle group are thought of as docile, and with them the teacher has least difficulty with discipline:

> Those children were much quieter, easier to work with. When we'd play our little games there was never any commotion. That was a very nice school to work in. Everything was quite nice about it. The children were easy to work with . . .

Children of the upper group are felt hard to handle in some respects, and are often termed "spoiled," "overindulged," or "neurotic"; they do not play the role of the child in the submissive manner teachers consider appropriate. One interviewee, speaking of this group, said:

> I think most teachers prefer not to teach in that type of school. The children are more pampered and, as we say, more inclined to run the school for themselves. The parents are very much at fault. The children are not used to taking orders at home and naturally they won't take them at school either.

Teachers develop methods of dealing with these discipline problems, and these tend to vary between social-class groups as do the problems themselves. The basic device used by successful disciplinarians is to establish authority clearly on the first meeting with the class:

> You can't ever let them get the upper hand on you or you're through. So I start out tough. The first day I get a new class in, I let them know who's boss. . . . You've got to start off tough, then you can ease up as you go along. If you start out easy-going, when you try to get tough they'll just look at you and laugh.

Having once established such a relation, it is considered important that the teacher be consistent in her behavior so that the children will continue to respect and obey her:

> I let them know I mean business. That's one thing you must do. Say nothing that you won't follow through on. Some teachers will say any-

---

[10] Miriam Wagenschein, "Reality Shock," master's thesis, University of Chicago, 1950, pp. 58–59.

thing to keep kids quiet, they'll threaten anything. Then they can't or won't carry out their threats. Naturally, the children won't pay any attention to them after that. You must never say anything that you won't back up.

In the difficult "slum" schools, teachers feel the necessity of using stern measures, up to and including physical violence (nominally outlawed):

Technically you're not supposed to lay a hand on a kid. Well, they don't, technically. But there are a lot of ways of handling a kid so that it doesn't show—and then it's the teacher's word against the kid's, so the kid hasn't got a chance. Like dear Mrs.—. She gets mad at a kid, she takes him out in the hall. She gets him stood up against the wall. Then she's got a way of chucking the kid under the chin, only hard, so that it knocks his head back against the wall. It doesn't leave a mark on him. But when he comes back in that room he can hardly see straight, he's so knocked out. It's really rough. There's a lot of little tricks like that that you learn about.

Where such devices are not used, there is recourse to violent punishment, "tongue lashings." All teachers, however, are not emotionally equipped for such behavior and must find other means:

The worst thing I can do is lose my temper and start raving. . . . You've got to believe in that kind of thing in order for it to work. . . . If you don't honestly believe it it shows up and the children know you don't mean it and it doesn't do any good anyway. . . . I try a different approach myself. Whenever they get too rowdy I go to the piano and . . . play something and we have rhythms or something until they sort of settle down. . . . That's what we call "softsoaping" them. It seems to work for me. It's about the only thing I can do.

Some teachers may also resort to calling in the parents, a device whose usefulness is limited by the fact that such summons are most frequently ignored. The teacher's disciplinary power in such a school is also limited by her fear of retaliation by the students: "Those fellows are pretty big, and I just think it would take a bigger person than me to handle them. I certainly wouldn't like to try."

In the school with children of the middle group no strong sanctions are required, mild reprimands sufficing:

Now the children at Z— here are quite nice to teach. They're pliable, yes, that's the word, they're pliable. They will go along with you on things and not fight you. You can take them any place and say to them, "I'm counting on you not to disgrace your school. Let's see that Z— spirit." And they'll behave for you. . . . They can be frightened, they have fear in them. They're pliable, flexible, you can do things with them. They're afraid of their parents and what they'll do to them if they get into trouble at school. And they're afraid of the administration. They're afraid of being sent down to the principal. So that they can be handled.

Children of the upper group often act in a way which may be interpreted as "misbehavior" but which does not represent a conscious attack on the teacher's authority. Many teachers are able to disregard such activity by interpreting it as a natural concomitant of the "brightness" and "intelligence" of such children. Where such an interpretation is not possible the teachers feel hampered by a lack of effective sanctions:

> I try different things like keeping them out of a gym period or a recess period. But that doesn't always work. I have this one little boy who just didn't care when I used those punishments. He said he didn't like gym anyway. I don't know what I'm going to do with him.

The teacher's power in such schools is further limited by the fact that the children are able to mobilize their influential parents so as to exert a large degree of control over the actions of school personnel.

It should be noted, finally, that discipline problems tend to become less important as the length of the teacher's stay in a particular school makes it possible for her to build a reputation which coerces the children into behaving without attempting any test of strength:[11]

> I have no trouble with the children. Once you establish a reputation and they know what to expect, they respect you and you have no trouble. Of course, that's different for a new teacher, but when you're established that's no problem at all.

III

The third area of problems has been termed that of *moral acceptability,* and arises from the fact that some actions of one's potential clients may be offensive in terms of some deeply felt set of moral standards; these clients are thus morally unacceptable. Teachers find that some of their pupils act in such a way as to make themselves unacceptable in terms of the moral values centered around health and cleanliness, sex and aggression, ambition and work, and the relations of age groups.

Children of the middle group present no problem at this level, being universally described as clean, well dressed, moderate in their behavior, and hard working. Children from the "better" neighborhoods are considered deficient in the important moral traits of politeness and respect for elders:

> Here the children come from wealthy homes. That's not so good either. They're not used to doing work at home. They have maids and servants of all kinds and they're used to having things done for them, instead of doing them themselves. . . . They won't do anything. For instance, if they drop a piece of cloth on the floor, they'll just let it lay, they wouldn't think of bending over to pick it up. That's janitor's work to them. As a matter of

---

[11] This is part of the process of job adjustment described in detail in Howard S. Becker, "The Career of the Chicago Public School Teacher," *American Journal of Sociology,* 57 (March, 1952).

fact, one of them said to me once: "If I pick that up there wouldn't be any work for the janitor to do." Well it's pretty difficult to deal with children like that.

Further, they are regarded as likely to transgress what the teachers define as moral boundaries in the matter of smoking and drinking; it is particularly shocking that such "nice" children should have such vices.

It is, however, the "slum" child who most deeply offends the teacher's moral sensibilities; in almost every area mentioned above these children, by word, action, or appearance, manage to give teachers the feeling that they are immoral and not respectable. In terms of physical appearance and condition they disgust and depress the middle-class teacher. Even this young woman, whose emancipation from conventional morality is symbolized in her habitual use of the argot of the jazz musician, was horrified by the absence of the toothbrush from the lives of her lower-class students:

> It's just horribly depressing, you know. I mean, it just gets you down. I'll give you an example. A kid complained of a toothache one day. Well, I thought I could take a look and see if I could help him or something so I told him to open his mouth. I almost wigged when I saw his mouth. His teeth were all rotten, every one of them. Just filthy and rotten. Man, I mean, I was really shocked, you know. I said, "Don't you have a toothbrush?" He said no, they were only his baby teeth and Ma said he didn't need a toothbrush for that. So I really got upset and looked in all their mouths. Man, I never saw anything like it. They were all like that, practically. I asked how many had toothbrushes, and about a quarter of them had them. Boy, that's terrible. And I don't dig that crap about baby teeth either, because they start getting molars when they're six, I know that. So I gave them a talking to, but what good does it do? The kid's mouth was just rotten. They never heard of a toothbrush or going to a dentist.

These children, too, are more apt than the other groups to be dishonest in some way that will get them into trouble with law enforcement officials. The early (by middle-class standards) sexual maturity of such children is quite upsetting to the teacher:

> One thing about these girls is, well, some of them are not very nice girls. One girl in my class I've had two years now. She makes her money on the side as a prostitute. She's had several children. . . . This was a disturbing influence on the rest of the class.

Many teachers reported great shock on finding that words which were innocent to them had obscene meanings for their lower-class students:

> I decided to read them a story one day. I started reading them "Puss in Boots" and they just burst out laughing. I couldn't understand what I had said that had made them burst out like that. I went back over the story and tried to find out what it might be. I couldn't see anything that would make them laugh. I couldn't see anything at all in the story. Later one of

the other teachers asked me what had happened. She was one of the older teachers. I told her that I didn't know; that I was just reading them a story and they thought it was extremely funny. She asked me what story I read them and I told her "Puss in the Boots." She said, "Oh, I should have warned you not to read that one." It seems that Puss means something else to them. It means something awful – I wouldn't even tell you what. It doesn't mean a thing to us.[12]

Warner, Havighurst, and Loeb note that "unless the middle-class values change in America, we must expect the influence of the schools to favor the values of material success, individual striving, thrift, and social mobility."[13] Here again, the "slum" child violates the teacher's moral sense by failing to display these virtues:

Many of these children don't realize the worth of an education. They have no desire to improve themselves. And they don't care much about school and schoolwork as a result. That makes it very difficult to teach them.

That kind of problem is particularly bad in a school like —. That's not a very privileged school. It's very under-privileged, as a matter of fact. So we have a pretty tough element there, a bunch of bums, I might as well say it. That kind you can't teach at all. They don't want to be there at all, and so you can't do anything with them. And even many of the others—they're simply indifferent to the advantages of education. So they're indifferent, they don't care about their homework.

This behavior of the lower-class child is all the more repellent to the teacher because she finds it incomprehensible; she cannot conceive that any normal human being would act in such a way. This teacher stresses the anxiety aroused in the inexperienced teacher by her inability to provide herself with a rational explanation for her pupils' behavior:

We had one of the girls who just came to the school last year and she used to come and talk to me quite a bit. I know that it was just terrible for her. You know, I don't think she'd ever had anything to do with Negroes before she got there and she was just mystified, didn't know what to do. She was bewildered. She came to me one day almost in tears and said, "But they don't want to learn, they don't even want to learn. Why is that?" Well, she had me there.

It is worth noting that the behavior of the "better" children, even when morally unacceptable, is less distressing to the teacher, who feels that, in this case, she can produce a reasonable explanation for the behavior. An example of such an explanation is the following:

---

[12] Interview by Miriam Wagenschein. The lack of common meanings in this situation symbolizes the great cultural and moral distance between teacher and "slum" child.

[13] Warner, Havighurst, and Loeb, *op. cit.,* p. 172.

I mean, they're spoiled, you know. A great many of them are only children. Naturally, they're used to having their own way, and they don't like to be told what to do. Well, if a child is in a room that I'm teaching he's going to be told what to do, that's all there is to it. Or if they're not spoiled that way, they're the second child and they never got the affection the first one did, not that their mother didn't love them, but they didn't get as much affection, so they're not so easy to handle either.

IV

We have shown that school teachers experience problems in working with their students to the degree that those students fail to exhibit in reality the qualities of the image of the ideal pupil which teachers hold. In a stratified urban society there are many groups whose life-style and culture produce children who do not meet the standards of this image, and who are thus impossible for teachers like these to work with effectively. Programs of action intended to increase the educational opportunities of the under-privileged in our society should take account of the manner in which teachers interpret and react to the cultural traits of this group, and the institutional consequences of their behavior.[14] Such programs might profitably aim at producing teachers who can cope effectively with the problems of teaching this group and not, by their reactions to class differences, perpetuate the existing inequities.

A more general statement of the findings is now in order. Professionals depend on their environing society to provide them with clients who meet the standards of their image of the ideal client. Social class cultures, among other factors, may operate to produce many clients who, in one way or another, fail to meet these specifications and therefore aggravate one or another of the basic problems of the worker-client relation (three were considered in this paper).

In attacking this problem we touch on one of the basic elements of the relation between institutions and society, for the differences between ideal and reality place in high relief the implicit assumptions which institutions, through their functionaries, make about the society around them. All institutions have embedded in them some set of assumptions about the nature of the society and the individuals with whom they deal, and we must get at these assumptions, and their embodiment in actual social interaction, in order fully to understand these organizations. We can, perhaps, best begin our work on this problem by studying those institutions which, like the school, make assumptions which have high visibility because of their variation from reality.

---

[14] One of the important institutional consequences of these class preferences is a constant movement of teachers away from lower-class schools, which prevents these schools from retaining experienced teachers and from maintaining some continuity in teaching and administration.

10. Education and status ascription[*]

E. DIGBY BALTZELL

Along with the decreasing importance of the hereditary principle in Western civilization, especially since the Enlightenment and the rise to power of the urban middle classes, men have been placed increasingly in the social hierarchy by their educational attainments. The American people, following the lead of such men of the Enlightenment as Thomas Jefferson and Benjamin Franklin, have traditionally placed more faith in universal education than in any particular political system. After all, democratic political institutions ultimately depend upon an educated and informed citizenry. More important perhaps, is the fact that education in America, from the very beginning, has been an important factor in assimilating the immigrant from foreign lands as well as a means of social mobility and the improvement of one's social status. In other words, in a highly utilitarian civilization such as ours, education has always been bound to pragmatic ends.

Benjamin Franklin, for example, advanced highly practical reasons for the founding of the *Academy* (later the University of Pennsylvania) in Philadelphia. His original prospectus, printed in the *Pennsylvania Gazette*, 24 August 1749, opened as follows:

> In the settling of new countries, the first care of the planters must be to provide and to secure the necessaries of life; this engrosses their attention, and affords them little time to think of anything further. We may therefore excuse our ancestors, that they established no ACADEMY or college in this province, wherein their youth might receive a polite and learned education. *Agriculture* and *mechanic arts,* were of the most immediate importance; the *culture* of *minds* by the *finer arts* and *sciences,* was necessarily postpon'd to times of more wealth and leisure.
>
> Since those times are come, and numbers of our inhabitants are both able and willing to give their sons a good education, if it might be had at home, free from the extraordinary expense and hazard in sending them abroad for that purpose; and since a proportion of men of learning is

*Reprinted with permission of The Macmillan Company from *Philadelphia Gentlemen* by E. Digby Baltzell, pp. 292–301, 319–20 and 326–32. © The Free Press, a Corporation 1958.

useful in every country, and those who of late years come to settle among us, are chiefly foreigners, unacquainted with our language, laws and customs; it is thought a proposal for establishing an ACADEMY in this province, will not now be deemed unseasonable.

At the same time that Franklin was making his proposal for founding an Academy, Edward Shippen, young Philadelphia aristocrat, illustrated this pragmatic American point of view towards education in the following letter written while traveling in Europe to his younger brother who was struggling through a private Latin school in Philadelphia: "If you ever travel," he writes in 1749, "you'll find men of letters are everywhere respected; you'll see the ascendency the knowing man has over the blockhead; you'll have a friend which will stand by you when all others fail. Be a man of learning and you'll be a man of consequence wherever you go." For generations Americans have followed this wise advice.

On the whole, in America social class position and educational attainment are positively correlated. On the other hand, the level of educational attainment does not differentiate the members of the American upper class from the rest of the elite. Of those Philadelphians listed in *Who's Who* in 1940, for example, approximately three-fourths were college graduates regardless of their social class origins. It was the type of educational institution attended, however, which differentiated the members of the upper class from the other members of the elite. It is the purpose of this chapter to show how the private secondary school—both the local day school and the boarding school — and certain fashionable eastern universities serve the sociological function of differentiating the upper classes in America from the rest of the population. In other words, in addition to their manifest and most important function, that of providing an education, these private educational institutions serve the latent function of acculturating the members of the younger generation, especially those not quite to the manor born, into an upper-class style of life. As the educative role of the family declines, as it must in a democratic as against an aristocratic age, the private school and college increasingly become a kind of surrogate family.

In social if not in educational terms the graduate of Groton and Harvard is subculturally as different from the graduate of the local high school and city college as the latter is from the laborer who left school in the eighth grade. Moreover, the Harvard of the clubs and the private school graduates is, in turn, very far removed from the Harvard world of the earnest scholars who have graduated from public high schools all over America. Charles McArthur of the Office of Tests at Harvard University, for example, has found some interesting differences between private and publicly educated Harvard students. Using Dr. Florence Kluckhohn's theoretical structure (see E. D. Baltzell, *Philadelphia Gentlemen, ibid.,* Chapter IV), he found that the public school boy's dominant values emphasized "the *Future* as the important time, the *Individual* as the important person, and *Doing* as the important aspect of personality." In contrast, he found that among the private school boys from "the Eastern upper class . . . the time most valued was the *Past,* the persons who matter bore a *Lineal relation* to oneself, and *Being* was the most valued aspect of the person." For example, the doing-oriented boys from the public schools make A's in Chemistry while the being boys are satisfied with a "gentleman's C"; the doing and future-oriented boys come to Harvard with a definite, usually pre-technical major in mind; the being and past-oriented boys usually drift into the Humanities. The public school boys worry about marks; but the deans find the private school boys more likely to be concerned about their personalities, whether they are going to make the right friends and the proper clubs. Interestingly enough, Dr. McArthur also found significant differences between these two types of Harvard boys when comparing the results of Thematic Apperception Tests in terms of Dr. Kluckhohn's theory. There were other extremely suggestive findings in this work at the Office of Tests at Harvard. The point to be made here, however, is that there are real differences between the privately and publicly educated subcultures in America.

Private school attendance clearly differentiated the members of the upper class from the rest of the Philadelphia elite in 1940. Of the Philadelphians listed in *Who's Who,* 41 per cent of those also listed in the *Social Register,* as against only 15 per cent of those who were not, reported attendance at some private school (see Table 1). If the private school is such an important part of the upper-class way of life, one is inclined to ask why more upper-class members did not

TABLE 1
Philadelphians in *Who's Who* in 1940—Secondary Education
as Related to Social Class

| Type of Schooling | Social Class | | | | | | Per Cent of Each Educ. Type in the Social Register |
| | Social Register | | Nonsocial Register | | Who's Who Total | | |
	No.	%	No.	%	No.	%	
Episcopalian Church boarding school†	14	(6)	1	(*)	15	(2)	94%
Other private schools	78	(35)	79	(15)	157	(20)	50%
No private schooling reported ‡	134	(59)	464	(85)	598	(78)	22%
Total	226	(100)	544	(100)	770	(100)	29%

*Less than 1 per cent.
†Three schools are included here—Groton School, St. Paul's School, and St. Mark's School.
‡In this book, parochial schools are not considered as private.

report a private school education. There are several reasons for this. First, there is the inevitable factor of inadequate reporting; many individuals list only their college or university in their *Who's Who* biographies. More important, however, is the fact that private school attendance is the best index of ascribed upper-class position, even more indicative than neighborhood, religion, or *Social Register* affiliation. One attends private school only if one's family can afford it. In other words, many of the members of the upper class in 1940 who did not go to private school presumably had achieved upper-class membership. The president of one of the city's leading banks, for example, was listed in the *Social Register* in 1940, lived in Chestnut Hill, went to the Episcopal Church, and belonged to the Rittenhouse Club (never a member of the Philadelphia Club, he was not taken into the Rittenhouse Club until after he became a bank president); he attended the city's public schools and did not go to college, however, and he was not listed in the *Social Register* until after his marriage into one of the wealthier Philadelphia families.

Finally, of course, it is important to realize that the importance of a private school education varies directly with the decline of the strength of the family. Thus the older generation (over sixty-five in 1940) were less likely to report a private school education than the younger members of the upper class (see Table 2). This difference was partly due to the fact that many of the older men were educated at home. George Wharton Pepper, for example, was educated by his mother until he went to the University; George W. Childs Drexel was educated by private tutors.

TABLE 2

Philadelphia Males in *Who's Who* in 1940–Secondary Education
as Related to Age and Social Class

	Social Class					
	Social Register		Nonsocial Register		Who's Who Total	
Secondary Schooling	65 & Over	Under 65	65 & Over	Under 65	65 & Over	Under 65
Private schooling	32%	46%*	16%	13%	22%	22%
No private schooling	68%	54%	84%	87%	78%	78%
Total	100%	100%	100%	100%	100%	100%
(Number of cases)	(94)	(112)	(185)	(304)	(279)	(416)

*Fourteen out of 15 of those who reported attendance at the three Episcopalian Church boarding schools were of the younger age group.

It is interesting that while the private school was of increasing importance within the upper class *(Social Register*–over 65, 32 per cent; under 65, 46 per cent), among the rest of the elite the younger generation were less likely to have attended private school than the older men (over 65, 16 per cent; under 65, 13 per cent). This is, of course, a reflection of the growth of the public secondary school in America during the last part of the nineteenth century. Of the older college graduates in this elite, for example, the private school may well have been the only available means of obtaining a secondary education at the time when they were of school age. In other words, as the public school has become available to all Americans, the private school then becomes the differentiating factor in a social class sense. At one time, however, education itself was the sole differentiating factor.

THE PRIVATE DAY SCHOOL IN PHILADELPHIA:
PROVINCIAL FAMILY-SURROGATE

Like Boston and other eastern seaboard cities, Philadelphia has an excellent system of private day schools. There are the well-known Quaker schools—Germantown Friends, Friends Select, in the center of the city, Friends Central, on the Main Line (all of which are co-educational), and the William Penn Charter School in Germantown which is for boys only. While many members of the upper class attend these Quaker schools, they are more likely to go to such boys' schools as the Protestant Episcopal Academy and the Haverford School, on the Main Line, or the Chestnut Hill Academy.

The William Penn Charter School is considered to be the oldest private school in Philadelphia, having been granted a charter by William Penn in 1689. It had been the custom among English Quakers to establish day schools "to which Friends were advised by the Yearly Meeting to send their children." Actually, Penn Charter was originally a part of the public school system in Philadelphia for most of its history. It was not until 1875 that the William Penn Charter School was opened as a private Quaker School for boys at Eight South Twelfth Street in the center of the city.

Germantown Academy is the oldest suburban day school in Philadelphia and possibly in America. Founded in 1760, it has been nonsectarian from the beginning. The main school building today is the oldest building in the United States which has been continuously devoted to secondary education. (In the 1830's, A. Bronson Alcott was a teacher at the school and his famous daughter, Louisa May Alcott, was born in Germantown in 1832. Although Alcott later became famous as the friend of Emerson and the leader of the Concord School of Philosophy, his teaching at Germantown was a failure. Somewhat of an idealist, in many ways a forerunner of the progressive school—he was interested in meaning rather than memory—he could not keep discipline.) As Germantown was a suburb by the end of the eighteenth century, there were several boarding schools for girls there as early as the 1830's.

Along with the suburban trend in the last part of the nineteenth century, Haverford School, on the Main Line, was opened as a part of Haverford College in 1884. It is now an independent and nonsectarian school. Although its charter goes back to 1861, Chestnut Hill Academy began its life in the fall of 1895 with thirty-five boys enrolled. In 1898, through the generosity of the Houston family, it moved into the old Wissahickon Inn, where it remains to this day (the building belonged to the Houstons until 1941).

THE PROTESTANT EPISCOPAL ACADEMY:
PROPER PHILADELPHIA FAMILY-SURROGATE

The Protestant Episcopal Academy has been intimately associated with Philadelphia's Anglo-Catholic gentry since the eighteenth century. According to Porter Sargent, who has published *A Handbook of Private Schools* for more than thirty years, "over sixty-five hundred boys of old Philadelphia families have attended the academy since 1850, and it is today the largest of the Episcopal schools."

On the first of January, 1785, a group of subscribers met at Christ Church to found the Protestant Episcopal Academy: they elected sixteen trustees, including Thomas Willing, Edward Shippen, Robert Morris, Francis Hopkinson, and, of course, the Reverend William White. School opened in April "on ye back part of a lot on ye east side of Fourth Street, a few feet south of Market Street." Benjamin Franklin lived next door. In 1788, the school moved to a newly constructed building between Sixth and Seventh on Chestnut Street. Noah Webster, of dictionary fame, taught mathematics and English, and Commodore Stephen Decatur and Bishop John Henry Hobart were among the first pupils.

Although the records are rather obscure, it is believed that the academy was run as a charity school between 1805 and 1846. Some support came from the government as it became necessary to get boys and girls off the street. The parents of the pupils at this time were required to take the pauper's oath.

The modern era at Episcopal Academy began in 1846. Under the leadership of Bishop Alonzo Potter, a boys' day school was opened and the Reverend George Emlen Hare (father of Bishop William Hobart Hare) was headmaster. In 1850, the Academy moved into a newly constructed school building on Locust Street several blocks below St. Mark's Church and convenient to the Rittenhouse Square neighborhood.

During Rittenhouse Square's "Golden Day," the sons of Proper Philadelphians were educated at the Episcopal Academy and the Delancey School. Founded by Henry Hobart Brown in 1877, Delancey School was at the corner of Seventeenth and Delancey Streets during the 1880's, a convenient location for the Rittenhouse Square gentry. The tone of the school is suggested by the names of the trustees in 1898 when the school was incorporated after the death of its founder. Among the eleven trustees were Thomas DeWitt Cuyler, president of the Rittenhouse Club; John H. Converse, later president of the Baldwin Locomotive Works; Effingham B. Morris, president of the Girard Trust Company between 1887 and 1928; J. Rodman Paul, Senator Pepper's former law partner; and Alexander Van Rensselear, A. J. Drexel's son-in-law.

In 1915 the Delancey School merged with the Episcopal Academy. The first class to graduate after the merger included the sons of many Philadelphia families mentioned in previous chapters. According to the class yearbook for that year, Horace Howard Furness Jayne was the class poet, John Frederick Lewis, "one of the strangest," Bertram Lippincott, "most original fellow in the class," Henry Rawle Pemberton, "most musical," Benjamin Rush, Jr., "leader in the class in regard to clothes," and Elias Wolf, who "was always riding around in his automobile."

The sixteen members of the board of trustees of the Academy in 1915 were representative Proper Philadelphians of the period. All of them were listed in the *Social Register;* ten were graduates of the University of Pennsylvania; three did not graduate from college; one, the youngest, was a graduate of Princeton, one of Trinity College, and Bishop Rhinelander was a Harvard man; all save two were members of either the Philadelphia (six members) or Rittenhouse (seven members) Clubs; eleven lived in the Rittenhouse Square neighborhood, two on the Main Line, three in Chestnut Hill, and one in Germantown. It is safe to assume that all were members of the Episcopal Church.

In response to the upper-class suburban trend, the Episcopal Academy moved to the Main Line in 1921. In that same year, Greville Haslam, a graduate and former master at St. Paul's School, became the first non-clerical headmaster. Upper-class suburbanization during this post-war period was a national phenomenon which can be accurately measured by the location of the fashionable private schools in the larger cities throughout America. Noble and Greenough, Proper Boston's most exclusive day school, for example, moved from Beacon Street to Dedham in 1922.

In 1940 the twenty trustees of the Academy were primarily Proper Philadelphians. The fact that three of the trustees were not listed in the *Social Register,* however, reflected the changes in the city's elite structure since the days before the First World War when all the trustees were quite naturally listed in the little black and orange book. As in 1915, of the seventeen Proper Philadelphia trustees, twelve were members of the Rittenhouse and Philadelphia Clubs. On the other hand, while a majority of the trustees in 1915 were alumni of the University of Pennsylvania, seven sons of Pennsylvania now shared the leadership of the school with three Princetonians, four Harvard men, a Yale man, and the headmaster and the Reverend John Mockridge, who were graduates of the Massachusetts Institute of Technology and Trinity College in Canada respectively. Finally, of course, the trustees now lived primarily in the suburbs—nine on the Main Line, two in Chestnut Hill, two in Germantown, and only four in the Rittenhouse Square area.

The move to the suburbs proved successful and the Academy grew in size all during the two post-war decades. By 1940 there were almost six hundred boys in the school who commuted each day from all parts of the city and its suburbs, from the Old York Road area, from Chestnut Hill and Germantown, and from Wallingford and Wawa. In contrast to the provincial Rittenhouse Square atmosphere of the pre-war years, the school enlarged its scope both geographically and socially. Like all the more fashionable country day schools, the Academy increasingly drew boys from more diverse social backgrounds, especially at the high school level. As many of the sons of the Proper Philadelphians, for example, began to go away to New England boarding schools for their last four or five years of secondary education, vacancies were created in the higher forms at Episcopal and other fashionable day schools. To fill this gap many boys came in from the public school system and spent their last few years at the Episcopal Academy. There is always a tendency to stress the exclusive aspects of all fashionable institutions. Actually, such institutions are always assimilating new material, as it were; in each generation capable boys with ambition and an eye to the main chance have gotten a start towards success through schoolboy "contacts" made at such schools as Episcopal. This is especially true of the sons of the new-rich. The private day schools, especially during the Depression, needed pupils who could pay full tuition. Newly rich fathers and mothers were, in turn, eager for their sons to meet "nice people." Moreover, the private school, with its personal supervision and consequently higher academic standards, often made it possible for these boys from the local high school to get into the better colleges.

PROPER PHILADELPHIA DAUGHTERS: PRE-DEBUTANTE EDUCATION

While most Proper Philadelphia gentlemen are products of Episcopal, Haverford, Penn Charter, or Chestnut Hill Academy, their wives are invariably alumnae of Springside School in Chestnut Hill, or the Shipley and Agnes Irwin schools along the Main Line. Springside and Shipley, founded in 1879 and 1894 respectively, were suburban schools from the very beginning. It is interesting that they were founded in the last part of the nineteenth century when Proper Philadelphians were moving out to these two suburbs in increasing numbers.

The Agnes Irwin School, the traditional Proper Philadelphia school for girls, was founded in the Rittenhouse Square neighborhood in 1869. Agnes Irwin, friend of S. Weir Mitchell, Horace Howard Furness, and Agnes Repplier, and a witty member of the "walking and talking" set in the early days of Mount Desert, was a nationally known educator of young ladies. As Porter Sargent puts it: "The more conservative of Philadelphia's elite still send their daughters to Miss Irwin's School as in the days before 1894 when her work here won her so great a reputation that she was called to be the first dean of Radcliffe College." Young ladies from both Chestnut Hill and the Main Line, as well as those from Rittenhouse Square, attended Miss Irwin's School until 1933 when the school moved from DeLancey Place out to Isaac H. Clothier's former estate in Wynnewood on the Main Line.

Although Philadelphia's most fashionable girls' school was founded and dominated for many years by Agnes Irwin, a strong-willed feminist and pioneer in women's education, most of the Irwin girls, even as of the nineteen-thirties, terminated their education at the secondary level and entered into the debutante world on graduation. All this has been changed since World War II. Daughters of even the most traditional and fashionable families now go on to college.

COLLEGE EDUCATION AND SOCIAL CLASS

Within the upper class, and especially along the eastern seaboard, colleges are socially stratified. Where one goes is far more important than going. It is more advantageous, socially, and economically, to have graduated from Harvard, Yale, or Princeton with a low academic standing than to have been a Phi Beta Kappa at some less fashionable institution. Thus the sixty-nine Philadelphians who were listed both in *Who's Who* in 1940 and the *Social Register* in 1900—the old-family core of the contemporary elite (see *Philadelphia Gentlemen,* Table 16, Chapter VIII)—limited themselves to attendance at the University of Pennsylvania, Haverford, Swarthmore, Harvard, Yale, and Princeton. The increasing importance attached to Harvard, Yale, and Princeton, moreover, is indicated by the fact that, while 50 per cent of the older men (over sixty-five) went to the University of Pennsylvania as against 3 per cent to the "big three," the younger men (under sixty-five) preferred the three fashionable universities (46 per cent) to the local University (40 per cent).

The pattern set by these old-family elite members was followed by the rest of the upper-class members of the Philadelphia elite. Of the Philadelphians listed in *Who's Who* in 1940, for example, over half of those also listed in the *Social Register* were graduates of the University of Pennsylvania, Harvard, Yale, or Princeton, while at least three-fourths of those not in the upper class were graduates of other institutions (Table 3). The figures in the last column of Table 3 provide a fairly accurate index of the prestige rankings of the various types of colleges and universities in America, at least as far as the Philadelphia upper class is concerned.

TABLE 3

Philadelphians in *Who's Who* in 1940—College
Attended as Related to Social Class

	Social Class						
	Social Register		Nonsocial Register		Who's Who Total		Per Cent in Social Register
College Attended	No.	%	No.	%	No.	%	
University of Pennsylvania ...	63	(28)	108	(20)	171	(22)	37%
Haverford-Swarthmore	8	(7)	12	(8)	20	(8)	40%
Other Philadelphia colleges ...	7		33		40		17%
Harvard	22		8		30		73%
Yale.....................	11	(23)	8	(5)	19	(10)	58%
Princeton.................	18		10		28		64%
Other Ivy colleges†	12	(5)	15	(3)	27	(4)	44%
All other colleges	36	(16)	204	(38)	240	(31)	15%
Noncollege graduates........	49	(22)	140	(26)	189	(25)	26%
No information			6	(1)	6	(*)	—
Total	226	(100)	544	(100)	770	(100)	29%

* Less than 1 per cent.

† This category includes—M.I.T., Columbia, Cornell, Dartmouth, Amherst, Trinity, Williams and the University of Virginia. By and large they are second choices for those of the upper class who for one reason or another do not go to one of the "big three."

HARVARD, YALE, AND PRINCETON:
NATIONAL UPPER-CLASS INSTITUTIONS

As far as the Board of Trustees was concerned, the University of Pennsylvania was still a very Proper Philadelphia institution in 1940. But graduates of other "Ivy League" universities were more likely to be listed in the Philadelphia *Social Register*. Of the Philadelphians listed in *Who's Who,* for instance, only 37 per cent of the University of Pennsylvania graduates, as against 73 per cent of the graduates of Yale, were also listed in the *Social Register* (see Table 3, above). Not only is the University considered to be socially inferior to Harvard, Yale, or Princeton; more important, upper-class loyalty to such local institutions as the University of Pennsylvania, Haverford, and even Swarthmore has been weakened throughout the twentieth century as fashionable Philadelphians have gone away increasingly to one of the three, nationally recognized, upper-class universities. While only 22 per cent of the older generation of the upper-class members of the Philadelphia elite (see Table 4) were graduates of Harvard, Yale, Princeton and other "Ivy League" institutions, this proportion was increased to 36 per cent among the younger men. At the same time, of course, the younger members of

TABLE 4
Philadelphia Males in *Who's Who* in 1940—College Attended
as Related to Age and Social Class

| | | Social Class | | | | |
| | Social Register | | Nonsocial Register | | Who's Who Total | |
College Attended	65 & Over	Under 65	65 & Over	Under 65	65 & Over	Under 65
Local institutions (University of Pennsylvania, Haverford, Swarthmore, other Philadelphia colleges)	42%	31%	27%	33%	32%	32%
Harvard-Yale-Princeton	18%	29%	5%	5%	10%	12%
Other Ivy colleges	4%	7%	2%	3%	3%	4%
All other colleges	15%	17%	37%	39%	29%	33%
Noncollege graduates	21%	16%	28%	21%	26%	19%
Total	100%	100%	100%	100%	100%	100%
(Number of cases)	(94)	(112)	(185)	(304)	(279)	(416)

the upper class were less likely to have graduated from the three local institutions (31 per cent as against 42 per cent). For the rest of the Philadelphia elite, local loyalty had remained the same over the generations. The trend to Harvard, Yale, and Princeton, then, was an upper class rather than an elite trend. In effect, these prestige institutions were not educating a larger proportion of Philadelphia's leaders, but more of its fashionable leaders.

In order to provide additional quantitative evidence of this centralizing trend, a 25 per cent sample of all the college graduates listed in the 1940 Philadelphia *Social Register* was obtained (see Table 5). This larger sample of upper-class Philadelphians illustrates this same trend in somewhat more detail. First, of the 990 college graduates in this sample taken from the *Social Register,* no less than

TABLE 5
Philadelphians in the 1940 *Social Register*—College Attended,
by Decade, 1870–1940

Decade Graduated	College Attended					
	Harvard	Yale	Princeton	Pennsyl-vania	All Other	Total
1870's	1	1	0	7	2	11
1880's	2	3	0	28	8	41
1890's	6	15	16	50	40	127
1900's	18	13	29	63	39	162
1910's	24	23	28	90	42	207
1920's	21	32	76	55	48	232
1930's	25	27	72	43	43	210
Total	97	114	221	336	222	990
Percentage Summary						
1870–1900	5%	10%	9%	48%	28%	179–100%
1900–1920	11%	10%	15%	42%	22%	369–100%
1920–1940	10%	13%	34%	22%	21%	442–100%
Total: 1870–1940	10%	12%	22%	34%	22%	990–100%

Source: In the *Social Register,* after the name of every male college graduate, his college and year of graduation are listed (i.e., P'36, H'08, PA'00, etc.). This sample was obtained by taking all the graduates listed on each fourth page of the 1940 Philadelphia *Social Register.*

78 per cent were graduates of either the University of Pennsylvania or Harvard, Yale, and Princeton. Most important, however, is the fact that the trend towards the "big three" continued throughout the whole period from 1870 to 1940, and was accelerated during the two decades following the First World War. While 48 per cent of the men who had graduated from college before the turn of the century went to the University of Pennsylvania, as against only 24 per cent to Harvard, Yale, and Princeton, the reverse was true of the graduates during the 1920's and 1930's; 22 per cent graduated from the local University compared to the 57 per cent who went away to one of the "big three."

The fashionable trend to Princeton was most pronounced. Princeton has, of course, educated the sons of the American upper classes since colonial times. Of the 230 men graduating from Princeton between 1766 and 1776 (then the College of New Jersey), James Madison became President of the United States, twelve sat in the Continental Congress, six sat in the Constitutional Convention, twelve were members of Congress, three were Judges of the Supreme Court of the United States, three Attorney-Generals, two foreign ministers, one Secretary of State, and one became Vice President. But the point to be made here is that only in F. Scott Fitzgerald's era of gin, jazz and the suburban country club, well-stocked with bond salesmen, did the Princetonian become an upper-class stereotype in America. Apparently Proper Philadelphians followed fashion. During the 1920's—and even through the Depression years when sending a son out of town to college was a considerable strain on the family budget—for the first time, more upper-class Philadelphians went to Princeton than to the University of Pennsylvania (see Table 5). Even old, and previously loyal, Pennsylvanians surrendered to the trend. Although most of the old trustee families in 1940, including Hopkinsons, Peppers, and Cadwaladers, still sent their sons to the University, both Adolph G. Rosengarten (Pennsylvania 1892) and Joseph Wharton Lippincott (Pennsylvania 1908), whose fathers had preceded them as trustees, sent their sons away to St. Paul's and Princeton in the post-war decades (their sons were Princeton 1927 and 1937 respectively). The trend is unabated and local pride continues to wane: President Gates' son remained a loyal Pennsylvanian, became a campus leader as an undergraduate, and later a trustee; Thomas Soverign Gates, III, however, went to St. Paul's and Harvard.

The New England boarding schools are closely connected by tradition with the fashionable universities. Approximately three-fourths of the Exeter boys have gone to Harvard for generations, just as their rivals at Andover have gone to Yale (in spite of this tradition, the class of 1929 at Princeton included fifty-seven Exeter and Andover alumni). Quite naturally, a vast majority of the Groton and St. Paul's boys go on to Harvard, Yale, or Princeton each year. In 1934 (see above, the discussion of the class of 1934 at St. Paul's) over 95 per cent of the 106 graduates of St. Paul's went to one of the "big three"; of the thirty-two Grotonians entering college that year, twenty-one went to Harvard, nine to Yale, and one each to Princeton and Cambridge, England.

The interrelationships among the family, the private school, and the university are illustrated by the following characteristics of three entering classes at Princeton:

Year of Entrance	Number in the Class	Per Cent Sons of Princeton Graduates	Per Cent Graduating Private School
1922	607	10.8	81.4
1930	631	15.8	84.9
1940	645	20.4	77.7

In spite of an admissions policy in these years which attempted to take boys on their merits, regardless of social background, over three-fourths of each class were products of private schools, and the amount of family in-breeding (sons of alumni) almost doubled in the course of two decades. The changing religious composition of the student body during the early decades of the twentieth century may be an additional clue to the changing class structure at Princeton. Of the 203 members of the class of 1900, for instance, 111 were Presbyterians and 36 were Episcopalians; of the 607 members of the class of 1926, on the other hand, 227 were Episcopalians as against 190 Presbyterians. Finally, the number of exclusive eating clubs at Princeton, the bane of such liberal reformers as Woodrow Wilson, multiplied during this same period. Of the eighteen eating clubs at Princeton in 1929, for instance, only two, Ivy (1879) and Cottage (1887) were in existence before 1890. Five came into being during the 1890's and the rest were founded in the twentieth century.

An intricate system of exclusive clubs, like the fraternities on less rarified American campuses, serves to insulate the members of the upper class from the rest of the students at Harvard, Yale, and Princeton. There are virtually "two nations" at Harvard. The private-school boys, with their accents, final clubs, and Boston debutante parties—about one-fifth of the student body—stand aloof and apart from the ambitious, talented, and less polished boys who come to Cambridge each year from public high schools over the nation. The Apley family, of J. P. Marquand's Boston, were members of the same club at Harvard for generations. George Apley explains the importance of the Harvard club to his son, John, in the following letter: "I am still quite well-known around the Club, you know, and your first object must be to 'make' the Club. I believe that everything else, including your studies, should be secondary to this. You may call this a piece of worldly counsel but it is worth while. I don't know what I should have done in life without the Club. When I leave Boston it is my shield. When I am in Boston it is one of my greatest diversions. The best people are always in it, the sort that you will understand and like. I once tried to understand a number of other people, but I am not so sure now that it was not a waste of time. Your own sort are the best friends and you will do well not to forget it."

While the Exeter and Andover graduates are likely to participate in the life of the whole college community, as members of the student council, editors, managers, debaters, and prom chairmen, the Groton and St. Paul's boys, on the whole, limit their social life to the club world. Porcellian and A.D., the top clubs at Harvard, are followed by Fly, Spee, Delphic, and Owl. Porcellian, founded in 1791 and including the loftiest names in Proper Boston history among its members, was the first college club in America. Owen Wister and his friend T. R. Roosevelt were both members of Porcellian. When asked about Porcellian, Owen Wister is said to have remarked: "Nothing has ever meant so much to me. It is a bond which can be felt but not analyzed." Although a few have belonged to Porcellian and A.D., most Proper Philadelphians are members of the Fly Club (F. D. Roosevelt's).

New Haven is marked by a somewhat more democratic atmosphere than Cambridge. The exclusive top drawer at Yale includes the Fence Club (Groton and St. Paul's), Delta Kappa Epsilon (Exeter and Andover), and Zeta Psi, as well as St. Anthony Hall, the leading fraternity at the Sheffield Scientific School. Perhaps the senior societies are even more important than the social clubs. The two most important are Skull and Bones, founded in 1832, and Scroll and Key, which opened ten years later. Each year Skull and Bones "taps" about fifteen or twenty of the campus leaders, football captains, editors of the *News,* and so forth, while Scroll and Key prefers the more polished members of the senior class. As Dixon Wecter puts it: "Skull and Bones has even been known to smile upon graduates of high schools; to Scroll and Key this anarchy would be unthinkable" (since World War II, a Negro was elected captain of the football team and tapped to Skull and Bones).

More homogeneous, more suburban than New Haven or Cambridge, the Princeton campus is both more democratic and more snobbish. Traditionally, almost two-thirds of the students have been members of one or another of the eighteen eating clubs (since World War II the policy calls for including the whole student body within clubland). The Ivy Club is the oldest (1879), wealthiest, and most exclusive of the Princeton eating clubs. For many Princetonians, to say "I am an Ivy man" is like the proud declaration of the ancient Roman, "I am a Roman citizen." Proper Philadelphia is tied to the Ivy Club in much the same way as Proper Boston is linked to Porcellian. Of the sixteen Board of Governors of the club in 1929 (all listed in the *Social Register* for various cities), six, including Edgar Allen Poe, Isaac W. Roberts, L. Caspar Wister, Fitz Eugene Dixon (P. A. B. Widener's grandson-in-law), and P. Blair Lee, president of the board, were residents of Philadelphia (Senator Blair Lee was one of the club's founders). Philadelphia alumni of the Ivy Club include descendants of William Disston, William Weightman, P. A. B. Widener, William L. Elkins, George D. Rosengarten, Isaac H. Clothier, and many Ingersolls and Robertses. It is worth noting that of all the graduates of Princeton listed in *Who's Who* from Philadelphia in 1940, only those who were members of the Ivy Club saw fit to list their undergraduate club affiliations in their *Who's Who* biographies.

Election to membership in an appropriate club has usually been the main concern of upper-class boys at Harvard, Yale, and Princeton. "Thirty years ago," writes George Biddle in his autobiography, "the standard at Harvard was established by the socially well born; and those who were not socially well born sensed this standard . . . by the measure of undergraduate and graduate prestige— college activities far outweighed scholarship; athletics outweighed undergraduate activities; social standing—the importance of club life—outweighed them all. At Harvard, then, the New England boarding-school boy went in for clubs—social success." In a similar vein, Arthur Stanwood Pier writes that, "of the boys who come to St. Paul's there are always some who have no serious interest in acquiring an education, and whose families do not encourage them to have such an interest. They go to college frankly to have a good time, to . . . make certain clubs; and having made their clubs they have acquired what they and their families regard as the hallmark of a college education—something more prized than the college diploma. College students may be classified into three groups; those who regard college as mainly an intellectual experience, those who regard it as both a social and an intellectual experience, and those who regard it as merely a social experience. By far the greater number of St. Paul's boys were found in the second of these categories, very few in the first, too many in the third."

PART IV

The school

as a social

system

The social systems of different schools will vary by purpose, geographical area, and the kind of community served. We are concerned here not so much with the differences in school systems but rather with some broad generalizations that may be suggested for most public schools. The school, as a part of society, is in many respects a reflection of the overall society. This is basically the relationship of the part to the whole, and the school is in many respects more a reflection of the social whole than it is an agency of social change. We will discuss some of the interrelationships of school and society, as well as some of the more important characteristics of the school as a social system, and the extent to which they are a reflection of dominant social influences.

EDUCATIONAL VALUES

A dominant American value is that education is both good and desirable. This value often assumes that formal education is basic to man's salvation and is, therefore, a social necessity for progress, and even survival. Yet, in reality, educators assume this value to a much stronger degree than does the general American public. Americans often pay lip service to the broad values of education but actually are interested only in the short-run, practical payoff. The school is often faced with the difficult problem of developing an educational

183

plan which is both philosophically sound and realistically salable. Therefore, the school is vitally concerned with how it is perceived by the community. The school, being financially dependent upon society, is placed constantly under pressure to prove that it is doing its job. This often results in schools being philosophically conservative and tending to reflect the dominant values of the community.

In recent years a value conflict has centered around the question of educational philosophy. Professional educators have, over the years, moved away from the traditional subject-matter orientation to one that is more student-oriented. The shift is reflected in the belief that the development of the "whole" child is basic to good education. This has led to a great deal of criticism's being directed at the educator because he is accused of ignoring or subordinating the traditional "basic skills." We are interested here not so much in the controversy as in the fact that the professional educator, unlike many other professionals, is subject to a great deal of social criticism and is often placed in an extremely defensive position. This illustrates the very tenuous nature of the school in relationship to society, and it also helps to explain the basic conservative nature of many schools.

SCHOOL ROLES

The following is a brief description of some of the important formal and informal roles played by adults and young people in the school system. A social role may be defined as a set of rights and obligations that goes with a position in a social system. The relationship of roles in a particular social setting is sometimes referred to as a role-set.[1] Sometimes the same social role will be differentially defined in changing social situations; for example, the role of the teacher is different in a role-set with other teachers than in one with students. We also know that while many roles are formal, that is, explicitly defined, many are also informal, defined implicitly through previous action and behavior patterns of individuals. For example, one dimension of the formal role of the teacher is to communicate knowledge, and one dimension of her informal role may be how it is done, as, democratically, autocratically, etc. Finally, it should be pointed out that the formal and informal role definitions often operate together in creating the overall role performance of the individual filling a general role. That is, the individual teacher may be good at communicating knowledge partially because of her informal role ability for doing so.

Formal Roles.   In most school systems the basic distinction between formal adult roles is between teacher and nonteacher (administrators, school nurses, clerks, etc.). The power structure of this basic set of role relationships is the nonteacher's (administrator's) having more power than the teacher. In most

---

[1] Harry M. Johnson, *Sociology: A Systematic Introduction* (New York: Harcourt, Brace & Co., 1960), p. 18.

schools the rights and obligations that go with the two types of formal roles are clearly defined. On the role level of teachers the interrelationships are essentially peer ones, though this is not always true in larger school systems where some teachers are quasi-administrators (for example, department heads).

The formal distribution of student roles is primarily centered around grade levels. The pupil is placed in a grade, usually by age, and is expected to accomplish certain goals and achieve promotion at the end of the school year to the next grade level, where he goes through essentially the same pattern. The pupil may also be expected to fill other formal role expectations—to participate in outside-the-classroom activities, to be cooperative and behave as a student should, according to the formal definitions of his role as student as perceived by the adults in the school system.

Informal Roles. To state the formal role expectations is to present only a part of the interpersonal relationships of the school. On the adult interaction level, the teachers essentially function as peers in the formal structure. But many informal definitions distinguish the real role variations between teachers. Different informal roles may be the result of sex or age differences; fields of interest; seniority in the particular school; reputation with the community, administration, or pupils; as well as many other factors. Frequently, the formal roles of teachers stress their similarity while the informal roles point out their differences.

Many times the informal definition of what constitutes a good student may be quite different from the formal. This is further complicated because the informal definitions of student roles come from teachers as well as from fellow students. What, for the teacher, is seen as a good student may even be different from the overall adult definition. For example, it may be the student who is submissive and shares the teacher's values. The informal values of the good student, judged by his peers, may also be quite different from the formal definitions. A part of this is related to the peer-group subculture, which is only partially influenced by the school system. There is often a basic contradiction between the formal school definition of a good student and how he is defined by other students. Fellow students often feel that he should not be too successful academically, that he should have his strongest identification with the world of his peers, and that he should take on their values rather than those of the adult-teacher world.

11. The school as a social environment*

EDGAR Z. FRIEDENBERG

Our free public high school has from the beginning discharged two paramount social functions, neither of which has burdened secondary education elsewhere to anything like the same extent. The first of these is to build a common pattern of values and responses among adolescents from a diversity of class and ethnic backgrounds; the high school is a very important unit in our traditional system of melting pots. The second has been to help youngsters, as we say, to better themselves. In most industrial countries this second function has by now assumed about as much importance as it has in the United States; but this is recent.

Until World War II secondary education of university preparatory quality in the rest of the world was essentially education for adolescents who had a reasonably high level of ascribed status. They came, as we used to say, from good homes; and, good or not, what they learned in school was culturally continuous with what they were used to at home. The same symbols had roughly the same meanings in both *ambiances.* In the United States, however, this was not true.

The public high school, being locally run, has generally deferred in various ways to the claims of status, devoting a preponderance of its resources and granting a preponderance of its rewards to solidly middle-class boys and girls to the relative neglect of lower-status youngsters, whom it often treats with great hostility. But its *own* folkways and traditions are not solidly middle-class; and if the higher-status youngsters are more favorably treated than their lower-status classmates, it must be recognized that the high school also extracts from them extra service as laboratory specimens for aspiring lower-status youth, and that the favor they receive is to some extent vitiated by the experience of immersion in a shabby-genteel and often envious environment for a period of years.

The melting pot and mobility functions of the high school are complementary. In combination, they are peculiarly potent. The atmosphere of the high school is permeated by the values they generate when combined. The combination is synergistic, and it really works. Taken as the high school directs, public

---

*Reprinted from College Admissions 10: The Behavioral Sciences and Education, published in 1963 by the College Entrance Examination Board, New York.

education efficiently produces the kind of individual who can, and does, operate to sustain and augment his own position in a limitless variety of situations; and who does so with a characteristic American style regardless of his antecedents. This is just as true of rich antecedents as poor, and probably truer. The American ideal of equality is nowhere stronger than in public education; and if its administrators tend to be "realistic" about status, they nevertheless keep a school in which an upper-class vocabulary or accent is informally corrected as surely as that of the slum; and the *insouciance* and spontaneity of rich and poor alike is reduced to the guarded good humor of the executive. In metropolitan areas, at least, the high school dropout rates for upper and lower-status students appear to be roughly comparable. Figures on this are not available to my knowledge, because schools do not directly record the social class of their students, and upper-status youngsters who leave public school for private school are not considered dropouts. But leave they do, in large proportions; and they are not always fleeing from the Negro. Even from the suburbs that have so far excluded Negroes, upper-class white parents manage to send their children to Chaminade or Country Day, and the Negroes they meet there may ask them home to dinner, if they like them.

Upper-class rejection of the public school of course reflects a variety of motives, including sheer snobbery and an often erroneous presumption that the private school selected can get its students into Ivy colleges. But it also reflects a search for what parents call higher standards. On examination these standards often turn out to be no higher than those of the public school, but decidedly different from them. No more and no better work may be demanded of students, but it is slightly different work, and it is demanded for different reasons. This is true, of course, only of those private schools that do, in fact, have a social function different from the public schools. To the extent that the school depends for patronage on the anxiety of ambitious and socially insecure parents, it will compound the defects of the public school and add a few of its own. All private schools in America, no doubt, receive many helpless adolescents from such sources; but there are still some schools in which these students do not set the tone and they may therefore find refuge and real help in working out the meaning of their own lives under the illumination of disciplined study. This is harder for the public school to provide under its twin mandate to serve as a melting pot and a rocket to the moon.

There is something to be learned from etymology. The original meaning of education as a "drawing-out" makes an important point about the process—the same point that John Dewey and the progressive education people, at their best, also made. Education, if it is to have any depth, must start with and be derived from the life-experience of the student, which is in some measure unique for every boy or girl. It must cultivate this experience with a disciplined and demanding use of the best resources offered by the humanities and the sciences—to help the individual understand the meaning of his own experience. The consequence of such education, though it clearly leads the student to share in a universal cultural heritage, is more fundamentally to *sharpen* his individuality, to clarify and emphasize to *him* the ways in which he is unique.

A school that serves as a melting pot must inhibit this process, not facilitate it. Its purpose is to establish a common response to certain key stimuli, regardless of how different the respondents started out to be. Not only the content becomes stereotyped; so do the values underlying it, for the function of the school is to make it unnecessary to take account of the differences that might have resulted from the heterogeneity of life. It often fails, of course, and the student's folder receives a notation that his personality is defective; that he underachieves or is immature or emotionally disturbed — perfectly true, too; regression and ritualized internal conflict are classical responses to unbearably painful pressure on the emerging self.

When, however, the mandate to contribute to social mobility is joined to the melting pot process, the result is far more inhibitory to education. The student now learns that it is no longer sufficient to give the same answer; he must learn to distinguish the *right* answer. And he must learn to do this reliably and, as nearly as possible, automatically while his inner voice continues to shriek that the answer is wrong. Of course, his inner voice gradually gets a lot softer and more plaintive, and may finally show up as nothing more than a symptom. At this juncture, however, it would be a little unfair to say that the student's values are stereotyped; a real value has emerged. It has become important to him to learn to give the right answer quicker and more often than the next boy, who is seen as a competitor rather than a person. And the inner voice is no longer irrelevant. It becomes, instead, the voice of the betrayer.

Professors Jacob W. Getzels and Philip W. Jackson in their recent work on *Creativity and Intelligence*[1] illustrate this process statistically. They drew their sample from a private, university-affiliated high school which afforded them, I should judge, an unusually abundant supply of the kind of "far-out" youngster that their methodology defines as creative. Their independent variables—that is, the criteria by which they assigned individual youngsters to their "high-creative" group—are essentially measures of "divergent thinking," as Professor J. P. Guilford of the University of Southern California defines this kind of mental activity in contrast to the "convergent thinking" of conventional high IQ students. Getzels and Jackson, in other words, started out by setting up a procedure in which the kind of adolescent who is especially prone to find a wealth of unconventional meanings in familiar material, and to use these meanings to arrive at perfectly workable but sometimes shockingly original solutions to problems, was contrasted with the kind of adolescent who is adept at setting such meanings aside as distractions and marching with power and determination along the path of conventional wisdom.

From a sample of 449 private high school students with a mean IQ of 129,

---

[1] (New York: John Wiley & Sons, Inc., 1962).

Getzels and Jackson selected 26 students who were in the top 20 per cent on their Guilford-type measures of creativity, but not in IQ, and 28 who were in the top 20 per cent in IQ, but not in creativity. The two groups were then compared with each other and with the total group of 449 on school performance as measured by standard achievement tests; teachers' preferences for having them, when identified by name, in class; and the quality and manner of their response to a series of pictures like those used in the Thematic Apperception Test.

Both groups did equally well on the subject-matter tests of school achievement, and better than the total group of 449. The teachers, however, preferred the high IQ students to both the "high creatives" and those who had not been included in either group; and though they did prefer the high creatives to the average student, the difference was too small to be statistically significant. It should be borne in mind that this was a private secondary school with an exceptionally intelligent student body, and teachers who, to some extent, had chosen to teach gifted students and were accustomed to them. But they nevertheless preferred school achievement to be expressed in conventional terms, which the creatives were unlikely to do.

Getzels and Jackson quote illustratively the following sample responses to one of their story-pictures. "One picture stimulus was perceived most often as a man in an airplane reclining seat returning from a business trip or conference. A high IQ student gave the following story: 'Mr. Smith is on his way home from a successful business trip. He is very happy and he is thinking about his wonderful family and how glad he will be to see them again. He can picture it, about an hour from now, his plane landing at the airport and Mrs. Smith and their three children all there welcoming him home again.' A high-creative subject wrote this story: 'This man is flying back from Reno, where he has just won a divorce from his wife. He couldn't stand to live with her any more, he told the judge, because she wore so much cold cream on her face at night that her head would skid across the pillow and hit him in the head. He is now contemplating a new skid-proof face cream.' "

This is perhaps sufficient to illustrate the contrasting cognitive styles of Getzels' and Jackson's high creatives and high IQ's, and also to suggest what it is that teachers dislike about the former. The youngsters in their high-creative sample *do* disrupt the social environment. You can lead them to the pot; but they just don't melt, they burn. Intelligent and perceptive critics of Getzels' and Jackson's work have pointed out that the actual power of the creative students to create anything worthwhile remains, at their age, unestablished; but their prickliness, hostility, and aggression show up on nearly every instrument of the study. Getzels and Jackson included among their procedures one of having each subject draw whatever they liked on a sheet of paper captioned "Playing Tag in the School Yard." The drawings of the high IQ subjects are literal and humorless, "stimulus-bound", the high creatives' drawings are fantastic and comical, with something of the quality of Till Eulenspiegel about them; but they are also gory.

Combining Getzels' and Jackson's Tables 10 and 11,[2] we get the following statistics on these drawings as they rate them:

	Type of Student	
	High IQ	High Creative
Number of students in sample	28	26
Humor present	5	14
Humor absent	23	12
Violence present	1	9
Violence absent	27	17

We do not, of course, know how this spiral of reciprocal hostility starts; whether the youngsters become hostile and sarcastic because they are punished for their originality, even though at first they express it openly, innocently, and warmly; or whether a youngster will only think and feel divergently if he starts with a certain detachment from and distrust of conventional, established attitudes and procedures. Most likely—say, on the basis of such a cogent analysis as that in Ernest G. Schachtel's brilliant and classic paper, "On Memory and Childhood Amnesia,"[3] the beginnings of creativity in the exploratory sensuality of childhood are quite free from hostility; they are innocent, though hardly chaste. But exploratory sensuality is punished long before the child gets to school, and certainly before he gets to high school. Among the initially gifted, the high creatives are perhaps those who have received enough affection through the total process that they can afford to respond to insult by getting angry and verbally swatting back. The high IQ's have been treated almost wholly as instruments of parental aspirations, even at home, and become anxious at any sign that they are getting off the track; anger and hostility are beyond their emotional means. The findings of Getzels and Jackson on the home background of their contrasting subjects bear this out.

But their most poignant data were obtained from an instrument that they called the Outstanding Traits Test. This consisted of 13 thumbnail descriptions of such traits as social skill, goal-directedness and good marks, using phrases like "Here is the student who is best at getting along with other people"; "Here is the student who is best able to look at things in a new way and to discover new ideas"; "Here is the outstanding athlete in the school," and so forth. The students in their sample were asked to rank these 13 descriptions in three different ways: as "preferred for oneself," as "favored by teachers," and as "believed predictive of adult success." The rank-order correlations obtained between the high IQ and high creative students as to how these traits contributed to later success was *unity;* as to what teachers preferred, it was 0.98. The high creative and high IQ students, in short, were in absolute agreement as to what traits

---

[2] *Ibid.,* p. 49. The tables indicate that the statistical probability of a chance difference between high IQ's and high creatives, as great as that shown here, is .02 or less.

[3] Included in *Metamorphosis* (New York: Basic Books, Inc., 1959), pp. 279–322.

would make a person succeed in adult life; they were virtually agreed as to what teachers liked in students—though the two ratings were not identical. Nevertheless, the correlation between the two groups' ratings of these traits as "preferred for oneself" was only 0.41. This can only be interpreted to mean that one or both of these groups believed that pleasing teachers and becoming successful was just not worth what it cost, even though they agreed completely as to what that cost would be.

Which group rejected the image of success that both shared? The data clearly permit me to resolve this question and end your suspense. Here, instead of correlations *between* the high IQ's and the high creatives, we need, of course, correlations *within* each group for the three possible bases of sorting. Here they are:

	Students	
Components of Correlation	*High IQ*	*High Creative*
Personal traits believed "predictive of success" and "favored by teachers"	0.62	0.59
Personal traits "preferred for oneself" and "believed predictive of adult success"	0.81	0.10
Personal traits "preferred for oneself" and "believed favored by teachers"	0.67	−0.25

I would interpret these statistics to mean that the high creatives cannot bring themselves to be what they believe success requires, and are even more strongly repelled by what the teacher demands. The correlation coefficients on the two "favored by teachers" categories are really very curious and interesting across the board. I find a .6 correlation here astonishingly low for *both* groups—with these *N*'s of 26 and 28 such a correlation has little statistical significance. While, for the high IQ's, the correlation between "preferred for oneself" and "predictive of success" is high, for the high creatives, it is negligible.

BOTH HIGH IQ'S, HIGH CREATIVES SHOW A NEED TO ACHIEVE

All these data could be explained very satisfactorily by the hypothesis that the high creatives, spontaneous and joyful as the happy-go-lucky Negro slave of song and story, just don't give a damn; that this is their way of singing "Hallelujah, I'm a bum." But it won't do. Using two standard measures of the need to achieve, David McClelland's *need: achievement* and Fred L. Strodtbeck's *V-score*, Getzels and Jackson were unable to find any significant differences between the two groups, or between either group and the total population of 449; the figures given for the high creatives are actually slightly higher on both measures. So we must turn for our interpretation to the relationship between the students and the school itself.

Both groups, I infer, see the teacher as on the side of success, but being too naive and square to be a very reliable guide as to how to go after it. Since the high IQ's are determined to *be* the kind of person who succeeds, this reduces the relevance of the teacher to him, but not the relevance of the school. Or to put it another way, the importance of the school as the monitor of his progress is quite enough to bring the high IQ to terms with it; and the terms are generous enough not to demand that he listen to what it actually says. To the high creative, the whole experience is rather frustrating and annoying, and relevant only because there is no viable alternative to high school for a middle-class adolescent. Lower-class adolescents who are not interested in economic success or who feel the school too suffocating can just drop out, go off on a kick, and let the authorities conceal their relief while they pretend to search for them. But this kind of direct action would cost the middle-class youngster his role, and cause him too much anxiety to be a satisfactory alternative. Generally he stays, and looks for ancillary satisfactions in specialized relationships with his peers, in sports or hobbies or sometimes sex and even love, building up a credential while inwardly rejecting the qualities the credential symbolizes.

For both groups, however, the function of the school becomes essentially liturgical, not epistemological. It isn't supposed to make sense. It is not appropriate to believe, disbelieve, or test what one is taught in school. Instead, one *relates* to it; one tries to figure out why this line has been taken rather than another, to figure out what response is expected, and give it.

The result is a peculiar kind of moral vacuity; a limitation of responsible *perception,* and therefore, of moral behavior, to situations that are wholly concrete and immediate. The public school is not primarily an educational institution. I have forgotten who first said that most Christians would feel equal consternation at hearing Christianity denounced and at seeing it practised; it ought, presumably, to have been Mary. But I am quite sure that this could justly be said of most Americans with respect to public education. In many ways, the relationship of the school to the community is like that of a TV station that carries mostly network programs but that is largely dependent on local advertising for support. Like the TV station, the school has its own technical staff, and such autonomy as it possesses is derived from their custody of the mysteries and the records, rather than from any considerable measure of popular deference to their authority. The entertainment provided is frequently of high quality and shrewdly geared to the public taste. Concessions to the intellect and culture, provided as a public service, tend to be more ponderous, conventional, and unconvincing. Though the staff likes to boast about how much of this sort of thing they program, they are self-conscious about it, and rather fearful. The commercials for the local way of life are interminable, boring, and egregiously dishonest, and the audience knows it. But they are hard to change for they are the real basis for the support the school receives. And they are effective, as good commercials are, not so much in stimulating an active desire for the product as in convincing the audience that only a social misfit would be without it.

STUDENTS PREPARE FOR NEXT STEP

What the students learn best in high school is how to function in and utilize a limited power network to achieve limited personal and social objectives. They learn how to get along and make ready for the next onward state. By the time they reach college, they are likely to be thoroughly impatient of anything else; and in our culture, college seldom tries their patience much; the process continues. To me, the most interesting finding in a recent study of medical students[4] is the righteous resentment with which the young medics respond to instruction in medical — to say nothing of social — theory. What they want from medical school is conventional knowledge and practical hints (what they call pearls) and a clear road to the practitioner's license. To get this they are willing to work like dogs; but they resist any suggestion that they work like a higher primate.

Doctors, of course, have notoriously high IQ's, and it is not astonishing that medical students should resemble Getzels' and Jackson's high IQ's in their characteristic cognitive style. But they are also quite creative, when they feel that circumstances and the American Medical Association permit; as are many high IQ's. Creativity and intelligence, like height and weight, are undoubtedly highly correlated. Getzels and Jackson adopted a classic design for their study to permit them to examine contrasts; just as biologists studying human metabolism might deliberately set out to study the differences between short, fat people and tall, thin ones. But both are exceptional, which is why the sample fell from 449 to 28 in one quadrant and 26 in the other. Had they chosen to study youngsters who were in the top 20 per cent in both creativity and IQ, they would probably have found 50 or so in the sample. How would *they* have fared in school?

Getzels and Jackson tell us nothing about this. My own understanding and observation of public education suggests that they would probably be very successful, indeed, and would be well received by the school and acquire a substantial proportion of positions of leadership. We would accept them as our best young Americans—executive material. And the school would teach them to be discreet: not to let their creativity get the upper hand, not to jeopardize their chances by antagonizing persons more stupid than themselves who might nevertheless turn up later on some committee that was passing on them. The pitch would be made on a high moral plane—usually in terms of keeping their availability so as not to impair their usefulness—but the net effect would be to convince the youngster that he ought not to get out of line or speak out of turn, if he hoped ultimately to put his creativity to use in the service of, say, General Electric or the United States Food and Drug Administration.

A statistic frequently cited in the United States is that we spend a little more on hard liquor than we do on public education. I have just finished reading a book which seems to me more striking in its educational implications than any

---

[4] Howard S. Becker, Blanche Geer, Everett S. Hughes, and Anselm L. Strauss, *Boys in White* (Chicago: University of Chicago Press, 1962).

work directly *about* education since Martin Mayer's *The Schools.*[5] This book is Theodore H. White's *The Making of the President 1960,*[6] and after reading it I find that datum shocking. We ought to be spending a *lot* more on hard liquor. We are going to need it, and besides, it works. But I have introduced Mr. White's book into this discussion, not primarily as a vivid portrait of the failure of public education to instruct a trustworthy electorate—though that, according to James Madison, was its essential function—but to allude to one particular passage as a specific illustration of creativity and what happens to it. Mr. White gives a circumstantial account of Richard Nixon's suspiciousness of the press and ineptness in communicating with it, which made the job of the reporters assigned to cover his campaign—for papers primarily committed to his support—almost impossible. The reporters themselves came to dislike and distrust Mr. Nixon and his program. In their dispatches, no hint of their actual feelings or personal appraisal appeared.

But, Mr. White reports: "Then having done their duty, they began frivolously to write imaginary dispatches of what they felt would be a more accurate transcription of their private understanding. I reproduce here a few leads of such dispatches as illustrations of what happens when the press feels itself abused.

" 'Guthrie Center, Iowa [read one] —Vice-President Nixon said today farmers should eat their way out of the surplus problem. . . .'

" 'Guthrie Center, Iowa [another] —Vice-President Nixon admitted today that the farm problem was too big for the Republican Party to handle. He said that if elected President, he would appoint Senator Hubert H. Humphrey as Secretary of Agriculture and let him wrestle with the problem. . . .'

" 'Guthrie Center, Iowa [another]—Vice-President Nixon today called on Pope John XXIII for guidance in finding a solution to the troublesome farm problems which have plagued Catholic, Jew and Protestant alike. . . .' " [7]

My point is that Mr. White also illustrates what doesn't happen even when the press feels itself abused. These "imaginary dispatches" may well afford "a more accurate transcription of their private understanding" than what the reporters actually transmitted. Their responsibility as reporters, I should say, included that of letting the public know not only what Mr. Nixon had said but what they thought he was actually like, properly labeled, of course, as a subjective judgment. This they were too canny to release until too late for it to do any good.

It is self-evident, I believe, that the quality of these imaginary dispatches is identical with the quality of the picture stories produced by the high creatives in Getzels' and Jackson's study, but the factually correct dispatches are the kind of response the high IQ's produce. The reporters, then, must have been both; but they had learned better than to be both when the chips were down and people were watching. They were not deliberately taught this in school, but school is a very good place in which to learn it.

---

[5] (New York: Harper & Bros., 1960).

[6] From *The Making of the President 1960,* by Theodore H. White. Copyright © 1961 by Atheneum House, Inc. Reprinted by permission of the publishers.

[7] *Ibid.,* pp. 274–75.

" 'One had to see Nixon entering a small Iowa village," Mr. White further writes, "the streets lined with schoolchildren, all waving American flags until it seemed as if the cavalcade were entering a defile lined by fluttering, peppermint-striped little banners . . . to see him at his best. . . . These people were his natural constituency, his idiom their idiom. . .' [8]

" '. . . He woke in Marietta, Ohio, on Monday, October 25th, to begin his last "peak" effort, and it was clear from his first speech of the day that he was at one with his audience as he had not been since he had passed through the corn fields of Iowa in the first week of the campaign. A sign outside the courthouse of Marietta, Ohio, read: *High School Debaters Greet World Debater*—the sign was apropos, and of the essence of this last trip as he revived. For he *was* a high-school debater, the boy who had, some thirty years before, won a Los Angeles *Times* prize for his high-school oration on the Constitution. He was seeking not so much to score home a message as to win the hearts of his little audiences. . . .' " [9]

It *is* a little like entering a defile. Some of us would prefer to enter a demurrer. On the basis of cognitive style I would infer that this would include a disproportionate number of high creatives. But how, in the present public high school, does one go about it?

One of the traditional forms of demurrer in our society is to get up and slowly walk away. We have always counted on pluralism as our most effective weapon against conformity and, in de Tocqueville's phrase, "the tyranny of the majority"; and I think it is one of the best social instruments that could be devised and inherent in the nature of democracy. For that reason, I am very much in favor of private and parochial schools. As a matter of social policy, I think they should receive some tax support. I am not a constitutional lawyer, and I cannot judge the legal merits of the argument that aid to church schools, granted at their request, would constitute the Congress making a law respecting an establishment of religion. Personally, I think this is a ridiculous interpretation of the First Amendment; but, then, the First Amendment has always been my favorite passage of the Constitution, and I am naturally reluctant to believe that it is against anything that I favor.

I am convinced that private schools—and in this country many of these are church-supported—contribute more to the general welfare even than they do to their own constituency. We so desperately need alternative life-styles and *ethical models that are related to a particular community and to the experience of life within it,* rather than recipes for tearing away from one's roots and learning to function smoothly among successively more affluent groups of strangers. As to the risk of encountering God, well, it is true that He can be very tricky. But I doubt if the encounter can be altogether avoided. It would certainly not harm any youngster—rather in the spirit of the New England gentlewoman who took up the study of Hebrew at the age of 85—to learn how to confront Him and thrash out those issues on which they were in disagreement. Adolescents gener-

---

[8] *Ibid.,* p. 277.
[9] *Ibid.,* p. 300.

ally get along very well with God, anyhow. The Creation is exactly the kind of thing they can imagine having done themselves, and they can sympathize with the kind of trouble He got Himself into by acting out His creative impulse. It is only in later life, the image having become somewhat tarnished, that the meeting tends to be rather embarrassing to both.

It is difficult to suggest practical ways in which the public school might represent and support a greater diversity of values and a less purely instrumental conception of learning. At present, the public high school lacks dignity. It is often incoherent. Whatever is learned of graciousness and leisure in English or art class—and it isn't likely to be much—is undercut by the food and the noise and standing in line in the cafeteria. The social studies class may discuss civil liberty, but the students still need a pass to walk through the hall and school disciplinary procedures are notably lacking in due process. The students are encouraged to get together in groups to discuss important issues, as long as there is somebody to represent all sides and the criticism doesn't go too deep. But there isn't any place to do it that is out of reach of the public address system announcing when you have to go to get your yearbook picture taken or directing Tom Brown to report to the principal's office *at once;* the efficiency of the p.a. system depends on the fact that you can't get away from it.

All these are trivia; what is not trivial is the continuous experience, day after day and year after year, of triviality itself; of being treated like a tiny unit in an administrative problem. So, really, it does add up; this is *how* you are taught not to take yourself too seriously. This is where you learn that whatever may be officially said, actual official decisions are made with the short-run purpose of getting the job done and keeping out of trouble. This is where you learn to keep your conversation brief, friendly, and to the point, instead of getting all hung up on ideas like an egghead or an Oxbridge don.

Of course, these things and worse occur in many private schools, which can also be barren and stultifying. But when they are, there is at least the theoretical possibility of appealing to an explicit educational tradition that transcends American middle-class practice to try and change them. These *are* basic American middle-class values, however; so there is not much use appealing there, though a smart public school administrator may develop considerable skill in identifying subgroups in his community that take education and youngsters more seriously. But it is a laborious and dangerous process. Public school administrators who try to give their communities better education than they are used to have a very short life expectancy. If you wish to see a case study of such a situation in detail, *Small Town in Mass Society,*[10] contains a superb one. But you know it already.

There is nothing wrong with the school as a social environment, except what is wrong with America. This is the grim truth on which such a study as James S.

---

[10] Arthur J. Vidich and Joseph Bensman (Princeton, N.J.: Princeton University Press, 1958).

Coleman's *The Adolescent Society* [11] seems to me to founder; though I also believe, as I have stated at some length, [12] that the kind of data gathered do not justify the inferences drawn. Even if Professor Coleman had convincingly established that "teen-age" culture is as trivial as he finds it to be, I would still reject his conclusion. The final sentences of his book read:

"To put the matter briefly, if secondary education is to be successful, it must successfully compete with cars and sports and social activities for the adolescent's attention in the open market. The adolescent is no longer a child, but will spend his energy in the ways he sees fit. It is up to the adult society to so structure secondary education that it captures this energy." [13]

Coleman reaches this conclusion on the basis of evidence that the adolescents in his 10-school, 8,000-youngster sample quite uniformly value achievement in athletics (for boys) and popularity (for girls) more than they do such recognition of scholarship as the high school affords. There is, of course, much more to his elaborate study; but, briefly, he finds that:

"Our adolescents today are cut off, probably more than ever before, from the adult society. . . . Our society has within its midst a set of small teen-age societies, which focus teen-age interests and attitudes on things far removed from adult responsibilities, and which may develop standards that lead away from those goals established by the larger society. . . . efforts can be made to redirect the whole society of adolescence itself, so that *it* comes to motivate the child in directions sought by the adult society." [14]

IN DEFENSE OF ADOLESCENTS

I think his statements are wrong, both logically and ethically, and I doubt if I can say why any more clearly than I did in the *Commentary* review earlier cited.

I would submit that, interpreted in their total relationship to American society, Coleman's findings may be more a credit to the adolescent society than an indictment of it. He himself points out that the top achievers are probably very far from being the ablest youngsters, because the brightest and most perceptive quickly learn to shun this particular competition. He also cites the recent and highly suggestive findings of Getzels and Jackson that teachers prefer youngsters who manifest their ability in conventional rather than creative ways. Coleman's policy proposals are intended to correct just these matters; but it is the level and conception of scholarship the youngsters have actually experienced in the high school as it now is that have led them to rate it way below athletics.

For in their experience, sports are at least real and manly; the competences they demand are true competences. They are a lot less likely to be

[11] (New York: Free Press of Glencoe, Inc., 1961).
[12] *Commentary*, Vol. 32, No. 5, pp. 445–47.
[13] James S. Coleman, *op. cit.*, p. 329.
[14] *Ibid.*, p. 9.

phony than the scholarship. I have seen boys from a tiny Louisiana high school, who had just defeated a major city high school team in a basketball tournament, come striding out of their locker room after the game, dressed once more in their farming clothes, and they looked magnificent. A girl who would not have dated one of them at that moment would have had to be singularly unimaginative. I have never seen these boys as they come out of their class in "Problems of Democracy," if they have one in their segregated high school, but I expect they look sheepish. They seemed to be the kind of boys who would know when they had been cheating.

Even within adult society, un-Greek as we are, athletics retains its place in the unconscious as something genuine and comparatively pure. When basketball players sell out, the public is shocked. When business executives are indicted for collusion, it is wearily amused. Coleman makes a far better case for the isolation of the adolescent society than he does for its triviality. Both its isolation and its triviality are largely responses to the greater triviality and corruption of much of our adult society. Their isolation is but an imperfect defense against our triviality; but it is the best they have, and the only way "teen-agers" have of gaining a little time and space in which to work out such meanings as their lives possess. I am reluctant to see this defense breached.[15]

One of the sailors in my company when I was in the Navy during World War II, had a stock proposal that he used to make with reference to any of our mates who was seriously annoying to him. "Let's ostracize him," he said. "You hold him, and I'll do it." Technically, what Coleman proposes is the exact contrary. But I am afraid it comes to the same thing in the end.

It seems to me, then, that I have no choice but to conclude on a note of satisfaction. As a social environment the public high school, by and large, functions very effectively. It is expected to socialize adolescents into the American middle-class, and that is just what it does. You can actually see it doing it. If that isn't what you want, go fight Livingston Street.

---

[15] Edgar Z. Friedenberg, *Commentary, op. cit.*, p. 447.

12. The school class as a social system: some of its functions in American society*

TALCOTT PARSONS

This essay will attempt to outline, if only sketchily, an analysis of the elementary and secondary school class as a social system, and the relation of its structure to its primary functions in the society as an agency of socialization and allocation. While it is important that the school class is normally part of the larger organization of a school, the class rather than the whole school will be the unit of analysis here, for it is recognized both by the school system and by the individual pupil as the place where the "business" of formal education actually takes place. In elementary schools, pupils of one grade are typically placed in a single "class" under one main teacher, but in the secondary school, and sometimes in the upper elementary grades, the pupil works on different subjects under different teachers; here the complex of classes participated in by the same pupil is the significant unit for our purposes.

THE PROBLEM: SOCIALIZATION AND SELECTION

Our main interest, then, is in a dual problem: first of how the school class functions to internalize in its pupils both the commitments and capacities for successful performance of their future adult roles, and second of how it functions to allocate these human resources within the role-structure of the adult society. The primary ways in which these two problems are interrelated will provide our main points of reference.

First, from the functional point of view the school class can be treated as an agency of socialization. That is to say, it is an agency through which individual personalities are trained to be motivationally and technically adequate to the performance of adult roles. It is not the sole such agency; the family, informal "peer groups," churches, and sundry voluntary organizations all play a part, as does actual on-the-job training. But, in the period extending from entry into

*From *Harvard Educational Review,* Vol. 29, No. 4 (Fall 1959), pp. 297–318.

Author's Note: I am indebted to Mrs. Carolyn Cooper for research assistance in the relevant literature and for editorial work on the first draft of this paper.

.irst grade until entry into the labor force or marriage, the school class may be regarded as the focal socializing agency.

The socialization function may be summed up as the development in individuals of the commitments and capacities which are essential prerequisites of their future role-performance. Commitments may be broken down in turn into two components: commitment to the implementation of the broad *values* of society, and commitment to the performance of a specific type of role within the *structure* of society. Thus a person in a relatively humble occupation may be a "solid citizen" in the sense of commitment to honest work in that occupation, without an intensive and sophisticated concern with the implementation of society's higher-level values. Or conversely, someone else might object to the anchorage of the feminine role in marriage and the family on the grounds that such anchorage keeps society's total talent resources from being distributed equitably to business, government, and so on. Capacities can also be broken down into two components, the first being competence or the skill to perform the tasks involved in the individual's roles, and the second being "role-responsibility" or the capacity to live up to other people's expectations of the interpersonal behavior appropriate to these roles. Thus a mechanic as well as a doctor needs to have not only the basic "skills of his trade," but also the ability to behave responsibly toward those people with whom he is brought into contact in his work.

While on the one hand, the school class may be regarded as a primary agency by which these different components of commitments and capacities are generated, on the other hand, it is, from the point of view of the society, an agency of "manpower" allocation. It is well known that in American society there is a very high, and probably increasing, correlation between one's status level in the society and one's level of educational attainment. Both social status and educational level are obviously related to the occupational status which is attained. Now, as a result of the general process of both educational and occupational upgrading, completion of high school is increasingly coming to be the norm for minimum satisfactory educational attainment, and the most significant line for future occupational status has come to be drawn between members of an age-cohort who do and do not go to college.

We are interested, then, in what it is about the school class in our society that determines the distinction between the contingents of the age-cohort which do and do not go to college. Because of a tradition of localism and a rather pragmatic pluralism, there is apparently considerable variety among school systems of various cities and states. Although the situation in metropolitan Boston probably represents a more highly structured pattern than in many other parts of the country, it is probably not so extreme as to be misleading in its main features. There, though of course actual entry into college does not come until after graduation from high school, the main dividing line is between those who are and are not enrolled in the college preparatory course in high school; there is only a small amount of shifting either way after about the ninth grade when the decision is normally made. Furthermore, the evidence seems to be that by far the most important criterion of selection is the record of school performance in elementary school. These records are evaluated by teachers and principals, and there are few cases of entering the college preparatory course against their advice. It is therefore not stretching the evidence too far to say broadly that the primary selective process occurs through differential school performance in elementary school, and that the "seal" is put on it in junior high school.[1]

The evidence also is that the selective process is genuinely assortative. As in virtually all comparable processes, ascriptive as well as achieved factors influence the outcome. In this case, the ascriptive factor is the socio-economic status of the child's family, and the factor underlying his opportunity for achievement is his individual ability. In the study of 3,348 Boston high school boys on which these generalizations are based, each of these factors was quite highly correlated with planning college. For example, the percentages planning college, by father's occupation, were: 12 per cent for semi-skilled and unskilled, 19 per cent for skilled, 26 per cent for minor white collar, 52 per cent for middle white collar, and 80 per cent for major white collar. Likewise, intentions varied by ability (as measured by IQ), namely, 11 per cent for the lowest quintile, 17 per cent for the next, 24 per cent for the middle, 30 per cent for the next to the top, and 52 per cent for the highest. It should be noted also that within any ability quintile, the relationship of plans to father's occupation is seen. For example, within the very important top quintile in ability as measured, the range in college intentions was from 29 per cent for sons of laborers to 89 per cent for sons of major white collar persons.[2]

The essential points here seem to be that there is a relatively uniform criterion of selection operating to differentiate between the college and the non-college contingents, and that for a very important part of the cohort the operation of this criterion is not a "put-up job"— it is not simply a way of affirming a previously determined ascriptive status. To be sure, the high-status, high-ability boy is very likely indeed to go to college, and the low-status, low-ability boy is very unlikely to go. But the "cross-pressured" group for whom these two factors do not coincide[3] is of considerable importance.

---

[1] The principal source for these statements is a study of social mobility among boys in ten public high schools in the Boston metropolitan area, conducted by Samuel A. Stouffer, Florence R. Kluckhohn, and the present author. Unfortunately the material is not available in published form.

[2] See table from this study in J. A. Kahl, *The American Class Structure* (New York: Rinehart & Co., 1953), p. 283. Data from a nationwide sample of high school students, published by the Educational Testing Service, show similar patterns of relationships. For example, the ETS study shows variation, by father's occupation, in proportion of high school seniors planning college, of from 35 per cent to 80 per cent for boys and 27 per cent to 79 per cent for girls. (From *Background Factors Related to College Plans and College Enrollment among High School Students* [Princeton, N.J.: Educational Testing Service, 1957]).

[3] There seem to be two main reasons why the high-status, low-ability group is not so important as its obverse. The first is that in a society of expanding educational and occupational opportunity the general trend is one of upgrading, and the social pressures to down-

Considerations like these lead me to conclude that the main process of differentiation (which from another point of view is selection) that occurs during elementary school takes place on a single main axis of *achievement.* Broadly, moreover, the differentiation leads up through high school to a bifurcation into college-goers and non-college-goers.

To assess the significance of this pattern, let us look at its place in the socialization of the individual. Entering the system of formal education is the child's first major step out of primary involvement in his family of orientation. Within the family certain foundations of his motivational system have been laid down. But the only characteristic fundamental to later roles which has clearly been "determined" and psychologically stamped in by that time is sex role. The postoedipal child enters the system of formal education clearly categorized as boy or girl, but beyond that his *role* is not yet differentiated. The process of selection, by which persons will select and be selected for categories of roles, is yet to take place.

On grounds which cannot be gone into here, it may be said that the most important single predispositional factor with which the child enters the school is his level of *independence.* By this is meant his level of self-sufficiency to relative guidance by adults, his capacity to take responsibility and to make his own decisions in coping with new and varying situations. This, like his sex role, he has as a function of his experience in the family.

The family is a collectivity within which the basic status-structure is ascribed in terms of biological position, that is, by generation, sex, and age. There are inevitably differences of performance relative to these, and they are rewarded and punished in ways that contribute to differential character formation. But these differences are not given the sanction of institutionalized social status. The school is the first socializing agency in the child's experience which institutionalizes a differentiation of status on nonbiological bases. Moreover, this is not an ascribed but an achieved status; it is the status "earned" by differential performance of the tasks set by the teacher, who is acting as an agent of the community's school system. Let us look at the structure of this situation.

THE STRUCTURE OF THE ELEMENTARY SCHOOL CLASS

In accord with the generally wide variability of American institutions, and of course the basically local control of school systems, there is considerable variability of school situations, but broadly they have a single relatively well-marked framework.[4] Particularly in the primary part of the elementary grades, i.e., the first three grades, the basic pattern includes one main teacher for the class, who

---

ward mobility are not as great as they would otherwise be. The second is that there are cushioning mechanisms which tend to protect the high status boy who has difficulty "making the grade." He may be sent to a college with low academic standards, he may go to schools where the line between ability levels is not rigorously drawn, etc.

[4] This discussion refers to public schools. Only about 13 per cent of all elementary and secondary school pupils attend non-public schools, with this proportion ranging from about

teaches all subjects and who is in charge of the class generally. Sometimes this early, and frequently in later grades, other teachers are brought in for a few special subjects, particularly gym, music, and art, but this does not alter the central position of the main teacher. This teacher is usually a woman.[5] The class is with this one teacher for the school year, but usually no longer.

The class, then, is composed of about 25 age-peers of both sexes drawn from a relatively small geographical area—the neighborhood. Except for sex in certain respects, there is initially no formal basis for differentiation of status within the school class. The main structural differentiation develops gradually, on the single main axis indicated above as achievement. That the differentiation should occur on a single main axis is insured by four *primary features* of the situation. The *first* is the initial equalization of the "contestants'" status by age and by "family background," the neighborhood being typically much more homogeneous than is the whole society. The *second* circumstance is the imposition of a common set of tasks which is, compared to most other task-areas, strikingly undifferentiated. The school situation is far more like a race in this respect than most role-performance situations. *Third,* there is the sharp polarization between the pupils in their initial equality and the *single* teacher who is an adult and "represents" the adult world. And *fourth,* there is a relatively systematic process of evaluation of the pupils' performances. From the point of view of a pupil, this evaluation, particularly (though not exclusively) in the form of report card marks, constitutes reward and/or punishment for past performance; from the viewpoint of the school system acting as an allocating agency, it is a basis of *selection* for future status in society.

Two important sets of qualifications need to be kept in mind in interpreting this structural pattern, but I think these do not destroy the significance of its main outline. The first qualification is for variations in the formal organization and procedures of the school class itself. Here the most important kind of variation is that between relatively "traditional" schools and relatively "progressive" schools. The more traditional schools put more emphasis on discrete units of subject-matter, whereas the progressive type allows more "indirect" teaching through "projects" and broader topical interests where more than one bird can be killed with a stone. In progressive schools there is more emphasis on groups of pupils working together, compared to the traditional direct relation of the individual pupil to the teacher. This is related to the progressive emphasis on co-operation among the pupils rather than direct competition, to greater permissiveness as opposed to strictness of discipline, and to a de-emphasis on formal marking.[6] In some schools one of these components will be more prominent,

22 per cent in the Northeast to about 6 per cent in the South. U.S. Office of Education, *Biennial Survey of Education in the United States, 1954–56* (Washington: U.S. Government Printing Office, 1959), chap. ii, "Statistics of State School Systems, 1955–56," Table 44, p. 114.

[5] In 1955–56, 13 per cent of the public elementary school instructional staff in the United States were men. *Ibid.,* p. 7.

[6] This summary of some contrasts between traditional and progressive patterns is derived from general reading in the literature rather than any single authoritative account.

and in others, another. That it is, however, an important range of variation is clear. It has to do, I think, very largely with the independence-dependence training which is so important to early socialization in the family. My broad interpretation is that those people who emphasize independence training will tend to be those who favor relatively progressive education. The relation of support for progressive education to relatively high socio-economic status and to "intellectual" interests and the like is well known. There is no contradiction between these emphases both on independence and on co-operation and group solidarity among pupils. In the first instance this is because the main focus of the independence problem at these ages is vis-à-vis adults. However, it can also be said that the peer group, which here is built into the school class, is an indirect field of expression of dependency needs, displaced from adults.

The second set of qualifications concerns the "informal" aspects of the school class, which are always somewhat at variance with the formal expectations. For instance, the formal pattern of nondifferentiation between the sexes may be modified informally, for the very salience of the one-sex peer group at this age period means that there is bound to be considerable implicit recognition of it— for example, in the form of teachers' encouraging group competition between boys and girls. Still, the fact of coeducation and the attempt to treat both sexes alike in all the crucial formal respects remain the most important. Another problem raised by informal organization is the question of how far teachers can and do treat pupils particularistically in violation of the universalistic expectations of the school. When compared with other types of formal organizations, however, I think the extent of this discrepancy in elementary schools is seen to be not unusual. The school class is structured so that opportunity for particularistic treatment is severely limited. Because there are so many more children in a school class than in a family and they are concentrated in a much narrower age range, the teacher has much less chance than does a parent to grant particularistic favors.

Bearing in mind these two sets of qualifications, it is still fair, I think, to conclude that the major characteristics of the elementary school class in this country are such as have been outlined. It should be especially emphasized that more or less progressive schools, even with their relative lack of emphasis on formal marking, do not constitute a separate pattern, but rather a variant tendency within the same pattern. A progressive teacher, like any other, will form opinions about the different merits of her pupils relative to the values and goals of the class and will communicate these evaluations to them, informally if not formally. It is my impression that the extremer cases of playing down relative evaluation are confined to those upper-status schools where going to a "good" college is so fully taken for granted that for practical purposes it is an ascribed status. In other words, in interpreting these facts the selective function of the school class should be kept continually in the forefront of attention. Quite clearly its importance has not been decreasing; rather the contrary.

THE NATURE OF SCHOOL ACHIEVEMENT

What, now, of the content of the "achievement" expected of elementary school children? Perhaps the best broad characterization which can be given is that it involves the types of performance which are, on the one hand, appropriate to the school situation and, on the other hand, are felt by adults to be important in themselves. This vague and somewhat circular characterization may, as was mentioned earlier, be broken down into two main components. One of these is the more purely "cognitive" learning of information, skills, and frames of reference associated with empirical knowledge and technological mastery. The *written* language and the early phases of mathematical thinking are clearly vital; they involve cognitive skills at altogether new levels of generality and abstraction compared to those commanded by the pre-school child. With these basic skills goes assimilation of much factual information about the world.

The second main component is what may broadly be called a "moral" one. In earlier generations of schooling this was known as "deportment." Somewhat more generally it might be called responsible citizenship in the school community. Such things as respect for the teacher, consideration and co-operativeness in relation to fellow-pupils, and good "work-habits" are the fundamentals, leading on to capacity for "leadership" and "initiative."

The striking fact about this achievement content is that in the elementary grades these two primary components are not clearly differentiated from each other. Rather, the pupil is evaluated in diffusely general terms; a *good* pupil is defined in terms of a fusion of the cognitive and the moral components, in which varying weight is given to one or the other. Broadly speaking, then, we may say that the "high achievers" of the elementary school are both the "bright" pupils, who catch on easily to their more strictly intellectual tasks, and the more "responsible" pupils, who "behave well" and on whom the teacher can "count" in her difficult problems of managing the class. One indication that this is the case is the fact that in elementary school the purely intellectual tasks are relatively easy for the pupil of high intellectual ability. In many such cases, it can be presumed that the primary challenge to the pupil is not to his intellectual, but to his "moral," capacities. On the whole, the progressive movement seems to have leaned in the direction of giving enhanced emphasis to this component, suggesting that of the two, it has tended to become the more problematical.[7]

The essential point, then, seems to be that the elementary school, regarded in the light of its socialization function, is an agency which differentiates the school class broadly along a single continuum of achievement, the content of

---

[7] This account of the two components of elementary school achievement and their relation summarizes impressions gained from the literature, rather than being based on the opinions of particular authorities. I have the impression that achievement in this sense corresponds closely to what is meant by the term as used by McClelland and his associates. Cf. D. C. McClelland *et al., The Achievement Motive* (New York: Appleton-Century-Crofts, Inc., 1953).

which is relative excellence in living up to the expectations imposed by the teacher as an agent of the adult society. The criteria of this achievement are, generally speaking, undifferentiated into the cognitive or technical component and the moral or "social" component. But with respect to its bearing on societal values, it is broadly a differentiation of *levels* of capacity to act in accord with these values. Though the relation is far from neatly uniform, this differentiation underlies the processes of selection for levels of status and role in the adult society.

Next, a few words should be said about the out-of-school context in which this process goes on. Besides the school class, there are clearly two primary social structures in which the child participates: the family and the child's informal "peer group."

FAMILY AND PEER GROUP IN RELATION TO THE SCHOOL CLASS

The school age child, of course, continues to live in the parental household and to be highly dependent, emotionally as well as instrumentally, on his parents. But he is now spending several hours a day away from home, subject to a discipline and a reward system which are essentially independent of that administered by the parents. Moreover, the range of this independence gradually increases. As he grows older, he is permitted to range further territorially with neither parental nor school supervision, and to do an increasing range of things. He often gets an allowance for personal spending and begins to earn some money of his own. Generally, however, the emotional problem of dependence-independence continues to be a very salient one through this period, frequently with manifestations by the child of compulsive independence.

Concomitantly with this, the area for association with age-peers without detailed adult supervision expands. These associations are tied to the family, on the one hand, in that the home and yards of children who are neighbors and the adjacent streets serve as locations for their activities; and to the school, on the other hand, in that play periods and going to and from school provide occasions for informal association, even though organized extracurricular activities are introduced only later. Ways of bringing some of this activity under another sort of adult supervision are found in such organizations as the boy and girl scouts.

Two sociological characteristics of peer groups at this age are particularly striking. One is the fluidity of their boundaries, with individual children drifting into and out of associations. This element of "voluntary association" contrasts strikingly with the child's ascribed membership in the family and the school class, over which he has no control. The second characteristic is the peer group's sharp segregation by sex. To a striking degree this is enforced by the children themselves rather than by adults.

The psychological functions of peer association are suggested by these two characteristics. On the one hand, the peer group may be regarded as a field for the exercise of independence from adult control; hence it is not surprising that it is often a focus of behavior which goes beyond independence from adults to the range of adult-*disapproved* behavior; when this happens, it is the seed bed from which the extremists go over into delinquency. But another very important function is to provide the child a source of non-adult approval and acceptance. These depend on "technical" and "moral" criteria as diffuse as those required in the school situation. On the one hand, the peer group is a field for acquiring and displaying various types of "prowess"; for boys this is especially the physical prowess which may later ripen into athletic achievement. On the other hand, it is a matter of gaining acceptance from desirable peers as "belonging" in the group, which later ripens into the conception of the popular teen-ager, the "right guy." Thus the adult parents are augmented by age-peers as a source of rewards for performance and of security in acceptance.

The importance of the peer group for socialization in our type of society should be clear. The motivational foundations of character are inevitably first laid down through identification with parents, who are generation-superiors, and the generation difference is a type example of a hierarchical status difference. But an immense part of the individual's adult role performance will have to be in association with status-equals or near-equals. In this situation it is important to have a reorganization of the motivational structure so that the original dominance of the hierarchical axis is modified to strengthen the egalitarian components. The peer group plays a prominent part in this process.

Sex segregation of latency period peer groups may be regarded as a process of reinforcement of sex-role identification. Through intensive association with sex-peers and involvement in sex-typed activities, they strongly reinforce belongingness with other members of the same sex and contrast with the opposite sex. This is the more important because in the coeducational school a set of forces operates which specifically plays down sex-role differentiation.

It is notable that the latency period sex-role pattern, instead of institutionalizing relations to members of the opposite sex, is characterized by an avoidance of such relations, which only in adolescence gives way to dating. This avoidance is clearly associated with the process of reorganization of the erotic components of motivational structure. The pre-oedipal objects of erotic attachment were both intra-familial and generation-superior. In both respects there must be a fundamental shift by the time the child reaches adulthood. I would suggest that one of the main functions of the avoidance pattern is to help cope with the psychological difficulty of overcoming the earlier incestuous attachments, and hence to prepare the child for assuming an attachment to an age-mate of opposite sex later.

Seen in this perspective, the socialization function of the school class assumes a particular significance. The socialization functions of the family by this time are relatively residual, though their importance should not be underestimated. But the school remains adult-controlled and, moreover, induces basically the same kind of identification as was induced by the family in the child's pre-oedipal stage. This is to say that the learning of achievement-motivation is, psychologically speaking, a process of identification with the teacher, of doing well in school in order to please the teacher (often backed by the parents) in the same sense in which a pre-oedipal child learns new skills in order to please his mother.

In this connection I maintain that what is internalized through the process of identification is a reciprocal pattern of role-relationships.[8] Unless there is a drastic failure of internalization altogether, not just one, but both sides of the interaction will be internalized. There will, however, be an emphasis on one or the other, so that some children will more nearly identify with the socializing agent, and others will more nearly identify with the opposite role. Thus, in the pre-oedipal stage, the "independent" child has identified more with the parent, and the "dependent" one with the child-role vis-à-vis the parent.

In school the teacher is institutionally defined as superior to any pupil in knowledge of curriculum subject-matter and in responsibility as a good citizen of the school. In so far as the school class tends to be bifurcated (and of course the dichotomization is far from absolute), it will broadly be on the basis, on the one hand, of identification with the teacher, or acceptance of her role as a model; and, on the other hand, of identification with the pupil peer group. This bifurcation of the class on the basis of identification with teacher or with peer group so strikingly corresponds with the bifurcation into college-goers and non-college-goers that it would be hard to avoid the hypothesis that this structural dichotomization in the school system is the primary source of the selective dichotomization. Of course in detail the relationship is blurred, but certainly not more so than in a great many other fields of comparable analytical complexity.

These considerations suggest an interpretation of some features of the elementary teacher role in American society. The first major step in socialization, beyond that in the family, takes place in the elementary school, so it seems reasonable to expect that the teacher-figure should be characterized by a combination of similarities to and differences from parental figures. The teacher, then, is an adult, characterized by the generalized superiority, which a parent also has, of adult status relative to children. She is not, however, ascriptively related to her pupils, but is performing an occupational role—a role, however, in which the recipients of her services are tightly bound in solidarity to her and to each other. Furthermore, compared to a parent's, her responsibility to them is much more universalistic, this being reinforced, as we saw, by the size of the class; it is also much more oriented to performance rather than to solicitude for the emotional "needs" of the children. She is not entitled to suppress the distinction between high and low achievers, just because not being able to be included among the high group would be too hard on little Johnny—however much tendencies in this direction appear as deviant patterns. A mother, on the other hand, must give *first* priority to the needs of her child, regardless of his capacities to achieve.

It is also significant for the parallel of the elementary school class with the

---

[8] On the identification process in the family see my paper, "Social Structure and the Development of Personality," *Psychiatry,* Vol. 21 (November, 1958), pp. 321–40.

family that the teacher is normally a woman. As background it should be noted that in most European systems until recently, and often today in our private parochial and non-sectarian schools, the sexes have been segregated and each sex group has been taught by teachers of its own sex. Given coeducation, however, the woman teacher represents continuity with the role of the mother. Precisely the lack of differentiation in the elementary school "curriculum" between the components of subject-matter competence and social responsibility fits in with the greater diffuseness of the feminine role.

But at the same time, it is essential that the teacher is not a mother to her pupils, but must insist on universalistic norms and the differential reward of achievement. Above all she must be the agent of bringing about and legitimizing a differentiation of the school class on an achievement axis. This aspect of her role is furthered by the fact that in American society the feminine role is less confined to the familial context than in most other societies, but joins the masculine in occupational and associational concerns, though still with a greater relative emphasis on the family. Through identification with their teacher, children of both sexes learn that the category "woman" is not co-extensive with "mother" (and future wife), but that the feminine role-personality is more complex than that.

In this connection it may well be that there is a relation to the once-controversial issue of the marriage of women teachers. If the differentiation between what may be called the maternal and the occupational components of the feminine role is incomplete and insecure, confusion between them may be avoided by insuring that both are not performed by the same persons. The "old maid" teacher of American tradition may thus be thought of as having renounced the maternal role in favor of the occupational.[9] Recently, however, the highly affective concern over the issue of married women's teaching has conspicuously abated, and their actual participation has greatly increased. It may be suggested that this change is associated with a change in the feminine role, the most conspicuous feature of which is the general social sanctioning of participation of women in the labor force, not only prior to marriage, but also after marriage. This I should interpret as a process of structural differentiation in that the same category of persons is permitted and even expected to engage in a more complex set of role-functions than before.

The process of identification with the teacher which has been postulated here is furthered by the fact that in the elementary grades the child typically has one teacher, just as in the pre-oedipal period he had one parent, the mother, who was the focus of his object-relations. The continuity between the two phases is also favored by the fact that the teacher, like the mother, is a woman. But, if she acted only like a mother, there would be no genuine reorganization of the pupil's

---

[9] It is worth noting that the Catholic parochial school system is in line with the more general older American tradition, in that the typical teacher is a nun. The only difference in this respect is the sharp religious symbolization of the difference between mother and teacher.

personality system. This reorganization is furthered by the features of the teacher role which differentiate it from the maternal. One further point is that while a child has one main teacher in each grade, he will usually have a new teacher when he progresses to the next higher grade. He is thus accustomed to the fact that teachers are, unlike mothers, "interchangeable" in a certain sense. The school year is long enough to form an important relationship to a particular teacher, but not long enough for a highly particularistic attachment to crystallize. More than in the parent-child relationship, in school the child must internalize his relation to the teacher's *role* rather than her particular personality; this is a major step in the internalization of universalistic patterns.

SOCIALIZATION AND SELECTION IN THE ELEMENTARY SCHOOL

To conclude this discussion of the elementary school class, something should be said about the fundamental conditions underlying the process which is, as we have seen, simultaneously (1) an emancipation of the child from primary emotional attachment to his family, (2) an internalization of a level of societal values and norms that is a step higher than those he can learn in his family alone, (3) a differentiation of the school class in terms both of actual achievement and of differential *valuation* of achievement, and (4) from society's point of view, a selection and allocation of its human resources relative to the adult role system.[10]

Probably the most fundamental condition underlying this process is the sharing of common values by the two adult agencies involved—the family and the school. In this case the core is the shared valuation of *achievement*. It includes, above all, recognition that it is fair to give differential rewards for different levels of achievement, so long as there has been fair access to opportunity, and fair that these rewards lead on to higher-order opportunities for the successful. There is thus a basic sense in which the elementary school class is an embodiment of the fundamental American value of equality of opportunity, in that it places value *both* on initial equality and on differential achievement.

As a second condition, however, the rigor of this valuational pattern must be tempered by allowance for the difficulties and needs of the young child. Here the quasi-motherliness of the woman teacher plays an important part. Through her the school system, assisted by other agencies, attempts to minimize the insecurity resulting from the pressures to learn, by providing a certain amount of emotional support defined in terms of what is due to a child of a given age level. In this respect, however, the role of the school is relatively small. The underlying foundation of support is given in the home, and as we have seen, an important supplement to it can be provided by the informal peer associations of the child. It may be suggested that the development of extreme patterns of alienation from the school is often related to inadequate support in these respects.

Third, there must be a process of selective rewarding of valued performance.

---

[10] The following summary is adapted from T. Parsons, R. F. Bates *et al., Family, Socialization and Interaction Process* (Glencoe, Ill.: Free Press, 1955), esp. chap. iv.

Here the teacher is clearly the primary agent, though the more progressive modes of education attempt to enlist classmates more systematically than in the traditional pattern. This is the process that is the direct source of intra-class differentiation along the achievement axis.

The final condition is that this initial differentiation tends to bring about a status system in the class, in which not only the immediate results of school work, but a whole series of influences, converge to consolidate different expectations which may be thought of as the children's "levels of aspiration." Generally some differentiation of friendship groups along this line occurs, though it is important that it is by no means complete, and that children are sensitive to the attitudes not only of their own friends, but of others.

Within this general discussion of processes and conditions, it is important to distinguish, as I have attempted to do all along, the socialization of the individual from the selective allocation of contingents to future roles. For the individual, the old familial identification is broken up (the family of orientation becomes, in Freudian terms, a "lost object") and a new identification is gradually built up, providing the first-order structure of the child's identity apart from his originally ascribed identity as son or daughter of the "Jones." He both transcends his familial identification in favor of a more independent one and comes to occupy a differentiated status within the new system. His personal status is inevitably a direct function of the position he achieves, primarily in the formal school class and secondarily in the informal peer group structure. In spite of the sense in which achievement-ranking takes place along a continuum, I have put forward reasons to suggest that, with respect to this status, there is an important differentiation into two broad, relatively distinct levels, and that his position on one or the other enters into the individual's definition of his own identity. To an important degree this process of differentiation is independent of the socio-economic status of his family in the community, which to the child is a prior ascribed status.

When we look at the same system as a selective mechanism from the societal point of view, some further considerations become important. First, it may be noted that the valuation of achievement and its sharing by family and school not only provides the appropriate values for internalization by individuals, but also performs a crucial integrative function for the system. Differentiation of the class along the achievement axis is inevitably a source of strain, because it confers higher rewards and privileges on one contingent than on another within the same system. This common valuation helps make possible the acceptance of the crucial differentiation, especially by the losers in the competition. Here it is an essential point that this *common* value on achievement is shared by units with different statuses in the system. It cuts across the differentiation of families by socio-economic status. It is necessary that there be realistic opportunity and that the teacher can be relied on to implement it by being "fair" and rewarding achievement by whoever shows capacity for it. The fact is crucial that the distribution of abilities, though correlated with family status, clearly does not coincide with it. There can then be a genuine selective process within a set of "rules of the game."

This commitment to common values is not, however, the sole integrative mechanism counteracting the strain imposed by differentiation. Not only does the individual pupil enjoy familial support, but teachers also like and indeed "respect" pupils on bases independent of achievement-status, and peer-group friendship lines, though correlated with position on the achievement scale, again by no means coincide with it, but cross-cut it. Thus there are cross-cutting lines of solidarity which mitigate the strains generated by rewarding achievement differentially.[11]

It is only *within* this framework of institutionalized solidarity that the crucial selective process goes on through selective rewarding and the consolidation of its results into a status-differentiation within the school class. We have called special attention to the impact of the selective process on the children of relatively high ability but low family status. Precisely in this group, but pervading school classes generally, is another parallel to what was found in the studies of voting behavior.[12] In the voting studies it was found that the "shifters"—those voters who were transferring their allegiance from one major party to the other—tended, on the one hand, to be the "cross-pressured" people, who had multiple status characteristics and group allegiances which predisposed them simultaneously to vote in opposite directions. The analogy in the school class is clearly to the children for whom ability and family status do not coincide. On the other hand, it was precisely in this group of cross-pressured voters that political "indifference" was most conspicuous. Non-voting was particularly prevalent in this group, as was a generally cool emotional tone toward a campaign. The suggestion is that some of the pupil "indifference" to school performance may have a similar origin. This is clearly a complex phenomenon and cannot be further analyzed here. But rather than suggesting, as is usual on common sense grounds, that indifference to school work represents an "alienation" from cultural and intellectual values, I would suggest exactly the opposite: that an important component of such indifference,

---

[11] In this, as in several other respects, there is a parallel to other important allocative processes in the society. A striking example is the voting process by which political support is allocated between party candidates. Here, the strain arises from the fact that one candidate and his party will come to enjoy all the perquisites—above all the power—of office, while the other will be excluded for the time being from these. This strain is mitigated, on the one hand, by the common commitment to constitutional procedure, and, on the other hand, by the fact that the nonpolitical bases of social solidarity, which figure so prominently as determinants of voting behavior, still cut across party lines. The average person is, in various of his roles, associated with people whose political preference is different from his own; he therefore could not regard the opposite party as composed of unmitigated scoundrels without introducing a rift within the groups to which he is attached. This feature of the electorate's structure is brought out strongly in B. R. Berelson, P. F. Lazarsfeld and W. N. McPhee, *Voting* (Chicago: University of Chicago Press, 1954). The conceptual analysis of it is developed in my own paper, " 'Voting' and the Equilibrium of the American Political System" in E. Burdick and A. J. Brodbeck (eds.), *American Voting Behavior* (Glencoe, Ill.: Free Press, 1959).

[12] *Ibid.*

including in extreme cases overt revolt against school discipline, is connected with the fact that the stakes, as in politics, are very high indeed. Those pupils who are exposed to contradictory pressures are likely to be ambivalent; at the same time, the personal stakes for them are higher than for the others, because what happens in school may make much more of a difference for their futures than for the others, in whom ability and family status point to the same expectations for the future. In particular for the upwardly mobile pupils, too much emphasis on school success would pointedly suggest "burning their bridges" of association with their families and status peers. This phenomenon seems to operate even in elementary school, although it grows somewhat more conspicuous later. In general I think that an important part of the anti-intellectualism in American youth culture stems from the *importance* of the selective process through the educational system rather than the opposite.

One further major point should be made in this analysis. As we have noted, the general trend of American society has been toward a rapid upgrading in the educational status of the population. This means that, relative to past expectations, with each generation there is increased pressure to educational achievement, often associated with parents' occupational ambitions for their children.[13] To a sociologist this is a more or less classical situation of anomic strain, and the youth-culture ideology which plays down intellectual interests and school performance seems to fit in this context. The orientation of the youth culture is, in the nature of the case, ambivalent, but for the reasons suggested, the antiintellectual side of the ambivalence tends to be overtly stressed. One of the reasons for the dominance of the anti-school side of the ideology is that it provides a means of protest against adults, who are at the opposite pole in the socialization situation. In certain respects one would expect that the trend toward greater emphasis on independence, which we have associated with progressive education, would accentuate the strain in this area and hence the tendency to decry adult expectations. The whole problem should be subjected to a thorough analysis in the light of what we know about ideologies more generally.

The same general considerations are relevant to the much-discussed problem of juvenile delinquency. Both the general upgrading process and the pressure to enhanced independence should be expected to increase strain on the lower, most marginal groups. The analysis of this paper has been concerned with the line between college and non-college contingents; there is, however, another line between those who achieve solid non-college educational status and those for whom adaptation to educational expectations at *any* level is difficult. As the acceptable minimum of educational qualification rises, persons near and below the margin will tend to be pushed into an attitude of repudiation of these expectations. Truancy and delinquency are ways of expressing this repudiation. Thus the very *improvement* of educational standards in the society at large may well be a major factor in the failure of the educational process for a growing number

---

[13] J. A. Kahl, "Educational and Occupational Aspirations of 'Common Man' Boys," *Harvard Educational Review,* Vol. 23 (Summer, 1953), pp. 186–203.

at the lower end of the status and ability distribution. It should therefore not be too easily assumed that delinquency is a symptom of a *general* failure of the educational process.

DIFFERENTIATION AND SELECTION IN THE SECONDARY SCHOOL

It will not be possible to discuss the secondary school phase of education in nearly as much detail as has been done for the elementary school phase, but it is worthwhile to sketch its main outline in order to place the above analysis in a wider context. Very broadly we may say that the elementary school phase is concerned with the internalization in children of motivation to achievement, and the selection of persons on the basis of differential capacity for achievement. The focus is on the *level* of capacity. In the secondary school phase, on the other hand, the focus is on the differentiation of *qualitative types* of achievement. As in the elementary school, this differentiation cross-cuts sex role. I should also maintain that it cross-cuts the levels of achievement which have been differentiated out in the elementary phase.

In approaching the question of the types of capacity differentiated, it should be kept in mind that secondary school is the principal springboard from which lower-status persons will enter the labor force, whereas those achieving higher status will continue their formal education in college, and some of them beyond. Hence for the lower-status pupils the important line of differentiation should be the one which will lead into broadly different categories of jobs; for the higher-status pupils the differentiation will lead to broadly different roles in college.

My suggestion is that this differentiation separates those two components of achievement which we labelled "cognitive" and "moral" in discussing the elementary phase. Those relatively high in "cognitive" achievement will fit better in specific-function, more or less technical roles; those relatively high in "moral" achievement will tend toward diffuser, more "socially" or "humanly" oriented roles. In jobs not requiring college training, the one category may be thought of as comprising the more impersonal and technical occupations, such as "operatives," mechanics, or clerical workers; the other, as occupations where "human relations" are prominent, such as salesmen and agents of various sorts. At the college level, the differentiation certainly relates to concern, on the one hand, with the specifically intellectual curricular work of college and, on the other hand, with various types of diffuser responsibility in human relations, such as leadership roles in student government and extracurricular activities. Again, candidates for post-graduate professional training will probably be drawn mainly from the first of these two groups.

In the structure of the school, there appears to be a gradual transition from the earliest grades through high school, with the changes timed differently in different school systems. The structure emphasized in the first part of this discussion is most clearly marked in the first three "primary" grades. With progression to the higher grades, there is greater frequency of plural teachers, though very generally still a single main teacher. In the sixth grade and sometimes in the fifth, a man as main teacher, though uncommon, is by no means unheard of. With junior high school, however, the shift of pattern becomes more marked, and still more in senior high.

By that time the pupil has several different teachers of both sexes[14] teaching him different subjects, which are more or less formally organized into different courses—college preparatory and others. Furthermore, with the choice of "elective" subjects, the members of the class in one subject no longer need be exactly the same as in another, so the pupil is much more systematically exposed to association with different people, both adults and age-peers, in different contexts. Moreover, the school he attends is likely to be substantially larger than was his elementary school, and to draw from a wider geographical area. Hence the child is exposed to a wider range of statuses than before, being thrown in with more age-peers whom he does not encounter in his neighborhood; it is less likely that his parents will know the parents of any given child with whom he associates. It is thus my impression that the transitions to junior high and senior high school are apt to mean a considerable reshuffling of friendships. Another conspicuous difference between the elementary and secondary levels is the great increase in high school of organized extracurricular activities. Now, for the first time, organized athletics become important, as do a variety of clubs and associations which are school-sponsored and supervised to varying degrees.

Two particularly important shifts in the patterning of youth culture occur in this period. One, of course, is the emergence of more positive cross-sex relationships outside the classroom, through dances, dating, and the like. The other is the much sharper prestige-stratification of informal peer groupings, with indeed an element of snobbery which often exceeds that of the adult community in which the school exists.[15] Here it is important that though there is a broad correspondence between the prestige of friendship groups and the family status of their members, this, like the achievement order of the elementary school, is by no means a simple "mirroring" of the community stratification scale, for a considerable number of lower-status children get accepted into groups including members with higher family status than themselves. This stratified youth system operates as a genuine assortative mechanism; it does not simply reinforce ascribed status.

The prominence of this youth culture in the American secondary school is, in comparison with other societies, one of the hallmarks of the American educational system; it is much less prominent in most European systems. It may be said to constitute a kind of structural fusion between the school class and the peer-group structure of the elementary period. It seems clear that what I have called the "human relations" oriented contingent of the secondary school pupils

---

[14] Men make up about half (49 per cent) of the public secondary school instructional staff. *Biennial Survey of Education in the United States, 1954–56, op. cit.,* chap. ii, p. 7.

[15] See, for instance, C. W. Gordon, *The Social System of the High School: A Study in the Sociology of Adolescence* (Glencoe, Ill.: Free Press, 1957).

are more active and prominent in extracurricular activities, and that this is one of the main foci of their differentiation from the more impersonally- and technically-oriented contingent. The personal qualities figuring most prominently in the human relations contingent can perhaps be summed up as the qualities that make for "popularity." I suggest that, from the point of view of the secondary school's selective function, the youth culture helps to differentiate between types of personalities which will, by and large, play different kinds of roles as adults.

The stratification of youth groups has, as noted, a selective function; it is a bridge between the achievement order and the adult stratification system of the community. But it also has another function. It is a focus of prestige which exists along side of, and is to a degree independent of, the achievement order focussing on school work as such. The attainment of prestige in the informal youth group is itself a form of valued achievement. Hence, among those individuals destined for higher status in society, one can discern two broad types: those whose school work is more or less outstanding and whose informal prestige is relatively satisfactory; and vice versa, those whose informal prestige is outstanding, and school performance satisfactory. Falling below certain minima in either respect would jeopardize the child's claim to belong in the upper group.[16] It is an important point here that those clearly headed for college belong to peer groups which, while often depreciative of intensive concern with studies, also take for granted and reinforce a level of scholastic attainment which is necessary for admission to a good college. Pressure will be put on the individual who tends to fall below such a standard.

In discussing the elementary school level it will be remembered that we emphasized that the peer group served as an object of emotional dependency displaced from the family. In relation to the pressure for school achievement, therefore, it served at least partially as an expression of the lower-order motivational system *out* of which the child was in process of being socialized. On its own level, similar things can be said of the adolescent youth culture; it is in part an expression of regressive motivations. This is true of the emphasis on athletics despite its lack of relevance to adult roles, of the "homosexual" undertones of much intensive same-sex friendship, and of a certain "irresponsibility" in attitudes toward the opposite sex—e.g., the exploitative element in the attitudes of boys toward girls. This, however, is by no means the whole story. The youth culture is also a field for practicing the assumption of higher-order responsibilities, for conducting delicate human relations without immediate supervision and learning to accept the consequences. In this connection it is clearly of particular importance to the contingent we have spoken of as specializing in "human relations."

We can, perhaps, distinguish three different levels of crystallization of these

---

16 J. Riley, M. Riley, and M. Moore, "Adolescent Values and the Riesman Typology" in S. M. Lipset and L. Lowenthal (eds.), *The Sociology of Culture and the Analysis of Social Character* (Glencoe, Ill.: Free Press, 1960).

youth-culture patterns. The middle one is that which may be considered age-appropriate without clear status-differentiation. The two keynotes here seem to be "being a good fellow" in the sense of general friendliness and being ready to take responsibility in informal social situations where something needs to be done. Above this, we may speak of the higher level of "outstanding" popularity and qualities of "leadership" of the person who is turned to where unusual responsibilities are required. And below the middle level are the youth patterns bordering on delinquency, withdrawal, and generally unacceptable behavior. Only this last level is clearly "regressive" relative to expectations of appropriate behavior for the age-grade. In judging these three levels, however, allowance should be made for a good many nuances. Most adolescents do a certain amount of experimenting with the borderline of the unacceptable patterns; that they should do so is to be expected in view of the pressure toward independence from adults, and of the "collusion" which can be expected in the reciprocal stimulation of age-peers. The question is whether this regressive behavior comes to be confirmed into a major pattern for the personality as a whole. Seen in this perspective, it seems legitimate to maintain that the middle and the higher patterns indicated are the major ones, and that only a minority of adolescents comes to be confirmed in a truly unacceptable pattern of living. This minority may well be a relatively constant proportion of the age cohort, but apart from situations of special social disorganization, the available evidence does not suggest that it has been a progressively growing one in recent years.

The patterning of cross-sex relations in the youth culture clearly foreshadows future marriage and family formation. That it figures so prominently in school is related to the fact that in our society the element of ascription, including direct parental influence, in the choice of a marriage partner is strongly minimized. For the girl, it has the very important significance of reminding her that her adult status is going to be very much concerned with marriage and a family. This basic expectation for the girl stands in a certain tension to the school's curricular coeducation with its relative lack of differentiation by sex. But the extent to which the feminine role in American society continues to be anchored in marriage and the family should not be allowed to obscure the importance of coeducation. In the first place, the contribution of women in various extra-familial occupations and in community affairs has been rapidly increasing, and certainly higher levels of education have served as a prerequisite to this contribution. At the same time, it is highly important that the woman's familial role should not be regarded as drastically segregated from the cultural concerns of the society as a whole. The educated woman has important functions *as wife and mother,* particularly as an influence on her children in backing the schools and impressing on them the importance of education. It is, I think, broadly true that the immediate responsibility of women for family management has been increasing, though I am very skeptical of the alleged "abdication" of the American male. But precisely in the context of women's increased family responsibility, the influence of the mother both as agent of socialization and as role model is a crucial one. This influence should be evaluated in the light of the general upgrading process. It is very doubtful whether, apart from any other considerations, the motivational prerequisites of the general process could be sustained without sufficiently high education of the women who, as mothers, influence their children.

CONCLUSION

With the general cultural upgrading process in American society which has been going on for more than a century, the educational system has come to play an increasingly vital role. That this should be the case is, in my opinion, a consequence of the general trend to structural differentiation in the society. Relatively speaking, the school is a specialized agency. That it should increasingly have become the principal channel of selection as well as agency of socialization is in line with what one would expect in an increasingly differentiated and progressively more upgraded society. The legend of the "self-made man" has an element of nostalgic romanticism and is destined to become increasingly mythical, if by it is meant not just mobility from humble origins to high status, which does indeed continue to occur, but that the high status was attained through the "school of hard knocks" without the aid of formal education.

The structure of the public school system and the analysis of the ways in which it contributes both to the socialization of individuals and to their allocation to roles in society is, I feel, of vital concern to all students of American society. Notwithstanding the variegated elements in the situation, I think it has been possible to sketch out a few major structural patterns of the public school system and at least to suggest some ways in which they serve these important functions. What could be presented in this paper is the merest outline of such an analysis. It is, however, hoped that it has been carried far enough to suggest a field of vital mutual interest for social scientists on the one hand and those concerned with the actual operation of the schools on the other.

13. Sponsored and contest mobility and the school system*

RALPH H. TURNER

This paper suggests a framework for relating certain differences between American and English systems of education to the prevailing norms of upward mobility in each country. Others have noted the tendency of educational systems to support prevailing schemes of stratification, but this discussion concerns specifically the manner in which the *accepted mode of upward mobility* shapes the school system directly and indirectly through its effects on the values which implement social control.

Two ideal-typical normative patterns of upward mobility are described and their ramifications in the general patterns of stratification and social control are suggested. In addition to showing relationships among a number of differences between American and English schooling, the ideal-types have broader implications than those developed in this paper: they suggest a major dimension of stratification which might be profitably incorporated into a variety of studies in social class; and they readily can be applied in further comparisons between other countries.

THE NATURE OF ORGANIZING NORMS

Many investigators have concerned themselves with rates of upward mobility in specific countries or internationally,[1] and with the manner in which school

---

*From *American Sociological Review,* Vol. 25 (December, 1960), pp. 855–67.

This is an expanded version of a paper presented at the Fourth World Congress of Sociology, 1959, and abstracted in the *Transactions* of the Congress. Special indebtedness should be expressed to Jean Floud and Hilde Himmelweit for helping to acquaint the author with the English school system.

[1] A comprehensive summary of such studies appears in Seymour M. Lipset and Reinhard Bendix, *Social Mobility in Industrial Society* (Berkeley and Los Angeles: University of California Press, 1959).

systems facilitate or impede such mobility.[2] But preoccupation with the *extent* of mobility has precluded equal attention to the predominant *modes* of mobility. The central assumption underlying this paper is that within a formally open class system that provides for mass education the organizing folk norm which defines the accepted mode of upward mobility is a crucial factor in shaping the school system, and may be even more crucial than the extent of upward mobility. In England and the United States there appear to be different organizing folk norms, here termed *sponsored mobility* and *contest mobility,* respectively. *Contest* mobility is a system in which elite[3] status is the prize in an open contest and is taken by the aspirants' own efforts. While the "contest" is governed by some rules of fair play, the contestants have wide latitude in the strategies they may employ. Since the "prize" of successful upward mobility is not in the hands of an established elite to give out, the latter cannot determine who shall attain it and who shall not. Under *sponsored* mobility elite recruits are chosen by the established elite or their agents, and elite status is *given* on the basis of some criterion of supposed merit and cannot be *taken* by any amount of effort or strategy. Upward mobility is like entry into a private club where each candidate must be "sponsored" by one or more of the members. Ultimately the members grant or deny upward mobility on the basis of whether they judge the candidate to have those qualities they wish to see in fellow members.

Before elaborating this distinction, it should be noted that these systems of mobility are ideal types designed to clarify observed differences in the predominantly similar English and American systems of stratification and education. But as organizing norms these principles are assumed to be present at least implicitly in people's thinking, guiding their judgments of what is appropriate on many specific matters. Such organizing norms do not correspond perfectly with the objective characteristics of the societies in which they exist, nor are they completely independent of them. From the complex interplay of social and economic conditions and ideologies people in a society develop a highly simplified conception of the way in which events take place. This conception of the "natural" is translated into a norm—the "natural" becomes what "ought" to be—and in turn imposes a strain toward consistency upon relevant aspects of the society. Thus the norm acts back upon the objective conditions to which it refers and has

---

[2] *Cf.* C. A. Anderson, "The Social Status of University Students in Relation to Type of Economy: An International Comparison," *Transactions of the Third World Congress of Sociology,* London, 1956, Vol. V, pp. 51–63; J. E. Floud, *Social Class and Educational Opportunity* (London: Heinemann, 1956); W. L. Warner, R. J. Havighurst, and M. B. Loeb, *Who Shall Be Educated?* (New York: Harper, 1944).

[3] Reference is made throughout the paper to "elite" and "masses." The generalizations, however, are intended to apply throughout the stratification continuum to relations between members of a given class and the class or classes above it. Statements about mobility are intended in general to apply to mobility from manual to middle-class levels, lower-middle to upper-middle class, and so on, as well as into the strictly elite groups. The simplified expressions avoid the repeated use of cumbersome and involved statements which might otherwise be required.

ramifying effects upon directly and indirectly related features of the society.[4]

In brief, the conception of an ideal-typical organizing norm involves the following propositions: (1) The ideal types are not fully exemplified in practice since they are normative systems, and no normative system can be devised so as to cope with all empirical exigencies. (2) Predominant norms usually compete with less ascendant norms engendered by changes and inconsistencies in the underlying social structure. (3) Though not fully explicit, organizing folk norms are reflected in specific value judgments. Those judgments which the relevant people regard as having a convincing ring to them, irrespective of the logic expressed, or which seem to require no extended argumentation may be presumed to reflect the prevailing folk norms. (4) The predominant organizing norms in one segment of society are functionally related to those in other segments.

Two final qualifications concerning the scope of this paper: First, the organizing folk norm of upward mobility affects the school system because one of the latter's functions is the facilitation of mobility. Since this is only one of several social functions of the school, and not the most important function in the societies under examination, only a very partial accounting of the whole set of forces making for similarities and differences in the school systems of United States and England is possible here. Only those differences which directly or indirectly reflect the performance of the mobility function are noted. Second, the concern of this paper is with the current dynamics of the situation in the two countries rather than with their historical development.

DISTINCTIONS BETWEEN THE TWO NORMS

Contest mobility is like a sporting event in which many compete for a few recognized prizes. The contest is judged to be fair only if all the players compete on an equal footing. Victory must be won solely by one's own efforts. The most satisfactory outcome is not necessarily a victory of the most able, but of the most deserving. The tortoise who defeats the hare is a folk-prototype of the deserving sportsman. Enterprise, initiative, perseverance, and craft are admirable qualities if they allow the person who is initially at a disadvantage to triumph. Even clever manipulation of the rules may be admired if it helps the contestant who is smaller or less muscular or less rapid to win. Applied to mobility, the contest norm means that victory by a person of moderate intelligence accomplished through the use of common sense, craft, enterprise, daring, and success-

---

[4] The normative element in an organizing norm goes beyond Max Weber's *ideal type*, conveying more of the sense of Durkheim's *collective representation; cf.* Ralph H. Turner, "The Normative Coherence of Folk Concepts," *Research Studies of the State College of Washington*, 25 (1957), pp. 127–36. Charles Wagley has developed a similar concept which he calls "ideal pattern" in his as yet unpublished work on Brazilian kinship. See also Howard Becker, "Constructive Typology in the Social Sciences," *American Sociological Review,* 5 (February, 1940), pp. 40–55.

ful risk-taking[5] is more appreciated than victory by the most intelligent or the best educated.

Sponsored mobility, in contrast, rejects the pattern of the contest and favors a controlled selection process. In this process the elite or their agents, deemed to be best qualified to judge merit, choose individuals for elite status who have the appropriate qualities. Individuals do not win or seize elite status; mobility is rather a process of sponsored induction into the elite.

Pareto had this sort of mobility in mind when he suggested that a governing class might dispose of persons potentially dangerous to it by admitting them to elite membership, provided that the recruits change character by adopting elite attitudes and interests.[6] Danger to the ruling class would seldom be the major criterion for choice of elite recruits. But Pareto assumed that the established elite would select whom they wished to enter their ranks and would inculcate the attitudes and interests of the established elite in the recruits.

The governing objective of contest mobility is to give elite status to those who earn it, while the goal of sponsored mobility is to make the best use of the talents in society by sorting persons into their proper niches. In different societies the conditions of competitive struggle may reward quite different attributes, and sponsored mobility may select individuals on the basis of such diverse qualities as intelligence or visionary capability, but the difference in principle remains the same.[7]

Under the contest system society at large establishes and interprets the criteria of elite status. If one wishes to have his status recognized he must display certain credentials which identify his class to those about him. The credentials must be highly visible and require no special skill for their assessment, since credentials are presented to the masses. Material possession and mass popularity are altogether appropriate credentials in this respect, and any special skill which produces a tangible product and which can easily be assessed by the untrained will do. The nature of sponsored mobility precludes these procedures, but assigns to credentials instead the function of identifying elite members to one another.[8]

---

[5] Geoffrey Gorer remarks on the favorable evaluation of the successful gamble in American culture: "Gambling is also a respected and important component in many business ventures. Conspicuous improvement in a man's financial position is generally attributed to a lucky combination of industry, skill, and gambling, though the successful gambler prefers to refer to his gambling as 'vision.'" *The American People* (New York: Norton, 1948), p. 178.

[6] Vilfredo Pareto, *The Mind and Society* (New York: Harcourt, Brace, 1935), Vol. 4, p. 1796.

[7] Many writers have noted that different kinds of societies facilitate the rise of different kinds of personalities, either in the stratification hierarchy or in other ways. *Cf.* Jessie Bernard, *American Community Behavior* (New York: Dryden, 1949), p. 205. A particularly interesting statement is Martindale's exploration of "favored personality" types in sacred and secular societies. Don Martindale and Elio Monachesi, *Elements of Sociology* (New York: Harper, 1951), pp. 312–78.

[8] At one time in the United States a good many owners of expensive British Jaguar automobiles carried large signs on the cars identifying the make. Such a display would have been unthinkable under a sponsored mobility system since the Jaguar owner would not care for the esteem of persons too uninformed to tell a Jaguar from a less prestigious automobile.

Accordingly, the ideal credentials are special skills that require the trained discrimination of the elite for their recognition. In this case, intellectual, literary, or artistic excellencies, which can be appraised only by those trained to appreciate them, are fully suitable credentials. Concentration on such skills lessens the likelihood that an interloper will succeed in claiming the right to elite membership on grounds of the popular evaluation of his competence.

In the sporting event there is special admiration for the slow starter who makes a dramatic finish, and many of the rules are designed to insure that the race should not be declared over until it has run its full course. Contest mobility incorporates this disapproval of premature judgments and of anything that gives special advantage to those who are ahead at any point in the race. Under sponsored mobility, fairly early selection of only the number of persons necessary to fill anticipated vacancies in the elite is desirable. Early selection allows time to prepare the recruits for their elite position. Aptitudes, inherent capacities, and spiritual gifts can be assessed fairly early in life by techniques ranging from divination to the most sophisticated psychological test, and the more naive the subjects at the time of selection the less likely are their talents to be blurred by differential learning or conspiracy to defeat the test. Since elitists take the initiative in training recruits, they are more interested in the latters' capabilities than in what they will do with them on their own, and they are concerned that no one else should first have an opportunity to train the recruits' talents in the wrong direction. Contest mobility tends to delay the final award as long as practicable to permit a fair race; sponsored mobility tends to place the time of recruitment as early in life as practicable to insure control over selection and training.

Systems of sponsored mobility develop most readily in societies with but a single elite or with a recognized elite hierarchy. When multiple elites compete among themselves the mobility process tends to take the contest pattern, since no group is able to command control of recruitment. Sponsored mobility further depends upon a social structure that fosters monopoly of elite credentials. Lack of such monopoly undercuts sponsorship and control of the recruitment process. Monopoly of credentials in turn is typically a product of societies with well entrenched traditional aristocracies employing such credentials as family line and bestowable title which are intrinsically subject to monopoly, or of societies organized on large-scale bureaucratic lines permitting centralized control of upward social movement.

English society has been described as the juxtaposition of two systems of stratification, the urban industrial class system and the surviving aristocratic system. While the sponsored mobility pattern reflects the logic of the latter, our impression is that it pervades popular thinking rather than merely coexisting with the logic of industrial stratification. Patterns imported into an established culture tend to be reshaped, as they are assimilated, into consistency with the established culture. Thus it may be that changes in stratification associated with industrialization have led to alterations in the rates, the specific means, and the rules of mobility, but that these changes have been guided by the but lightly challenged organizing norm of sponsored mobility.

SOCIAL CONTROL AND THE TWO NORMS

Every society must cope with the problem of maintaining loyalty to its social system and does so in part through norms and values, only some of which vary by class position. Norms and values especially prevalent within a given class must direct behavior into channels that support the total system, while those that transcend strata must support the general class differential. The way in which upward mobility takes place determines in part the kinds of norms and values that serve the indicated purposes of social control in each class and throughout the society.

The most conspicuous control problem is that of ensuring loyalty in the disadvantaged classes toward a system in which their members receive less than a proportional share of society's goods. In a system of contest mobility this is accomplished by a combination of futuristic orientation, the norm of ambition, and a general sense of fellowship with the elite. Each individual is encouraged to think of himself as competing for an elite position so that loyalty to the system and conventional attitudes are cultivated in the process of preparation for this possibility. It is essential that this futuristic orientation be kept alive by delaying a sense of final irreparable failure to reach elite status until attitudes are well established. By thinking of himself in the successful future the elite aspirant forms considerable identification with elitists, and evidence that they are merely ordinary human beings like himself helps to reinforce this identification as well as to keep alive the conviction that he himself may someday succeed in like manner. To forestall rebellion among the disadvantaged majority, then, a contest system must avoid absolute points of selection for mobility and immobility and must delay clear recognition of the realities of the situation until the individual is too committed to the system to change radically. A futuristic orientation cannot, of course, be inculcated successfully in all members of lower strata, but sufficient internalization of a norm of ambition tends to leave the unambitious as individual deviants and to forestall the latters' formation of a genuine subcultural group able to offer collective threat to the established system. Where this kind of control system operates rather effectively it is notable that organized or gang deviancy is more likely to take the form of an attack upon the conventional or moral order rather than upon the class system itself. Thus the United States has its "beatniks"[9] who repudiate ambition and most worldly values and its delinquent and criminal gangs who try to evade the limitations imposed by conventional means,[10] but very few active revolutionaries.

These social controls are inappropriate in a system of sponsorship since the

---

[9] See, e.g., Lawrence Lipton, *The Holy Barbarians* (New York: Messner, 1959).

[10] *Cf.* Albert K. Cohen, *Delinquent Boys: The Culture of the Gang* (Glencoe, Ill.: Free Press, 1955).

elite recruits are chosen from above. The principal threat to the system would lie in the existence of a strong group the members of whom sought to *take* elite positions themselves. Control under this system is maintained by training the "masses" to regard themselves as relatively incompetent to manage society, by restricting access to the skills and manners of the elite, and by cultivating belief in the superior competence of the elite. The earlier that selection of the elite recruits is made the sooner others can be taught to accept their inferiority and to make "realistic" rather than phantasy plans. Early selection prevents raising the hopes of large numbers of people who might otherwise become the discontented leaders of a class challenging the sovereignty of the established elite. If it is assumed that the difference in competence between masses and elite is seldom so great as to support the usual differences in the advantages accruing to each,[11] then the differences must be artificially augmented by discouraging acquisition of elite skills by the masses. Thus a sense of mystery about the elite is a common device for supporting in the masses the illusion of a much greater hiatus of competence than in fact exists.

While elitists are unlikely to reject a system that benefits them, they must still be restrained from taking such advantage of their favorable situation as to jeopardize the entire elite. Under the sponsorship system the elite recruits—who are selected early, freed from the strain of competitive struggle, and kept under close supervision—may be thoroughly indoctrinated in elite culture. A norm of paternalism toward inferiors may be inculcated, a heightened sensitivity to the good opinion of fellow elitists and elite recruits may be cultivated, and the appreciation of the more complex forms of aesthetic, literary, intellectual, and sporting activities may be taught. Norms of courtesy and altruism easily can be maintained under sponsorship since elite recruits are not required to compete for their standing and since the elite may deny high standing to those who strive for position by "unseemly" methods. The system of sponsorship provides an almost perfect setting for the development of an elite culture characterized by a sense of responsibility for "inferiors" and for preservation of the "finer things" of life.

Elite control in the contest system is more difficult since there is no controlled induction and apprenticeship. The principal regulation seems to lie in the insecurity of elite position. In a sense there is no "final arrival" because each person may be displaced by newcomers throughout his life. The limited control of high standing from above prevents the clear delimitation of levels in the class system, so that success itself becomes relative: each success, rather than an accomplishment, serves to qualify the participant for competition at the next higher level.[12] The restraints upon the behavior of a person of high standing, therefore, are principally those applicable to a contestant who must not risk the

---

[11] D. V. Glass, editor, *Social Mobility in Britain* (Glencoe, Ill.: Free Press, 1954), pp. 144–45, reports studies showing only small variations in intelligence between occupational levels.

[12] Gorer, *op. cit.*, pp. 172–87.

"ganging up" of other contestants, and who must pay some attention to the masses who are frequently in a position to impose penalties upon him. But any special norm of paternalism is hard to establish since there is no dependable procedure for examining the means by which one achieves elite credentials. While mass esteem is an effective brake upon over-exploitation of position, it rewards scrupulously ethical and altruistic behavior much less than evidence of fellow-feeling with the masses themselves.

Under both systems, unscrupulous or disreputable persons may become or remain members of the elite, but for different reasons. In contest mobility, popular tolerance of a little craftiness in the successful newcomer, together with the fact that he does not have to undergo the close scrutiny of the old elite, leaves considerable leeway for unscrupulous success. In sponsored mobility, the unpromising recruit reflects unfavorably on the judgments of his sponsors and threatens the myth of elite omniscience; consequently he may be tolerated and others may "cover up" for his deficiencies in order to protect the unified front of the elite to the outer world.

Certain of the general values and norms of any society reflect emulation of elite values by the masses. Under sponsored mobility, a good deal of the protective attitudes toward and interest in classical subjects percolates to the masses. Under contest mobility, however, there is not the same degree of homogeneity of moral, aesthetic, and intellectual values to be emulated, so that the conspicuous attribute of the elite is its high level of material consumption—emulation itself follows this course. There is neither effective incentive nor punishment for the elitist who fails to interest himself in promoting the arts or literary excellence, or who continues to maintain the vulgar manners and mode of speech of his class origin. The elite has relatively less power and the masses relatively more power to punish or reward a man for his adoption or disregard of any special elite culture. The great importance of accent and of grammatical excellence in the attainment of high status in England as contrasted with the twangs and drawls and grammatical ineptitude among American elites is the most striking example of this difference. In a contest system, the class order does not function to support the *quality* of aesthetic, literary, and intellectual activities; only those well versed in such matters are qualified to distinguish authentic products from cheap imitations. Unless those who claim superiority in these areas are forced to submit their credentials to the elite for evaluation, poor quality is often honored equally with high quality and class prestige does not serve to maintain an effective norm of high quality.

This is not to imply that there are no groups in a "contest" society devoted to the protection and fostering of high standards in art, music, literature, and intellectual pursuits, but that such standards lack the support of the class system which is frequently found when sponsored mobility prevails. In California, the selection by official welcoming committees of a torch singer to entertain a visiting king and queen and "can-can" dancers to entertain Mr. Khrushchev illustrates how American elites can assume that high prestige and popular taste go together.

FORMAL EDUCATION

Returning to the conception of an organizing ideal norm, we assume that to the extent to which one such norm of upward mobility is prevalent in a society there are constant strains to shape the educational system into conformity with that norm. These strains operate in two fashions: directly, by blinding people to alternatives and coloring their judgments of successful and unsuccessful solutions to recurring educational problems; indirectly, through the functional interrelationships between school systems and the class structure, systems of social control, and other features of the social structure which are neglected in this paper.

The most obvious application of the distinction between sponsored and contest mobility norms affords a partial explanation for the different policies of student selection in the English and American secondary schools. Although American high school students follow different courses of study and a few attend specialized schools, a major educational preoccupation has been to avoid any sharp social separation between the superior and inferior students and to keep the channels of movement between courses of study as open as possible. Recent criticisms of the way in which superior students may be thereby held back in their development usually are nevertheless qualified by the insistence that these students must not be withdrawn from the mainstream of student life.[13] Such segregation offends the sense of fairness implicit in the contest norm and also arouses the fear that the elite and future elite will lose their sense of fellowship with the masses. Perhaps the most important point, however, is that schooling is presented as an opportunity, and making use of it depends primarily on the student's own initiative and enterprise.

The English system has undergone a succession of liberalizing changes during this century, but all of them have retained the attempt to sort out early in the educational program the promising from the unpromising so that the former may be segregated and given a special form of training to fit them for higher standing in their adult years. Under the Education Act of 1944, a minority of students has been selected each year by means of a battery of examinations popularly known as "eleven plus," supplemented in varying degrees by grade school records and personal interviews, for admission to grammar schools.[14] The remaining students attend secondary modern or technical schools in which the

---

[13] See, e.g., *Los Angeles Times,* May 4, 1959, Part I, p. 24.

[14] The nature and operation of the "eleven plus" system are fully reviewed in a report by a committee of the British Psychological Society and in a report of extensive research into the adequacy of selection methods. See P. E. Vernon (ed.), *Secondary School Selection: A British Psychological Inquiry* (London: Methuen, 1957); and Alfred Yates and D. A. Pidgeon, *Admission to Grammar Schools* (London: Newnes Educational Publishing Co., 1957).

opportunities to prepare for college or to train for the more prestigeful occupations are minimal. The grammar schools supply what by comparative standards is a high quality of college preparatory education. Of course, such a scheme embodies the logic of sponsorship, with early selection of those destined for middle-class and higher-status occupations, and specialized training to prepare each group for its destined class position. This plan facilitates considerable mobility, and recent research reveals surprisingly little bias against children from manual laboring-class families in the selection for grammar school, when related to measured intelligence.[15] It is altogether possible that adequate comparative study would show a closer correlation of school success with measured intelligence and a lesser correlation between school success and family background in England than in the United States. While selection of superior students for mobility opportunity is probably more efficient under such a system, the obstacles for persons not so selected of "making the grade" on the basis of their own initiative or enterprise are probably correspondingly greater.

That the contrasting effects of the two systems accord with the social control patterns under the two mobility norms is indicated by studies of student ambitions in the United States and in England. Researches in the United States consistently show that the general level of occupational aspiration reported by high school students is quite unrealistic in relation to the actual distribution of job opportunities. Comparative study in England shows much less "phantasy" aspiration, and specifically indicates a reduction in aspirations among students not selected following the "eleven-plus" examination.[16] One of the by-products of the sponsorship system is the fact that at least some students from middle-class families whose parents cannot afford to send them to private schools suffer severe personal adjustment problems when they are assigned to secondary modern schools on the basis of this selection procedure.[17]

This well-known difference between the British sorting at an early age of students into grammar and modern schools and the American comprehensive high school and junior college is the clearest application of the distinction under discussion. But the organizing norms penetrate more deeply into the school systems than is initially apparent. The most telling observation regarding the direct normative operation of these principles would be evidence to support the author's impression that major critics of educational procedures within each country do not usually transcend the logic of their respective mobility norms. Thus the British debate about the best method for getting people sorted accord-

---

[15] J. E. Floud, A. H. Halsey, and F. M. Martin, *Social Class and Educational Opportunity* (London: Heinemann, 1956).

[16] Mary D. Wilson documents the reduction in aspirations characterizing students in British secondary modern schools and notes the contrast with American studies revealing much more "unrealistic" aspirations; see "The Vocational Preferences of Secondary Modern School-children," *British Journal of Educational Psychology*, 23 (1953), pp. 97–113. See also Ralph H. Turner, "The Changing Ideology of Success," *Transactions of the Third World Congress of Sociology, 1956*, London, Vol. V, esp. p. 37.

[17] Pointed out by Hilde Himmelweit in private communication.

ing to ability, without proposing that elite station should be open to whosoever can ascend to it. Although fear of "sputnik" in the United States introduced a flurry of suggestions for sponsored mobility schemes, the long-standing concern of school critics has been the failure to motivate students adequately. Preoccupation with motivation appears to be an intellectual application of the folk idea that people should *win* their station in society by personal enterprise.

The functional operation of a strain toward consistency with the organizing norms of upward mobility may be illustrated by several other features of the school systems in the two countries. First, the value placed upon education itself differs under the two norms. Under sponsored mobility, schooling is valued for its cultivation of elite culture, and those forms of schooling directed toward such cultivation are more highly valued than others. Education of the non-elite is difficult to justify clearly and tends to be half-hearted, while maximum educational resources are concentrated on "those who can benefit most from them"— in practice, this means those who can learn the elite culture. The secondary modern schools in England have regularly suffered from less adequate financial provision, a higher student-teacher ratio, fewer well trained teachers, and a general lack of prestige in comparison with the grammar schools.[18]

Under contest mobility in the United States, education is valued as a means of getting ahead, but the contents of education are not highly valued in their own right. Over a century ago Tocqueville commented on the absence of an hereditary class "by which the labors of the intellect are held in honor." He remarked that consequently a "middling standard is fixed in America for human knowledge." [19] And there persists in some measure the suspicion of the educated man as one who may have gotten ahead without really earning his position. In spite of recent criticisms of lax standards in American schools, it is in keeping with the general mobility pattern that a Gallup Poll taken in April, 1958, reports that school principals are much more likely to make such criticisms than parents. While 90 per cent of the principals thought that ". . . our schools today demand too little work from the students," only 51 per cent of the parents thought so, with 33 per cent saying that the work was about right and six per cent that schools demanded too much work.[20]

Second, the logic of preparation for a contest prevails in United States schools, and emphasizes keeping everyone in the running until the final stages. In primary and secondary schools the assumption tends to be made that those who are

---

[18] Less adequate financial provision and a higher student-teacher ratio are mentioned as obstacles to parity of secondary modern schools with grammar schools in *The Times Educational Supplement,* February 22, 1957, p. 241. On difficulties in achieving prestige comparable with grammar schools, see G. Baron, "Secondary Education in Britain: Some Present-Day Trends," *Teachers College Record,* 57 (January, 1956), pp. 211–21; and O. Banks, *Parity and Prestige in English Secondary Education* (London: Routledge and Kegan Paul, 1955). See also Vernon, *op. cit.,* pp. 19–22.

[19] Alexis de Tocqueville, *Democracy in America* (New York: Knopf, 1945), Vol. I, p. 52.

[20] An earlier Gallup Poll had disclosed that 62 per cent of the parents opposed stiffened college entrance requirements while only 27 per cent favored them. Reported in *Time,* April 14, 1958, p. 45.

learning satisfactorily need little special attention while the less successful require help to be sure that they remain in the contest and may compete for the
final stakes. As recently as December, 1958, a nationwide Gallup Poll gave
evidence that this attitude had not been radically altered by the international
situation. When asked whether or not teachers should devote extra time to the
bright students, 26 per cent of the respondents replied "yes" and 67 per cent,
"no." But the responses changed to 86 per cent "yes" and only nine per cent
"no" when the question was asked concerning "slow students."[21]

In western states the junior college offers many students a "second chance"
to qualify for university, and all state universities have some provision for sub-
standard high school students to earn admission.

The university itself is run like the true contest: standards are set competi-
tively, students are forced to pass a series of trials each semester, and only a
minority of the entrants achieve the prize of graduation. This pattern contrasts
sharply with the English system in which selection is supposed to be relatively
complete before entrance to university, and students may be subject to no
testing whatsoever for the first year or more of university study. Although
university completion rates have not been estimated accurately in either country,
some figures are indicative of the contrast. In American institutions of higher
learning in 1957–1958, the ratio of bachelor's and first-professional degrees to
the number of first-time degree-credit enrollments in the fall four years earlier
was reported to be .610 for men and .488 for women.[22] The indicated 39 and
51 per cent drop-out rates are probably underestimates because transfers from
two-year junior colleges swell the number of degrees without being included in
first-time enrollments. In England, a study of the careers of individual students
reports that in University College, London, almost 82 per cent of entering students between 1948 and 1951 eventually graduated with a degree. A similar
study a few years earlier at the University of Liverpool shows a comparative
figure of almost 87 per cent.[23] Under contest mobility, the object is to train as
many as possible in the skills necessary for elite status so as to give everyone a
chance to maintain competition at the highest pitch. Under sponsored mobility,
the objective is to indoctrinate elite culture in only those presumably who will
enter the elite, lest there grow a dangerous number of "angry young men" who
have elite skills without elite station.

Third, systems of mobility significantly affect educational content. Induction
into elite culture under sponsored mobility is consistent with an emphasis on
school *esprit de corps* which is employed to cultivate norms of intra-class loyalty
and elite tastes and manners. Similarly, formal schooling built about highly

---

[21] Reported in the *Los Angeles Times,* December 17, 1958, Part I, p. 16.

[22] U.S. Department of Health, Education, and Welfare, Office of Education, *Earned Degrees Conferred by Higher Education Institutions, 1957–1958* (Washington, D.C.: Government Printing Office, 1959), p. 3.

[23] Nicholas Malleson, "Student Performance at University College, London, 1948–1951," *Universities Quarterly,* 12 (May, 1958), pp. 288–319.

specialized study in fields wholly of intellectual or aesthetic concern and of no "practical" value serves the purpose of elite culture. Under contest mobility in the United States, in spite of frequent faculty endorsement of "liberal education," schooling tends to be evaluated in terms of its practical benefits and to become, beyond the elementary level, chiefly vocational. Education does not so much provide what is good in itself as those skills, especially vocational skills, presumed to be necessary in the competition for the real prizes of life.

These contrasts are reflected in the different national attitudes toward university students who are gainfully employed while in school. More students in the United States than in Britain are employed part-time, and relatively fewer of the American students receive subsidies toward subsistence and living expenses. The most generous programs of state aid in the United States, except those applying to veterans and other special groups, do not normally cover expenses other than tuition and institutional fees. British maintenance grants are designed to cover full living expenses, taking into account parental ability to pay.[24] Under sponsored mobility, gainful employment serves no apprenticeship or testing function, and is thought merely to prevent students from gaining the full benefit of their schooling. L. J. Parry speaks of the general opposition to student employment and asserts that English university authorities almost unanimously hold that "... if a person must work for financial reasons, he should never spend more than four weeks on such work during the whole year."[25]

Under contest mobility, success in school work is not viewed as a sufficient test of practical merit, but must be supplemented by a test in the world of practical affairs. Thus in didactic folk tales the professional engineer also proves himself to be a superior mechanic, the business tycoon a skillful behind-the-counter salesman. By "working his way through school" the enterprising student "earns" his education in the fullest sense, keeps in touch with the practical world, and gains an apprenticeship into vocational life. Students are often urged to seek part-time employment, even when there is no financial need, and in some instances schools include paid employment as a requirement for graduation. As one observer describes the typical American view, a student willing to work part-time is a "better bet" than "the equally bright student who receives all of his financial support from others."[26]

Finally, training in "social adjustment" is peculiar to the system of contest mobility. The reason for this emphasis is clear when it is understood that adjustment training presumably prepares students to cope with situations for which there are no rules of intercourse or for which the rules are unknown, but in which the good opinions of others cannot be wholly ignored. Under sponsored

---

[24] See, e.g., C. A. Quattlebaum, *Federal Aid to Students for Higher Education,* Washington, D.C.: Government Printing Office, 1956; and "Grants to Students: University and Training Colleges," *The Times Educational Supplement,* May 6, 1955, p. 446.

[25] "Students' Expenses," *The Times Educational Supplement,* May 6, 1955, p. 447.

[26] R. H. Eckelberry, "College Jobs for College Students," *Journal of Higher Education,* 27 (March, 1956), p. 174.

mobility, elite recruits are inducted into a homogeneous stratum within which there is consensus regarding the rules, and within which they succeed socially by mastering these rules. Under contest mobility, the elite aspirant must relate himself both to the established elite and to the masses, who follow different rules, and the elite itself is not sufficiently homogeneous to evolve consensual rules of intercourse. Furthermore, in the contest the rules may vary according to the background of the competitor, so that each aspirant must successfully deal with persons playing the game with slightly different rules. Consequently, adjustment training is increasingly considered to be one of the important skills imparted by the school system.[27] That the emphasis on such training has had genuine popular support is indicated by a 1945 *Fortune* poll in which a national sample of adults was asked to select the one or two things that would be very important for a son of theirs to get out of college. Over 87 per cent chose "Ability to get along with and understand people;" and this answer was the second most frequently chosen as the *very* most important thing to get out of college.[28] In this respect, British education may provide better preparation for participation in an orderly and controlled world, while American education may prepare students more adequately for a less ordered situation. The reputedly superior ability of "Yankees" to get things done seems to imply such ability.

To this point the discussion has centered on the tax-supported school systems in both countries, but the different place and emphasis of the privately supported secondary schools can also be related to the distinction between sponsored and contest mobility. Since private secondary schools in both countries are principally vehicles for transmitting the marks of high family status, their mobility function is quite tangential. Under contest mobility, the private schools presumably should have little or no mobility function. On the other hand, if there is to be mobility in a sponsored system, the privately controlled school populated largely with the children of elite parents would be the ideal device through which to induct selectees from lower levels into elite status. By means of a scholarship program, promising members of lesser classes could be chosen early for recruitment. The English "public" schools, in fact, have incorporated into their charters provisions to insure that a few boys from lesser classes will enter each year. Getting one's child into a "public" school, or even into one of the less prestigeful private schools, assumes an importance in England relatively unknown in the United States. If the children cannot win scholarships the parents often make extreme financial sacrifices in order to pay the cost of this relatively exclusive education.[29]

How much of a role private secondary schools have played in mobility in

[27] Adjustment training is not a necessary accompaniment of contest mobility. The shift during the last half century toward the increased importance of social acceptability as an elite credential has brought such training into correspondingly greater prominence.

[28] Reported in Hadley Cantril (ed.), *Public Opinion 1935-1946* (Princeton: Princeton University Press, 1951), p. 186.

[29] For one account of the place of "public" schools in the English educational system, see Dennis Brogan, *The English People* (New York: Knopf, 1943), pp. 18–56.

either country is difficult to determine. American studies of social mobility usually omit information on private *versus* tax-supported secondary school attendance, and English studies showing the advantage of "public" school attendance generally fail to distinguish between the mobile and the nonmobile in this respect. However, during the nineteenth century the English "public" schools were used by *nouveaux riches* members of the manufacturing classes to enable their sons to achieve unqualified elite status.[30] In one sense, the rise of the manufacturing classes through free enterprise introduced a large measure of contest mobility which threatened to destroy the traditional sponsorship system. But by using the "public" schools in this fashion they bowed to the legitimacy of the traditional system—an implicit acknowledgement that upward mobility was not complete without sponsored induction. Dennis Brogan speaks of the task of the "public" schools in the nineteenth century as "the job of marrying the old English social order to the new."[31]

With respect to mobility, the parallel between the tax-supported grammar schools and the "public" schools in England is of interest. The former in important respects have been patterned after the latter, adopting their view of mobility but making it a much larger part of their total function. Generally the grammar schools are the vehicle for sponsored mobility throughout the middle ranges of the class system, modelled after the pattern of the "public" schools which remain the agencies for sponsored mobility into the elite.

EFFECTS OF MOBILITY ON PERSONALITY

Brief note may be made of the importance of the distinction between sponsored and contest mobility with relation to the supposed effects of upward mobility on personality development. Not a great deal is yet known about the "mobile personality" nor about the specific features of importance to the personality in the mobility experience.[32] However, today three aspects of this experience are most frequently stressed: first, the stress or tension involved in striving for status higher than that of others under more difficult conditions than they; second, the complication of interpersonal relations introduced by the necessity to abandon lower-level friends in favor of uncertain acceptance into higher-level circles; third, the problem of working out an adequate personal scheme of values in the face of movement between classes marked by somewhat variant or even contradictory value systems.[33] The impact of each of these three

[30] A. H. Halsey of Birmingham University has called my attention to the importance of this fact.

[31] *Op. cit.*, pp. 24–25.

[32] *Cf.* Lipset and Bendix, *op. cit.*, pp. 250 ff.

[33] See, e.g., August B. Hollingshead and Frederick C. Redlich, *Social Class and Mental Illness* (New York: Wiley, 1958); W. Lloyd Warner and James C. Abegglen, *Big Business Leaders in America* (New York: Harper, 1955); Warner *et al.*, *Who Shall Be Educated? op. cit.*; Peter M. Blau, "Social Mobility and Interpersonal Relations," *American Sociological Review*, 21 (June, 1956), pp. 290–300.

mobility problems, it is suggested, differs depending upon whether the pattern is that of the contest or of sponsorship.

Under the sponsorship system, recruits are selected early, segregated from their class peers, grouped with other recruits and with youth from the class to which they are moving, and trained specifically for membership in this class. Since the selection is made early, the mobility experience should be relatively free from the strain that comes with a series of elimination tests and long-extended uncertainty of success. The segregation and the integrated group life of the "public" school or grammar school should help to clarify the mobile person's social ties. (One investigator failed to discover clique formation along lines of social class in a sociometric study of a number of grammar schools.[34]) The problem of a system of values may be largely met when the elite recruit is taken from his parents and peers to be placed in a boarding school, though it may be less well clarified for the grammar school boy who returns each evening to his working-class family. Undoubtedly this latter limitation has something to do with the observed failure of working-class boys to continue through the last years of grammar school and into the universities.[35] In general, then, the factors stressed as affecting personality formation among the upwardly mobile probably are rather specific to the contest system, or to incompletely functioning sponsorship system.

It is often taken for granted that there is convincing evidence to show that mobility-oriented students in American secondary schools suffer from the tendency for cliques to form along lines predetermined by family background. These tendencies are statistically quite moderate, however, leaving much room for individual exceptions. Furthermore, mobility-oriented students usually have not been studied separately to discover whether or not they are incorporated into higher-level cliques in contrast to the general rule. Nor is it adequately demonstrated that the purported working-class value system, at odds with middle-class values, is as pervasive and constraining throughout the working class as it is conspicuous in many delinquent gangs. The model of contest mobility suggests, then, that there is more serious and continuing strain over the uncertainty of attaining mobility, more explicit and continued preoccupation with the problem of changing friendships, and more contradictory learning to inhibit the acquisition of a value system appropriate to the class of aspiration than under sponsored mobility. But the extent and implications of these differences require fuller understanding of the American class system. A search for personality-forming experiences specific to a sponsorship system, such as the British, has yet to be made.

---

[34] A. N. Oppenheim, "Social Status and Clique Formation among Grammar School Boys," *British Journal of Sociology,* 6 (September, 1955), pp. 228–45. Oppenheim's findings may be compared with A. B. Hollingshead, *Elmtown's Youth* (New York: Wiley, 1949), pp. 204–42. See also Joseph A. Kahl, *The American Class Structure* (New York: Rinehart, 1957), pp. 129–38.

[35] Floud *et al., op. cit.,* pp. 115 ff.

CONCLUSION: SUGGESTIONS FOR RESEARCH

The foregoing discussion is broadly impressionistic and speculative, reflecting more the general impression of an observer of both countries than a systematic exploration of data. Relevant data of a variety of sorts are cited above, but their use is more illustrative than demonstrative. However, several lines of research are suggested by this tentative analysis. One of these is an exploration of different channels of mobility in both England and the United States in an attempt to discover the extent to which mobility corresponds to the mobility types. Recruitment to the Catholic priesthood, for example, probably strictly follows a sponsorship norm regardless of the dominant contest norm in the United States.

The effect of changes in the major avenues of upward mobility upon the dominant norms requires investigation. The increasing importance of promotion through corporation hierarchies and the declining importance of the entrepreneurial path of upward mobility undoubtedly compromise the ideal pattern of contest mobility. The growing insistence that higher education is a prerequisite to more and more occupations is a similar modification. Yet, there is little evidence of a tendency to follow the logic of sponsorship beyond the bureaucratic selection process. The prospect of a surplus of college-educated persons in relation to jobs requiring college education may tend to restore the contest situation at a higher level, and the further possibility that completion of higher education may be more determined by motivational factors than by capacity suggests that the contest pattern continues within the school.

In England, on the other hand, two developments may weaken the sponsorship system. One is positive response to popular demand to allow more children to secure the grammar school type of training, particularly by including such a program in the secondary modern schools. The other is introduction of the comprehensive secondary school, relatively uncommon at present but a major plank in the labour party's education platform. It remains to be determined whether the comprehensive school in England will take a distinctive form and serve a distinctive function, which preserves the pattern of sponsorship, or will approximate the present American system.

Finally, the assertion that these types of mobility are embedded in genuine folk norms requires specific investigation. Here, a combination of direct study of popular attitudes and content analysis of popular responses to crucial issues would be useful. Perhaps the most significant search would be for evidence showing what courses of action require no special justification or explanation because they are altogether "natural" and "right," and what courses of action, whether approved or not, require special justification and explanation. Such evidence, appropriately used, would show the extent to which the patterns described are genuine folk norms rather than mere by-products of particular structural factors. It would also permit determination of the extent to which acceptance of the folk norms is diffused among the different segments of the populations.

14.   Bureaucracy and teachers' sense of power*

GERALD H. MOELLER

Over the span of our nation's history, teaching has ranked low among the occupations available to young people. The typical eighteenth-century teacher who paid for his passage to this country by being indentured to the highest bidder and the contemporary teacher who views greater prestige as the panacea for his professional ills express a common dissatisfaction with their respective positions in the social order.

Poorly paid, insecure in their jobs, and surrounded by petty restrictions, teachers, nonetheless, are regarded by the public with apparent respect and, perhaps, affection. Underlying this, however, is pity for women who failed to find husbands and for men who avoided "real" life by retiring to the classroom. Parents and other citizens in the community have discovered the political inability of teachers to change unfavorable school policies and tax rates. There seems little question that in matters that really count the popularly ascribed role of the teacher, more often than not, is one of impotence to shape his social environment.

It is a matter of conjecture whether teachers agree with this stereotype of themselves. However, it would seem that many of them have, indeed, learned that their authority hangs by a slender thread in encounters with the community of parents. Exhorted to be "professional" and, therefore, self-directed and autonomous in judgment, teachers may feel themselves surrounded by restrictions imposed by the policy structure of their school systems and by their superiors' idiosyncracies of leadership. The dangers in this situation are apparent. If teachers think they are unable to make an impact upon their occupational environment, they may divert their energy from teaching pupils to other activities, avocational or vocational, which are more meaningful to them.

Many factors may induce such a state. The results of a growing body of research have shown that an individual's perception of where he belongs relative to the community power structure is multiply determined.[1] For example, Camp-

*From the *School Review*, Vol. 72, No. 3 (Summer 1964), pp. 137–57.

[1] Wayne E. Thompson and John E. Horton, "Political Alienation as a Force in Political Action," *Social Forces,* Vol. 38 (1960), pp. 190–95. This article succinctly summarizes and presents results emerging from research in this area.

bell, Gurin, and Miller, in a study of voter behavior during the 1952 Presidential election, found both sex and socioeconomic factors associated with feelings of political efficacy.[2] Men had a higher sense of political efficacy than women; and persons with higher incomes, more extensive educational training, and higher social status felt greater power with respect to public affairs than their less advantaged counterparts. The extent to which a person feels capable of affecting the course of events, whether within the local community or the society at large, may well be a highly generalized attitude. Shipton and Belisle, after showing a close relationship between feelings of local inefficacy among school patrons and their inclination to agree with stereotyped criticisms concerning the schools, suggested that powerlessness reflected "some generalized feelings of futility and dissatisfaction which are projected upon either local government or public education in general."[3] Similarly, Douvan proposed that the feeling of political efficacy is intimately related to a fundamental attribute of personality, the psychological energy which a person has at his disposal.[4]

Since attitudes are learned, it follows that persons who learned that there is a high probability of changing conditions through persistent action will have a different attitude toward existing social conditions than persons who learned that social conditions are impervious to change. It is proposed that teachers who were reared in middle- and upper-class families learned, in a generalized manner, that they could effect changes, while those from lower-class homes learned the futility of such activity. If these attitudes persist into adult life, as Child has indicated,[5] then teachers may initially come to their jobs with different expectations regarding their power in any social system.

Ultimately, whatever orientations or expectations a teacher may have toward power in the abstract will converge with the effects of the school organization and social system, since the organizational structure of the school system both determines and is determined by the social ethos of its members. Accordingly, the focus in this study was directed at organizational complexity and its human antecedents which have been treated by sociologists as a problem of "bureaucracy."

The concept of bureaucracy provided a means for identifying a number of interrelated organizational dimensions which might be found in school systems in company with various effects upon teachers. Such effects, presumably, included sense of power, or, conversely, powerlessness, a concept which, too, has been the subject of recent interest and research among sociologists and social psychologists.

In this study the central issue was the teacher's sense of power with respect

---

[2] Angus Campbell, Gerald Gurin, and Warren E. Miller, *The Voter Decides* (Evanston, Ill.: Row, Peterson & Co., 1954), p. 187.

[3] James M. Shipton and Eugene L. Belisle, "Who Criticizes the Public Schools?" *Phi Delta Kappan,* Vol. 37 (1956), pp. 303–7.

[4] Elizabeth Douvan, "The Sense of Effectiveness and Response to Public Affairs," *Journal of Social Psychology,* Vol. 47 (1958), pp. 111–26.

[5] Irvin L. Child, "Socialization," in Gardner Lindzey (ed.), *Handbook of Social Psychology* (Reading, Mass.: Addison-Wesley Publishing Co., 1954), p. 681.

to the school system at large—his sense of ability or inability to influence the organizational forces which so importantly shape his destiny. It was not the teacher's feelings about himself and his position with respect to the classroom, nor to the profession, nor to the larger society in which he lives which engaged this investigation. Rather, it was the teacher's sense of power vis-à-vis his school system, as the system varied with regard to its bureaucratization, toward which the study was directed.

Finally, meshed within the organizational structure of the school system are certain situational and social factors which serve to enhance or reduce the teacher's feelings of power. Specifically, cues provided by positions of power he has held in the system (i.e., committee chairmanships and other *ad hoc* decision-making positions), particularistic obligations incurred with administrators,[6] the style of leadership exercised by the chief administrator, and the professional associations and other sources of corporate power upon which he depends, may indicate to the teacher the extent of his potential influence on policy decisions affecting the school system.

While organizational structure may affect individuals in a number of different ways, the issue in this study was restricted to the teacher's sense of powerlessness to influence school system policy.[7] Presumably, school systems in the process of becoming larger and more complex adopt more and more of the elements of bureaucracy. Teachers in such systems are confronted with increased regulations, structuring of the curriculum, and other bureaucratic devices for coordination and control. The major hypothesis, then, was that bureaucracy in school system organization induces in teachers a sense of powerlessness to affect school system policy. Positively stated, it was predicted that the general level of sense of power in a school system varies inversely to the degree of bureaucratization in that system. Secondary hypotheses held that intraschool-system variations in sense of power are induced by factors lying within the individual teacher and his immediate social environment.

METHOD

To test the hypotheses, twenty school systems employing from 37 to 700 full-time teachers were selected from the St. Louis metropolitan area.[8] Super-

---

[6] An interpersonal relationship is said, in Parsons' terms, to be particularistic when each participant evaluates the relationship in terms of his own and the other individual's personal relations. On the other hand, a relationship is universalistic when each individual evaluates the other as an instance of a general class of persons, irrespective of personal elements. A more complete discussion may be found in Talcott Parsons and Edward A. Shils, *Toward a General Theory of Action* (Cambridge, Mass.: Harvard University Press, 1952), p. 81.

[7] Gerald H. Moeller, "The Relationship between Bureaucracy in School System Organization and Teachers' Sense of Power" (unpublished Ed.D. dissertation, Washington University, 1962). This study was part of a larger project performed pursuant to SAE Contract 9009, project No. 929, with the United States Office of Education, "Teacher Perception of Administrator Behavior," W. W. Charters, Jr., Principal Investigator.

[8] The school systems participating in the study are located in St. Louis and Jefferson Counties in Missouri and in Madison and St. Clair Counties in Illinois.

intendents of these systems were visited by members of the research staff for authorization to contact teachers who were selected from faculty lists by the use of a table of random numbers. Twenty elementary and twenty secondary teachers were chosen, whenever possible, from each school district to receive questionnaires. By additional contacts with non-responding teachers, the research staff brought the final return to 88 per cent of the total, or 692 responses. In order to estimate the bias represented by the non-returns, comparisons were made of the sense-of-power scores of teachers who returned the questionnaire soon after the initial mailing and those who required additional contacts. These differences were found to be insignificant, suggesting that the 12 per cent who did not respond might not differ significantly either.

Since the bureaucratic model had been selected as the means for investigating the influence of organizational structure upon the teacher's sense of power, it was necessary either to find a suitable measure of bureaucratization or to construct one. After an unsuccessful search of the literature such a measure was constructed, using the characteristics of bureaucracy as described by Blau.[9] In an absolute sense, it must be pointed out, American public school systems are highly bureaucratized organizations, governed by a complex body of law and characterized by an elaborate division of labor and a formal structure of administrative authority. Teachers and other employees are certified for their jobs on criteria of technical competence and typically are promoted on the basis of seniority. In some school systems, teachers are protected in their employment by tenure. Consequently, distinctions drawn among school systems necessarily must be within a relatively narrow range on a continuum of bureaucratization.

Using an eight-item forced-choice instrument, a group of persons with first-hand knowledge of the school systems in the study made judgments which provided the data for ordering the twenty school systems on a bureaucracy scale. The method of scaling the data followed in general the procedures outlined by Riley, Riley, and Toby for construction of an object scale, that is, data from individuals combined to represent collective responses.[10] Each of the twenty school systems was rated by three, four, or five judges. If a majority of judges chose the "bureaucratic" alternative on a given item, a plus was entered for the school; if less than a majority chose the "bureaucratic" alternative, a minus was entered. In this way a single set of ratings over the eight items was obtained for each school system based upon the majority response of the system's judges. This provided the primary data upon which the scale analysis was performed.

Following scale analysis a pattern descriptive of the most to the least bureaucratic school systems emerged (Table 1). On this bureaucracy continuum school systems could be scaled from type 0 to type 8. A school system to which none of the items applied was scored 0 (least bureaucratic), while a school system to

---

[9] Peter M. Blau, *Bureaucracy in Modern Society* (New York: Random House, 1956), pp. 28–33.

[10] Matilda W. Riley, J. W. Riley, Jr., and J. Toby, *Sociological Studies in Scale Analysis* (New Brunswick, N.J.: Rutgers University Press, 1954), chap. V.

which all items applied was scored 8 and was considered "most bureaucratic." In order for a system to be considered most bureaucratic, or scale type 8, all characteristics had to be positive. While the coefficient of reproducibility was found to be .93, the limited number of objects used in scale analysis indicated the need for further evaluation of the data.[11] The question of interrater reliability was most evident. Following the analysis of variance design reported by Ebel when several raters are used, interrater reliability was computed to be .47.[12]

TABLE 1
Scale Items Describing Most to Least Bureaucratic School Systems

Item *	Scale Type
Uniform course of study	8
Communication through established channels	7
Uniform hiring and dismissing procedures	6
Secure tenure for non-teaching personnel	5
Explicit statement of school policies	4
Clearly delimited area of responsibility	3
Specified lines of authority	2
Standard salary policies for new teachers	1

*Systems characterized by none of the above were scaled 0.

In this design it is impossible to take out the between-rater variance which must go into the error term; this is one reason for the low interrater correlation.

These questions indicated the advisability of further analysis. Accordingly, a parallel scale analysis of the data was pursued in an attempt to describe the amount of bureaucracy each judge saw in the school systems. In this case, it was the subjects, the judges, who were scored, and not the objects of their judgments, the school systems. The purpose in obtaining scores for subjects as well as for objects (for judges as well as for school systems) was to determine whether or not the bureaucracy score achieved by a school system was an artifact of the kind of judges who happened to rate that system. Conceivably, a school system could achieve a high bureaucracy score by having as its judges persons who were inclined to see a large amount of bureaucracy in any school they rated. Indeed, the subject scale of bureaucracy (for judges) indicated systematic differences between judges in their inclinations to choose the bureaucracy alternative in rating school systems.

To test this possibility, cross-tabulations of subject and object scores were made to determine correlation. The correlation as estimated by the coefficient of contingency was virtually zero. Hence, school scores appear to be independent of the characteristics of the judges by this test.

---

[11] The coefficient of reproducibility is the quantity of one minus the number of errors divided by the number of item responses.

[12] R. L. Ebel, "Estimation of the Reliability of Ratings," *Psychometrika*, Vol. 16 (1951), pp. 407–24.

In sum, the purpose in undertaking these scale analyses of the bureaucracy ratings was to avoid the uninspected assumptions which would have been involved in an arbitrary, although simple, construction of a bureaucracy index. Only a study conducted on a far larger sample of ratings could verify the unidimensionality which this measure was presumed to possess.

The teacher's sense of power, or the feeling that he can influence the policy direction of the school system, constituted the major issue and dependent variable of the study. Sense of power was conceived of as a continuum upon which teachers may be ordered; at one extreme are those who feel unlimited in the degree to which they can affect school system policy, and, at the other end are those who feel totally powerless to influence its direction in any way. Powerlessness was used as Seeman has defined it, "the expectancy or probability held by the individual that his own behavior cannot determine the occurrence of the outcomes, or reinforcements, he seeks." [13]

Since an extensive search of the literature revealed no measure of sense of power adaptable to teachers in the social context of the school, it was necessary to construct such a measure. To this end, a set of Likert-type questionnaire items was prepared, tested on a scaling sample of one hundred teachers, and subjected to scale analysis. Six items, whose marginal distributions were well distributed over a range between 0.2 and 0.8, whose cutting points were separated from one another, and whose error counts were low, were selected for the final measure. These six items constituting the sense-of-power scale are listed in Table 2 by order of difficulty, from highest to least high in sense of power:

TABLE 2
Sense of Power Scale

Item	Response	Scale Type
In the school system where I work, a teacher like myself:		
Considers that he has little to say over what teachers will work with him on his job	Disagree	6
Usually can find ways to get system-wide policies changed if he feels strongly enough about them	Agree	5
Feels he does not know what is going on in the upper levels of administration	Disagree	4
Feels he has little to say about important system-wide policies relating to teaching	Disagree	3
Never has a chance to work on school committees which make important decisions for the school system	Disagree	2
Believes he has some control over what textbooks will be used in the classrooms	Agree	1
(Reserved for respondents who indicated the powerless response to each of the above)	...	0

---

[13] Melvin Seeman, "On the Meaning of Alienation," *American Sociological Review*, Vol. 24 (1959), p. 784.

Later, using the responses of the teachers in the main study, scale analysis was again conducted to determine whether unidimensionality could be cross-validated on a different population. The six items again scaled in the same order as before with a coefficient of reproducibility of *.93* when chance reproducibility was found to be .85.

In addition to the sense-of-power scale the teacher questionnaire included indexes of differences among the systems in teachers' exposure to powerlessness-producing effects and in the selection of powerlessness-prone teachers. Specifically included were factors related to particularism in administrator-teacher relations; positions of authority held in the system; repressive authority exercised by the superintendent; teachers' social origins; accessibility of teachers to corporate groups; and sex, length of service, and teaching level.

A measure of the particularism in the teacher-administrator relationship was constructed to determine whether school officials interacted with teachers impersonally or in a highly personal manner conducive to the formation of reciprocal obligations in the framework of their official roles. It was considered that, while universalism might conceivably be considered a goal in some school systems, its attainment was virtually impossible. Hence, all interpersonal interaction between teachers and administrators was on a continuum of particularism bounded by absolute impartiality of treatment or universalism at one pole and extreme partiality at the other. In the measure of particularism, visiting relationships between administrators and teachers were assigned highest weight (3), other teachers who used first names with administrators were assigned a medium weight (2), while all others were assigned a low weight (1).

A measure of the positions of authority teachers had held in their school systems was formed by including all teachers who had been chairmen of committees in the high category and all others in the low category. It was found that committee chairmanship constituted almost the only position full-time classroom teachers held in the power hierarchy of the school. Marginal comments on returned questionnaires indicated that other jobs were viewed as menial extra chores which, if anything, served to emphasize, rather than reduce, the teacher's sense of powerlessness.

Other measures similarly used as control and explanatory variables were an index of repressive authority perceived by teachers to exist in their relations with the superintendent; a measure of corporate power in which teachers were asked, if possible, to name a teachers' organization capable of changing unpopular administrative decisions; and measures of teachers' socioeconomic origins, sex, length of service, and teaching level.

RESULTS

The major hypothesis was denied. Contrary to the hypothesis, teachers in bureaucratic school systems were significantly higher in sense of power than were those in less fully bureaucratized systems ($F = 19.18$, $p < .01$). When teachers were grouped by school system, the more bureaucratic organizations were higher in teacher sense of power than were the less bureaucratic organizations (Spearman rank correlation coefficient $[r_s]$ = .40, p < .05). The question confronting us at this point was whether the logic underlying the hypothesis was at fault or whether disproportionate weighting of specific power-inducing or power-reducing elements in the population had led to this result, masking the effect of organization upon teachers' sense of power. Accordingly, proportions of teachers in the various subgroups noted in Table 3 were examined and held constant when disproportionate in subsequent analyses of bureaucracy and sense of power. Those subgroups considered disproportionate were length of service, social class origins, particularism, repressive authority, and corporate groups. Sex, teaching level, and positions of authority did not differ by more than 1 per cent between high and low bureaucratic systems and were, on this basis, considered proportionate.

The summarized results of the analyses of bureaucracy and sense of power, holding constant disproportionate subgroups, may be seen in Table 4. What is, perhaps, most striking about these findings is the pervasiveness of the bureaucratic variable in its effect upon teachers. Only in one instance, the group of fourteen teachers who chose the welfare committee as a corporate source of power, did teachers in the low bureaucratic systems exceed their high bureaucratic colleagues in sense of power. The low number of teachers involved (total twenty-six) indicates that this is not a dominant factor in the hypothesized relationship.

At this juncture the research strategy pointed toward further examination of the factors other than organization to which sense of power is sensitive.

Particularism in the Administrator-Teacher Relationship. Particularistic ties between teachers and administrators were more prevalent in low bureaucratic systems than in the high bureaucratic ones. As shown in Table 3, 43 per cent of the high-service teachers reported visiting relationships or high particularism in the low bureaucratic systems compared to 27 per cent of the teachers in the high bureaucratic systems. Yet, teachers in the high bureaucratic systems with personal ties with administrators were significantly higher in sense of power than those lacking such ties (χ^2 = 6.79, p < .01). Apparently, particularism held no significance for sense of power among the high-service teachers in the low bureaucratic systems (χ^2 = .50), or among low-service teachers in high bureaucratic systems (χ^2 = .38), or in low bureaucratic systems (χ^2 = .04).

Particularistic connections between teachers and administrators in bureaucratic systems were infrequent. It seems reasonable that, if only a few teachers have access to the administrator in an informal, social way, those teachers who do have access will have a higher sense of power than those without such ties.

On the other hand, in the low bureaucratic systems, particularistic ties were relatively easy to acquire and may have become commonplace; for example, any teacher wishing to do so could establish visiting relationships with the administrator. The openness of this avenue in the low bureaucratic systems may have

TABLE 3
Characteristics of the Teacher Population

Teacher Characteristics	High Bureaucratic Systems		Low Bureaucratic Systems	
	Per Cent	N	Per Cent	N
All Teachers				
Length of service: *				
0–3 years	33	109	44	139
4+ years	67	221	56	178
Total	100	330	100	317
Social class origins: *				
Professional	19	62	10	32
Managerial	26	84	19	58
Clerical	9	28	10	31
Labor	26	85	33	103
Farm	20	69	28	89
Total	100	328	100	313
Elementary:				
Male	4	13	5	16
Female	41	134	40	129
Secondary:				
Male	29	93	30	90
Female	26	81	25	75
Total	100	321	100	310
High-Service Teachers Only (4+ Years)				
Positions of authority:				
High	47	104	48	85
Low	53	116	52	92
Total	100	220	100	177
Particularism: *				
High	27	60	43	77
Low	73	160	57	101
Total	100	220	100	178
Repressive authority: *				
High	30	58	34	53
Medium	47	93	51	79
Low	23	45	15	24
Total	100	196	100	156
Corporate groups: *				
Union	14	30	6	10
Welfare committee	6	12	8	14
Local organization	65	141	54	92
No organization	15	33	32	55
Total	100	216	100	171

* Factors considered disproportionately distributed and hence subjected to further analysis as intervening variables in the relationship of bureaucracy and sense of power.

made particularism appear ineffective in enhancing any one teacher's sense of power.

Positions of Authority Held by Teachers in the School System.   The proportions of teachers with high service reporting positions of authority in high and low bureaucratic systems were remarkably similar, as noted in Table 3. However, when such positions and sense of power were compared, a significant relation-

TABLE 4
Sense-of-Power Means for Variables Disproportionately Distributed
in High and Low Bureaucratic School Systems

Teacher Characteristics	High Bureaucratic Systems		Low Bureaucratic Systems		Comparisons
	Means	N	Means	N	
Length of service:					
0–3 years	3.06	109	2.46	139	Hi vs. Lo Bur, $F = 26.93$**;
4+ years	3.19	221	2.55	178	Hi vs. Lo Serv, $F = 3.29$**
Social class origins:					
Professional	3.29	62	2.81	32	Hi vs. Lo Bur, $F = 20.51$**;
Managerial	3.15	84	2.41	58	between origins, $F = 2.40$*
Clerical	3.32	28	2.25	31	
Labor	2.75	85	2.21	103	
Farm	3.23	69	2.83	89	
Particularism:					
High	3.73	60	2.64	77	Hi vs. Lo Bur, $F = 3.80$; Hi
Low	3.01	160	2.50	101	vs. Lo Part, $F = 61.45$**
Repressive authority:					
High	2.29	58	1.53	53	Hi vs. Lo Bur, $F = 12.60$**;
Medium	3.33	93	2.81	79	repressive authority, $F =$
Low	3.98	45	3.33	24	20.70**
Corporate groups:					
Union	3.63	30	2.60	10	Hi vs. Lo Bur, $F = .31$; or-
Welfare committee	4.33	12	4.71	14	ganizations vs. no organi-
Local association	4.56	141	3.39	92	zations, $F = 12.54$**; be-
No organization	3.09	33	2.78	55	tween organizations, $F = 9.75$**

*Significant at less than 0.05 level.
**Significant at less than 0.01 level.

ship was found among the teachers in the high bureaucratic systems ($\chi^2 = 4.56$, $p < .05$) but not among the teachers in the low bureaucratic systems ($\chi^2 = .23$). Again, as in the results of comparisons of particularism and sense of power, teachers in the low bureaucratic systems did not see positions of authority as a route to power.

Administrator's Reputation for Repressive Authority.   The extent to which teachers in high or low bureaucratic systems saw their superintendent as exercising restrictive and oppressive authority over the faculty depressed their sense of power accordingly ($F = 20.70$, $p < .01$, as shown in Table 4).

One element of bureaucratic administration is the reliance upon reason or rationality to achieve organizational objectives. Hence, it had been anticipated that in the high bureaucratic systems where rationality was the administrative mode, few teachers would report repressive authority in relations with the administration. But, as noted in Table 3, this was not borne out in the findings which showed larger numbers of teachers reporting repressive authority in the high bureaucratic than in the low bureaucratic systems. Apparently, rationality in bureaucratic organization does not preclude the use of restrictive and coercive measures. As Gouldner has noted, bureaucracies may be punishment-centered, using compulsion and sanctions, or bureaucracies may be representative and use human relations techniques, feedback, and education to attain compliance with organizational objectives.[14] Or it may be that teachers with strong aspirations to autonomy may see *all* administrative direction or structure as repressive authority, incompatible with their professional roles.

Corporate Group Membership. Teachers with organizational ties, as noted in Table 4, were found to possess a significantly higher sense of power than teachers without such corporate instruments of power. And teachers in the bureaucracies felt that such organizations were more readily available to them than did their colleagues in the less bureaucratized systems (Table 3). Again the pervasive effect of bureaucracy was in evidence. With one exception (the welfare committee) members of organizational groups in the bureaucracies had a higher sense of power than did their counterparts in the low bureaucratic systems. In the high bureaucratic systems 65 per cent of the teachers saw the local teachers organization as the most potent source of power available to them compared to 54 per cent in the low bureaucratic systems. Unions appeared to sustain sense of power in 14 per cent of the high bureaucratic teachers and in 6 per cent of the low bureaucratic teachers. The welfare committee, which usually consisted of a group of teachers chosen by popular vote, was the choice of 6 per cent of the high bureaucratic teachers and 8 per cent of the low bureaucratic group. Interestingly, the latter group had the highest sense of power scores when the data were classified by groups. The analyses of teacher groups again pointed up both the variability of teachers in their orientations to power and the strength of the bureaucratic variable in determining a system-wide level of sense of power.

Social-Class Origins of Teachers. The home background of teachers in their formative years appeared to be a factor in sense of power. When all teachers, irrespective of school system, were grouped by social origins, sense of power ranked, from high to low, as follows: professional, farm, business-managerial, clerical-white collar, and labor (between origins $F = 2.40$, $p < .05$, in Table 4). The high sense of power of teachers reared on farms brings into question the use of economic indicators in measurement of power. The knowledge that their environment is controllable may, indeed, characterize groups other than the upper strata of society. In each grouping, however, the teachers from the bureau-

---

14 Alvin W. Gouldner, "Organizational Analysis, in Robert K. Merton and Leonard S. Cottrell, Jr. (eds.), *Sociology Today* (New York: Basic Books, 1959), p. 403.

cracies indicated higher sense of power than did similar teachers in the low
bureaucratic systems ($F = 20.51$, $p < .01$, in Table 4).

 Sex and Teaching Level. Male teachers felt themselves more powerful than
did female teachers ($F = 10.30$, $p < .01$, data not shown) and elementary teachers, as a group, more powerful than secondary ($F = 12.63$, $p < .01$, not shown).
With one exception, however, the differences between groups were relatively
small. This group, the male elementary teachers, was smallest in size (29 men to
263 women in the elementary grades) and had the highest sense of power.

 Length of Service. As noted in Table 3, teacher turnover was less evident in
the bureaucracies, with 67 per cent of the teachers having 4 or more years of
service, than in the low bureaucratic systems, with 56 per cent of the teachers in
this category. This stability of employment was accompanied by higher sense of
power (relative to the low bureaucratic systems) at all points in the teachers'
careers ($F = 26.93$, $p < .01$, in Table 4 and, graphically, in Fig. 1). Particularly

FIGURE 1
Sense of Power among Teachers in High Bureaucratic Systems (Dotted Line)
and among Teachers in Low Bureaucratic Systems (Solid Line)

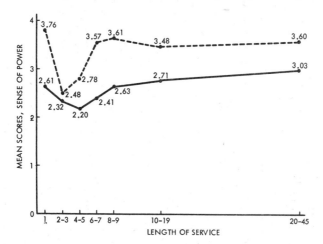

striking in Figure 1 is the shape of the curves in high and low bureaucratic
systems when teachers' careers were viewed longitudinally. First-year teachers
had a high sense of power which dropped and then rose again in the second- to
fifth-year group to a point where it remained rather constant for the more senior
teachers in the sample. Since these data are cross-sectional, selective factors may
have operated, first, to eliminate those with high sense of power and, later, those
with low sense of power. In any event, the pattern similarity between high and
low bureaucratic systems suggests that length of service relates to sense of power
in a manner unrelated to bureaucracy.

 As further noted in Figure 1, first-year teachers in the contrasting organizations differed strikingly in sense of power. A *t*-test showed that this difference

was significant at less than the 0.05 level. These data, however, were obtained after the first-year respondents had been teaching for 5 months, and the data might have looked different had they been collected earlier in the year. But, the total evidence suggests no organizational effects on sense of power unique to bureaucratized or non-bureaucratized systems.

The foregoing results are summarized in Figure 2, which shows those variables augmenting or reducing a teacher's sense of power in the school systems studied.

FIGURE 2
Summary of Major Findings: Variables Augmenting (Solid Line) or
Reducing (Dotted Line) a Teacher's Sense of Power

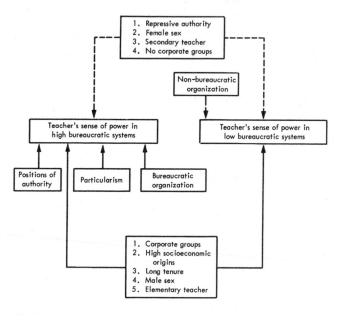

SENSE OF POWER AND POLICY

Sense of power to influence the policy direction of the school system was found to be high in the bureaucratic systems when teachers as individuals, when school system means, and when all other subgroups of teachers were compared. In contrast, sense of power was consistently low among teachers in the low bureaucratic school systems.

It is the position taken here that the firm policy of the more heavily bureaucratized school systems enhanced rather than reduced a teacher's sense of power. As functionaries of organized school systems, teachers are in no sense "free" agents but are subject to many restrictions imposed by law, local customs, limited finances, and, perhaps, by their own indecision. The issue, therefore, is not one of policy direction of the administration versus professional autonomy of teachers, as is so often proposed in current debate; rather, the issue appears to be policy direction versus capricious, infirm, and poorly conceived decisions made by the administration in response to each new challenge generated within or outside of the school system.

It seems apparent in the low bureaucracy schools that nearly everyone—teachers, parents, and the general public—has access to the administrative policy-makers on a friendship basis—or realizes that he can go to the superintendent if he chooses. This, in effect, tends to devalue this avenue, for if everyone has access, then all should benefit equally. Since particularism pervades the entire teaching staff of a low bureaucratic system, relatively few are disenfranchised and the possibility for invidious comparisons of power is greatly reduced. Without the stabilizing benefit of a comprehensive and uniform written set of rules for the school system, many decisions arise for which adequate policy is unavailable. This, it would seem, leads teachers in the low bureaucratic systems to be uncertain as to such decisions and the element of unpredictability inherent in the system tends to abrogate their sense of power. In short, only in an orderly, understandable, and predictable organization can any individual expect to influence the direction the organization will take. This factor seems crucial in the low sense of power of the low bureaucratic teachers and leads to the postulation of predictability as a major organizational element differentiating the high and low bureaucratic systems. Teachers who know that most events will follow a prescribed course and will be dealt with in a predictable and rational manner are in a much better position to influence these events than are teachers who never know what action the administration will take. In such an ambiguous situation, teachers must view each new situation with foreboding, not knowing which cues are dependable guides for action.

In systems characterized by firm policy, we may postulate that teachers' knowledge of that policy is, in itself, a form of power. When policy is applicable to all, then any individual who knows the rules by which the system is governed is able to predict how any particular situation will be handled. This factor enables the teachers in the bureaucratic school systems, by the expedient of learning the rules, to anticipate how the administration will act in most problems confronting it. More importantly, knowledge of policy enables teachers to know the most effective course of action to take in order to influence the policy-maker. Accordingly, in the bureaucratic school systems, firm policy enables teachers to predict events accurately, providing an effective basis for action and thereby enhancing sense of power. With the advantage of a firm policy structure, teachers in the bureaucracies, as a group, have a higher general sense of power than teachers in the low bureaucratic systems.

A REASSESSMENT OF BUREAUCRACY AND SENSE OF POWER

From the findings reported in this study have emerged a number of postulates regarding bureaucracy in the public school setting. Certainly bureaucracy, as a rational and, hence, predictable form of organization, does not induce in teachers feelings of powerlessness or alienation from the system. The greater predictability seems to stem from the published policy of these systems which assures teachers of specific avenues of communication up the line to the decision-making centers of the administration. Then, too, the rationality of the bureaucracies presses toward effectiveness of operation and efficiency in employment of personnel, insuring teachers the best possible working conditions within the limits of available resources.

By definition the low bureaucratic school systems are less complex organizations with fewer and less explicit written policies. Without specified rules to guide them, administrators of these systems must rely on unanticipated decisions or on traditional community norms—either of which are subject to misunderstanding and, hence, are less predictable than a well-defined policy structure would be.

When the focus is shifted from the school system organization to the individual teacher, the dimension of comparative evaluation becomes relevant. Each member of a social system learns his role in that system and, in so doing, assesses his power in relation to others. This knowledge of relative position in the power hierarchy enables teachers with greater service, of higher social-class origins, and the males in elementary schools to score high on sense of power whether they were employed in high or low bureaucratic systems.

In short, sense of power appears to be influenced by many diverse variables lying within the teacher himself, in his past, in his social groups, in his relations with his superiors, and in the organizational structure of the school in which he is employed. The general level of sense of power seems to be limited by the organizational variable. Bureaucracy provides the teacher with an understandable and predictable ethos in which to pursue his profession. This predictability, far from reducing sense of power, sets a higher level of sense of power than is found in the less bureaucratized school organizations. To the general level of sense of power set by the organization of the school system the teacher brings his own personal characteristics which differentiate him from his colleagues and enable him to make comparisons of his power in relation to that held by others. Thus, the school system sets the general level of sense of power and the teacher varies from this level by his own personal orientation toward power.

15. The professional prestige of classroom teachers: a consequence of organizational and community status*

HOLGER R. STUB

Ever since the rise of mass education the public school classroom teacher has been faced with a status dilemma,[1] a fact which has contributed to certain problems currently facing American education. The persistent debate over whether the teacher is a professional, the continued preponderance of females in teaching, the large number of persons who leave teaching after a short stay, the lower academic abilities of many who become teachers, and inconsistencies in the public attitude toward teaching as an occupational choice are illustrative of the problems involving the teacher's role and status.

*This study was supported by a grant-in-aid from the Faculty Research Committee of Temple University.
[1] This is only a small selection of the large number of works dealing with the status of teachers: Willard Waller, *Sociology of Teaching* (New York: John Wiley & Sons, 1932); Wilbur B. Brookover, *A Sociology of Education* (New York: American Book Co., 1955); Ronald G. Corwin, *A Sociology of Education* (New York: Appleton-Century-Crofts, 1965); Myron Lieberman, *Education as a Profession* (Englewood Cliffs, N.J.: Prentice-Hall, 1956); Mary Vlick, "Historical Status of the Teacher," *Educational Forum*, Vol. 22 (March, 1958), pp. 341–48; Willard E. Goslin, "Forces Undermining Professional Status," *Childhood Education*, Vol. 34 (February, 1963), pp. 272–73; Patrick J. Groff, "The Social Status of Teachers," *Journal of Educational Sociology*, Vol. 36 (September, 1962), pp. 20–25; Donald Walkout, "The Teacher Image in America," *Journal of Higher Education*, Vol. 32 (January, 1961), pp. 31–36; S. Rettig and B. Passamanick, "Status and Job Satisfaction of Public School Teachers," *School and Society*, Vol. 87 (March 14, 1959), pp. 113–16; G. G. Gordon, "Conditions of Employment and Service in Elementary and Secondary Schools: Teacher Status and Role Expectations," *Review of Educational Research*, Vol. 33 (October, 1963), p. 382; Hazel Davis *et al.*, "Economic, Legal, and Social Status of Teachers," *Review of Educational Research*, Vol. 33 (October, 1963), pp. 398–414; National Education Association, *The Status of the American Public School Teacher* (Washington, D.C.: NEA, 1957).

A number of underlying social and economic factors are involved in these problems of status. Some of these factors are closely related to the organization of the school and its consequences for the status and prestige of the teacher in the community. This paper will attempt to analyze the relationship between the teacher's status within the organized structure of the school and in the community itself.

The following definitions will be used in analyzing the relationship between these two statuses.[2] In general, the concept of status refers to (1) one's position relative to others in a social context; (2) the deference or prestige granted by others within that context. Status is thus defined both in structural and social-psychological terms.[3] The teacher's role will be viewed in terms of two analytically different statuses. *Community status* will refer to the teacher's status and prestige in the community.[4] An empirical referent of this status involves others' opinions of teaching as an occupation (occupational prestige) and its place relative to other occupations held by community members. The term *organizational status* will refer to the teacher's position and prestige within the organized structure of the school.[5]

Status "on the job" is a significant determinant of status in the community, in that occupation has become a critical variable in shaping one's social norms, self-definition, and expectations for the behavior of others. Caplow considers occupation crucially important in modern societies; he states that occupation serves "as a measure of a man."[6] A critical aspect of the teacher's occupational role is revealed in the recurrent debate over whether teaching can be called a profession. This issue has important ramifications for the teacher's community and organizational status.

---

[2] These definitions are similar to the two types of status relations defined by Burleigh Gardner and David G. Moore, *Human Relations in Industry* (Homewood, Ill.: Richard D. Irwin, Inc., 1955), pp. 103 ff. They distinguish one kind of status involving not only differences in rank, but also the right to give orders (organizational status). The other type of status does not involve this right, but expresses relative rank or superiority and inferiority (community status).

[3] The theoretical basis for the present use of this concept is derived from Linton on one hand, and from Weber on the other.

[4] The concept of community is another ambiguous and difficult term, but hopefully the context of the present paper will provide the necessary referents for this discussion.

[5] Barnard uses a similar distinction in his concept of *functional status,* which is a general attribute and refers to such groups as "different callings, trades, crafts, métiers, division of labor, specialization, and professions." This kind of status does not depend on authority and jurisdiction and is generally what I mean by community status. Scalar status (Barnard's term) is similar to my use of organizational status. It refers to position in an organizational hierarchy wherein amount of formal authority is the criterion of one's position in the structure. According to Barnard, scalar status is "determined by (1) the relationship of superordination or subordination in a chain of command or formal authority and (2) by jurisdiction." See Chester I. Barnard, "Functions and Pathology of Status Systems in Formal Organizations," in William F. Whyte (ed.), *Industry and Society* (New York: McGraw-Hill Book Co., 1946), pp. 48–49.

[6] Theodore Caplow, *The Sociology of Work* (Minneapolis: University of Minnesota Press, 1954), p. 31.

THE TEACHER AS A PROFESSIONAL

Both teachers and nonteachers are apparently unsure of the teacher's position vis-à-vis the traditional professions. A recent survey has investigated whether the members of a particular community considered high school teachers as professionals. The results are strongly in the affirmative—over 96 percent of the population views high school teaching as a profession. Nevertheless, other evidence indicates that teaching may not qualify as a profession. For example, frequently those who say they regard teaching as a profession do not seriously consider it as an acceptable occupational choice for their children.[7] This discrepancy may stem, in part, from the fact that most teachers are severely limited in their occupational autonomy and are ignored in the determination of school policy.

> Teachers have virtually no control over their standards of work. They have little control over the subjects to be taught; the materials to be used; the criteria for deciding who should be admitted, retained, and graduated from training schools; the qualifications for teacher training; the forms to be used in reporting pupil progress; school boundary lines and the criteria for permitting students to attend; and other matters that affect teaching.[8]

The lack of status inherent in certain aspects of the teacher's role is further illustrated by the NORC study of occupational prestige. Reiss has analyzed the findings from the NORC study and noted that, in contrast to most of the professional or semiprofessional occupations listed in the study, school teaching is most devalued by those with the highest socioeconomic background.[9] Respondents at the lowest socioeconomic level assign the highest percentages of negative evaluations to most of the other occupations in the same category, whereas prosperous and middle-class persons vary slightly one way or the other. Thus, only at the lower socioeconomic levels does teaching have the prestige accorded other professions. However, the greater value assigned by the lower strata to teaching seems to be based primarily on the fact that this occupation offers a feasible avenue of social mobility for lower class individuals. Its prestige as an occupation is therefore relative to its place in the job market.

The problem of professional status for teachers is intensified by the fact that teachers are trained to view themselves as professionals. But the new teacher quickly learns that there are few rewards for behaving in a manner consistent with his professional training.[10] According to Gerstl,

> the greatest fact of life of teaching is . . . likely to strike as a culture shock: the recognition that the teacher is an employee. The demands of

---

[7] Lieberman, *op. cit.,* p. 465.

[8] Corwin, *op. cit.,* p. 241.

[9] Albert Reiss, *Occupation and Social Status* (Glencoe, Ill.: Free Press, 1961), pp. 276, 295. Additional data is presented in Robert W. Richy, William H. Fox, and Charles E. Fauset, "Prestige Ranks of Teaching," *Occupations,* Vol. 30 (October, 1951), pp. 33–37.

[10] Chandler Washburne, "The Teacher in the Authority System," *Journal of Educational Sociology,* Vol. 30 (May, 1957), p. 394.

pedagogy must be placed against (and often subservient to) those of bureaucracy—the world of Delany cards, attendance sheets, supply requisitions, toilet passes, and fire drill regulations.[11]

The activities that constitute the teaching occupation occur under circumstances that affect the attainment of professional status. The work of the school teacher is under constant neighborhood and community surveillance. Parents receive continuous information (both accurate and distorted) from their children. Parents must contend with the rules of the school in managing their home life—this is especially true for mothers of elementary school children. However, in return the school does free the mothers from responsibility for their children for a few hours a day. The mothers of a community are some of the key judges of teachers, and it is they who can confer or deny prestige or deference to a given teacher and to teachers generally. When problems arise, mothers are the ones who must be impressed or defended against, depending upon the observer's perspective. Mothers are particularly important since they provide their children with opinions and attitudes about teachers from kindergarten well into junior high school.

The handiwork of the teacher and school is much more visible on a continuous basis than that of other professional occupations. Although visible, the teacher's work is not necessarily understood. Gerver and Bensman point out that the process by which members of an occupation gain recognition as experts is related to social visibility and distance.

> Experts do not arrive in society spontaneously but are the result of a complex process of institutional development, claims for recognition as experts, and the granting of social recognition is the *social visibility* of those claiming expertness and the *social distance* of the conferring groups from the alleged experts. The more distant groups, i.e., those least technically qualified, grant recognition which is based not upon a knowledge of expert procedures, methods and information, but instead upon the imputed consequences of expert action. . . . The recognition of expertness, then, varies with the social distance of the conferring groups and their criteria of recognition.[12]

In terms of social visibility and distance, teachers apparently occupy a particular place relative to receiving recognition as experts. School teachers are highly visible to almost all the status conferring groups in the community.[13] Although the least educated families may feel socially distant from teachers,

---

[11] Joel E. Gerstl, "Education and the Sociology of Work," in Donald Hansen and Joel E. Gerstl (eds.), *On Education—Sociological Perspectives* (New York: John Wiley & Sons, 1967), p. 247.

[12] Israel Gerver and Joseph Bensman, "Toward a Sociology of Expertness," *Social Forces*, Vol. 32 (March, 1954), pp. 226–27.

[13] Teachers "are the sanctioning agents for the young, the guardians of morals, the arbiters of conduct, and it is in this status that they are remembered by all adults from their own childhood. In truth, teachers constitute a kind of conscience in society, and their status is that of the conscience—recognized as fundamentally important, but neglected as much as

their own school experience provides them with a range of information and opinions about teachers, which is not true for other experts in our society. Although many Americans do feel competent to judge some aspects of the teacher's work, they are uncertain about the consequences of the "expert action" of teachers. The traditionally high levels of anti-intellectualism, the strong emphasis on experience, and the attributing of success to one's personal characteristics, makes the teacher's expertness open to question. The so-called "school of hard knocks" has received some of the credit that might otherwise have been accorded the teaching profession. The apparent ineffectiveness of education in bettering the lives of those most socially distant from teachers (the lower socioeconomic strata) does not help to promote high status for teachers.

The recent success of teachers in winning better salaries and working conditions, commensurate with a professional image, has resulted partly from a recognition that the expert actions of teachers may have important consequences. The teacher's community and organizational status has probably been enhanced by a growing awareness of educational achievement as an increasingly critical variable in social mobility.

A client seeking services among the established professions is much freer in his choice of a professional than in education. Consequently, the level of surveillance or visibility of the established professions is decreased. The relative lack of information about the inner workings of law, medicine, and similar professions can facilitate the promotion of illusions, myths, and favorable professional images. However, high visibility prevents public school teachers from utilizing certain kinds of image-enhancing techniques. With respect to gaining status and prestige for teachers, one might argue that educators should not be overly concerned with informing parents about the latest pedagogical theories and the development of new strategies, such as the "new math." However, if the teacher must rely on parents to augment the educational process, then sufficient information and knowledge to meet educational goals must be shared. There is considerable evidence showing that parental behavior can facilitate the educational process, but whether such behavior includes technical aspects of pedagogy is questionable.

The conditions imposed by lay control of American schools also increase the teacher's difficulties in attaining full professional status. Most public schools are characterized by relatively low tolerance for variation in behavior within the school. A substantial share of the demand for conformity is a result of external pressures for a standardized product. Coser notes that external pressures on a group or organization tend to reduce internal tolerance, a fact which not only affects the student's life, but also narrows the teacher's range of "individual autonomy."[14]

---

possible." Frederic W. Terrien, "The Occupational Role of Teachers," *Journal of Educational Sociology,* Vol. 29 (September, 1955), pp. 14–20. See also J. W. Getzels and E. G. Guba, "The Structure and Role Conflict in the Teaching Situation," *ibid.,* p. 30.

[14] Lewis Coser, *The Function of Social Conflict* (Glencoe, Ill.: Free Press, 1956), p. 103.

Educators have written and implied that local lay control inhibits the professionalization of school teachers. Intuitively, this seems reasonable, in terms of the school's place in society. The fact that the school system is "open" at the top and bottom makes internal professional controls very difficult to enforce. At the top of the structure are the laymen on the school boards, and at the bottom are the children, who also in a sense, represent the community. Thus, external intrusions at either end of the school structure can potentially be extreme and create conditions of unpredictability. Such a situation can in turn be detrimental to the development of professional norms and values. In general, the school board end of the school hierarchy structure apparently poses less of a threat to the formation of a viable set of internal professional norms and values than we could expect. In a recent article Kerr argues that school boards may actually function more as agencies of legitimation than as controlling and innovating bodies representing the community.[15] School administrations, headed by the superintendent, are apparently not wholly ineffective in coopting school board members. The size and complexity of many school systems places the superintendent and his immediate staff in the position of experts, which implies considerable influence over the lay board. This type of situation can favor the development of professionalism within the school. This situation probably only holds true in relatively large and complex systems.

However, the literature contains some discordant notes on school administration in general and on superintendency in particular. Many books dealing with the role of the superintendent overlook the fact that the superintendent should function in a social context involving other professionals (i.e., the teaching staff). One recent textbook referred to superintendents with the rather euphemistic title of "status leader." The author found it necessary to justify the use of an authority system headed by the superintendent in the otherwise democratically oriented structure of the American school. The following characteristics were given in describing this authoritative role of "status leader":

1. He is employed by an individual, a board, or a company.
2. He is responsible to his employer for getting defined work done.
3. This work is done by others responsible to him.
4. He is usually chosen by an employer who places him over other workers.
5. His continued employment rests upon the judgment of the employer.
6. His authority comes from his employer.
7. His authority, selection, and continuance are wholly or in major part beyond the control of the group responsible to him.
8. He has a large measure of authority in selecting those who work for him, in determining how their work shall be done, and in determining whether or not they shall remain at work.[16]

---

[15] Norman D. Kerr, "The School Board as an Agency of Legitimation," *Sociology of Education,* Vol. 38 (Fall, 1964), pp. 34–59.

[16] Van Miller and Willard B. Spalding, *The Public Administration of American Schools* (Yonkers-on-the-Hudson: World Book, 1958), p. 494.

These characteristics could just as easily describe the authority position of the executive head of a private corporation; they come close to describing the position of commanding officers of military units. There is no mention either of authority based on expertise or professional training and competence, or of the shared authority and need for consensus implicit in a collegial structure.[17] In one instance the professionalization of superintendents was discussed, but no reference was made to the profession of teaching.[18] Whether this implies that the former are professionals and the latter are not, or that there are two different types of professionals in the public schools was not made clear.

The concern over the professional status of teachers has led some educators to note that such status depends partially on the degree to which teachers participate in the social affairs of the community.[19] However, amount of social participation is probably more a *consequence* than a cause of low status.[20] Promoting community participation in order to enhance the teacher's status reflects a common approach to certain problems—the treatment of symptoms rather than causes. Other professionals participate in social affairs to the degree determined by their status, particular style of life, and the traditional community expectations regarding social involvement. There is probably a minimum level of necessary social participation for any particular occupational group that effectively claims professional standing. However, there is no one-to-one relationship between high status and participation in community affairs. For example, the type and amount of social participation is substantially different for doctors and scientists, although both areas are associated with high professional status.

Bureaucratization and the teacher as a professional

The status dilemma of the teacher is closely related to the fact that schools, of necessity, have become more bureaucratically organized. According to Corwin, the recent past has seen a dual evolution of professional and bureaucratic principles in education. Despite the development of some aspects of professionalism,

> the employee status of teachers has been reinforced, first by a strong tradition of local, lay control over education, and then by the subsequent

---

[17] Max Weber, *The Theory of Social and Economic Organization,* translated and edited by A. M. Henderson and Talcott Parsons (New York: Oxford University Press, 1947), pp. 392 ff.

[18] H. A. Moore, Jr., *Studies in School Administration* (Washington, D.C.: American Association of School Administrators, 1957).

[19] L. W. Drabick, "Teacher's Day: Analysis of Professional Role Perceptions," *Educational Administration and Supervision,* Vol. 45 (November, 1959), pp. 329–36; Roy C. Buck, "The Extent of Social Participation Among Public School Teachers," *Journal of Educational Sociology,* Vol. 33 (April, 1960), pp. 311–19.

[20] Madaline K. Remmhein, Marth L. Ware, and Jean Flanigan, "Economic, Legal and Social Status of Teachers," *Review of Educational Research,* Vol. 28 (June, 1958), pp. 242–55.

growth of complex school systems, which have required more administrative control to maintain coordination.[21]

Bureaucratization is also occurring in medicine and law, but under different circumstances. The professional status of doctors and lawyers was fully established before the onset of bureaucratization and thus had to be fully taken into account in introducing new bureaucratic principles of organization and conduct. As a result, new types of bureaucratic structures have evolved, especially designed for the professional and his activities. In education, however, the new bureaucracies have not been adapted to a teaching corps already possessing full professional rights and responsibilities. For this reason bureaucratic principles have sometimes taken precedence over emerging professional principles among teachers.

Despite many of the presumably negative consequences of bureaucratization for the professions, the process may actually have produced some positive results for the professionalization of teachers. In a recent study, teachers in school systems defined as high in bureaucratic characteristics report a greater "sense of power" with respect to influencing school policy than do teachers employed in school systems rated low in bureaucracy. The study concludes that "bureaucracy provides the teacher with an understandable and predictable ethos in which to pursue his profession."[22]

Although certain features of bureaucratic structure may aid the process of professionalization, the teacher must gain what has been called "individual authority"[23] in order to qualify as a professional. He must be free to make professional decisions based on his own expert judgment rather than on the basis of directives issued by his superiors in the bureaucratic structure. Such authority is of the collegial type; it is characterized by Goss' discussion of how professional norms function in authority structures within the medical profession:

> When both supervisor and supervised are physicians, the control-oriented behavior of each is largely predetermined by established professional norms and values which both know and accept in advance. Relatively little mutual adjustment of role expectations is therefore required on the part of either person. . . .[24]

The status of the teacher within the school

Since bureaucratization in the public school has occurred under conditions that deemphasize the professional status of teachers, a hierarchical- rather than

---

[21] Ronald G. Corwin, "Professional Persons in Public Organizations," *Educational Administration Quarterly,* Vol. 1 (Autumn, 1965), p. 4.

[22] Gerald H. Moeller, "Bureaucracy and Teachers' Sense of Power," *School Review,* Vol. 72 (Summer, 1964), p. 152. [Pp. 236–50 of this volume.]

[23] Logan Wilson, *The Academic Man* (New York: Oxford University Press, 1942), p. 73; L. Vrick (ed.), *Dynamic Administration: The Collected Papers of Mary Parker Follett* (New York: Harper & Bros., 1940), pp. 227–81.

[24] Mary E. W. Goss, "Influence and Authority Among Physicians in an Out-Patient Clinic," *American Sociological Review,* Vol. 26 (February, 1961), p. 50.

collegial-type authority system has developed. This situation is exemplified by the mode of instituting and following rules within the school, as well as by many teachers' perceptions of authority figures.

Systems of rules govern much of the behavior of professionals and employees, but rules that ordinarily apply to professionals are more diffuse and abstract. Regulations for employees are frequently unconditionally binding, whereas those applicable to professionals are stated or perceived as alternatives. Teachers are frequently subject to apparently unconditional rules:

> For example, rules stating that personnel [teachers] may not leave the building until 3:30 and that they may not leave the premises without permission of the administration defines them as employees.[25]

There is evidence that classroom teachers *view* themselves as employees in a hierarchical and authoritarian structure. In a recent study a teacher is quoted as saying:

> After all, he's the principal, he is the boss, what he says should go, you know what I mean. . . . He's the Principal and he's the authority, and you have to follow his orders; that's all there is to it.[26]

Becker characterizes the authority structure of the school as a "small, self-contained system of social control."[27] This small world containing principal and teachers results in a structure which is more predictable (and hence, more satisfactory) than a structure involving several ranks of teachers along with the administrative ranks of principals and assistant principals. It is implied that this simple two-rank structure protects the teacher and the administrator from lay persons in the community. The major functionary in the protective relationship is the principal. However, the principal often fails to support fully the action of a teacher. In this case, the teacher lacks sufficient authority and prestige to ward off or effectively counter an attack from an offended parent or disturbed citizen.[28]

In many ways the teacher's status position in the school can be compared to that of a foreman in a factory. Like the foreman, the teacher is the "man in the middle," subject to conflicting social demands from above and below. Both teacher and foreman are key functionaries in implementing organizational goals, and both hold positions quite distant from the level of large-scale decision making in the two types of structures. The two occupational roles require the utilization of considerable social skill in interpersonal relations, in order to gain close cooperation on one hand, and to maintain the status of expert and authority on the other. The teacher and foreman both lack the unambiguous status

---

[25] Corwin, *op. cit.,* p. 238.

[26] Howard S. Becker, "The Teacher in the Authority System of the Public School," in A. Etzioni (ed.), *Complex Organizations* (New York: Holt, Rinehart, and Winston), p. 246.

[27] Becker, *op. cit.,* p. 251.

[28] This may be further reflected in the fact that the type of principal is a crucial variable in determining the quality of the school. See Edward Gross, "Sociological Aspects of Professional Salaries in Education," *Educational Record,* Vol. 41 (April, 1960), p. 137.

necessary for maintaining a consistent degree of autonomy, yet both roles demand a measure of independence in order to be effectively fulfilled.

One factor involved in creating these status dilemmas for the teacher is reflected in the conception of power and decision making held by many Americans. Clayton cogently discusses the relationship between the professionalization of teachers and current premises underlying conceptions of power. He refers to Lynd and Galbraith, and states that Americans in general have refused to deal adequately with problems of power.

> "We Americans," says Professor Lynd, "have an uneasy awareness that organized power, as we know it and use it, and democracy as we profess it, do not fit well together. And this leaves us for the most part busy with, but reticent about, power."

This orientation seems to result in

> the refusal to recognize power while jealously guarding it, the use of euphemisms to disguise the possession of power, the vagueness and equivocation that cover up who is responsible for what, and the consequent exposure of the society as a whole to the risks of legerdemain when the control of power is short-circuited. . . . [Consequently,] when power is wielded over others and covered up by equivocation, there is no way to reduce its arbitrary character. It becomes power to manipulate and to sustain the practice of manipulation rather than power to engage in and extend a professional activity.[29]

The decision-making process found in the public school system has suffered from this kind of malaise, at least since the rise of mass education.

The status and authority structure of the school

The ambiguity surrounding the professionalization of teachers, the exposure to criticism and intervention because of high visibility and local lay control, the occurrence of bureaucratization before teachers had realized full professional status, and current conceptions of power in American society have all contributed to the development of schools with authority structures inimical to the professionalization of teachers. As noted earlier, teachers have little or no control over most major aspects of the educational process. Power is wielded by ex-teachers who have become administrators, and classroom teachers are virtually powerless as a group. The situation has resulted in a rather drastic polarization of two major groups—teachers versus administrators. This polarity is reflected in the increasing militancy and unionism among teachers in an effort to achieve higher salaries.

---

[29] A. Stafford Clayton, "Professionalization and Problems of Power," *Journal of Teacher Education,* Vol. 16 (March, 1965), pp. 72–73. [The reference made is to Robert S. Lynd, "Power in American Society as Resource and Problem," in Arthur Kornhauser (ed.), *Problems of Power in American Democracy* (Detroit: Wayne State University Press, 1957), p. 7.]

This polarity, which has been spurred by the awareness that power lies in teacher solidarity and common action, results partly from the simple two-level status structure of the school. When virtually all the major functionaries in a polarized status structure—namely, teachers—are on the same status level, the *informal* status system assumes added significance. The teacher's lack of opportunity for promotion, as well as the availability of other formal means of recognition for merit and achievement, tends to direct status demands along other lines. This process eventuates in the elaboration of the informal system of relationships found in all organized structures.

In the school the informal system has become the major device for achieving status. Within this informal system status can be achieved by assignment to a more prestigeful school, for example (i.e., a school which contains students from high-status families). This constitutes a status gain through horizontal movement within the system.[30] Personal contacts and friendships with a high-status teacher, building custodian, principal, superintendent, or school board member can also lead to the influence and privileges symbolic of higher status.

The earlier reference to the positive relationship between schools with a high level of bureaucratization and teachers' "sense of power" illustrates the relationship between bureaucratization and the informal status system in the school.[31] Moeller notes that in low-bureaucracy schools nearly everyone—including teachers, parents, and interested laymen—has equal access to the superintendent, access based primarily on friendship and informality. Such unstructured arrangements tend to devalue access to the top authority as a major avenue of influence, and lend a degree of ambiguity and unpredictability to the authority system. This type of situation can lead to an atmosphere of intrigue and manipulation.

Although a bureaucratized school does not preclude the development of an informal system, it does routinize the degree of access to authority figures. Only individuals with rank (both formal and informal) have ready access to the top executive. Within the more bureaucratically structured school, teachers can ascertain those with rank in the *informal* system by determining who has access to the individuals in authority. By this means, teachers can make some kind of systematic judgment about their own current status and their future prospects for status and influence. The importance of the informal status system results from the lack of a formal system.

According to certain equalitarian ideas, teachers and those in other "dedicated" occupational groups should be unconcerned with matters of status. However, it is quite evident that "nearly all members of formal organizations may be

---

[30] Robert E. Herriot and Mary Hoyt St. John, *Social Class and the Urban School* (New York: John Wiley & Sons, 1966), p. 9 [cited from: Bobby J. Chandler, Lindley J. Stiles, and John I. Kitsuse, *Education in Urban Society* (New York: Dodd, Mead & Co., 1962), pp. 3-35]; Helen E. Amerman, "Perspective for Evaluating Intergroup Relations in a Public School System," *Journal of Negro Education,* Vol. 26 (1957), pp. 108–20; and Hermine I. Popper, *How Difficult Are Difficult Schools?* (New York: Public Education Association, 1959).

[31] Moeller, *op. cit.,* pp. 153–56.

observed to be much preoccupied with matters of status."[32] Reliance on an informal status system is conducive to the wielding of power based on personal and semiprivate dealings among administrators, lay people, and individual teachers. As noted earlier, authority systems of such a nature readily lead to the kind of arbitrary and manipulative behavior that are contrary to the type of power wielding inherent in professional and collegial structures.

The status system of an organization provides rewards and incentives, which have, in turn, a direct effect on the problem of variation in abilities among teachers. It is a truism that teachers do not all have equal ability. Although the lay public may have difficulty in assessing the abilities of teachers, other teachers and administrators can evaluate these abilities to some extent, on the basis of shared criteria. The problem of cooperation among persons with unequal ability faces all kinds of complex organizations. Barnard states that

. . . individuals of superior ability and those of inferior ability can comfortably work together only on a basis of physical or social segregation. If no formal segregation is established, either friction and noncooperation occur or there is spontaneous informal segregation. . . .

Some of the consequences for the individuals concerned are that:

To be lumped with inferiors in ability seems an unjust withholding of recognition, an injury to the integrity of the person. Their escape from this position will probably be more individualistic than those of inferior abilities who must more often resort to group solidarity. One escape or attempt to escape for the superior individual is to try and organize the group, to adopt a function of leadership, or to dominate without authority. Another is to leave the group. . . .[33]

The lack of variability of status positions for classroom teachers may account partially for the emergence of group solidarity. Solidarity does aid in pressuring school boards; however, it may reflect in part what Barnard characterizes as the mode of response of teachers who cannot adequately meet the demands of organizational roles, as well as of superior teachers seeking informal leadership in school affairs. Escape from the group—leaving the field of teaching altogether—is apparently another response of some potentially superior teachers.[34]

The foregoing discussion underlines the ambiguity of rewards characteristic of the status system of the school. There is evidence that the breadth of the status system (e.g., the "opportunity for promotion") is an important element in making one school more desirable than another. An analysis of the individual's

[32] Barnard, *op. cit.*, p. 50.

[33] *Ibid.*, pp. 61–62.

[34] Robert L. Thorndike and Elizabeth Hagen, "Men Teachers and Ex-Teachers: Some Attitudes and Traits," *Teachers College Record*, Vol. 62 (January, 1961), pp. 306–16. This study indicates that of the male teachers and ex-teachers who took aptitude tests for the Air Force in 1943, the ex-teachers were significantly superior to those still in teaching in the areas of mathematics, arithmetic reasoning, and reading comprehension. In addition, the ex-teachers had a 25 percent greater income.

status situation both inside and outside the organized work structure must consider the relationship between "need" (or motivation) for achievement and the prestige of the occupational role. Research supporting Barnard's assertions indicates that persons with strong motivation for achievement tend to be attracted to activities which can provide an unambiguous indication of their competence.[35] A study of scientists in a large research center shows that recognition and rewards (through promotion and other means) constitute very important incentives, both in fostering further achievement and in job satisfaction.[36] In the field of teaching the criteria of excellence and the system of granting rewards are extremely ambiguous. Since such ambiguity has important consequences for the self-definition of teachers, it implies that those with a strong desire for achievement will find the field unsatisfactory.[37]

Some critical observations can be made in comparing school administrators with teachers. For example, Lieberman notes that

> . . . [salary] differentials between administrators and teachers are greater than the differentials between administrators and practitioners in any other profession. . . . in many professions the differentials either do not exist at all or exist in favor of the practitioners rather than the administrators. Doctors often receive several times the income of their hospital administrators.[38]

At present, there are no opportunities for teachers to attain salaries that are comparable to those of other professionals—unless they abandon the classroom for administrative posts. Since size of salary is an important status symbol, this situation undeniably acts to hinder professionalization among teachers.

THE STATUS SITUATION OF COLLEGE PROFESSORS VERSUS SCHOOL TEACHERS

In the literature on the status of the teacher, one rarely encounters comparisons of college professors and school teachers, despite the apparent logic for making such comparisons. It is possible that the teacher's perception of the status of the college professor is less favorable than that of the "free" professions, and thus does not serve as a very desirable model for comparisons. Lieber-

---

[35] David C. McClelland, John W. Atkinson, Russell A. Clark, and Edgar L. Lowell, *The Achievement Motive* (New York: Appleton-Century-Crofts, 1953); Eugene Burnstein, Robert Moulton, and Paul Liberty, Jr., "Prestige vs. Excellence as Determinants of Role Attractiveness," *American Sociological Review,* Vol. 28 (April, 1963), p. 213.

[36] Barney G. Glaser, *Organization Scientists: Their Professional Careers* (New York: Bobbs-Merrill, 1964), chaps. 1, 3.

[37] Raymond Kuhler and Wilbert Dipbrze, *Motivational and Personality Factors in the Selection of Elementary and Secondary Teaching as a Career* (Washington, D.C.: United States Department of Health, Education, and Welfare, Office of Education, Cooperative Research Project [Syracuse, N.Y.: Syracuse University], 1959). This study indicates that prospective public school teachers do, in fact, exhibit *lower* needs for achievement, autonomy, and change than other professionally directed groups.

[38] Lieberman, *op. cit.,* p. 403.

man comments on the inability of college professors to gain the status honor and attendant privileges (particularly higher income) commensurate with full professional status. He claims that public school teachers can be criticized for being too much like college professors.[39] He is probably right with respect to winning income and developing impregnable professional organizations. However, there is still a great difference in occupational prestige between professors and school teachers—a level of prestige apparently not wholly contingent upon high income.

Some differences in the community status of professors and school teachers are related to differences in the organizational status of both types of teachers. The professor's position in a college or university usually provides a considerable amount of individual autonomy in his performance as teacher, scholar, counselor, surrogate parent, and administrator. He has professional status at the same time that he functions within an organized structure. He has rank *as a professor* within the academic structure, a fact of substantial consequence with respect to such important status criteria as income, tenure, special privileges (e.g., offices, telephones, a private library, etc.), and authority within the decision-making system of the faculty. Part of the professor's status and prestige is based on the fact that the administrative officers of the university or college exercise only limited control over the faculty. Students soon learn that faculty members have important professional prerogatives, especially when the students try to bring administrative pressure to bear, or when they see that important decisions are made by committees of faculty members. Of course, having a few intellectual celebrities on a faculty contributes both to organizational and community status.

Compared to that of the public school, the status system (or reward and incentive system) of the college is structurally similar to the reward systems used in dealing with other professionals within complex organizations. It provides the incentives associated with the "opportunity for promotion." Many lawyers, clergymen, "organizational" scientists, and professional experts working in government, church bureaucracies, and industrial organizations function within structures that provide a range of rank and status differences, based on merit and achievement.

The lack of infallible criteria for measuring teaching ability in public schools[40] and colleges is not sufficient reason to eliminate all other criteria of teacher role performance in the two educational settings. The common argument for automatic salary increases based on time in service and number of graduate credits apparently grows out of the lack of precision in judging teaching merit. This argument has some validity, but it should not exclude using imprecise criteria for judging teaching ability *plus* criteria for evaluating additional important aspects of teachers' roles. If teachers are to assume professional rights and

[39] Lieberman, *op. cit.,* pp. 506 ff.

[40] Walter H. Worth, "Can Administrators Rate Teachers?" *Canadian Administration,* Vol. 1 (October, 1961), pp. 1–6; A. S. Barr, "Wisconsin Studies of the Measurement and Prediction of Teacher Effectiveness, Summary of Investigation," *Journal of Experimental Education,* Vol. 30 (September, 1961), pp. 5–156.

privileges, some of them must lead others, develop new methods and techniques, write new textbooks, conduct educational experimentation and research, administer supplementary programs, select appropriate books and teaching aids, determine pupil composition of classes and special groupings, take on extracurricular activities (which must be done by persons with talent rather than by those who primarily need additional money), and be involved in numerous other nonclassroom *teaching* functions.

The argument for eliminating all criteria for judging and rewarding merit is based primarily on the real and/or apparent capriciousness of some school boards and administrators in dispensing rewards in the past, as well as on the difficulties inherent in developing an equitable reward system in large, complex school systems. The obvious hiatus in income, prestige, and authority between school administrators and teachers is an important factor in mobilizing teachers to demand (and in some instances to effect) a reward system that prevents certain kinds of inequities. But, in this process another inequity is introduced—namely, that merit and achievement cannot be adequately rewarded.

Clearly, the types of reward systems found among professionals in many large organizations, including colleges and universities, are rarely observed in the public schools. This difference apparently has important implications for the status dilemmas that have plagued public school teachers for a long time. Barnard emphasizes the use of a status system in developing incentives and responsibility. He states that

> the scarcity of effective incentives calls for the use of many kinds of incentives; and their wise use requires, especially in larger organizations, their systematic use.

The only status system that differentiates superior and inferior teaching performance in the contemporary public school is an informal reward system, which, by its very nature, cannot be systematically used to provide incentives. Formal status provides

> . . . prestige for its own sake, as a reinforcement of the ego, as security for the integrity of the person. . . . a status system is a strong and probably an indispensable developer of the sense of responsibility and therefore, of stability and reliability. . . . the function of status in creating and maintaining dependable behavior is probably indispensable.[41]

All of these qualities are fundamental to an effectively functioning school.

CONCLUSIONS

The previous discussion suggests that the present narrow, essentially two-level, status structure of the American public school is inadequate for the further development of teaching as a profession. A change in the status system could

---

[41] Barnard, *op. cit.,* pp. 68–69.

have a number of important consequences for the teacher's organizational and community status. A considerable body of theory and research indicates that the teacher's status, both in the school and community, would be indirectly enhanced by an expansion of the internal status arrangements of the school. This expansion would eliminate identical official rank for all classroom teachers and establish a variety of official ranks. The educational literature provides some support for this approach.[42] However, the most relevant and available model of such an existing status system is to be found in American universities and colleges. It is possible that ranks comparable to instructor, assistant professor, associate professor, and professor could be introduced into the public school structure. For example, the following labels might be used: associate teacher (noncertified), teacher (beginning certified teacher), career teacher (major category of experienced teachers with tenure), and master teacher (those with great teaching abilities and other special skills).

At this point we can briefly explore some of the possible practical consequences of expanding the status structure of the school to include several official levels of status and of developing a concomitant wider range of rewards.

1.   An increase in the range of statuses might stimulate the development of better criteria for determining the worth and competence of classroom teachers. Currently, seniority and college credits are the major criteria for granting the rewards of small salary increases and/or transfer to a high-status school.

2.   Providing a wider range of opportunity for promotion and achievement would put teaching more on a par with the other professions, and help to attract and retain a greater number of the most competent and ambitious college graduates.

3.   An expanded status system would probably decrease the use of horizontal mobility as a major avenue for gaining status, and thus facilitate a more equitable distribution of teacher talents throughout a given school system. Real opportunities for promotion might help to eliminate current demands for "combat pay" for teaching in difficult schools. As an alternative, the administration could offer promotions at a faster rate for teachers who could successfully meet the challenges of the more problematic schools.

4.   A change in the ranking system could provide the teacher with a choice of behavior in deciding how best to earn rewards for his work. Most organizations manned by professionals (hospitals, universities, clinics, research laboratories, etc.) specify several different kinds of activities that can lead to higher rank *without* completely changing one's major function (i.e., leaving the classroom, in the case of teachers).

5.   A system with a range of statuses more comparable to that used in

---

[42] Max R. Goodson, "Differentiating the Profession of Teaching," *School and Society,* Vol. 86 (May 24, 1958), pp. 239–40; Edward Gross, "Sociological Aspects of Professional Salaries in Education," *Educational Record,* Vol. 41 (April, 1960), pp. 130–37. Gross states that salaries should be determined by merit, which implies a system of ranking.

colleges and universities might help to close the status gap between teachers and professors.

6.   Laymen on the school board, as well as parents of children in or out of school, have no really adequate way to judge a teacher's merits. A ranking system might provide a useful, although sometimes imperfect, criterion.

7.   The development of a more formal and visible ranking system for classroom teachers could bring the decision-making process more into the open, or at least under scrutiny in the manner described by Professor Lynd in his discussion of "participative power."[43]

8.   A ranking system among teachers implies that high-ranking teachers would evaluate their lower ranking professional peers in deciding on promotions, etc.[44] Although such a system does not guarantee the wisest and best judgment, it is probably superior to placing merit judgments exclusively in the hands of bureaucratically oriented administrators.

9.   The suggested system of ranks might contribute to the conditions necessary for legislating increased salaries for teachers. If through an expanded ranking system the teacher could gain more prestige both inside and outside the school, the need for higher salaries might be more readily recognized by the lay public.

10.   Similarly, such a system might also lead to a greater use of other symbols of rank and privilege than size of salary. Although this topic is unpopular with equalitarian-oriented teachers, it appears nevertheless to be an important one. There is considerable impressionistic evidence supporting the idea that private offices, telephones, parking spaces, and freedom of movement constitute important status symbols for the professional, without which the teacher has difficulty in claiming professional status.

A number of these possible consequences of an expanded status system in the public school can be empirically tested. The establishment of schools organized in a manner which would allow such empirical evaluation would be of utmost importance for the future of the teaching profession and, in turn, the public school.

---

[43] Lynd, *op. cit.,* p. 7.

[44] Such a system of evaluation would obviously be very difficult to implement in many large urban school systems. However, current attempts at decentralization, utilizing, for example, the "house plan" (which is being considered in the Philadelphia school system), which virtually establishes smaller schools within the large urban high school, might ultimately make collegial evaluation a feasible aspect of the status and reward system.

PART V

The teacher

The teacher is a member of an occupational group which is labeled as a profession, but which, in many respects, lacks some of the major criteria of professional status. First, the occupation of teaching has for many years been characterized by long hours and low pay. This has changed some in recent years, but the teacher still puts in longer hours for less pay than is the case in most comparable professions. Second, unlike most professionals the teacher has a limited amount of prestige in the eyes of the community and this has influenced both the recruitment of new and the retention of old teachers. Third, there is also some evidence that teachers are not recruited from the most intellectually competent or motivated of college students[1] and that some students become teachers because of inability in other more demanding academic areas. This is not a criticism of the many able teachers, but it does point out a social reality—that when the rewards, both financial and psychic, are low, it is difficult to recruit and retain the most able individuals in an occupation. There follows a discussion of some occupational aspects of education and the teacher.

SOCIAL CLASS

There was a time in the United States when teachers were recruited principally from the middle class, but this has changed greatly in recent years. Today many teachers are being recruited from the lower-middle and upper-lower classes.[2] This is more often the case in the recruitment of males than of females.

---

[1] William H. Whyte, Jr., *The Organization Man* (New York: Simon and Schuster, 1956), p. 83.

[2] Wilbur B. Brookover, *A Sociology of Education* (New York: American Book Co., 1955), p. 276.

Many individuals in becoming teachers have attained personal social mobility because they have moved from their lower-class origins to a more middle-class level. The variety of social backgrounds might lead one to expect a broad range of social class values presented by teachers. In reality such is not the case, because often middle-class values acquired through occupational mobility may be more rigid and binding than when the same values are of an ascribed nature.

There is another possible problem related to the teacher who has successfully achieved social mobility — an overidentification with the means that brought about her success, that of formal education. Because the middle-class teacher of lower class origins has in her own mind been socially successful through the means of formal education plus the taking on of education as an occupation, it may seem that this is the correct behavior pattern to be followed by all "worthwhile" young people of lower class background. But the reality of an individual situation may show that such an assumption is not always justified. Extended formal education may be inappropriate for some individuals because of counter-value pressures, other interests, or lack of intellectual ability.

THE FEMALE WORLD

The majority of all teachers are women, and this is particularly true in elementary education.[3] In the learning of future adult sex roles by pupils, this may have unfortunate consequences. It means that children through the first six or eight grades have a limited contact with male teachers. The problem is not so much around the formal role of the teacher as it is with the student perception of the informal aspects of teaching and teachers. The youngster in the elementary grades sees only a few adult males and this means that most of the informal adult role behavior available to him is coming from women.[4] Add to this the female-centered home, and it can be seen that children are growing up in essentially a world dominated by female adults.

The female world has important consequences for both boys and girls. For boys it means a limited number of adult males to learn from and to emulate in preparing for their future adult sex roles. The few available adult male models in the school may be one reason for the high identification with athletes and athletics on the part of young American boys. The one male they often see in the school is the gym teacher, and he provides them with an area of learning that is essentially male.[5] The male gym teacher showing his students how to play basketball is being masculine in his teaching of a very definitely male activity. Young girls are also affected because of the limited contact with adult male models. They often get a distorted image of the female role and lack the opportunity to understand the male role and how it is a part of the total male-female role-set.

In the female teaching population there is frequently a high turnover; many

---

[3] *Ibid.*, p. 276.
[4] *Ibid.*, pp. 246–47.
[5] *Ibid.*, pp. 246–47.

young women in elementary education are teaching only until they enter their own childbearing years. Often students have the image of the female teacher role not as a first choice of possible adult roles, but rather as only temporary until she can leave to have children of her own. Or the student sees teaching as a substitute for marriage and motherhood.[6] While those images are not necessarily accurate they do often distort the image the student has in regard to female teachers.

Finally the female-dominated elementary school has had adverse effects on the recruitment of male teachers. The handling of children is seen as essentially a female function in the American society, and so long as most elementary teachers are female this stereotype will probably be perpetuated. One consequence of this stereotype is that many males are afraid of some loss of masculinity if they enter elementary education. Furthermore, many men who do go into elementary education go in with the idea of moving as soon as possible away from teaching and into administration. These men often share the general image that young children should be taught by women, and conveniently hold to a belief that men should be administrators over female teachers.

COMMUNITY DEFINITIONS

The occupational role of the teacher must also be viewed in the broader perspective of the community. How the community views the teacher, the rewards given, the obligations expected, will have a strong influence on the recruitment and the self-satisfaction of the teacher in regard to her occupational role. With urbanization the teacher has in many ways been removed from the informal social control of the community. In the large city the teacher has some degree of autonomy and may have a personal life that is less apt to be under the constant scrutiny of the community than was the case in the rural and small town setting of the past. While the social pressures on the teacher have decreased, they have not disappeared. The teacher in many respects is still in, but not of, the community. In general, the teacher's personal life is still expected to personify the highest ideals of middle-class morality, and the teacher is often expected by parents to be a better model than are the parents themselves.

But what may be even more difficult for the teacher to accept today is the old saw that "those that can, do; those that can't, teach." As a result of this belief teachers often find themselves restricted from many types of community activities. Often, the activities they are asked to join are of a "do good" nature with a minimum amount of power and influence. In effect, the teachers' community activities are often of a "busy work" nature with a limited amount of social or personal prestige.

Teachers, because of their formal education, may be interested in a pattern of life that they cannot financially afford. They often find themselves with

---

[6] *Ibid.*, p. 247.

values and interests in cultural areas beyond their standard of living. Other professionals in the community, as a result of educational achievement, are often financially able to pursue interests that one expects of the well-educated individual. Often, the teacher must try to adjust champagne tastes to a beer salary.

CAREER PATTERNS

As has been pointed out, the teacher has a curious career pattern when it is contrasted with many other professions. In the past, one means of occupational success for the teacher was to move into school administration. Today this is usually done through specialized formal education related to administration and is no longer a direct occupational movement from teaching. For teachers not interested in the formal training necessary for administration there is little room for movement within the occupation. Seniority and related salary differences may often be the only meaningful difference for most teachers, but even here the range between the beginner and the veteran is not great. This has implications for the ambitious, the highly motivated and the talented. When mobility within the occupation is restricted, where are they going to go?

There are few other occupations where one enters and has little chance of movement because the role system is so undifferentiated in regard to rewards, prestige, authority, and responsibility. This may, in part, account for the mobility of teachers from one school to another—but even here the change factor is not one of role difference, but rather the same role being played in different school systems. The high mobility rate of teachers out of education may be due to the teacher's seeking a different and more satisfying occupational role.

16. The teacher *

ALMA S. WITTLIN

Education may be defined as a process of shaping behavior. In a general sense every waking moment of life from birth to death is an educational experience, for better or for worse. The function of the educator is to effect behavioral changes in specified groups of people, and to do so in a planned and goal-directed manner.

Storage and dissemination of knowledge are among the great energy-saving devices of mankind. The teacher is one of the foremost guardians and transmitters of knowledge. He occupies a shunting point between generations: he may reinforce the continuation of traditions; or he may be a factor in unsettling or in reshaping them. And he may perform either of these functions with a greater or lesser consciousness of his role. Directly or circuitously he may be a powerful force molding society. A single teacher may accelerate the fruition of talent in hundreds of individuals, neglect or warp it; he may further or stifle potentials for creativity or waywardness. A teacher's trade is concerned with the human condition, with human promise and destiny.

The teacher claims to be a *professional.* Contrary to an amateur, a professional person assumedly possesses a body of knowledge and of skills, and he uses them with confidence. It would not befit him to skip from dabbling in one thing to trifling with another; he is to be earnest, persistent and accurate in his work. A dilettante may engage in a pursuit for the built-in recompense of doing or toying, but a professional person is entitled to a monetary reward. Certain professional people, however, are expected to put service to others before personal profit. In this respect, the image of the educator has common traits with that of the healer of the sick.

According to dictionary lore the terms "vocation" and "profession" are to some degree interchangeable, but while a vocation often presupposes routine jobs, a profession enshrines the meaning of a calling and an avowal to a higher purpose. In logical conclusion the respect of his fellow men would seem to be due the teacher, as well as a wide scope in decision-making that would be commensurate with his status. The setting of special standards and their enforcement are among the privileges of a professional group and of its members.

In Martin Luther's judgment the teacher's vocation was next to that of the

*Reprinted with permission from DAEDALUS, Journal of the American Academy of Arts and Sciences, Boston, Mass. Fall 1963. "The Professions."

ministry. In *Sartor Resartus,* Thomas Carlyle referred to teachers as to "fashioners of souls," who ought to be "world-honored dignitaries" like generals and field marshals. Notables of England, Sweden and Hungary vied for the counsel of the seventeenth-century schoolmaster and writer on education John Amos Comenius, the son of a Czech miller. Johann Pestalozzi's schools in Switzerland were places of pilgrimage in the early nineteenth century. The philosopher Johann Herbart was among the visitors, and Johann Fichte referred to the educator in his "Addresses to the German Nation." Later in the century Friedrich Froebel's Kindergarten was a subject of international admiration, in which Charles Dickens joined with the French historian Jules Michelet and with Giuseppe Garibaldi, the leader of the newly unified Italy.

In a period of accelerated change the teacher's function acquires special significance. The era of automated industry, of computers performing operations hitherto reserved to the human brain, of global intercourse and of space exploration demands a quickened pace in lifting increasing numbers of people to higher levels of education: ". . . never before were men and nations compelled, by inescapable challenge, to learn so much, so fast, so well." "Indeed, this is a revolutionary era . . . calling for a new and better life. But I wonder if it is not true to say that there has been no comparable revolution—and perhaps no revolution at all—in the realm of education?" These two statements were made at the International Centennial Conference at Vassar College in 1962, by Emmet John Hughes and Ralph J. Bunche respectively.

In the course of the last decade teachers have been severely criticized for failing in their tasks. There is young Johnny who after several years of schooling cannot read. There are the dropouts from high school, estimated to be 4 out of 10 students, and referred to by Dr. James Conant as social dynamite. There are the graduates of an education known as liberal or liberalizing who show little sensitive regard for humane values in their daily lives and who remain stubbornly immature in spite of their credits for courses in Greek history or in literature. Teachers are often accused of incompetence in the subject matter they teach. To make up for the omissions of science teachers, scientists feel challenged to take time off from their research and college teaching to act as school reformers from the high school down to the grades. Scholars, businessmen and union leaders are demanding that students receive instruction in economics and other significant aspects of their present environment. The ratio of private to public schools rose from 10.9 per cent to 14 per cent between 1950 and 1960, and is an index of the dissatisfaction of parents with public schools.

One of the contributors to the first symposium on "Automation and the Challenge to Education," held in Washington, D.C. in 1961, the economist Dr. Walter Buckingham, Director of the School of Industrial Management at the Georgia Institute of Technology, Atlanta, called for teachers of ". . . higher quality . . . who are creative, courageous, imaginative, intelligent, sensitive, personable." He expressed his conviction that "teachers of this caliber are capable of stirring a student's imagination so that he can develop his own potentialities. Dull, uninspiring teachers may well force students into the ranks of those who are indifferent, even hostile, to knowledge and reason."[1]

Public schools are accused of anti-intellectualism and of offering cafeteria-style curricula, superficial and discontinuous, requiring neither concentration nor precision. Teachers are blamed for being popularity seekers instead of representing legitimate authority. The question is raised, what function does a school teacher first and foremost fulfill—that of an instructor, of a custodian or of a social worker? The professional status of the school teacher is altogether questioned on the grounds of his limited autonomy, of his restrictions in decision-making concerning what and how he teaches, and of his position as a strictly supervised employee.

Any attempt at a judicious and constructive evaluation of criticisms and of their causes must begin with an analysis in which each symptom of a complex syndrome would appear in isolation, with the help of which the hierarchy of the symptoms and their possible relations to each other could be better understood. Both the teacher and his habitat require examination: the school, the society, and the legacies of the past which live on in the minds of men. If teachers are accused of being supervisees, to what extent and in what respect are they responsible for shortcomings in education? Who is the master-mind behind them who carries the main burden of responsibility? Or is it a group-mind, and if so, what is its composition? Does society wish the teacher to be in this position, does it tolerate such circumstances, or is there an insufficient general awareness of the situation?

The number of elementary and secondary teachers in the United States may approach one million and a half. How can such a large contingent of human beings be uniformly assessed and judged—like a homogenized mass? There are men and women among them, people from 22 to 65 years of age, and representatives of a variety of religious and political persuasions. There are natives of all states and graduates of a wide range of colleges and universities; people without any academic degree and holders of advanced degrees. There are grade-school teachers who take care of all subjects, instructors of physics or of literature for advanced high school students, and teachers of driving an automobile. What may be the specific traits characterizing so many people of such heterogeneous backgrounds?

The place of direct impact of formal education on the pupil is in the classroom, and in considerable measure in the interaction between teacher and pupil. As I. L. Kandel said, "To erect fine buildings and to seek to meet the needs and abilities of all individuals who desire to avail themselves of the opportunity so generously offered without providing teachers with qualifications commensurate with the ideal is a sham." Yet the teacher in the American classroom has only a

---

[1] L. H. Evans and G. E. Arnstein (eds.), *Automation and the Challenge to Education*, Proceedings of a Symposium (Washington, D.C.: National Education Association, 1962).

very limited power of decision-making. In their book *The Role of Schools in Mental Health,* W. Allinsmith and G. W. Goethals listed among the main functions of a teacher's immediate superior, as item number one, "to make decisions"[2] and they note: "Teachers have unclear perceptions of the policy-making processes and practices in the school system." In a publication of the U.S. Office of Education, *Elementary School Administration and Organization,* of 1960, by Stuart E. Dean, the main role of the school principal is described as that of a supervisor of instruction. In fact, the principal's autonomy is bridled by the central office of his school system. If he retains 41.8 per cent authority in assigning pupils to classes and 23 per cent authority in matters of pupils' promotion, little is left of important decisions to the classroom teacher. Lack of democratic administration procedures and of a share in policy-making were among the main causes of poor teacher morale recorded in a survey made by the George Peabody College for Teachers in Nashville, Tennessee.

Owing to the increasing pressure of public demand for better academic standards in the schools, the scholastic achievements of an elementary teacher may currently serve as a recommendation for a post, contrary to a previously prevailing distrust on the part of administrators of overqualified teachers. The physical appearance of a candidate for a teaching position is, however, still receiving considerable attention; it is questionable whether any very able teacher with some physical disability or deformity would be hired. Of primary importance is the teacher's conformity with existing standards. The code of ethics of the National Education Association demands that a teacher accept the community's pattern of behavior.

Parents, members of the P.T.A., and other citizens are vociferous in expressing their views on school matters. They criticize, advise, and demand the institution of certain courses and the abolition of others; they argue in favor of or against strict discipline or children's right to creative self-expression, though they would hardly take it upon themselves to compete with their physician or with their legal adviser in matters which require professional expertise. As Sterling M. McMurrin, former U.S. Commissioner of Education, pointed out in his introduction to J. D. Koerner's *Miseducation of American Teachers,* the average citizen has taken it for granted that teaching is a profession appropriate for persons of second- or third-rate ability.[3] The public's attitude toward the teachers of the growing generations is, however, rarely based on solid facts. As Mr. Devereux Josephs, chairman of President Eisenhower's Committee on Education Beyond High School, said, "The public knows more about potato prices, the number of hogs slaughtered, and the status of bank loans than it knows about its schools."

If salaries are to be considered as an index of status, teachers rank lower than

---

[2] W. Allinsmith and G. W. Goethals, *The Role of Schools in Mental Health,* Monograph Series No. 7, Joint Commission on Mental Health (New York: Basic Books, 1962).

[3] James D. Koerner, *The Miseducation of American Teachers* (Boston: Houghton Mifflin, 1963).

members of other professions. After considerable improvement in the last few years, the average yearly salary of a public school teacher has risen to a little more than $5000. About 15 per cent of teachers earn less than $3500, although according to the U.S. Department of Labor's estimate the average city worker needs more than $6200 per year to maintain an accepted standard of living. There may be a few hundred high school teachers who earn about $10,000 yearly, a paltry sum for similarly successful physicians or attorneys.

The present status of the teacher is the result of conditions reaching back into a distant past. There is a plurality of antecedents rather than a single step-by-step sequence of cause and effect—economic and political determinants together with ambivalent human attitudes which obfuscated and distorted the rational perception of a changing environment. In ancient Greece philosophers were highly honored teachers, and fees were deemed acceptable only among Sophists. The men who taught children to read, to write and to memorize passages from poetic history accepted a meager pay and enjoyed little respect. The original *paidagogos* was a servant whose function was literally implied in his title—he had to lead the boy to and from school. In the traditional Chinese school for young pupils the schoolmaster was by definition a man who had failed intellectually. Having fallen short of the requirements at a civil service examination he stooped to the job of compelling boys to the confrontation of ideographs and to the memorization of hardly understood texts. To meet the unprecedented demand for teachers on an elementary level misfits and invalids were sometimes considered equal to the task of teaching. Russian theological seminaries disposed of some of their undesirable students by turning them over to the new common schools under Peter the Great. In Frederick the Great's Prussia invalids of the army were promoted, or demoted, to teachers.

The low opinion of the rank-and-file schoolmaster in Europe spread to the New World, and a seventeenth-century Rector of Annapolis recorded that on the arrival of every ship containing bondservants or convicts, schoolmasters were offered for sale but that they did not fetch as good prices as weavers, tailors and other tradesmen. Eighteenth-century rural families in America often had tutors in their houses who lived like people "on alms." When the instruction of "petties," or young children, became necessary in great numbers, instructors were sometimes "poor women or others whose necessities compelled them to undertake it as a mere shelter from beggary." In referring to conditions in 1823, Arthur Bestor quoted a previous author: "The common schools are, in not a few instances, conducted by individuals who do not possess one of the qualifications of an instructor; and in very many cases, there is barely knowledge enough to keep the teacher at a decent distance from the scholars."[4] In his Annual Report of 1842 the state superintendent of public instruction of Michigan wrote that "an elementary school, where the rudiments of an English education only are taught . . . requires a female of practical common sense, with amiable and

---

[4] Arthur Bestor, *The Restoration of Learning* (New York: Knopf, 1955).

winning manners, a patient spirit, and a tolerable knowledge of the springs of human action."

The monitorial schools of the early nineteenth century seemed ideally to fit the early state of industrial civilization. Pupils were cheaply mass produced, down to $1 per year. The scholars, who first learned their lessons from the teacher, conveyed exactly the same lesson to other children, ten to every monitor. The financial expenditure was limited to a wage for a single teacher and to the maintenance of a single hall. Western man was under the spell of an unprecedented experience: of the realization of abundance produced by the inanimate power of machines. Since the dawn of memory human fate had been identified with toil in striving for the bare necessities of life, except for the conspicuous consumption indulged in by small elites. The harnessing of the wind and of the muscle power of animals had eased the grind, but millennia had to pass before energy became plentiful with James Watts' steam engine and with the use of electric power transmitted over distances. The increasing demands of industry on labor and the extension of the ballot made improved general education imperative. Large-scale mechanisms were needed for education, mind-factories comparable to those factories used in the manufacture of goods. In the 'thirties of the nineteenth century a superintendent in Chicago became known for his motto: "Organize, deputize, supervise," which he recommended to schools in imitation of big business. The analogy of the industrial plant, of assembly lines and of speed was haunting human minds (and may still have a grip on them). In 1916 a book appeared in Boston on *Public School Administration,* by E. P. Cubberly, in which it was stated that ". . . the schools are, in a sense, factories in which the raw materials are to be shaped into products to meet the various demands of life." According to this philosophy the educator was allotted the modest role of a copyist of patterns.

The United States was the first country in the world to provide free public schooling beyond the elementary level, and American education was becoming a colossal enterprise. In 1900, 17 million students went to school; their present number is close to 50 million. As Paul Woodring wrote, "Many people seem satisfied merely to have more schools, bigger schools, and to keep children in them for a longer period of time."[5] It is in the nature of any large enterprise involving many people and masses of materials to crystallize into a corporate structure. Big business followed the example of governments and of armies, and was in its turn followed by big-scale education. But for all the bureaucracy and hierarchy, for all the chains of command and delays of action which are entailed in corporate structure, business in competitive society could hardly have survived without remaining flexible, without retaining scope for autonomy and spontaneity in its strategic managerial posts where a salaried person had to have something of the character of an entrepreneur, of a risk-taking innovator. In the schools, however, where products do not lend themselves to the same quick

---

[5] Paul Woodring, *New Directions in Teacher Education* (New York: Fund for the Advancement of Education, 1957).

evaluation as marketable merchandise, the figure occupying the strategically most significant post, the teacher in the classroom, was deprived of most of his opportunities for decision-making, for spontaneous and original action. He was demoted to an employee on the bottom link of a long chain of command which winds its way from the state governor's office and the chambers of the state legislature to state boards and state education departments, further down to local school boards and offices of superintendents, and from them to the principals of individual schools. A host of statisticians, supervisors, guidance officers, counselors, testing experts and other specialists supply a supporting cast which in Myron Lieberman's terms leads "to a splitting, not a fusion of power and technical competence" and to "a power structure which is inconsistent with the professional status of the teacher."[6]

All these educator figures may have their relevance, but as in any interaction among human beings their roles have to be subtly defined and teamwork has to replace hierarchy to make each individual productive without debilitating others. It has been shown, for example, that the presence of guidance officers may deprive some teachers of a sense of individual responsibility needed by an adult for successful performance. The school superintendent may feel somewhat akin to a corporation executive, he may receive the highest salary in his occupational group and appear in the beam of publicity as the authoritative representative of the school system; yet in fact he is a short-term employee of the local school board, which is mainly composed of laymen, if he is not occupying an elective office of partisan-political denomination. When Abraham Flexner in 1908 wrote his historical report on "Medical Education in the United States and Canada," which was based on extensive studies made under the sponsorship of the Carnegie Foundation, he recommended that all state medical boards which judged on such matters as the accreditation of medical schools and the licensing of doctors should be composed of doctors and not of laymen. A publication of the Council of State Governments, "Occupational Licensing in the States," recorded in 1952 that all or the majority of members of professional boards of dentists and of attorneys had to be practitioners of the profession in all the states of the union. A similar ruling existed in 42 states with regard to barbers, in 41 states with regard to beauticians, and in 5 states with regard to teachers.

Even now, in the 'sixties, educational boards in many states are still largely or exclusively composed of laymen. They exercise authority over teacher accreditation, salaries and tenure, the selection of courses, the adoption or rejection of textbooks or the keeping of deviant pupils in ordinary classrooms, sometimes in opposition to a superintendent's request for special classes for such students. No lay adviser would defy a hospital administrator or doctor with the immoral request of accommodating in a general ward patients suffering from an infectious or mental disease.

Two specific examples will illustrate actions of lay boards or ignorant citizens.

---

[6] Myron Lieberman, *Education as a Profession* (Englewood Cliffs, N.J.: Prentice-Hall, 1956); *The Future of Public Education* (Chicago: University of Chicago Press, 1960).

The community of Levittown, New York, is the topic of a report of an investigation conducted in 1962 under the auspices of the National Education Association and the New York State Teachers Association. One of the numerous controversies between the community and the schools was centered on the letter of a housewife to the superintendent of the local schools, in which she protested the use of the cantata, "The Lonesome Train," which describes the journey of the train bearing Lincoln's body from Washington, D.C. to Springfield, Illinois, for burial, and which was allegedly written and scored by "known communists" and therefore communist propaganda. This happened in 1955, but the temper of the community has not subsided, as could be witnessed recently when the Levittown school board voted 5 to 2 to ban a textbook, *Subcontinent of India,* by an established author of history books and professor at Fairleigh Dickinson University, on the grounds that the author, Emil Lengyel, had sometime in the past been a member of objectionable organizations. The trustee who made the motion had read the book and did not object to its contents. These are merely two of the numerous happenings at Levittown which hamper the education of children.

When Gordon Lish, a teacher of English at Mills High School in Burlingame, California, was dismissed by the school board but was offered help in finding another school job, he answered: "I don't want one . . . teaching is not a man's job. They won't let you be one and they don't pay a man's salary. I used to think teaching was the most rewarding thing you could do, but I have begun to care less and less. Yet just walking away from this seems like an immoral decision." Mr. Lish was fired for spending time on the editing of a literary quarterly, *Genesis West,* among whose contributors were Stephen Spender, Kenneth Rexroth and Mark Harris. He was also blamed for reciting the Allegiance to the Flag too rapidly and for telling his students that they were free not to crouch beneath their desks during nuclear attack drills.

It is encouraging to learn that the new superintendent of the New York City schools, Dr. Calvin E. Gross, hopes to establish "administrative control points" manned "by individuals, not committees." In his opinion decentralization of authority in schools is needed, and a wider margin for the delegation of responsibility.

Why do people choose teaching as a career? There is a preponderance of teachers from the lower or lower middle socio-economic groups of the population. To them teaching means advancement in social status. In the case of women it is one of the traditional occupations, and there are in the public schools of the United States 73 women teachers to 27 men. Up to about 1939, teachers' salaries were higher than the wages of employees in industry, and this served as an additional inducement. The financial picture changed, however. In 1952 a classroom teacher's average annual salary was 1.4 per cent below the average annual income of all employed persons, while that of industrial employees was 12.9 per cent above it. [It ought to be noted that from 1952 to the present, teachers' salaries have gained in momentum.] Between 1904 and 1953 the purchasing power of the income of a coal miner and of a railroad switchtender increased by 163 per cent and 134 per cent respectively, while the elementary school teacher's purchasing power rose by 60 per cent, and that of a high school teacher and a college professor by even less. The disparity between white and blue collar incomes lessened. Furthermore, teacher training extended over a longer period of time, and so did the school year. While industrial and office work decreased from a six-day work week of at least 48 hours to a five-day work week of not more than 40 hours between 1904 and 1953, children's school terms increased in length by about 23 per cent.

In spite of the lengthening period of teacher training, it is still short if compared with the preparation for other professions such as medicine or law, and this aspect in itself may encourage some people to choose education as a career. Secondary school teachers receive a much more thorough training in a specific subject matter than teachers for elementary schools, but are at present required to show credit in such courses as Educational Psychology, Educational Measurement or School Procedure.

"When national samples of education students are compared with comparable samples of students in other curricular areas, they consistently fall below the liberal arts, science and engineering groups. . . . Under conditions now prevailing in the country as a whole . . . the field of education is not competing successfully with other professions in drawing the high-caliber personnel that it so urgently needs," wrote Robert D. North in *Education of Teachers: New Perspectives* in 1958.[7] In a Selective Service Qualification Test of 1955, the I.Q.'s of students majoring in nine different areas were compared. Engineers scored highest; physical scientists and mathematicians came next, with students of humanities following them; students of education appeared at the bottom of the list. In another study, made in Philadelphia, high school students scored higher than students in a teacher training college. The image of the prospective school teacher might look brighter if such comparisons were repeated at present, after several years of increasing demand by critics for better teachers; but these and similar often-quoted statistics still leave a very incomplete image of the prospective teacher. Supposing that the student of education of 1963 compares more favorably with his counterpart in economics or in physics than he did five years ago, how will he compare after several years of teaching? Furthermore, is the "I.Q." the most relevant characteristic of people? Or are there other "queues"— such as for example an A.Q., a C.Q. and a F.Q.— measures for ambiguity tolerance, for adaptation to change, for flexibility? And which endowments, or lack of them, may motivate people to choose teaching as a career? So far we have invested our faith in the I.Q.

---

[7] Robert D. North, "The Teacher Education Student: How Does He Compare Academically with Other College Students?" in *The Education of Teachers: New Perspectives* (Washington, D.C.: National Commission on Teacher Education and Professional Standards, N.E.A., 1958).

What discourages people from teaching? The attitudes of families and of friends act in varying degrees as deterrents, especially if the candidate for the teaching career is a male. As Allinsmith and Goethals reported, he is told, "You can do better than that." The neutral attitude toward the girl who intends to teach may acquire an acid tone if she wants to teach in the elementary school. A liberal arts student will consider elementary school teaching as an acceptable female occupation but as an undesirable way of living for a man.

There is a strange contradiction between the prestige in which students of "Ivy League" colleges or liberal arts colleges hold teaching and their rating of the contribution the teacher makes to society. In terms of social prestige a secondary teacher may rank at the bottom of twelve occupations, on a par with salesmen and small-business proprietors, even though above elementary school teachers. As a contributor to society he rises to the fourth rank from the top, above lawyers, engineers and business executives, and below medical doctors and ministers of religion.

"A continuing hardship under which public schools operate is the annual loss of a substantial number of their experienced teachers. Each year many thousands leave the profession permanently. . . ." — "The public school . . . is not only unable to hold experienced teachers . . . but it does not attract enough of the able young men and women of each new generation. . . . In the elementary schools where the total need is the greatest, the annual supply of new teachers is least adequate in numbers. Why do one-fourth of the young people who go to the effort and expense of completing teacher education turn away at the point of employment?" These are statements and questions of the authors of *Conditions of Work for Quality Teaching,* published under the auspices of the Department of Classroom Teachers, N.E.A. in 1959. One of the answers, found by a touring investigator of Ohio State University, is that "able teachers are deeply dissatisfied; many are leaving the schools because of working conditions . . ." Teaching loads are too heavy, pupils too numerous, clerical routines and community projects too distracting from the professional purpose. Salaries are inadequate, buildings and equipment are unsatisfactory.

There are beginnings of changes to the better, even though insular and unevenly distributed throughout the country, and often as yet in the preparatory phase of discussion and experiment. There is a growing awareness of the need for a teacher's competence in subject matter. A questionnaire on this aspect issued in 1959 to secondary teachers elicited from two thirds of them the answer that a thorough familiarity with subject matter is "very important" or "important." More than one fourth of the responding teachers were at least part of the time working outside their field of major preparation. A recently released study of the National Science Foundation, *Secondary School Science and Mathematics Teachers, Characteristics and Service Loads,* stresses the problems arising in schools owing to the wrong teacher assignment pattern. With comparatively few students requiring courses in physics or chemistry, specialists teach only one or two courses in their discipline and spend the rest of their time on subjects in which they have no formally acquired competence. A no more desirable alternative is the teacher of physics who had a single one-year college course in the subject, or none at all.

The specialized teacher in the elementary school is gaining ground in the face of still considerable opposition. There is no evidence in support of the old wives' tale of children being in need of a single teacher as a substitute mother, and of their experiencing insecurity when changing teachers or rooms. Children, like people of all ages, are profitably stimulated by a change of environment, in the form of both things and people. The elementary school curriculum having proliferated greatly from its original narrow task of teaching the rudiments of the three R's, no single person can be competent to teach it all adequately. It may be that the reading difficulties of children are to a considerable measure due to the incompetence of instructors in this difficult skill, whatever the method of teaching may be. The growing acceptance of Team Teaching may not yet have defeated the prejudice against specialist teachers in grade schools, but it serves as a serious challenge.

Team Teaching incorporates several budding new approaches to teaching as well as to learning. Ideally, school time is divided into three parts—into large assemblies, small discussion groups, and children's individual work combined with consultations with teachers. An assembly for 150 children frees two or three teachers for preparation and evaluation of lessons; teachers gain opportunities to teach the subjects in which they feel competent. Children learn to use time on independent study and to avail themselves of the facilities of the library and of mechanical aids. Theoretically, this approach tends to make for a higher ratio of school staff to pupils, but a constant awareness of pitfalls is needed to make the principles come alive in daily practice. A fine exposition of developed Team Teaching on the secondary level is offered in the publication *Images of the Future,* by J. Lloyd Trump, sponsored by the National Association of Secondary School Principals of the N.E.A. in 1958. Instructional staff is divided into full-time professional or career teachers, who may be specialists or general teachers; instructional assistants who may work part time; clerks; general aides; community consultants and staff specialists. The customary sixteen teachers working together some 150 hours weekly are replaced by five full-time teacher specialists and five full-time generalists, by 200 hours of instructional assistance, 100 hours of clerking, and 50 hours of miscellaneous help. The annual cost is over $2000.00 less than the expenditure for traditional staffing.

The consultation between an individual pupil or a few pupils with a teacher in the quiet of his study is a modern adaptation of a teaching situation which has proved effective over thousands of years. The original was, and still is, the parent who interacts with his child or children. "And thou shalt teach [the Laws] diligently unto thy children, and shalt talk of them when thou sittest in thine house and when thou walkest by the way," is a command of the Bible, in the sixth chapter of Deuteronomy, to the father of the family in ancient Israel.

It was no doubt taken for granted that both parents trained their children in the traditional skills of simple farming, husbandry and domestic arts. Variations of the theme were still common in rural parts of Europe in the nineteenth century. The master-craftsman and the private tutor were substitute figures of the parent-educator. There is again the personal relationship, the bond between an elder and one or a few disciples. There is mutual trust, intimacy and spontaneity. The apprentice is an heir of the master-craftsman, and a tutor spiritually fathers his disciple. In medieval, feudal society the son of a noble spent fourteen years as a page and a squire to a knight. In ancient Egypt governmental officials started their careers as apprentices. In Athens a youth received his education by watching men in public places and listening to their speeches.

Another new avenue is opened up by the ungraded elementary school, in which pupils of different ages are grouped together during lessons in which they show comparable ability. Not only the pupils gain in this manner, both the fast and the slow, but teachers are faced by fewer obstacles. Since every fifth American is supposed to change his residence every year, classes have to shelter many transients from different states whose scholastic equipment varies greatly. On the occasion of a test given to registrants for Selective Service every other Mississippian failed, while the men from Montana did best, with only 2.5 per cent failures. If students of comparable ability are grouped together, learning acquires a new quality. They have an opportunity not only to absorb facts and postulates but to engage in inquiry and to learn how to learn—which may be the most important basic skill in the preparation for an unknown future.

How do we get better teachers in greater numbers? Obviously an extended period of study will be of help, but in my personal opinion it will not necessarily give us the benefit of teachers of a greater intellectual power than we have now. The longer and better courses will benefit only those who are fit to study any subject at any depth and who continue to study while they teach; who are inquisitive, who have a scholarly bent of mind, and who realize the complexities of a teacher's task, be it in a physics laboratory, with a group of fourth graders, or in a kindergarten. Students of this caliber would hardly be content with the sterile atmosphere in some of the teacher training institutions. If college instructors do not continue some scholarly pursuit themselves, they can hardly elicit curiosity and intellectual delight in their students. Both teachers of children and their teachers in colleges and universities must, indeed, have scholarly interests in two domains: in a subject matter and in child development. Another currently advocated reform, extended internship, should provide good results. Yet all approaches ultimately depend on the quality of the people who go into the teaching profession and on their working conditions in schools—on their chances to maintain such good mental health as would allow them to use their talents and their training. No teacher should be allowed to spend more than three lesson-sessions daily in a group-teaching situation with students, and least of all with children. Every school teacher should have a daily period for quiet study—like his colleague in colleges and universities. There is concern in schools over "the sheer constancy of teacher contacts with children" and that teachers might be "taxed to the point of fatigue and diminishing returns," as Stuart Dean put it.

Mental health problems among teachers have not gone unobserved, but they are an unpopular topic. Dr. Clarence O. Senior, a professor of sociology at Brooklyn College and a member of the board of the New York City schools, referred, according to reports, to "mentally-disturbed teachers" in the city's schools, who "hate children." In 1962 a pamphlet entitled "Mental Health" appeared in a series, *What Research Says to the Teacher,* by R. V. Peck and J. V. Mitchell, under the auspices of the American Education Research Association and the Department of Classroom Teachers of the N.E.A. They pointed out: "If the research on the mental health of school children is still incomplete, it is vast by comparison with studies on the mental health of members of the school staff."

Peck and Mitchell's publication lists some of the tasks a teacher has to fulfill: He has to make careful observations of a child's developing abilities and skills; provide the appropriate experiences just at the right time; be on hand with exciting and worthwhile experiences when the time is ripe; provide opportunities for self-esteem and the utilization of unique abilities; encourage the child's creativity at every turn; help the child to discover and understand himself as a person; understand the defense mechanisms of anxious children who without such understanding may become poor learners and aggressive, antisocial citizens; and create a desire for learning and an eagerness for life in the minds of the students because he himself feels that way about learning and life. . . . This list of tasks and roles is far from being complete.

No human being remains free of anxieties when teaching subjects in which he has no competence. Nobody can enjoy good mental health—a combination of stability and flexibility, of self-confidence and self-criticism, of vigorous curiosity and subtle sensitivity—while spending his working hours without interruption with children; with other adults issuing orders and acting as superiors; trying to play diverse and incompatible roles; in constant noise and under pressure which lead either to the disintegration of personality or to the numbing of the mind. The effectiveness of our teachers is as much a problem of good mental health as of numbers of academic credits. As the late Dr. T. A. C. Rennie of Cornell University wrote in his prologue to *Mental Health in the Metropolis,* by Leo Srole, published in 1962: "We have reached the point in psychiatric development where many psychiatrists feel deeply impelled to turn their interest outward from the individual . . . to the community, to the total cultural scene."[8] The cultural scenes of the school and the classroom are awaiting multidisciplinary research in which the psychiatrist would join with the specialist in psychosomatic medicine, with the clinical psychologist and with the behavioral scientist. In this way we may get definite evidence of the superhuman perfor-

---

[8] Leo Srole *et al., Mental Health in the Metropolis,* Series in Social Psychiatry (New York: McGraw-Hill, 1962), Vol. I.

mance society is expecting of the school teacher. Efforts connected with space medicine are supplying us with a most valuable tool, with a miniaturized transmitter, no larger than a pack of cigarettes, which can be attached to the teacher's body or clothing while he works in the classroom and goes about his business in school. The pupils would be unaware of its presence, and the teacher would hardly remain conscious of it after an initial trial. In this manner several physical modalities of a person can be recorded simultaneously—heartbeat and respiration, skin temperature and blood pressure, possibly the electrical action of the brain. The apparatus is being used in other group-action situations; why not in schools? Psychological tests alone would bring evidence of many of these aspects, but their combination with tests of physiological conditions holds the promise of a far greater convincing power.

The future of a nation may be affected by the acceptance of a new teacher concept in the schools below college level, and especially in the elementary school. A single teacher deals with at least fifteen hundred children during his career. An inquiry of the proposed kind might defeat objections to the employment of part-time teachers in elementary schools: the ones who are there full time physically are not always mentally present. Under stress and fatigue they turn into husks in human shape and react no longer to all signals of inquiry or of distress which come from their pupils.

According to forecasts we shall need an increase of 160 per cent in teachers by 1966. To reach the quota every other college graduate would have to become a teacher instead of every twentieth as at present. How then can we cut down on the teaching time of elementary and secondary school teachers? The answer seems simple: the occupation must not be allowed to remain a drudgery, a series of frustrations, a condition of constant fatigue and of too little autonomy in the classroom. Under changed conditions we shall not only get greater numbers of teachers, but greater numbers of better teachers, and we shall keep them. The improvement will begin with a new self-selection fitting new standards and new expectations.

There is a considerable pool of fine potential teachers among the married women who want to work and who are prepared to spend time and money on training, provided that it will lead to a satisfactory occupation. There are women in their thirties who as young girls may have raised their sights to careers as medical doctors, scholars or lawyers, had they not married and raised a family. Deriving satisfaction from their home life and hesitating to embark on a training of five or more years, many of them would probably be interested in being trained as specialized elementary school teachers. We need suitable training opportunities for such women, first of all on the undergraduate level, and partly based on self-study and examination. This in itself would provide a needed pilot project, in preparation of the years of acute shortage of college instructors. There ought to be part-time positions for these women, or for any specialized school teacher who wishes to spend only two hours in the classroom and to do his preparation and continuous further study at home, in libraries, or in laboratories at any time of the day or of the evening.

Lieberman considers a change in the power structure of the public school, in the layman-administrator-teacher relationship, as need number one. Bestor demands that an end be put to the "interlocking directorate" of education departments and administrators; he would like to see the entire university shaping a new breed of teachers. Rickover points out that homogenized education does justice to no one. These and other recommendations are facets of the same problem. And so is the one that is here proposed.

The concept of education as investment in human beings has for a long time been familiar among economists from Adam Smith to Alfred Marshall, but the consciousness of people in general has only slightly been touched by the call for "investment in human resources," imperative as it is. We have too long been conditioned to investment in durable things, in inanimate objects and materials. Accordingly vast sums are spent on research and development of goods in industry in contrast to trifling sums of money for research on learning and teaching; and what there is of it has in fact very little to say to the teacher. Our current national expenditure on public education in the United States is $25 billion, about 5 per cent of the gross national product. Five per cent of the total expenditure on education would seem to be an adequate figure to begin research on education, about $1,250,000,000. In actual practice we are spending no more than 0.1 per cent on this type of research. The U.S. Office of Education receives less for research grants than the Department of Agriculture or the Department of the Interior.

Dollar figures reflect human attitudes. It is estimated that we are spending from $15 to $20 billion every year on the leisure-time use of automobiles, rather close to the sum devoted to public education. We are supposedly spending more money on alcohol, tobacco and cosmetics than on public education, although the percentage of personal income spent on education has been rising, from 2.1 per cent in 1950 to an estimated 5.5 per cent in 1970. Our personal incomes are two to twenty times as high as the incomes of people in other countries, and we are the consumers of almost half of all goods produced on this planet. Changes in the education of future generations are hinged on our values, on our choices and on our courage rather than on the availability of funds.

17.   The role of the teacher

in the social structure

of the high school *

C. WAYNE GORDON

PURPOSE AND SCOPE

This paper will examine some of the complexities of the teachers' role in the social structure of the high school.[1] The analysis will be primarily concerned with those aspects of social organization which impinge directly on the teacher in the classroom.

This discussion will rely chiefly on a research of the social organization of a high school previously reported as "The Social System of a High School," referred to here as Wabash High.[2] Wabash is a midwestern metropolitan community, a four-year high school in a detached suburb, with a student population of 576. Lower middle class members predominate, but all socio-economic levels are significantly represented. There is diversity of socio-economic levels to confront the teacher with a sufficient status range and power system to introduce the maximum of complexities related to social class which have been reported in other school and community studies.[3] The number of students is sufficiently

*From the *Journal of Educational Sociology,* Vol. 29 (1955), pp. 21–29. By permission of author and the *Journal of Educational Sociology.*

[1] The concept of role used here is that of Talcott Parsons and Edward A. Shils, with the assistance of James Olds, "Values, Motives and Systems of Action," in Parsons and Shils (eds.), *Toward a General Theory of Action* (Cambridge: Harvard University Press, 1951), p. 190; and Theodore M. Newcomb, "Role Concepts in Social Psychology" (paper delivered at the 1948 meetings of the American Psychological Association); Gross, Neal, and Ward S. Mason, "Role Conceptualization and Empirical Complexities" (paper delivered at the 1953 meeting of the American Sociological Society).

[2] C. Wayne Gordon, "The Social System of a High School" (paper delivered at the American Sociological Society as a summary of a larger study first reported by the writer); C. Wayne Gordon, "The Social System of a High School" (unpublished Ph.D. thesis, Washington University, St. Louis, Missouri, 1952). The complete study will be published by Glencoe, Ill.: Free Press.

[3] August B. Hollingshead, *Elmtown's Youth* (New York: John Wiley & Sons, Inc., 1949). W. Lloyd Warner, Robert J. Havighurst, and Martin B. Loeb, *Who Shall Be Educated?* (New York: Harper & Bros., 1944).

small to permit the development of a social system in which the members interact sufficiently with one another to establish a clearly defined set of relationships which have a stable character.

Data on the teacher is from three major sources: (1) school records, (2) two hundred personal documents written by upper grade students on their school careers with special reference to classroom performance, (3) the writer's field diary as a participant observer and classroom teacher in the Wabash school system for ten years.

THE STRUCTURAL CONTEXT OF THE TEACHERS' ROLE

The Wabash study revealed three major aspects of the high school organization to be relevant to an analysis of the teachers' role. Viewed as systems of expectations which define behavior they are: (1) the formal organization of the school which prescribes learning achievement, (2) the system of student organization usually referred to as extracurricular activities, and (3) the network of interpersonal relationships defined by friendship choice referred to here as the informal system.[4]

1. The formal system of expectations:
   a) Incorporates the expectations of learning achievement as a technical system for communicating and evaluating the acquisition of knowledge. The grading system embodies the requisite student roles. It also incorporates
   b) The authority system which governs the conditions for learning and defines the relationships between (1) teacher and pupil, (2) teacher and principal, (3) teacher and parents, (4) teacher and colleagues.
2. The informal system which consists of a network of personal and social relations in grade-sex groups and between them. School-wide it is a system of parallel grade-sex groups which are intergroup differentiated by grade rank and intragroup differentiated into prestige cliques. Thus, the individual may be viewed in relation to his prestige rank in a primary group, the clique, his grade-sex group, his school membership, and his socio-economic position determined by the status of his family in the community. Status in the adolescent system ranges from the "big wheel" at the top to the unincorporated isolates at the bottom. The mean per cent of members isolated was 26.7 for boys and 15.7 for girls, all grades included. The perspective of the individual and that of others in relation to him incorporate his status as an individual within these various group structures. The entire informal system is integrated around prestige seeking.
3. The system of student organizations which both integrates and differentiates the system. Extensive differentials in the amount of participation define and differentiate the social position of the members of

---

[4] The formal-informal distinctions used here are those used by C. I. Barnard, *The Functions of the Executive* (Cambridge: Harvard University Press, 1948), p. 73.

the group. Social status is compounded by fulfillment of differentially valued statuses. The range of deference dispersion, i.e., the difference between the most esteemed and least esteemed individuals, tends to conform to the range in the amount of participation. This results in accenting status differentials based on social class differences. Discussions of social class influences within the school tend to overlook the tremendous drive for differentiated status among members who are essentially of the same socio-economic position and the extensive socialized anxiety related to status seeking which is associated with it. The result is to introduce a greater amount of power into the influence system of the informal group and a strain to conformity. This power in Wabash was given legitimate authority within formal school organization which was invested in a powerful student council, and a large number of other formal organizations, fifty altogether, with some 464 formal statuses which could wield some kind of legitimate authority. The most significant influence was the sense of power which was manifest in the informal system. It posed a constant source of conflict to the teacher. In the words of one harrassed teacher, "Jones and his gang terrify me," we have the testimony of the extent to which the "big wheel" who was well integrated into the informal group and the formal student organizations can exercise influence in conflict with the legitimate authority of the teacher.

The chief general finding of the Wabash study was that the dominant motivation of the adolescent was to achieve and maintain a generalized social status within the organization of the school. General social status is regarded as the position held as a consequence of the various specific statuses he achieves throughout his high school career. At the action level, the dominant motivation of the adolescent will be to accept the roles of the informal group. This view suggests that the orientation of the individual is best understood and predicted given his position within the general system of action in the school-wide social system; for instance, the classroom behavior will be conditioned by his relation to his peers which introduces a general tendency to conflict with those performances which the teacher seeks to define. We are not proposing a simple dichotomy between the formal expectations and those of the informal group, rather two definitions of the situation compatible at times between teacher and students and having varying degrees of acceptability among students.

IMPLICATIONS FOR THE TEACHER'S ROLE: SOURCE OF STRAIN

The structural context of the school presents the incumbent of the teacher's role with the task of continuous integration and adjustment of conflicting expectations. There was a significant range of adaptation among teachers in their capacity to harmonize the conflicting tendencies. There also was a great range in the amount of personal anxiety teachers experienced in relation to their efforts to carry on the teaching function. It is further noted that some typical modes of adaptation are made by teachers over a period of years as they routinized their functions in such a way as to minimize the amount of personal stress which they experience in a situation of endemic conflict.

The institutionally prescribed function of the teacher is to insure the enactment of roles related to learning achievement according to a specified range of standards. The range of standards defined by the grading system represents the instrumental goals of the system. Viewed within the achievement-ascription distinction proposed by Talcott Parsons, the high school primarily defines achievement values and roles both as a functioning institution and in relation to the socialization of its members to a technical social order.[5] The task of the teacher is to insure the essential performances. By virtue of her adult status, her personal orientation to knowledge, and as custodian of the institutionally prescribed tasks, the teacher tends to seek performances from students according to standards somewhat higher than those which the adolescent group will set for itself. There results an incompatibility in the learning output norms which the teacher seeks to resolve.

In spite of the competitive-achievement orientation of the high school, the teacher is confronted with powerful ascriptive tendencies within the system. The Wabash study reveals the same ascriptive influences of the social class system which have been reported by Warner, Hollingshead, and others.[6] The drive for ascriptive rewards operates both at the value level which introduces subjective biases in the grading system and at the power level in which teachers assign rewards and punishments with the awareness that direct and indirect consequences may result from not doing so. Hollingshead demonstrated the tendency for teachers who originated from the local community to be able to ascribe success to members of the higher socio-economic groups because they "understood" the backgrounds of the students.[7] The Wabash data show likewise that the longer a teacher works in the community the more likely he was to accept the social class controls of the community in his assignment of rewards and punishments. The values of the teacher which define rewards in relation to achievement determine that consciously ascribed success is usually attended by personal conflict.

The clearly defined status system in the informal student group described above which coincides somewhat with the social class system and extends itself through differential participation also generates potent tendencies for the most prestigeful group to be ascribed success.

A further basis of conflict for the teacher arises in relation to the basic conflict in educational philosophy which expresses the influence of the competitive achievement social order to insist on a product from the high school which can

---

[5] Pattern variable distinctions used through the paper are those used by Talcott Parsons, *The Social System* (Glencoe, Ill.: Free Press, 1951).

[6] Warner, *op. cit.;* Hollingshead, *op. cit.*

[7] Hollingshead, *op. cit.*

be rated and labeled according to his achievement capacity on the one hand and the influence of educational theory with a concern for the personality development within the learning experience which poses for the teacher the obligation to ascribe minimum success as an investment in the personality development of all students and particularly the least advantaged ones.

A final ascriptive tendency results in that most students expect more. Merton has mentioned the tendency for most Americans to desire about 20 per cent more in income than they receive. It could be said of students that most want at least 20 per cent more than they are assigned.

THE AUTHORITY SYSTEM

Comment on the authority system will be confined to the role of the teacher as intermediate between students and principal. The duty of the teacher is to maintain order both as a condition for learning and because it symbolizes her competence. Teaching competence is difficult to assess, but disorder is taken as a visible sign of incompetence by colleagues, principal, parents, and students. In a situation of conflict the teacher has constant anxiety for his ability to control. A significant amount of conflict results from the requirements of the two sets of expectations which operate in the classroom, those represented by the teacher and those which the informal system defines.

Interaction within the student group is the most frequent cause of conflict between the authority of the teacher and the expectations of the informal group. The teachers' definition of orders makes many of the actions within the student group a threat to authority. Teachers tend to accept noise, confusion, humor and horseplay to a point where it becomes a challenge to authority. Consequently, talking, whispering, inattention, may be viewed as a challenge to authority. The following eighty-one cases of eviction from classroom in a one-year period indicate the nature of offenses for which the principal's office was employed for discipline:

Disturbance of the group.	33
Talking without permission	27
Talking back to the teacher	14
Throwing objects	4
Other	3
Total	81

Reasons given for eviction by teachers are not necessarily the real cause for eviction. They are rather symptoms of strain in teacher to individual student or teacher group relationships. They are both an indication of a mode of adaptation of teachers to the informal group structure and the adaptation of students to the teacher's definition of the expectations of the classroom.

Since eviction from class is a serious crisis in the relationships of students and teachers, eviction is a conservative index of the real conflict which occurs. The classroom situation may be characterized roughly as: (1) conflict of sufficient crisis proportion to result in eviction, with the enlistment of the principal's office to resolve it; (2) conflict of crisis proportions in which the teacher absorbs the conflict without resort to the principal; (3) conflict is minimized or non-existent as a result of the way in which the teacher articulates the requirements of both the formal and informal groups.

Reasons for absorbing conflict in the classroom have been discussed by Howard Becker in connection with the tri-partite relation to authority among students, teacher, and principal.[8] The extent to which the principal will support the formal expectations of the system by an exercise of authority will determine the kind of authority role the teacher may assume in the classroom. Students and teachers alike seek to avoid the crisis of eviction from classroom. It affects both the status of the teacher and student in relation to the formal authority system. Student evictions affect student status because they become a factor in grading, establish a formal record of non-conformity, and may result in expulsion from the group. Teacher status is likewise adversely affected. When the burden of classroom control is shifted to the office of the principal, it calls attention to the problems which he usually prefers not to have made public beyond the classroom. Changes in the exercise of authority from the principal's office result in a greater diffusion of power throughout the school system among both teachers and pupils. In Wabash the number of classroom evictions over a three-year period were for successive years respectively 160, 81, and 50. Reduction in the number of evictions was related to the dissemination of a rumor among the teachers that "the principal has a little black book in which he records the number of students which teachers send to the office. When he gets ready to rate your teaching he looks in the little black book and decides your salary increase for the next year." It appeared that the greater the support the principal gives the teachers' authority, the more likely the formal institutional role of the teacher will be utilized to coordinate the classroom. The less willing the principal is to support the teachers' institutional authority, the more likely that the teacher will absorb conflict in his classroom role, and the more likely he will be to resort to personalized leadership, and face a situation of endemic conflict. Waller has pointed out the hazards of personalized leadership because only the virtuoso can sustain it.[9] The personality of the teacher under such a situation will be exposed. An additional consequence is to shift a balance of power into the hands of students. Here differentials in status among teachers will affect their ability to exercise power and their sense of adequacy since the ability to control is equated with the ability to teach. The Wabash study shows that the least secure teachers in tenure are the ones least likely to be supported by colleagues, principal, parents, and the most likely to attack from students.

---

[8] Howard S. Becker, "The Teacher in the Authority System of the Public School," *Journal of Educational Sociology,* November, 1953.

[9] Willard Waller, *The Sociology of Teaching* (New York: John Wiley & Sons, Inc., 1932).

TEACHER ROLE AND THE INFORMAL SYSTEM

In Wabash the teacher role was conditioned by the fact that he faced in the classroom a system of student organization which was differentiated by grade rank, grade achievement, sex, social class, and prestige cliques which were value differentiated by their participation in both the formally organized and informal student culture. The system as mentioned above exercised a potent influence over behavior. The dominant motivation was to accept the role of the informal group or differentially defined roles within value differentiated cliques or simply the role of subordinate to an overwhelming status system by the unincorporated and incorporated members. There was a consequent muting of action in this direction of teacher-presented expectations.

The teacher perspective of the classroom is one in which behavior is defined according to an ideally conceived classroom situation in which performances approximate the ability and knowledge of the students. According to this perspective discussion operates in ping-pong fashion between teacher and pupils and among pupils limited only by considerations of knowledge and limitations of personality. The teacher accepts the personal limitations of pupils as part of the educational situation. The student understands the teacher's perception of the situation and rules of its operation. However, the student calculates his relation to two sets of status positions; those of students of variously rated performance and those of the informal group; namely, adolescent in relation to same sex and opposite sex, "dater-nondater," athlete-nonathlete, "brain," "big wheel" or "nonwheel" and "fruits" (derogated group), clique member and isolate. Each of the above labels defines roles which incorporate expectations counter to those of the teacher. Teacher defined roles which are not accepted result in strain in the role of the teacher. The teacher with insight into the informal system may articulate both sets of roles in such a way as to fulfill the requirements of the teacher with a minimum of disturbance to the informal group. The unsophisticated teacher may lack the insight and technique or both to harmonize the two systems. He may attack the status system head-on and precipitate conflict.

The informal system with its congeries of ingroups operates as a personalized system of relations significantly motivated by affective response. The teacher as the authority who controls the system seeks to control the system in the direction of affective neutrality. As the coordinator of the system, custodian of the formal sanctions, and dispenser of scarce rewards, he tends to increase or reduce the total anxiety of the incumbents of the system by the use of varying amounts of expressive affect in the communication process. The security and protection which students are afforded within the clique and congeniality groups may be adequate to the needs of the students. Furthermore, it may be disrupted by the way in which the teacher manipulates the reward system. The tension and anxiety is reduced by the manipulation of the symbols or gestures of varying and affective content by the teacher. Thus he will afford the maximum security to students if he expresses and bestows at least a minimum of esteem on every student. Evidence from social class and school studies suggests that teachers display a wide range in the amount of esteem and affective response for various categories of students. The Wabash drop-out of 30% appeared to be directly related to the least esteemed and disesteemed students. We are suggesting that an adequate conception of motivation for the teacher is that which has been demonstrated in the studies in industrial sociology. The problem in the teacher's role consists in that he sometimes accepts the significance of affective response in maintaining student morale and motivation toward his objectives within an institutional framework based on a sanction and reward system of hedonistic psychology. The accompanying ambivalence constitutes a dilemma. He must define goals for students who are widely different in value orientation to his expectations. There is a discrepancy between the values of the teacher and the students. Equally important is the great diversity of values within the student group. The teacher will tend to present and express the values of the able minority without impunity from the formal authority system. However, the values of his professional role decree a 100 per cent consensus on the goals he presents. If he cares for the consequences, he will have anxiety over the lack of interest on the part of the least motivated group. He will be led to strenuous efforts to sustain the interest of the group with the resulting charge on his physical and emotional resources. If he teaches for 30 hours a week, meeting between 130 to 150 students daily, the necessity to reduce the stress will be considerable.

TEACHER ROLE IN RELATION TO STUDENT ORGANIZATIONS

We have mentioned the function of participation in student activities as a means for defining the general status of the student in the school-wide informal system. The result is a status system with a powerful ascriptive tendency. The teacher may accept this system dominated by "big wheels" with its ascriptive tendencies or he may insist on the achievement values of the institutional system with its narrow deference range admitted in the classroom among superior to failing students. To reject the status system of the students is to risk the sanctions of the informal group.

A second tendency of the system of student organizations which results from the extreme differentials in the amount of participation among most active and least active students is the differential association which is produced among most active students and teachers and least active students and teachers. The differential association results in diffuse affectively toned relationships with some students compared to specific affectively neutral relations with the nonparticipants. The result is to particularize with those he knows well in the distribution of rewards and apply universalistic standards with greater affective neutrality in the distribution of rewards and punishments to least active, least known students. For instance, Freshmen make lower grades because teachers know them much less well in addition to the usually accepted fact that they are less sophisticated in the grade getting culture. We seem to need a distinction between grade getting and grade achievement, if by achievement we mean quality of performance and by grade getting the loss of objectivity which accompanies personalizing relationships as well as the manipulation by students of the teacher in the assignment of rewards which accompanies the process.

The more involved the teacher becomes in the student activity program the more likely he is to be influenced by particularistic tendencies. When he does he violates the standards of the universalistic or "fair" teacher defined by the institutional values and professional ethics of the teacher. He faces conflict with students in either case.

The teacher who is not involved in the student activity program will be less sensitive to the status differentiation of the informal system and therefore more universalistic with all members. Lacking the personal influence of association he may risk the conflict with the politically potent informal student group. He may likewise gain the esteem of the "underdog status" group.

More attention needs to be given to other than social class factors in teacher student relationships. For instance, in Wabash Miss Jones was generally regarded to be an able scholar who had high performance expectations of students. She was considered to be "fair," i.e., "just" in her grading by most students. But reputation of "fair" tended to be qualified by members of different groups. Upper middle class members sometimes thought her "unfair" because she resisted social class ascriptive tendencies. Lower class thought her very "fair" because she practiced a not too subtle form of "underdog" ascription. It should be noted that she was by origin of working class background. Mr. Higby, on the other hand, who affected a manner of rigid universalism was thought by lower class members to be "unfair" and by all to particularize in favor of more attractive physically mature girls.

TEACHERS' ADAPTATIONS TO THE STRUCTURE

The foregoing discussion of the complexities of the teaching situation adds up to a situation of continuous stress in the teachers' role. An adaptation to the conditions of the situation leads the teacher to seek to adjust the various pressures in order to protect his personality. Adjustments tend to be worked out privately or in intimate congeniality groups. The problems of the classroom are not shared on a colleague-wide basis due to the competitiveness of the status system among teachers. The success ideology of the school states that "successful teachers do not have problems"; therefore the most disturbing problems of the teacher tend to be regarded as unique to his situation and therefore are private. His greatest anxieties are not expressed. The teacher perspective with its failure to incorporate the reality of the social structure in which he works prevents him from seeing problems as a consequence of this generic structure. Such a perspective would be necessary in order that teachers define problems as general rather than special and private. Such a solution is necessary to relieve high school teachers of the sources of anxiety in the role and socialize them to the reality of the social structure of the high school within an analytical framework which may replace the current moralistic evaluative one.

18.   The teacher in the authority system of the public school *

HOWARD S. BECKER

Institutions can be thought of as forms of collective action which are somewhat firmly established.[1] These forms consist of the organized and related activities of several socially defined categories of people. In service institutions (like the school) the major categories of people so defined are those who do the work of the institution, its functionaries, and those for whom the work is done, its clients. These categories are often subdivided, so that there may be several categories of functionaries and several varieties of client.

One aspect of the institutional organization of activity is a division of authority, a set of shared understandings specifying the amount and kind of control each kind of person involved in the institution is to have over others: who is allowed to do what, and who may give orders to whom. This authority is subject to stresses and possible change to the degree that participants ignore the shared understandings and refuse to operate in terms of them. A chronic feature of service institutions is the indifference or ignorance of the client with regard to the authority system set up by institutional functionaries; this stems from the fact that he looks at the institution's operation from other perspectives and with other interests.[2] In addition to the problems of authority which arise in the internal life of any organization, the service institution's functionaries must deal with such problems in the client relationship as well. One of their preoccupations tends to be the maintenance of their authority definitions over those of clients, in order to assure a stable and congenial work setting.

This paper deals with the authority problems of the metropolitan public school teacher. I have elsewhere described the problems of the teacher in her relations with her pupils,[3] and will here continue that discussion to include the

*From the *Journal of Educational Sociology,* Vol. 27 (1953), pp. 128–41. This paper is based on research done under a grant from the Committee on Education, Training, and Research in Race Relations of the University of Chicago.

[1] Cf. E. C. Hughes, "The Study of Institutions," *Social Forces,* Vol. 20 (March, 1942), pp. 307–10.

[2] See my earlier statement in "The Professional Dance Musician and His Audience," *American Journal of Sociology,* Vol. 57 (September, 1951), pp. 136–44.

[3] Howard S. Becker, "Social-Class Variations in the Teacher-Pupil Relationship," *Journal of Educational Sociology,* Vol. 25 (April, 1952), pp. 451–65. [Pp. 155–66 this volume.]

teacher's relations with parents, principals, and other teachers. The following points will be considered in connection with each of these relationships: the teacher's conception of her rights and prerogatives, her problems in getting and maintaining acceptance of this conception on the part of others, and the methods used to handle such problems. The picture one should get is that of the teacher striving to maintain what she regards as her legitimate sphere of authority in the face of possible challenge by others. This analysis of the working authority system of the public school is followed by a discussion which attempts to point up its more general relevance. The description presented here is based on sixty long and detailed interviews with teachers in the Chicago public schools.[4]

TEACHER AND PARENT

The teacher conceives of herself as a professional with specialized training and knowledge in the field of her school activity: teaching and taking care of children. To her, the parent is a person who lacks such background and is therefore unable to understand her problems properly. Such a person, as the following quotation shows, is considered to have no legitimate right to interfere with the work of the school in any way:

> One thing, I don't think a parent should try and tell you what to do in your classroom, or interfere in any way with your teaching. I don't think that's right and I would never permit it. After all, I've a special education to fit me to do what I'm doing, and a great many of them have never had any education at all, to speak of, and even if they did, they certainly haven't had my experience. So I would never let a parent interfere with my teaching.

Hers is the legitimate authority in the classroom and the parent should not interfere with it.

Problems of authority appear whenever parents challenge this conception, and are potentially present whenever parents become involved in the school's operation. They become so involved because the teacher attempts to make use of them to bolster her authority over the child, or because they become aware of some event about which they wish to complain. In either case the teacher fears a possible challenge of her basic assumption that the parent has no legitimate voice with regard to what is done to her child in school.

In the first instance, the teacher may send for the parent to secure her help in dealing with a "problem child." But this is always done with an eye to possible consequences for her authority. Thus, this expedient is avoided with parents of higher social-class position, who may not only fail to help solve the problem but may actually accuse the teacher of being the source of the problem

---

[4] Details of method are reported in Howard S. Becker, "Role and Career Problems of the Chicago Public School Teacher" (unpublished Ph.D. dissertation, University of Chicago, 1951).

and defend the child, thus materially weakening the teacher's power over her children:

> You've got these parents who, you know, they don't think that their child could do anything wrong, can't conceive of it. If a teacher has to reprimand their child for something they're up in arms right away, it couldn't be that the child did anything wrong, it must be the teacher. So it's a lot of bother. And the children come from those kind of homes, so you can imagine that they're the same way.

The teacher feels more secure with lower-class parents, whom she considers less likely challengers. But they fail to help solve the problem; either ignoring the teacher's requests or responding in a way that increases the problem or is personally distasteful to the teacher.

> [They] have a problem child, but you can't get them to school for love or money. You can send notes home, you can write letters, you can call up, but they just won't come.
>   If you send for [the child's] parents, they're liable to beat the child or something. I've seen a mother bring an ironing cord to school and beat her child with it, right in front of me. And, of course, that's not what you want at all.

This tactic, then, is ordinarily dangerous in the sense that the teacher's authority may be undermined by its consequences. Where it is not dangerous, it tends to be useless for strengthening authority over the child. This reinforces the notion that the parent has no place in the school.

Parents may also become involved in the school's operation on their own initiative, when they come to complain about some action of the school's functionaries. Teachers recognize that there are kinds of activity about which parents have a legitimate right to complain, for which they may legitimately be held responsible, although the consequences of the exercise of this right are greatly feared. They recognize, that is, that the community, in giving them a mandate to teach, reserves the right to interfere when that mandate is not acted on in the "proper" manner. As Cooley put it:

> The rule of public opinion, then, means for the most part a latent authority which the public will exercise when sufficiently dissatisfied with the specialist who is in charge of a particular function.[5]

Teachers fear that the exercise of this latent authority by parents will be dangerous to them.

One form of this fear is a fear that one will be held responsible for any physical harm that befalls the child:

> As far as the worst thing that could happen to me here in school, I'd say

[5] Charles Horton Cooley, *Social Organization* (New York: Charles Scribner's Sons, 1927), p. 131.

it would be if something awful happened someplace where I was supposed to be and wasn't. That would be terrible.

This, it is obvious, is more than a concern for the child's welfare. It is also a concern that the teacher not be held responsible for that welfare in such a way as to give the parents cause for complaint, as the following incident makes clear:

> I've never had any trouble like that when the children were in my care. Of course, if it happens on the playground or someplace where I'm not there to watch, then it's not my responsibility, you see. . . . My children have had accidents. Last year, two of the little boys got into a fight. They were out on the playground and Ronald gave Nick a little push, you know, and one thing led to another and pretty soon Nick threw a big stone at Ronald and cut the back of his head open. It was terrible to happen, but it wasn't my fault, I wasn't out there when it happened and wasn't supposed to be. . . . Now if it had happened in my room when I was in there or should have been in there, that's different, then I would be responsible and I'd have had something to worry about. That's why I'm always careful when there's something like that might happen. For instance, when we have work with scissors I always am on my toes and keep looking over the whole room in case anything should happen like that.

Another area in which a similar fear that the parents will exercise their legitimate latent authority arises is that of teaching competence; the following incident is the kind that provokes such fears:

> There was a French teacher—well, there's no question about it, the old man was senile. He was getting near retirement. I think he was sixty-four and had one year to go to retire. The parents began to complain that he couldn't teach. That was true, of course, he couldn't teach any more. He'd just get up in front of his classes and sort of mumble along. Well, the parents came to school and put so much pressure on that they had to get rid of him.

The teachers' fear in these and similar situations is that intrusion by the parents, even on legitimate grounds, will damage their authority position and make them subject to forms of control that are, for them, illegitimate—control by outsiders. This fear is greatest with higher class groups, who are considered quick to complain and challenge the school's authority. Such parents are regarded as organized and militant and, consequently, dangerous. In the lower-class school, on the other hand:

> We don't have any PTA at all. You see, most of the parents work; in most families it's both parents who work. So that there can't be much of a PTA.

These parents are not likely to interfere.

To illustrate this point, one teacher told a story of one of her pupils stabbing another with a scissors, and contrasted the reaction of the lower-class mother with that to be expected from the parents of higher status whose children she now taught:

> I sure expected the Momma to show up, but she never showed. I guess the Negroes are so used to being squelched that they just take it as a matter of course, you know, and never complain about anything. Momma never showed up at all. You take a neighborhood like the one I'm teaching in now, why, my God, they'd be sueing the Board of Education and me, and there'd be a court trial and everything.

It is because of dangers like this that movement to a school in such a neighborhood, desirable as it might be for other reasons, is feared.[6]

The school is for the teacher, then, a place in which the entrance of the parent on the scene is always potentially dangerous. People faced with chronic potential danger ordinarily develop some means of handling it should it become "real" rather than "potential," some kind of defense. The more elaborate defenses will be considered below. Here I want to point to the existence of devices which teachers develop or grow into which allow them some means of defense in face-to-face interaction with the parent.

These devices operate by building up in the parent's mind an image of herself and of her relation to the teacher which leads her to respect the teacher's authority and subordinate herself to it:

> Quite often the offense is a matter of sassiness or backtalk. . . . So I'll explain to the parent, and tell him that the child has been sassy and disrespectful. And I ask them if they would like to be treated like that if they came to a group of children. . . . I say, "Now I can tell just by looking at you, though I've never met you before, that you're not the kind of a person who wants this child to grow up to be disrespectful like that. You want that child to grow up mannerly and polite." Well, when I put it to them that way, there's never any argument about it. . . . Of course, I don't mean that I'm not sincere when I say those things, because I most certainly am. But still, they have that effect on those people.

The danger may also be reduced when the teacher, over a period of years, grows into a kind of relationship with the parents of the community which minimizes the possibilities of conflict and challenge:

> If you have a teacher who's been in a school twenty years, say, why she's known in that community. Like as not she's had some of the parents as pupils. They know her and they are more willing to help her in handling the children than if they didn't know who she was.

If the teacher works in the same neighborhood that she lives in she may acquire a similar advantage, although there is some evidence that the degree of advantage is a function of the teacher's age. Where she is a middle-aged woman whose

---

[6] See Howard S. Becker, "The Career of the Chicago Public School Teacher," *American Journal of Sociology,* Vol. 57 (March, 1952), p. 475.

neighborhood social life is carried on among those women of similar age who are the parents of her pupils, the relationship gives her a distinct advantage in dealing with those same women in the school situation. If, however, she is a younger woman, parents are likely to regard her as "a kid from the neighborhood" and treat her accordingly, and the danger of her authority being successfully challenged is that much greater.

In short, the teacher wishes to avoid any dispute over her authority with parents and feels that this can be accomplished best when the parent does not get involved in the school's operation any more than absolutely necessary. The devices described are used to handle the "parent problem" when it arises, but none of them are foolproof and every teacher is aware of the ever-present possibility of a parent intruding and endangering her authority. This constant danger creates a need for defenses and the relations of teacher and principal and of teachers to one another are shaped by this need. The internal organization of the school may be seen as a system of defenses against parental intrusion.

TEACHER AND PRINCIPAL

The principal is accepted as the supreme authority in the school:

> After all, he's the principal, he is the boss, what he says should go, you know what I mean. . . . He's the principal and he's the authority, and you have to follow his orders. That's all there is to it.

This is true no matter how poorly he fills the position. The office contains the authority, which is legitimated in terms of the same principles of professional education and experience which the teacher uses to legitimate her authority over parents.

But this acceptance of superiority has limits. Teachers have a well-developed conception of just how and toward what ends the principal's authority should be used, and conflict arises when it is used without regard for the teachers' expectations. These expectations are especially clear with regard to the teacher's relationships with parents and pupils, where the principal is expected to act to uphold the teacher's authority regardless of circumstances. Failure to do this produces dissatisfaction and conflict, for such action by the principal is considered one of the most efficient defenses against attack on authority, whether from parents or pupils.

The principal is expected to "back the teacher up"—support her authority—in all cases of parental "interference." This is, for teachers, one of the major criteria of a "good" principal. In this next quotation the teacher reacts to the failure of a principal to provide this:

> That's another thing the teachers have against her. She really can't be counted on to back you up against a child or a parent. She got one of our teachers most irate with her, and I can't say I blame her. The child was being very difficult and it ended up with a conference with the parent,

principal, and teacher. And the principal had the nerve to say to the parent that she couldn't understand the difficulty, none of the other teachers who had the child had ever had any trouble. Well, that was nothing but a damn lie, if you'll excuse me. . . . And everybody knew it was a lie. . . . And the principal knew it too, she must have. And yet she had the nerve to stand there and say that in front of the teacher and the parent. She should never have done that at all, even if it was true she shouldn't have said it. [Interviewer: What was the right thing to do?] Well, naturally, what she should have done is to stand behind the teacher all the way. Otherwise, the teacher loses face with the kids and with the parents and that makes it harder for her to keep order or anything from then on.

This necessity for support is independent of the legitimacy of the teacher's action; she can be punished later, but without parents knowing about it. And the principal should use any means necessary to preserve authority, lying himself or supporting the teacher's lies:

You could always count on him to back you up. If a parent came to school hollering that a teacher had struck her child, Mr. D— would handle it. He'd say, "Why, Mrs. So-and-So, I'm sure you must be mistaken. I can't believe that any of our teachers would do a thing like that. Of course, I'll look into the matter and do what's necessary but I'm sure you've made a mistake. You know how children are." And he'd go on like that until he had talked them out of the whole thing.

Of course the teacher would certainly catch it later. He'd call them down to the office and really give them a tongue lashing that they wouldn't forget. But he never failed them when it came to parents.

Not all principals live up to this expectation. Their failure to support the teacher is attributed to cowardice, "liberalism," or an unfortunate ability to see both sides of a question. The withholding of support may also, however, be a deliberate gesture of disapproval and punishment. This undermining of the teacher's authority is one of the most extreme and effective sanctions at the principal's command:

[The teacher had started a class project in which the class, boys and girls, made towels to be given to the parents as Christmas presents.] We were quite well along in our project when in walked this principal one day. And did she give it to me! Boy! She wanted to know what the idea was. I told her it was our Christmas project and that I didn't see anything the matter with it. Well, she fussed and fumed. Finally, she said, "Alright, you may continue. But I warn you if there are any complaints by fathers to the Board downtown about one of our teachers making sissies out of their boys you will have to take the full responsibility for it. I'm not going to take any responsibility for this kind of thing." And out she marched.

Teachers expect the same kind of support and defense in their dealings with pupils, again without regard for the justice of any particular student complaint.

If the students find the principal a friendly court of appeal, it is much harder for the teacher to maintain control over them.[7]

The amount of threat to authority, in the form of challenges to classroom control, appears to teachers to be directly related to the principal's strictness. Where he fails to act impressively "tough" the school has a restless atmosphere and control over pupils is difficult to attain. The opposite is true where the children know that the principal will support any action of a teacher.

> The children are scared to death of her [the principal]. All she has to do is walk down the hall and let the children hear her footsteps and right away the children would perk up and get very attentive. They're really afraid of her. But it's better that way than the other.

Such a principal can materially minimize the discipline problem, and is especially prized in the lower-class school, where this problem is greatest.

The principal provides this solid underpinning for the teachers' authority over pupils by daily acts of "toughness," daily reaffirmations of his intention to keep the children "in line." The following quotation contrasts successful and unsuccessful principal activity in this area:

> For instance, let's take a case where a teacher sends a pupil down to the office. . . . When you send a child down to this new principal, he goes down there and he sits on the bench there. . . . Pretty soon, the clerk needs a messenger and she sees this boy sitting there. Well, she sends him running all over the school. That's no punishment as far as he's concerned. Not at all.
>
> The old principal didn't do things that way. If a child was sent down to the office he knew he was in for a rough time and he didn't like it much. Mr. G— would walk out of his office and look over the children sitting on the bench and I mean he'd look right through them, each one of them. You could just see them shiver when he looked at them. Then he'd walk back in the office and they could see him going over papers, writing. Then, he'd send for them, one at a time. And he'd give them a lecture, a real lecture. Then he'd give them some punishment, like writing an essay on good manners and memorizing it so they could come and recite it to him the next day by heart. Well, that was effective. They didn't like being sent to Mr. G—. When you sent someone there that was the end of it. They didn't relish the idea of going there another time. That's the kind of backing up a teacher likes to feel she can count on.

The principal is expected to support all teachers in this way, even the chronic complainers who do not deserve it:

> If the principal's any good he knows that the complaints of a woman like that don't mean anything but he's got to back her just the same. But he

---

[7] Cf. *The Sociology of Georg Simmel,* trans. Kurt Wolff (Glencoe: Free Press, 1950), p. 235: "The position of the subordinate in regard to his superordinate is favorable if the latter, in his turn, is subordinate to a still higher authority in which the former finds support."

knows that when a teacher is down complaining about students twice a week that there's nothing the matter with the students, there's something the matter with her. And he knows that if a teacher comes down once a semester with a student that the kid has probably committed a real crime, really done something bad. And his punishments will vary accordingly.

The teacher's authority, then, is subject to attack by pupils and may be strengthened or weakened depending on which way the principal throws the weight of his authority. Teachers expect the principal to throw it their way, and provide them with a needed defense.

The need for recognition of their independent professional authority informs teachers' conceptions of the principal's supervisory role. It is legitimate for him to give professional criticism, but only in a way that preserves this professional authority. He should give "constructive" rather than "arbitrary" orders, "ask" rather than "snoop." It is the infringement of authority that is the real distinction in these pairs of terms. For example:

> You see, a principal ought to give you good supervision. He ought to go around and visit his teachers and see how they're doing—come and sit in the room awhile and then if he has any constructive criticism to make, speak to the teacher about it privately later. Not this nagging bitching that some of them go in for, you know what I mean, but real constructive criticism.
>
> But I've seen some of those bastards that would go so far as to really bawl someone out in public. Now that's a terrible thing to do. They don't care who it's in front of, either. It might be a parent, or it might be other teachers, or it might even be the kids. That's terrible, but they actually do it.

Conflict arises when the principal ignores his teachers' need for professional independence and defense against attacks on authority. Both principal and teachers command sanctions which may be used to win such a conflict and establish their definition of the situation: i.e., they have available means for controlling each other's behavior. The principal has, as noted above, the powerful weapon of refusing to support the teacher in crucial situations; but this has the drawback of antagonizing other teachers and, also, is not available to a principal whose trouble with teachers stems from his initial failure to do this.

The principal's administrative functions provide him with his most commonly used sanctions. As administrator he allocates extra work of various kinds, equipment, rooms, and (in the elementary school) pupils to his teachers. In each category, some things are desired by teachers while others are disliked—some rooms are better than others, some equipment newer, etc. By distributing the desired things to a given teacher's disadvantage, the principal can effectively discipline her. A subtle use of such sanctions is seen in this statement:

> *Teacher:* That woman really used to run the school, too. You had to do just what she said.

Interviewer: What did she do if you "disobeyed?"

Teacher: There were lots of things she could do. She had charge of assigning children to their new rooms when they passed. If she didn't like you she could really make it tough for you. You'd get all the slow children and all the behavior problems, the dregs of the school. After six months of that you'd really know what work meant. She had methods like that.

Such sanctions are ineffective against those few teachers who are either eccentric or determined enough to ignore them. They may also fail in lower-class schools where the teacher does not intend to stay.[8]

The sanctions teachers can apply to a principal who does not respect or protect their authority are somewhat less direct. They may just ignore him: "After all if the principal gets to be too big a bother, all you have to do is walk in your room and shut the door, and he can't bother you." Another weapon is hardly a weapon at all—making use of the power to request transfer to another school in the system. It achieves its force when many teachers use it, presumably causing higher authorities to question the principal's ability:

I know of one instance, a principal of that type, practically every teacher in her school asked to leave. Well, you might think that was because of a group that just didn't get along with the new principal. But when three or four sets of teachers go through a school like that, then you know something's wrong.

Finally, the teachers may collectively agree on a line of passive resistance, and just do things their way, without any reference to the principal's desires.

In some cases of extreme conflict, the teachers (some of whom may have been located in the school for a longer period than the principal) may use their connections in the community to create sentiment against the principal. Cooperative action of parents and teachers directed toward the principal's superiors is the teachers' ultimate sanction.

The principal, then, is expected to provide a defense against parental interference and student revolt, by supporting and protecting the teacher whenever her authority is challenged. He is expected, in his supervisory role, to respect the teacher's independence. When he does not do these things a conflict may arise. Both parties to the conflict have at their disposal effective means of controlling the other's behavior, so that the ordinary situation is one of compromise (if there is a dispute at all), with sanctions being used only when the agreed-on boundaries are overstepped.

COLLEAGUE RELATIONS

It is considered that teachers ought to cooperate to defend themselves against authority attacks and to refrain from directly endangering the authority of another teacher. Teachers, like other work groups, develop a sense that they share

---

[8] See Becker, "The Career of the Chicago Public School Teacher," *op. cit.,* pp. 472–73.

a similar position and common dangers, and this provides them with a feeling of colleagueship that makes them amenable to influence in these directions by fellow teachers.

Challenging of another teacher so as to diminish her authority is the basic crime:

> For one thing, you must never question another teacher's grade, no matter if you know it's unjustified. That just wouldn't do. There are some teachers that mark unfairly. A girl, or say a boy, will have a four "S" report book and this woman will mark it a "G". . . . Well, I hate to see them get a deal like that, but there's nothing you can do.

Another teacher put it more generally: "For one thing, no teacher should ever disagree with another teacher or contradict her, in front of a pupil." The result in terms of authority vis-à-vis students is feared: "Just let another teacher raise her eyebrow funny, just so they [the children] know, and they don't miss a thing, and their respect for you goes down right away." With regard to authority threats by parents it is felt that teachers should not try to cast responsibility for actions which may provoke parental interference on another teacher.

Since teachers work in separate rooms and deal with their own groups of parents and pupils, it is hard for another teacher to get the opportunity to break these rules, even if she were so inclined. This difficulty is increased by an informal rule against entering another teacher's room while she is teaching. Breaches of these rules are rare and, when they do occur, are usually a kind of punishment aimed at a colleague disliked for exceeding the group work quotas or for more personal reasons. However, the danger inherent in such an action—that it may affect your own authority in some way or be employed against you—is so feared that it is seldom used.

In short, teachers can depend on each other to "act right" in authority situations, because of colleague feeling, lack of opportunity to act "wrong," and fear of the consequences of such action.

DISCUSSION

I have presented the teacher as a person who is concerned (among other things) with maintaining what she considers to be her legitimate authority over pupils and parents, with avoiding and defending against challenges from these sources. In her view, the principal and other teachers should help her in building a system of defenses against such challenges. Through feelings of colleagueship and the use of various kinds of sanctions, a system of defenses and secrecy (oriented toward preventing the intrusion of parents and children into the authority system) is organized.

This picture discloses certain points of general relevance for the study of institutional authority systems. In the first place, an institution like the school can be seen as a small, self-contained system of social control. Its functionaries (principal and teachers) are able to control one another; each has some power to influence the other's conduct. This creates a stable and predictable work setting, in which the limits of behavior for every individual are known, and in which one can build a satisfactory authority position of which he can be sure, knowing that he has certain methods of controlling those who ignore his authority.

In contrast the activities of those who are outside the professional group are not involved in such a network of mutual understanding and control. Parents do not necessarily share the values by which the teacher legitimates her authority. And while parents can apply sanctions to the teacher, the teacher has no means of control which she can use in return, in direct retaliation.

To the teacher, then, the parent appears as an unpredictable and uncontrollable element, as a force which endangers and may even destroy the existing authority system over which she has some measure of control. For this reason, teachers (and principals who abide by their expectations) carry on an essentially secretive relationship vis-à-vis parents and the community, trying to prevent any event which will give these groups a permanent place of authority in the school situation. The emphasis on never admitting mistakes of school personnel to parents is an attempt to prevent these outsiders (who would not be subject to teacher control) from getting any excuse which might justify their intrusion into and possible destruction of the existing authority system.

This suggests the general proposition that the relations of institutional functionaries to one another are relations of mutual influence and control, and that outsiders are systematically prevented from exerting any authority over the institution's operations because they are not involved in this web of control and would literally be uncontrollable, and destructive of the institutional organization, as the functionaries desire it to be preserved, if they were allowed such authority.[9]

---

[9] Cf. Max Weber: "Bureaucratic administration always tends to be an administration of 'secret sessions': in so far as it can, it hides its knowledge and action from criticism. . . . the tendency toward secrecy in certain administrative fields follows their material nature: everywhere that the power interests of the domination structure toward *the outside* are at stake . . . we find secrecy." In H. H. Gerth and C. Wright Mills, *From Max Weber: Essays in Sociology* (New York: Oxford University Press, 1946), p. 233.

19. Docility, or giving teacher what she wants*

JULES HENRY

This essay deals with one aspect of American character, the process whereby urban middle-class children in elementary school acquire the habit of giving their teachers the answers expected of them. Though it could hardly be said that I deal exhaustively with this matter, what I do discuss, using suggestions largely from psychoanalysis and communications theory, is the signaling process whereby children and teacher come to understand each other or, better, to pseudo-understand each other, within the limited framework of certain schoolroom situations.

I think it will be readily understood that such a study has inter-cultural significance and interesting biosocial implications. The smooth operation of human interaction, or "transaction," if one prefers the Dewey and Bentley decor, requires that in any culture much of the give and take of life be reduced to a conventional, parsimonious system of quickly dicipherable messages and appropriate responses. These messages, however, are different in different cultures, because the give and take of life is different in different cultures. At a simple level, for example, a Pilaga Indian paints his face red when he is looking for a sexual affair with a woman, whereas were an American man to paint his face red, the significance of this to other Americans would be quite different. Behaviors that have been variously called signal, cue, and sign are as characteristic of the animal world as they are of the human, and in both groups tend to be highly specific both with respect to themselves (signs, signals, cues) and with respect to the behavior they release in those for whom they are intended. Since, furthermore, each culture tends to standardize these, it would seem that any study of such behaviors, or rather behavior systems, in humans in any culture would throw light on two problems: (1) What the signal-response system is; and (2) How humans learn the system.

Since in humans the mastery of a signal-response system often involves the emotional life, and since in this paper on docility I am dealing with urban American middle-class children, it will readily be seen that a study of the manner

*From *The Journal of Social Issues,* Vol. 2 (1955), pp. 33–41.

in which they learn the signal-response system called docility carries us toward an understanding of the character of these children.

When we say a human being is docile we mean that, without the use of external force, he performs relatively few acts as a function of personal choice as compared with the number of acts he performs as a function of the will of others. In a very real sense, we mean that he behaves mostly as others wish him to. In our culture this is thought undesirable, for nobody is supposed to like docile people. On the other hand, every culture must develop in its members forms of behavior that approximate docility; otherwise it could not conduct its business. Without obedience to traffic signals transportation in a large American city would be a mess. This is a dilemma of our culture: to be able to keep the streets uncluttered with automotive wrecks, and to fill our armies with fighting men who will obey orders, while at the same time we teach our citizens not to be docile.

It is to be supposed that, although the basic processes as outlined are universal, every culture has its own way of creating the mechanism of docility. It will be the purpose of the rest of this paper to examine the accomplishment of docility in some American middle-class schoolrooms. The study was carried out by several of my graduate students and me. Names of persons and places are withheld in order to give maximum protection to all concerned.

In the following examples I shall be concerned only with demonstrating that aspect of docility which has to do with the teacher's getting from the children the answers she wants; and I rely almost entirely on verbal behavior, for without cameras it is impossible to record non-verbal signals. The first example is from the second grade.

1.   The children have been shown movies of birds. The first film ended with a picture of a baby bluebird.

Teacher: Did the last bird ever look like he would be blue?

The children did not seem to understand the slant of the question, and answered somewhat hesitantly: Yes.

Teacher: I think he looked more like a robin, didn't he?

Children, in chorus: Yes.

In this example one suspects that teacher's intonation on the word "ever" did not come through as a clear signal, for it did not create enough doubt in the children's minds to bring the right answer, "No." The teacher discovered that her signal had not been clear enough for these seven year-olds, so she made it crystal clear the second time, and got the "right" response. Its correctness is demonstrated by the unanimity of the children's response, and the teacher's acceptance of it. Here the desire of the teacher, that the children shall acknowledge that a bird looks like a robin, is simple, and the children, after one false try, find the correct response.

In the next example we see the relation of signal to cultural values and context:

2a.   A fourth grade art lesson. Teacher holds up a picture.

Teacher: Isn't Bobby getting a nice effect of moss and trees?

Ecstatic Ohs and Ahs from the children. . . .

2b.   The art lesson is now over.

Teacher: How many enjoyed this?

Many hands go up.

Teacher: How many learned something?

Quite a number of hands come down.

Teacher: How many will do better next time?

Many hands go up.

Here the shifts in response are interesting. The word "nice" triggers a vigorously docile response, as does the word "enjoy." "Learned something," however, for a reason that is not quite clear, fails to produce the desired unanimity. On the other hand, the shibboleth, "better next time" gets the same response as "enjoyed." We see then that the precise triggering signal is related to important cultural values; and that the value-signal must be released in proper context. One suspects that the children's resistance to saying they had learned something occurred because "learned something" appeared out of context. On the other hand, it would be incorrect to describe these children as perfectly docile.

3.   The children have just finished reading the story, "The Sun, Moon, and Stars Clock."

Teacher: What was the highest point of interest—the climax?

The children tell what they think it is. Teacher is aiming to get from them what she thinks it is, but the children give everything else but. At last Bobby says: When they capture the thieves.

Teacher: How many agree with Bobby?

Hands, hands, hands.

In this example the observer was not able to record all the verbal signals, for they came too fast. However, it is clear that hunting occurred, while the children waited for the teacher to give the clear signal, which was "(I) agree with Bobby."

In all the examples given thus far, the desired answer could be indicated rather clearly by the teacher, for the required response was relatively unambiguous. Even so, there was some trouble in obtaining most of the answers. In the example that follows, however, the entire situation becomes exceedingly ambiguous because emotional factors in the children make proper interpretation of teacher's signals difficult. The central issue is that teacher and children are seen to have requirements that are complementary on one level, because teacher wants the children to accept her point of view, and they want to be accepted by her; but these requirements are not complementary on a different level, because the children's emotional organization is different from the teacher's. Hence exact complementarity is never achieved, but rather a pseudo-complementarity which enables teachers and pupils to extricate themselves from a difficult situation. The example comes from a fifth-grade schoolroom:

4.   This is a lesson on "healthy thoughts" for which the children have a special book that depicts specific conflictful events among children. There are

appropriate illustrations and text, and the teacher is supposed to discuss each incident with the children in order to help them understand how to handle their emotions.

One of the illustrations is of two boys, one of whom is griping because his brother has been given something he wants himself—a football, I think. The other is saying his brother couldn't help being given it—they'll both play with it.

(Observer is saying that this sibling pair is illustrated by three boys: (1) The one who has received the ball. (2) The one who is imagined to react with displeasure. (3) The one who is imagined to react benignly and philosophically, by saying: My brother couldn't help being given the football; we'll use it together.)

Teacher: Do you believe it's easier to deal with your thoughts if you own up to them, Betty?

Betty: Yes it is, if you're not cross or angry.

Teacher: Have you any experience like this in the book, Alice?

Alice tells how her brother was given a watch and she envied him and wanted one too, but her mother said she wasn't to have one until she was fifteen, but now she has one anyway.

Teacher: How could you have helped—could you have changed your thinking? How could you have handled it? What could you do with mean feelings?

Alice seems stymied; she hems and haws.

Teacher: What did Susie (a character in the book) do?

Alice: She talked to her mother.

Teacher: If you talk to someone you often feel that "It was foolish of me to feel that way. . . ."

Tommy: He says he had an experience like that. His cousin was given a bike, and he envied it. But he wasn't ugly about it. He asked if he might ride it, and his cousin let him, and then I got one myself; and I wasn't mean or ugly or jealous.

Here the process of signal development is intricate, and children and teacher do not quite manage to arrive at a mutually intelligible complex of signals and behavior. The stage is set by the presentation of a common, but culturally unacceptable situation: A child is pictured as envious of the good luck of his sibling. Since American culture cannot accept two of its commonest traits, sibling rivalry and envy, the children are asked by teacher to acknowledge that they are "bad," and to accept specific ways of dealing with these emotions. The children are thus asked to fly in the face of their own feelings, and, since this is impossible, the little pigeons never quite get home. This is because teacher and pupil wants are not complementary.

It will have been observed that at first Alice does well, for by docilely admitting that it is good to own up to evil, she correctly interprets the teacher's wish to hear her say that the ancient ritual of confession is still good for the soul; and she continues docile behavior by giving a story of her own envy. However, eventually she muffs the signal, for she says she was gratified anyway; she did get a watch. And the reason Alice muffs the signal is that her own impulses dominate over the signals coming in from the teacher. Teacher, however, does not reject Alice's story but tries, rather, to get Alice to say she could have "handled" her thoughts by "owning up" to them and talking them over with someone. Alice, however, stops dead because she cannot understand the teacher. Meanwhile Tommy has picked up the signal, only to be misled by it, just as Alice was. By this time, however, the matter has become more complex: Tommy thinks that because teacher did not reject Alice's story it is "correct." Teacher's apparent acceptance of Alice's story then becomes Tommy's signal; therefore he duplicates Alice's story almost exactly, except that a bike is substituted for a watch. Like Alice he is not "mean" or "ugly" or "jealous," not because he "dealt with" his thoughts in the culturally approved-but-impossible manner, but because he too got what he wanted. So far, the only part of the message that is getting through to the children from the teacher is that it is uncomfortable—not wrong—to be jealous, et cetera. Thus the emotions of the children filter out an important part of the message from the teacher.

We may summarize the hypotheses up to this point as follows:

1)   By virtue of their visible goal-correcting behavior the pupils are trying hard to be docile with respect to the teacher.

2)   They hunt for signals and try to direct their behavior accordingly.

3)   The signals occur in a matrix of cultural value and immediate circumstance.

4)   This fact at times makes interpretation and conversion into action difficult.

5)   A basis in mutual understanding is sought, but not quite realized at times.

6)   The children's internal signals sometimes conflict with external ones and thus "jam the receiver."

7)   Both children and teacher want something. At present we may say that the children want acceptance by the teacher, and teacher wants acceptance by the children.

8)   However it is clear, because of the mix-up that may occur in interpreting signals, as in the lesson on healthy thoughts, that the desires of teacher and pupil are sometimes not quite complementary.

9)   Teacher must avoid too many frustrating (painful) failures like that of Alice, otherwise lessons will break down.

As we proceed with this lesson, we shall see how teacher and pupils strive to "get on the same wave length," a condition never quite reached because of the different levels of organization of teacher and pupil; and the unawareness of this fact on the part of the teacher.

Two boys, the "dialogue team," now come to the front of the class and dramatize the football incident.

Teacher, to the class: Which boy do you think handled the problem in a better way?

Rupert: Billy did, because he didn't get angry . . . It was better to play together than to do nothing with the football.

Teacher: That's a good answer, Rupert. Has anything similar happened to you, Joan?

Joan can think of nothing.

(Observer notes: I do not approve of this business in action, though I have not yet thought it through. But I was intermittently uncomfortable, disapproving and rebellious at the time.)

Sylvester: I had an experience. My brother got a hat with his initials on it because he belongs to a fraternity, and I wanted one like it and couldn't have one; and his was too big for me to wear, and it ended up that I asked him if he could get me some letters with my initials, and he did.

Betty: My girl-friend got a bike that was 26-inch, and mine was only 24; and I asked my sister what I should do. Then my girl-friend came over and was real nice about it, and let me ride it.

Teacher approves of this, and says: Didn't it end up that they both had fun without unhappiness? (Observer notes: Constant questioning of class, with expectation of affirmative answers: that wasn't this the right way, the best way, etc. to do it?)

Here we note that the teacher herself has gone astray, for on the one hand her aim is to get instances from the children in which they themselves have been yielding and capable of resolving their own jealousy, etc., while on the other hand, in the instance given by Betty, it was not Betty who yielded but her friend. The child immediately following Betty imitated her since Betty had been praised by the teacher:

Matilde: My girl-friend got a 26-inch bike and mine was only 24; but she only let me ride it once a month. But for my birthday my mother's getting me a new one, probably (proudly) a "28." (Many children rush in with the information that "28" doesn't exist.) Matilde replies that she'll probably have to raise the seat then, for she's too big for a "26."

This instance suggests more clearly, perhaps, than the others, another possible factor in making the stories of the children end always with their getting what they want: the children may be afraid to lose face with their peers by acknowledging they did not get something they wanted.

As we go on with this lesson, we shall see how the children's need for substitute gratification and their inability to accept frustration prevent them from picking up the teacher's message. As we continue, we shall see, how, in spite of the teacher's driving insistence on her point, the children continue to inject their conflicts into the lesson, while at the same time they gropingly try to find a way to gratify the teacher. They cannot give the right answers because of their conflicts; teacher cannot handle their conflicts because she cannot perceive them. The lesson goes on:

Teacher: I notice that some of you are only happy when you get your own way. (Observer noticed too, horrified.) You're not thinking this through, and I want you to. Think of an experience when you didn't get what you want. Think it through. (Observer wonders: Are the children volunteering because of expectations: making desperate efforts to meet the expectation, even though they do not quite understand it?)

Charlie: His ma was going to the movies and he wanted to go with her; and she wouldn't let him; and she went off to the movies; and he was mad; but then he went outside and there were some kids playing baseball, so he played baseball.

Teacher: But suppose you hadn't gotten to play baseball? You would have felt hurt because you didn't get what you wanted. We can't help feeling hurt when we are disappointed. What could you have done? How could you have handled it? (Observer notes: Teacher is not getting what she wants, but I am not sure the kids can understand. Is this a function of immaturity, or of spoiling by parents? Seems to me the continued effort to extract an idea they have not encompassed may be resulting in reinforcement for the one they have got—that you eventually get the watch, or the bicycle, or whatever.)

Charlie: So I can't go to the movies; so I can't play baseball; so I'll do something around the house.

Teacher: Now you're beginning to think! It takes courage to take disappointments. (Turning to the class) What did we learn? The helpful way. . . .

Class: is the healthy way!

Thus the lesson reaches this point on a note of triumphant docility, but of pseudo-complementarity. If the teacher had been able to perceive the underlying factors that made it impossible for these children to accept delayed gratification or total momentary frustration, and had handled that problem, instead of doggedly sticking to a text that required a stereotyped answer, she would have come closer to the children and would not have had to back out of the situation by extracting a parrot-like chorusing. The teacher had to get a "right" answer, and the children ended up giving her one, since that is what they are in school for. Thus on one level teacher and pupils were complementary, but on another they were widely divergent. This is the characteristic condition of the American middle-class schoolroom.

If we review all the verbal messages sent by the teacher, we will see how hard she has worked to get the answer she wants; how she has corrected and "improved" her signaling in response to the eager feedback from the children:

1) Do you believe it's easier to deal with your thoughts if you own up to them, Betty?

2) Have you any experience like this in the book, Alice?

3) What could you do with mean feelings?

4) What did Susie (in the book) do?

5) (Rupert says that Billy, the character in the book, handled the problem in the better way because he did not get angry.) That's a good answer, Rupert.

6) (Betty tells how nice her girl-friend was, letting her ride her bike.) Teacher approves of this and says: Didn't it end up that they both had fun without unhappiness?

7) I notice that some of you are happy only when you get your own way.

8) What could you have done (when you did not get your own way)?

9) Now you're beginning to think. It takes courage to take disappointments. What did we learn? The helpful way. . . . and the class responds, is the healthy way.

DISCUSSION AND CONCLUSIONS

This paper has been an effort to describe the mental docility of middle-class American children *in their classrooms*. It says nothing about the home or the play group. The analysis shows how children are taught to find the answer the teacher wants, and to give it to her. That they sometimes fail is beside the point, because their trying so hard is itself evidence of docility; and an understanding of the reasons for failure helps us to see why communication breaks down and pseudo-understanding takes its place. When communication breaks down it is often because complementarity between sender (teacher) and receivers (pupils) is not exact; and it is not exact because teacher and pupils are at different levels of emotional organization.

We may now ask: Why are these children, whose phantasies our unpublished research has found to contain so many hostile and anxious elements, so docile in the classroom? Why do they struggle so hard to gratify the teacher and try in so many ways, as our protocols show, to bring themselves to the teacher's attention?

We might, of course, start with the idea of the teacher as a parent-figure, and the children as siblings competing for teacher's favor. We could refer to the unresolved dependency needs of children of this age, which make them seek support in the teacher, who then manipulates this seeking and the children's sibling rivalry in order, as our unpublished research suggests, to pit the children against each other. Other important factors, however, that appear in the middle-class schoolrooms, ought to be taken into consideration. For example, our research shows the children's tendency to destructively criticize each other, and the teacher's repeated reinforcement of this tendency. We have taken note, in our research, of the anxiety in the children as illustrated in the stories they tell and observed that these very stories are subjected to carping criticism by other children, the consequence of which would be anything but an alleviation of that anxiety. Hence the schoolroom is a place in which the child's underlying anxiety may be heightened. In an effort to alleviate this he seeks approval of the teacher, by giving right answers, and by doing what teacher wants him to do under most circumstances. Finally, we cannot omit the teacher's need to be gratified by the attention-hungry behavior of the children.

A word is necessary about these classrooms in middle class. The novel *Blackboard Jungle*, by Evan Hunter, describes schoolroom behavior of lower-class children. There we see them solidly against the teacher, as representative of the middle class. But in the classes we have observed we see the children against each other, with the teacher abetting the process. Thus, as the teacher in middle-class schools directs the hostility of the children toward one another (particularly in the form of criticism), and away from herself, she reinforces the competitive dynamics within the middle class itself. The teacher in the lower-class schools, on the other hand, appears to become the organizing stimulus for behavior that integrates the lower class, as the children unite in expressing their hostility to the teacher.

In conclusion, it should be pointed out that the mental docility (or near docility) achieved in these middle-class schoolrooms is a peculiar middle-class kind of docility. It is not based on authoritarian control backed by fear of corporal punishment, but rather on fear of loss of love. More precisely, it rests on the need to bask in the sun of the teacher's acceptance. It is not fear of scolding or of physical pain that makes these children docile, but rather fear of finding oneself outside the warmth of the inner circle of teacher's sheltering acceptance. This kind of docility can be more lethal than the other, for it does not breed rebellion and independence, as struggle against authoritarian controls may, but rather a kind of cloying paralysis; a sweet imprisonment without pain. Looking at the matter from another point of view, we might say that were these children not fearful of loss of love they would be indifferent to the teacher's messages. In a sense what the teacher's signals are really saying is: "This is the way to be loved by me; and this is the way I want you to love me."

20. *Sociological aspects of professional salaries in education* *

EDWARD GROSS

In the literature on educational salaries, an oft-repeated theme may be stated in the form of a syllogism:

Professionals, such as doctors and lawyers, receive large incomes.
Teachers are professionals.
Therefore, teachers should receive high incomes.

Clearly, something is wrong. The conclusion should read that teachers *do* receive high incomes, and we know they do not. Since there seems no doubt that teachers are professionals, we are left only with the major premise, and the data from occupational research suggest that it is, at best, only roughly true.[1] Such professionals as social workers, nurses, clergymen, artists, police detectives, and researchers do not earn very high salaries. On the other hand, some professionals do—lawyers, doctors, professional criminals, for example—but not even all of them.

What I am questioning is the frequent tendency to take doctors' and lawyers' incomes as our models for our conception of educational salaries. If we examine the various ways in which income is derived from occupations, we find we can divide them into three main categories: (1) income derived from one's own entrepreneurial activity by selling goods or services in a free market—for example,

---

*From *Educational Record,* Vol. 41 (April, 1960), pp. 130–37.

Author's Note: I am indebted to Professor Jack London for valuable suggestions and criticisms, and to Professor Albert D. Waterman for critical reading of an early draft.

[1] For a good general discussion of income, see H. P. Miller, *Income of the American People* (New York: John Wiley & Sons, 1955).

For specific data by occupation, see Department of Commerce, Bureau of the Census, *Population Census Report,* Vol. IV, part I, chap. B, "Occupational Characteristics," 1956.

For an excellent reworking of these data to overcome problems presented by the omnibus character of census categories, see L. G. Thomas, *The Occupational Structure and Education* (Englewood Cliffs, N.J.: Prentice-Hall, 1956), especially chap. 6 and Appendix B.

independent craftsmen, independent professionals, and businessmen; (2) payment received from a firm on the basis of its earnings in a competitive market; and (3) income from occupations subsidized out of taxation or philanthropic sources—for example, government employees and employees of nonprofit organizations such as social work agencies, hospitals, universities, and schools.[2] We see here the difficulties of making comparisons from one category to another, and some occupations can even be found in all three categories. An engineer may be in private practice taking fees as a consulting engineer; he may be on the payroll of a factory where his salary will depend on the earnings of the factory as a whole; or he may be part of an engineering corps in the Army. Even teachers exist in all three categories—the music teacher who charges per pupil, the trainer in the personnel department of a factory, and the teacher in a public school. Depending on where one practices one's occupation, one's market position is different, and correspondingly the forces determining the size of one's income will also be different.

Let us look more closely at this matter. The professionals, as a group, are supposed to concentrate on doing the best possible job that they can.[3] Attention is ideally to be concentrated only on the professional problem presented by the case at hand, and such matters as personal friendship and the ethnic group, religion, race, or social class of the client are assumed to be irrelevant. Among these things that are irrelevant is money. "The professional, it has been said, does not work in order to be paid: he is paid in order that he may work."[4] Here we encounter a paradox. A British student of occupations states it this way:

> The professions . . . are respectable because they do not strive for money, but they can only remain respectable if they succeed, in spite of this pecuniary indifference, in making quite a lot of money, enough for the needs of a gentlemanly life.[5]

In the United States, the "gentlemanly life" may not concern us much, but we do recognize that a teacher cannot concentrate her best efforts on her job if she is tired because she has to have a second job or because she is constantly anxious about finances. Then too, the doctor behaves as if he were not interested in sordid money. He may refuse money offered him directly, preferring that his secretary shall send a bill. However, his services are supposed to be so valuable that money is expected to roll in, virtually unsolicited. The client should feel

---

[2] This categorization is drawn from Talcott Parsons, "A Revised Analytical Approach to the Theory of Social Stratification," in Reinhard Bendix and Seymour M. Lipset (eds.), *Class, Status and Power* (Glencoe, Ill.: Free Press, 1953), pp. 121–22.

[3] For a discussion, in detail, of the criteria of professionalization, see Edward Gross, "Some Suggestions for the Legitimation of Industrial Studies in Sociology," *Social Forces*, Vol. 33 (1955), pp. 233–39.

[4] T. H. Marshall, "The Recent History of Professionalism in Relation to Social Structure and Social Policy," *Canadian Journal of Economics and Political Science*, Vol. 5 (1939), p. 325.

[5] *Ibid.*, p. 326.

that the services he has received are beyond a price: after all, what price can one put on one's health? The bill he pays is little more than a token payment. But from time to time the money does not roll in unsolicited, and then the professional may behave in a most businesslike way, such as calling in person at one's home or turning the bill over to a collection agency. Teachers are in this position. Their services are also valuable beyond price, but the money does not seem to roll in. Why not?

We secure a clue by looking at salaries from a sociological point of view. This does not, of course, present a full explanation but one that is an essential part of the picture. In some discussions of income one encounters references to the "importance to society" of some occupation as justifying its high pay. Yet one could spend a fruitless hour discussing the relative importance of teaching the young and burying the dead without explaining why the latter yields more income than the former.

We must ask what position in society the occupation has. Society, like any person in it, will pay as little for any service as it can. Therefore, the reward for a service depends, in part at least, on what society can be forced to pay, a situation that makes pay frequently a matter of power.[6] From this point of view, a service in high demand places those who supply it in a strong power position. If it is in high demand *and* of an emergency character, then those who supply it (doctors, lawyers, plumbers, TV repairmen, drug smugglers) can demand more money than those who supply services that can, relatively speaking, be postponed (architects, librarians, many types of researchers, gardeners, rug-shampooers).

A strong power position is also enjoyed by those whose service is in demand and is rare, either because of natural scarcity (beauty, talent, risk of injury or death), long preparation, or because of scarcity through restriction of entry to the occupation.

In teaching, the demand seems to be high, but the service is not usually of an emergency character. Perhaps psychiatrists might be a better comparison group for teachers than would the ordinary medical doctor, but psychiatrists are also fee-takers, and the latter are often (though not always) in a better power position than salaried personnel. Teachers are not fee-takers, and most of us would not want the income of the teacher to rest on the number of students he has. Nor can their power position be increased appreciably, in my opinion, by resorting to such tactics as strikes which seem inappropriate for purveyors of an essential service, as they are inappropriate for policemen, firemen, and soldiers.

If educators wish to increase their power position, their major recourse, it seems to me, is that of keeping their numbers down. It is important not to misunderstand this point. I do not advocate deliberate restriction to the end of an increase in power position. Such a mercenary line of action would surely

---

[6] For a discussion of income from the point of view of power, see Edward Gross, *Work and Society* (New York: Thomas Y. Crowell Co., 1958), pp. 120–22.

fail and be rejected, quite properly, by the professional himself since he is dedicated to service to the society and not power over it. But all professions carefully restrict entry to ensure that practitioners will be properly trained and qualified and to increase the ease of control of those already in the profession so that proper standards may be maintained.

The teaching profession certainly would and does concur on the desirability of those goals. It would be desirable to guard them carefully and not let standards fall on the grounds that teachers must be provided at any cost. If *these* goals are kept continually in the center, then the power of the profession will increase *indirectly* and thereby the twin goals of high standards and high income may be more easily pursued.

Related to numbers is the deleterious effect on income provided by the presence of a reservoir population which moves in and out of the occupation to satisfy current pressing needs. An example is teen-agers seeking pocket money who take farm jobs during the harvest. Often willing to take low wages and uninterested in long-term considerations, they depress the wages of regular farm laborers. In teaching, the largest such group consists of married women who move in and out, depending on the economic status of their families, and who, like the teen-agers, may be willing to work for low wages and be uninterested in long-term considerations.

There is nothing wrong, per se, with hiring such persons, provided that their mere availability and cheapness do not influence us to close our eyes to gaps in their qualifications. And one important gap is their lack of a commitment to the profession. Few would care to have a lung removed by a man who was temporarily back in to help out in the shortage of pulmonary specialists.

On the subject of numbers, we should bear one other factor in mind. Even a country as rich as the United States has a limit to its ability to pay for services. A small group, physical scientists, for example, may be able to double or triple its wages without affecting total costs very much. But should a large group try to do so, a severe strain is imposed on the economy.[7] And teachers are becoming such a large group.

Lieberman[8] estimates that if teachers were actually to receive the average income of doctors, the wage bill alone would exceed by $2 billion per year the entire cost of public education. As the numbers of pupils in schools go up, we should speak, it seems to me, not of the increased need for teachers, but of the increased need for teaching. We may ask not only where will the teachers come from but also how can we more effectively use the teachers we have? There are unanswered questions here about effects on size of class and teaching efficiency which space does not permit me to discuss, but they do not, I believe, present insuperable problems.

---

[7] See T. Caplow, *The Sociology of Work* (Minneapolis: University of Minnesota Press, 1954), pp. 145–46.

[8] M. Lieberman, *Education as a Profession* (Englewood Cliffs, N.J.: Prentice-Hall, 1956), p. 413.

I have emphasized power position as a factor in income determination because I believe it is a major and practical avenue for the increase of teachers' income. What of the role of prestige in salary determination? In general, prestige and size of income are positively related, but it is often difficult to say which is cause and which is effect. The money that persons of prestige may enjoy does not come by magic—there must be an intervening mechanism for converting prestige to money; for example, a sports hero may earn a great deal of money through the endorsement of a commercial product. I am not advising teachers to endorse LePage's glue or Eberhard Faber pencils, for the primary intervening mechanism for teachers is the legislature.

In the case of socialist countries, an occupation with high prestige will have high income by government fiat. Thus in the Soviet Union teachers' salaries parallel those of physicians, whereas in Israel manual laborers' salaries are not far from those of physicians. If the prestige of teachers in the United States rises, legislators may feel they can justify higher salaries for teachers to their constituents. However, even here numbers are of central importance. In the Middle Ages, the occupation of scribe had high prestige only as long as few persons could write. Prestige is lost if it is spread around too much. It also seems to be elevated if the members of an occupation have strong identification with their work and conceive of their function not simply as the rendering of a service but as having the character of a mission. To that end, professional organizations which help define appropriate behavior and control anomalous behavior seem to be universal.

Up to this point, I have dwelt on certain problems presented by the size of salaries, and in so doing I reflect the concern I find in the literature. It is certainly important, perhaps of first importance, but it should not lead us to ignore the symbolic significance of money. To take a simple illustration: when we give a tip to the waitress, we not only add to her income but we also tell her what we think of her services. In this connection, recent research on the social-class origin of teachers is relevant.[9]

In the years before the 1920's, teachers came mainly from middle-class homes. Teaching was also one of the few respectable occupations for women and attracted even women from upper-class homes. But with urbanization, the great growth of the school population, the growth of teacher-training schools, and the availability of other occupations for women, the social composition of the teaching profession has changed. A number of studies show that now the majority of teachers come from lower-middle or lower class homes. A recent study by Wattenberg[10] in a large city found that 45 percent of teachers under forty years of age came from working-class families, with only 35 percent com-

---

[9] For a good discussion of the social origins of teachers, see R. J. Havighurst and B. L. Neugarten, *Society and Education* (Boston: Allyn and Bacon, 1957), chap. 16.

[10] W. Wattenberg *et al.,* "Social Origins of Teachers: Facts from a Northern Industrial City," in L. J. Stiles (ed.), *The Teacher's Role in American Society* (New York: Harper & Bros., 1957), chap. 2.

ing from middle-class families. The city was an industrial one, but other studies elsewhere show a similar pattern.[11]

We know from other sociological research that money has different meanings to persons in different social classes.[12] Also, occupational research shows that when persons think about their salaries, they tend to compare themselves with certain others who act as points of reference for the evaluation of their own progress.[13] One such comparison group appears to be one's former schoolmates. If a teacher comes from the middle class, most of his former middle-class schoolmates are probably not in teaching, but are in middle-class occupations and are probably earning more money, perhaps a great deal more, than he is. Since money is the main difference, he is likely to be highly conscious of it and be keenly desirous of increasing his pay.

By contrast, if the teacher is from a working-class family, his former schoolmates are probably in skilled or semi-skilled jobs, and are earning about the same or only a little more money than he is. The striking contrast, to him, will be the white-collar features of teaching, and he will tend to feel strongly the value of the hours, the security, and the prestige of his position. If the teacher was upwardly mobile, again social class will be important. The boy from a working-class family who was ambitious will be gratified at being a teacher at all. His family and perhaps his ethnic group, if he has one, will proudly point him out as "one of our boys who made it." By contrast, the boy from a middle-class family who becomes a teacher has not, by that token, risen. If he is upwardly mobile, we may expect him to try to improve his position by pressing for more money or aggressively seeking an administrative position.

Let us look next at the problem of salary differentials. In industrial sociological research it has been found that differences in wages and salaries are not interpreted solely in terms of the groceries they will buy but in terms of group comparisons. The question, in other words, is, not only how am I doing in terms of my ability to pay the family's bills, but also how am I doing in comparison to somebody else?[14] In industry no one questions the validity of wage differentials per se. Even in factories with a straight seniority system it is accepted as perfectly proper that punch-press operators should receive a lower hourly wage than tool- and die-makers. The reason for this acceptance is that the justification for the difference—superior skill—is accepted as a legitimate criterion by both punch-press operators and tool- and die-makers. The seniority system functions

---

[11] See, for example, W. S. Elsbree, *The American Teacher* (New York: American Book Co., 1939); F. Greenhoe, *Community Contacts and Participation of Teachers* (Washington, D.C.: American Council on Public Affairs, 1941); and E. C. Valentine, "The Occupational Expectations of Three Normal School Student Groups" (Master's thesis, University of Chicago, 1950).

[12] The literature here is extensive. An insightful summary is found in J. A. Kahl, *The American Class Structure* (New York: Rinehart & Co., 1957).

[13] Excellent illustrative cases are to be found in W. F. Whyte *et al.*, *Money and Motivation* (New York: Harper & Bros., 1955), especially chaps. 8 and 10.

[14] See for example, *ibid.*, pp. 213–15.

as a floor to ensure everyone a minimum wage and as a reward for loyalty and continuous service.

In education, the preparation or single-salary schedule can have a similar function. In addition, of course, amount of preparation and experience may be assumed to have a positive correlation with teaching efficiency. However, it is difficult to see how, if that is *all* one has, one can attract and hold persons with special talents, such as science or mathematics teachers, when there is competition for such persons from noneducational powers and sources.

In one firm in which I did research, the company was faced with the task of hiring key-punch operators to punch IBM cards. Key-punching is similar to typing but requires less training. Yet the company was forced to pay key-punch operators more than typists in order to attract them to the position. The typists were unhappy with the situation but took solace from their claim that key-punch operators were little better than "machine slaves": the key-punch operators, who were mostly typists who had learned the new skill, felt the pay difference to be no more than adequate recognition of the risk they were taking in their new jobs since the demand for key-punch operators was not as high as for typists. There was grumbling, but everyone recognized that the company had to pay them the higher wage since they knew the company would never pay one cent more than it had to. No one, except the key-punch operators, thought they were being paid for superior work.

Similarly, if one must pay the science teacher more to hold him, I doubt that anyone except science teachers thinks that their subject is more valuable than others. The problem is one of market contingencies, and, whether we like it or not, this is a simple fact of life.

This brings us to the subject of merit rating, the object of much current controversy. One reads of the problems of assessing teacher efficiency and of who is to do the rating—difficult, but not impossible to settle. The use of pupil performance as a criterion has been suggested, and that *is* liable to serious abuses. It is comparable to paying the physician according to the number of cures he can report. In some ancient legal codes, a physician might be put to death if the patient died, a situation that must have led physicians to select their cases carefully and reject those who needed help the most. If teachers' salaries are related to students' class success, teachers may, with clear conscience, begin giving heavy homework assignments and pressuring their students, whereas a few teachers, without clear conscience, might begin to give easier examinations. But these dangers too can be examined and possibly controlled.

Community service is mentioned as a possible basis for merit rating and is usually rejected as "nonprofessional." I suppose it is, but community service is found very widely among all professionals, and sometimes for the most mercenary reasons. The gynecologist may join public service organizations in which he has no interest whatsoever in order to build a favorable public image of himself and so attract patients. But speaking more generally, since the professional is the guardian of our most vital activities, we expect from him not merely that he be competent but that he should be beyond reproach. He is inevitably, therefore, something of a public figure, and his private life is the object of careful scrutiny. How far this should go is a matter for debate, but one seldom does away with it completely.

In sum, merit rating presents problems, but none of them is insuperable. The major consideration should be to see that it is done in an objective manner that is in accord with the teacher's conception of what is right and necessary. The administrator who decides not to hire a highly qualified mathematics teacher on the grounds that the salary to attract him would anger the teachers on the staff is, it seems to me, performing a disservice, not only to students and parents, but to the faculty itself. No man wishes to find himself on the same faculty with incompetents, and morale and turnover may be expected to be affected. Nor does such an administrator really avoid the problem. The English teacher will grumble to learn that a competent science teacher makes more money than she does; but will she not also grumble, and more loudly, when she finds that an *incompetent* science teacher is being paid the *same* as she is? The need, in my view, is for a careful examination of the criteria for evaluation of specialty and performance—and I think this should be a subject for research—the explanation of these criteria to teachers and the securing of their consent, and, finally, the assignment of salary differences strictly in accord with these criteria.

But what shall these criteria be? We make a serious mistake and take action we shall later regret if Russian success in launching satellites leads us to panic into offering high salaries to science teachers to the neglect of all else. A physical education instructor who had seen the Russian Bolshoi ballet told me we should pay higher salaries to attract physical education instructors to the schools since he felt the Russian emphasis on calisthenics was responsible for the excellence of the ballet. In other words, we should not let the criteria be determined for us but should examine our value system and make decisions we can live with and justify to the world at large. Excellence of teaching, performance levels, and training would probably constitute basic criteria, while others should be the object of research. We need more knowledge of what abilities and types of training contribute to effective teaching.

I have given attention primarily to salaries as such. Yet a great deal of industrial sociological research argues for the proposition that salary is only one of a complex of forces which motivate the worker. It may be the most important, but it is not the only one.

In an extensive study of school superintendents in Massachusetts, headed by Neal Gross, one problem examined was the type of situation in which the superintendent was exposed to contradictory pressures from different groups around him. Two problems were found to involve the most contradictory pressure—teacher salary recommendations and budget recommendations. In connection with salary, for example, school superintendents reported that they were under pressure from eighteen different kinds of groups to go one way or the other.[15]

---

[15] N. Gross, W. S. Mason, and A. W. McEachern, *Explorations in Role Analysis: Studies of the School Superintendency Role* (New York: John Wiley & Sons, 1958), chap. 16.

For example, groups that pressured him to try to keep salaries down were politicians, business organizations and influential businessmen, taxpayers associations, and town finance committee or city council. On the other hand, groups that pressured him to push salaries up ever skyward were church groups, labor unions, P.T.A.'s, personal friends, service clubs, school committee, *and* teachers. One other interesting "group" also pressured the superintendent—the committee of one known as "my wife"—so that he had no escape even at home.

I bring up Gross's study because it highlights a vital point in any salary discussion: teachers do not simply want money; they want and value a superintendent who seems to be on their side and to be sympathetic with their needs. At the same time, a superintendent who tries to increase salaries and fails, through no fault of his, will create a favorable attitude among teachers toward working in his school system, even though the teachers have no more money than before.

This generalization is not mere speculation but is supported by solid research. This research goes back to the most famous pioneer experiment in industrial sociology, that at the Hawthorne works of the General Electric Company.[16] A small group of women, assembling telephone equipment, performed feats of productivity that were beyond management's dreams, but no one knew why. The experiment was designed to do no more than test the efficiency of workers under different illumination conditions. Every few weeks, the lights in the workroom were changed. When more powerful lights were put in, productivity went up, as expected. But when the lights were weakened, productivity also went up. And once, when the maintenance man came in, removed the lights, and replaced them with lights of identical strength, productivity went up even higher! What was the mystery? The women explained it very simply. It was because of the very fact that they were being experimented upon when the company was trying to find out what lighting the women preferred. One woman commented that this was the first time in her ten years at the plant that management had done something that proved it was concerned about her.

This effect is not peculiar to factory workers. The most important single factor in job satisfaction has been found to be the supervisor. In the school situation this is the principal and superintendent, usually. Francis S. Chase,[17] in a study of over two thousand teachers in forty-three states, found a close correspondence between ratings teachers gave to superintendents, principals, and supervisors and the degree of their satisfaction with the school system and with their jobs. When the teachers were asked which factor contributed most to job satisfaction, over 88 percent replied: the leadership of the principal.

Miriam Wagenschein,[18] in a study of beginning elementary teachers in Chi-

---

16 F. J. Roethlisberger and W. J. Dickson, *Management and the Worker* (Cambridge, Mass.: Harvard University Press, 1940).

A good popular treatment is to be found in Stuart Chase, *Men at Work* (New York: Harcourt, Brace & Co., 1945), pp. 15–20 and *passim.*

17 F. S. Chase, "Factors Productive of Satisfaction in Teaching" (Ph.D. dissertation, University of Chicago, 1951).

18 M. Wagenschein, "Reality Shock: A Study of Beginning Elementary School Teachers" (Master's thesis, University of Chicago, 1950).

cago, found the principal to be the most important single factor in making a school a "good" one. And what do teachers want from their administrators that makes these people such crucial figures in their evaluation of their jobs?

Howard Becker[19] and Joseph Yarbrough,[20] in separate studies, found that the most highly sought-after feature was support in stress, as in discipline cases or cases involving understanding and respect.

These studies represent only beginnings, and we need more research on what teachers value and why they do so. We need to understand their motivation and the place of salary in the total structure of incentives. And we must be careful that we do not dismiss such a finding as "teachers wish support from their administrators" as mere common sense. Some of the most exciting research now going on in sociology is the testing of the great body of common-sense beliefs that are widely held. One, for example, is the belief that it is more difficult to get ahead in America now than it used to be in the days of Rockefeller and Vanderbilt, and the evidence denies this claim.

So we want to know, not simply how much money teachers want, but what money means to them, and how important superintendents, principals, fellow teachers, power groups in the community, and pupils are in the teacher's picture of his job and his profession. We want, in other words, to know how we can create a climate in which the teacher and superintendent can take pride in their profession, enjoy one another's high esteem, and concentrate on the task of giving youngsters the tools and knowledge with which they can, perhaps, solve the world problems that we, of this generation, are forcing them to face.

---

[19] H. S. Becker, "Role and Career Problems of the Chicago Public School Teacher" (Ph.D. dissertation, University of Chicago, 1951).

[20] J. Yarbrough, "Morale is a Number of Things," *Illinois Education,* Vol. 38 (1949), pp. 130–31.

PART VI

Higher

education

Higher education in America has evolved from a small and highly specialized educational effort to a mammoth diversified establishment. The early colleges were perceived to have relatively few clear-cut functions—to train acceptable clergymen and provide a liberal education for gentlemen. Since the early days of Harvard, Yale, and Brown, the colleges and universities have increased to over 2,000 in number, and provide specialized training in almost all conceivable scholarly disciplines and occupational specialties. The proliferation of institutions of higher education has to a great extent been due to the many new and diverse social, economic, and political functions which they have performed.

An important social function of the college or university is the key role it plays in status mobility and status retention or stability for large segments of the American population. The children of the immigrants in the great migration from Europe of 1890 to 1910 provided early signs of a trend involving higher education as a significant element in upward mobility for some of the new Americans. The large urban universities, particularly of the great metropolitan centers of New York, Boston, Philadelphia, and Chicago, along with the land-grant universities of the Middle West, became the educational vehicles for upward mobility and occupational education. A subsequent increase in college enrollments resulted from the G.I. Bill of Rights of World War II. This large-scale educational subsidy brought a new social stratum into American colleges. Boys whose families had not dreamed of seeing their sons in college were suddenly confronted with a chance for a free college education. Thus, the place of higher education as a prominent factor in the social and economic mobility of large numbers of American males has now reached full awareness in our society. Many believe that attendance in college is so important in determining one's life chances that it ought to be the right of everyone to have easy access to a college or university. And states like California and New York are allocating millions to try to reach this goal.

The changes in attitude toward higher education have been further stimulated by what C. Wright Mills referred to as the decline of the "old middle classes."[1] These social strata were comprised of small- to medium-sized retailers, entrepreneurs, and the like. An important element in the family structure of the old middle classes was that the family business was passed on to the son or son-in-law. Therein the family possessed a legacy of economic and social value that could be inherited by succeeding generations. This resulted in stability and continuity in the style of life for most middle-class families.

In contrast, the "new middle classes" are comprised primarily of white-collar workers, executives, and others whose employment is within large bureaucratic structures—they are organization men. For these strata of the population the only effective legacy (if it can be defined as a legacy) a family can provide is the economic resources needed for gaining a higher education, plus, of course, the norms and values that lead to the motivations necessary for success in school. In an age of bureaucracy few can inherit either a business or enough wealth to insure the continuity and class stability of the family for succeeding generations. Each new generation must find its own place in the bureaucratized world of business and government. This apparent fact has revolutionized attitudes toward higher education among the middle strata of the United States. For all those seeking social mobility or status maintenance from one generation to the next, one or more college degrees have become critical goals. How college functions for those who fail to get degrees is the subject of one of the papers in this section.

The important changes in the social and economic functions of higher education are closely related to the great expansion in size of college student populations and those who operate the educational establishment. The aforementioned G.I. Bill of Rights brought a flood of students into college. What appeared to some as a temporary upsurge in student ranks has become accepted as normal since the 1950's. The new strata that were brought in as a result of the G.I. Bill, the apparent need for education in climbing the social ladder, and the technical demands of a bureaucratically organized industrial state, have brought not only new students but new and diverse courses, curricula, research institutes, and thoroughly transformed some of the older traditional features of the academic community.

From a certain point of view, attendance at college may function as an initiation rite for considerable numbers of American youth. Riesman and Jencks state that:

---

[1] C. Wright Mills, *White Collar* (New York: Oxford University Press, 1951).

In general, what a college does is to "nationalize" the student, taking him out of his ethnic, religious, geographic, and social parishes, and exposing him to a more cosmopolitan world in which the imagination is less restricted by preconception and ignorance.[2]

It has been pointed out that "emancipation from the older generation" takes place at colleges of all levels of excellence.[3] The lunch-counter sit-ins were devised and carried out by students from Negro colleges, Negroes who saw the old order as not only an anachronism but an insult to human dignity.

The colleges also serve a decided economic function in postponing the annual entry into the labor market of thousands of young people. During this postponement some are kept out of the labor force for many years: for example, girls who marry before or immediately after the baccalaureate and then start to raise families. College attendance allows the young male to mature while he is being tested and sifted into either a discipline or a vocational field where he can be trained for a place in the national economic structure. In a period of decreasing blue-collar jobs and expanding semiprofessional and professional white-collar jobs, the colleges and universities have functioned to facilitate the transition in the demands of the national labor market. The college, as the locus of initiating rites, aging and maturing, marriage market, and some time devoted to liberal learning and intellectual development, appears to be functional in providing social types who can partially, at least, meet the demands of a rapidly changing society.

The relatively substantial period of time devoted to college during the formative years of youth has led to the formation of collegiate subcultures. Although the subcultural element may vary from coast to coast, the themes are essentially the same. The greatest difference among these subcultures is probably found between the small rural residential college and the large urban university. Although relatively little is known of the college subculture, it is evident that the norms and values that arise and are perpetuated by the student subculture are an important factor in determining the nature of relationships between students (e.g., upper and lower classmen), faculty and students, and students and adults outside of the collegiate community. Much of what the faculty may wish to achieve in certain areas of persuasion and the dissemination of ideas can be greatly hindered or enhanced by the nature of the subculture. At large universities many administrators and faculty members know little or nothing about the student subculture, the informal networks of communication, or the characteristics of student leaders. Consequently, many attempts to facilitate communication and learning fail or are only minimally successful.

It has been obvious for some years that a substantial number of the largest universities have been beset by the problems that follow the bureaucratization of many aspects of college administration. Universities have become gigantic

---

[2] David Riesman and Christopher Jencks, "The Viability of the American College," in Nevitt Sanford (ed.), *The American College: A Psychological and Social Interpretation of the Higher Learning* (New York: John Wiley & Sons, 1962), p. 77.

[3] *Ibid.*, p. 77.

corporate structures with payroll, investment, and procurement functions that dwarf many large businesses. This has brought the academician face-to-face with the executive-manager types needed to manage such large enterprises, as well as their bureaucratically organized staff, clerical, and maintenance personnel. Large universities are currently in a period in which the faculties and administrations are competing for power in determining the major policies within the university structure.

Despite the large-scale changes and the challenge posed by higher education, as in primary and secondary education, sociologists have been slow to conduct studies of colleges and universities. The apparent importance of the collegiate period in the lives of an ever-increasing segment of the population is, however, stimulating added interest and new investigations are in the making.

21. A social theory of intellectual development *

CHRISTIAN BAY

INSTITUTIONS AND RATIONALITY

All persistent patterns of human interaction, whether formally organized or not, will in this chapter be termed *institutions*. And all attempts, by one or more individuals, to choose maximally effective means to promote given purposes will be termed *rationality*. Any human behavior that is explicable neither in terms of conformity to institutions nor in terms of effort toward rationality will for present purposes be termed *incongruent* behavior, a category that includes purely impulsive or expressive behavior as well as idiosyncratic, autistic, and ego-defensive behavior.

In the study of any enduring social process, including any educational process, it may be fruitful to try to distinguish between its institutional and its rational determinants and components. It is a fundamental assumption in this chapter that any continuing process of human interaction is the outcome of conflicting pressures toward conformity and toward rationality, modified only slightly by incongruent individual behavior. This is not to imply that individual contributions to cooperative enterprises are slight; rather, it is claimed that individual contributions attain great significance only to the extent that they are either highly expressive of traditions or are of considerable help in the solving of pressing problems.

A *problem* is any discrepancy between what is and what is desired, or between what may come to pass and what we might hope for. Some problems are posed by hazards, others by hopes. Survival raises one kind of problem; another kind is raised by the urge to adorn and improve human existence. Some problems are

*From Nevitt Sanford (ed.), *The American College* (New York: John Wiley & Sons, 1962), pp. 972–1006.

I want to thank two of my friends, Andrzej Malewski of Warsaw, Poland, and Sethard Fisher of San Andreas, California, for good advice during my work on this chapter. Also, I have benefited from the thinking of five students who discussed higher education with me for six weeks during a summer session course in Argumentative Discourse at the University of California in Berkeley: Miss Judith Crawford, Mr. Carl A. Flegal, Mrs. Anna Bow Lim, Mr. T. David McFarland, and Mr. Dirk A. Plummer.

inherent in our human condition and press themselves upon us unless we individually are sheltered from them or can imagine that we are; other problems emerge with the formulation of purposes in the minds of human beings. Problems in the former category are concerned with the preservation or protection of what is valued, those in the latter category with progress or advancement toward what would be more valued.

All problems have this much in common: they stimulate efforts toward rationality. If there should be a total absence of problems in a community, people would live entirely according to traditional customs, and there would be no thinking and hardly any consciousness of being human. An aboriginal tribe may, theoretically speaking, survive for millennia without much social and cultural change if it is sheltered from enemies, fed by a bountiful nature, and prevented from expanding greatly in numbers. As soon as serious problems of preservation present themselves, however, a premium is placed on supplementing customs with rationality. And the basic trend over the many centuries of expanding civilization has been toward increasing stress on rationality and reduced emphasis on purely institutional patterns of behavior. The more serious and complex the problems, the more reason itself, and procedures to encourage the use of reason, become institutionalized; in the more advanced societies, new organizations are continually being created for purposes of solving problems. At this stage the distinction between problems of preservation and problems of progress has become blurred, since preservation in a changing world may well depend on comparable rates of progress in different societies. At any rate a written language, literature, political and legal institutions, and much else have developed, in the service of preservation and progress. And so have processes of higher education.

Even though human rationality and its organizational devices keep expanding, institutions do not become unimportant. In fact, rationality can displace institutional patterns only in given situations and for the moment; rational reforms either are abandoned soon or else they become institutionalized, and become transformed during this process. Institutions are the tissues of the enduring community. One might say that while reason proposes, institution disposes. Patterned regularities and predictability are the prerequisites of any interaction among individuals; neither a social order nor even a conscious self would be possible without the kind of stability of the social universe that enduring institutions provide. What characterizes a society that is oriented toward advanced rationality, then, is not a dearth of institutions but a capacity to place each institution—not all of them at once—under scrutiny to see if it works well. Adverse findings do not necessarily lead to a call for the abolition of the institution, but they suggest at the very least the value of research efforts to identify alternative ways of doing things, alternatives with a more favorable balance of advantages over disadvantages.

The system of science is the most advanced and complicated instrument of human rationality; and the system of higher education is the most advanced organization for the long-term improvement and expansion of human rationality and of science. Because our modern society has become so complex, and because its complexity continually appears to increase or even accelerate, we depend on increasingly complex and specialized sciences to help us tackle our problems. And we depend on a continually expanding and advancing educational system to provide not only the needed specialists of the general and applied sciences, but also the cultural perspectives and the constant reappraisals of purposes within which science can remain a means to human ends rather than become a soulless end in itself.

The fact that striving or effort of any kind presupposes some kind of problem or difficulty is a fundamental principle of individual development as well as of social and cultural history. Within the personality this principle can be illustrated by the challenge-response model, any striving is seen as a consequence of tension or disequilibrium, and the implied goal of any striving is the reduction of the tension and the re-establishment of an equilibrium. This model serves to illustrate not only the cycles of elementary physiological drives such as hunger; at this level of abstraction the dynamics is presumably the same also for much more complicated strivings such as intellectual effort. When referring to the elementary drives toward the satisfaction of physiological requirements one may speak of a fundamental "rationality of the organism" (compare Krech and Crutchfield, 1948, pp. 168–173), since its survival depends on these strivings; and one may well adopt as a fundamental working hypothesis the proposition that all secondary or psychologically based strivings are analogously rational, too, in the limited sense of serving some immediate function for the personality.

Growth and maturation in the child can take place only when mere repetition no longer works well. The child's accustomed responses may become inadequate either owing to changes in his own developing physiology with the ensuing changes in the nature of his primary and secondary drives, or because his parents or peers come to expect more mature behavior as he grows older; both things keep happening, of course, in the life of every child. To the extent that he can cope with these problems and frustrations, he not only grows but matures; whenever they overwhelm him, neurotic developments ensue.

This last possibility makes it necessary to be explicit about three fundamentally different types of motivations for mental effort. Without problems, it has been implied, an individual could theoretically live wholly according to fixed habits, with little effort and indeed little consciousness required. However, every child faces problems of at least two kinds: how to be accepted by or win approval of parents or peers, and how to understand why they behave as they do and thus anticipate their future reactions. The former problem is resolved by palatable opinions; the latter by the development of beliefs that are realistic and that improve the child's capacity to understand and predict. For the adult, too, to hold and express a given opinion may serve primarily the purpose of facilitating his immediate social acceptance, or the purpose of cognitive enlightenment of his universe. Some opinions, however, may serve a third kind of purpose that may be called ego defensive: they serve to allow the individual a psychological escape from reminders of problems and past events with which he could not cope and which now persist unconsciously as sources of much anxiety.

Sarnoff and Katz have illustrated these three motivational bases of opinions with the example of anti-Negro prejudice (Sarnoff and Katz, 1954; Sarnoff, Katz, and McClintock, 1954).[1] For a young white person who grows up in the American Deep South, a belief that Negroes are racially inferior may in the first place serve the *rationality* function of explaining what could otherwise be a cognitive problem: how does it happen that Negroes everywhere seem to be in socially inferior positions? Alternately, or in addition, such a belief may serve the *social-acceptance* function in that it saves the person from getting into scrapes with parents or neighbors. Thirdly, the same belief may serve the *ego-defense* function, too: a person who has experienced early overpowering humiliations may be neurotically anxious about his worth as a human being, and it may serve to reassure him somewhat if he can believe that he is superior to some racially, at least, if in no other way.

To understand the motivational basis of an opinion makes it possible to understand how it can be influenced. A rationality-motivated belief can presumably be influenced by new knowledge; a conformity-motivated belief can be influenced by statements issued by opinion leaders within the group to which the person belongs or aspires to belong; while a belief that serves ego-defense functions is a hardy perennial that may be subjected to change only in the course of psychoanalysis or some other sequence of fairly profound experience. It should be added that many of our beliefs and attitudes probably serve more than one of these kinds of motives; this circumstance sometimes means that we are pulled in opposite directions at the same time, and respond with neurotic impulses, indecisive acts, and vague language.

In a limited sense each type of motivation, or tension, is a rational basis for the appropriate opinion, in that the opinion does serve some immediate function for the personality. However, if a time perspective is added, the question of rationality comes in a different light. Ego-defensive opinions may for the moment help keep anxieties in check but are in the long run self-defeating in that they also help prevent the individual from seeing and grappling with the sources of his anxiety. Conforming opinions make for temporary external adjustment but keep the individual from gaining a broader understanding of himself and of society, an understanding that could help him anticipate his own future needs and society's changing requirements. Only what have been called rationality-motivated opinions indicate a type of response to problems that is constructive

---

[1] Similar psychological categories are developed and applied in Smith, Bruner, and White (1956). Some recent revisions and applications of the theory referred to in the text are found in the Summer, 1960, issue of *Public Opinion Quarterly,* which is edited by Daniel Katz; see especially Katz (1960).

in terms of the individual's long-range needs, to say nothing of the fortunes of the society in which he has a stake as a citizen. The term *rational,* consequently, will from here on be used with reference to task-oriented efforts only, and never to self-oriented or ego-defense-oriented efforts.

Relatively simple traditional societies may require very little rational effort on the part of their members, as we have seen. Complex modern societies, on the other hand, require a great deal of rational intelligence of many of their members, and this is the ultimate reason for the existence of colleges and universities. It does not follow, unfortunately, that the colleges actually deliver the intellectual power they are assigned to produce. In fact, most of them fall far short of producing even a moderate proportion of graduates who have been educated to utilize their own minds effectively for meaningful purposes of their own choice.

Why is this so? One obvious explanation is that there are and have been divergent views on what higher education ought to accomplish. Another is that the practices of educators and administrators may not be appropriate to their purposes, particularly not during periods of rapid socio-economic change. Riesman and Jencks have shown . . . that a college is likely to serve many nonintellectual functions and may have to look for much of its support on that basis. . . . Stewart places the American college in a broader historical context, and makes it clear that the *universitas* has always been a political organization, whatever else it has been, which has depended on its own foreign and domestic policies to protect its corporate well-being as well as higher learning. And Pinner argues . . . that the cultivation of intellectual excellence and of new knowledge with necessity brings about social conflict; for many of the comfortable insights cherished by men of habit or of vested interest are vulnerable indeed to the challenge of new ideas and insights.

The present chapter attempts to develop some general propositions to explain why universities generally fail to educate most of their students. Much of what will be said is presumably as applicable to the ancient universities of Bologna or of Paris as to Michigan State or any other modern American university; yet many circumstances have changed. The failure of the universities in our time is on a vaster scale, for the obvious reason, among others, that they have become so many and frequently so large. Our discussion will focus on the present and the future rather than the past; and we proceed on the bold assumption of our time that the university is duty bound to open its gates to all persons who can and who want to become educated, regardless of whether or not they can pay for what they get. "America needs all its brain power," is one familiar rationale for this; our preference is for another: "Individuals need to grow as much as they are capable of; this is what America is for."

Our theoretical point of departure is in a fundamental hypothesis that has been stated already: that all organizations, however rational in design, tend to become transformed as they endure and become institutionalized. But the dynamics of this process needs study, with particular reference to the college;

and this kind of study needs some clarification of concepts. In the next section I shall attempt to define and discuss some key concepts in the study of what may be called the erosion of rationality in the processes of higher education. Utilizing these concepts, I shall in the third section assume that the main purpose of the college is to help develop rational, independent, intellectual individuals and then proceed to review various factors in the college community and in the larger society that seem to militate against the achievement of that purpose. In a fourth and final section I shall seek to account for the fact that some students nevertheless do become well educated, and to support the view that many more students—theoretically all—could, with incentives possible under different social circumstances, gain a fuller use of their rational faculties.

SOME KEY CONCEPTS

This chapter attempts a contribution to a *social theory* of *intellectual development*. This kind of theory is not an alternative to personality theory, but a supplement which emphasizes developmental determinants in the social surroundings of the individuals concerned; in this instance, of college students.

"Intellectual development," though of course a crucial concept, will nevertheless here be given a somewhat open-ended definition. The reference is to man's rational faculties, the extent to which the person becomes able to question conventional and habitual beliefs and develops a truly autonomous individual outlook on the basic issues of life and of society. "Intellectual" will mean roughly the same as "rational" in the sense developed in the foregoing; more precisely the reference of "intellectual" is to a rationality for the whole person and for his whole life-span. A person is an *intellectual*, one might say, to the extent that his mind produces and utilizes the insight—into himself, into others, into the nature of society—that is required for coping with and anticipating the problems of living a full life and of facing death with serenity. The long-range rationality associated with "intellectual" is also a broad-gauge rationality, moreover, in the sense that the intellectual recognizes his stake in an enlightened society and in enlightened citizenship on his own part. It is this propensity of the developed intellect that makes a rich and continuing supply of intellectuals not only an advantage but a necessity for a civilization if it is to survive in a complex and rapidly changing world.

The student's social surroundings should for present purposes of analysis be viewed as a variety of *social systems*. "System" here refers to "a set of related components constituting a whole that is separated from other systems by a boundary of some kind." A social system is conceived as being composed, not of individuals, but "of the actions of individuals, the principal units of which are roles and the constellations of roles" (Parsons and Shils, 1953, p. 197). Like Chinese boxes, large social systems contain a succession of subsystems. And, what is more important, many social systems overlap, so that most individuals in a complex society belong to a variety of social systems. Sometimes overlapping systems are in harmony, but sometimes they are in conflict, and the man in the middle is torn. Both the persons and the social systems involved may change in response to the stress engendered by conflicting role expectations, but the amounts and directions of change, if any, may be difficult to predict.

The American society as a whole can be considered one large social system that can be analyzed in terms of an almost infinite variety of subsystems. Higher education in the United States, too, is one social system of which the many colleges and universities are the most obvious subsystems. Within each college, professors and students may for various purposes of analysis be said to form separate subsystems, criss-crossed for other purposes by other systems in which professors and students are united, for example along the lines of the various sciences or fields of study.

Every new rational venture, for example, a new college, or department, or type of course, creates a new social system. The difficulty of keeping a new venture rational should be apparent already from the fact that each individual who takes on a role in the new system continues at the same time to play many of his familiar roles in other systems, of which his habitual or deliberate kinds of behavior are component parts.

New social systems frequently are the result of deliberately planned human efforts; if so, they are *organizations* as well as social systems. A college, for example, is a deliberately established social system; it is an organization with explicit rules of procedure, including rules for determining who makes the important decisions, under what circumstances, utilizing what procedures, and guided by what criteria. By "organized"—a word used frequently also in the foregoing pages—is simply meant: deliberately arranged with some purposes in mind. Generally speaking, organizations are established in order to solve problems; that is, in order to expand the rational at the expense of the institutional components of social interaction.

However, as already stated as a fundamental hypothesis, no organization works entirely according to its rational design. Even the procedures for making decisions are invariably moulded in directions that deviate from those on the organizational chart. Partly, this may be because no planners, however well-informed and wise, are capable of making rules that fit all future situations. Partly, also, because social systems (like systems of ideas and other cultural systems) develop a momentum of their own, so far insufficiently explored by students of behavior; the merging and meshing of new institutions with old lead to unanticipated types of stresses and opportunities, which are influenced also by varying personalities of individuals in key roles at crucial moments. Partly, again, leadership groups in any social organization may be in a position to utilize their prerogatives of leadership to bolster their own power at the expense of other groups or potential groups within the organization. Every stable organization, to conclude, has presumably developed some informal compromise between deliberate plans with purposes in mind, unanticipated stresses and incentives, and general tendencies toward entrenchment of leadership, of privilege, and of institutional stability. This informal structure is often referred to as the "informal organization" in contrast to the deliberately planned "formal organization."

Most American colleges are stable formal organizations, within which a variety of informal organizations or social systems operate. It is always legitimate to ask to what extent the informal institutions tend to defeat the purposes which the organization should serve. But if we want to pursue this inquiry, we need to focus on what the college experience means to the student.

Individual human behavior is nearly always, it is safe to assume, a succession of compromises, often preconsciously or unconsciously developed, between what the person would most want to do and what the relevant social system seems to require of him. Yet the analysis of behavior is vastly more complicated than this statement would suggest, because the personality throughout its life cycle keeps adapting to and incorporating aspects of various social systems, while the systems in turn are moulded and further developed by influential persons. Although it might, for most purposes, be sterile to discuss personal behavior apart from its social determinants, it would be equally fruitless, except for highly abstract and remote purposes, to discuss social processes apart from individual perspectives. Indeed, the most fruitful focus for inquiries into most social processes is probably in the area where personality theory and social theory overlap: the perspective of the individual who is confronted by a social system and induced to assume some kind of *role* in relating to other individuals and to the system.

The concept of role has for a number of years, even decades, been prominently displayed in the theory of the fundamental behavioral sciences—psychology, sociology, and social anthropology. "The world is a stage"; so plausible is the concept of role, that it has been widely used in entertaining as well as in serious literature, in fiction as well as nonfiction, in articulate discussions as well as in the vernacular. Since the concept needed no justification, neither has it by and large received, in the behavioral sciences, the amount of attention commensurate with its general explanatory assignments. In consequence, the more specific explanatory uses of the role concept have been few; as Neiman and Hughes observed in 1951, relatively few testable hypotheses had employed it (1951, p. 149; cf. Sarbin, 1954, p. 255).

One reason for the limited practical use of the role concept until recently has surely been the insidious ambiguity of the term. As Levinson has pointed out in a recent paper (1959), even some of the most articulate and careful theorists of modern sociology have tended to overburden the term "role" with at least three operationally quite separate meanings: organizational role-demands; personal role-definitions; and actual role-behavior, or personal tendencies to act in relation to given roles. "Role-demand" is, as Levinson points out, a sociological concept, in the sense that the term usually refers to supposed requirements of the organization or social system; "role-definition" and "role-behavior," on the other hand, are both psychological concepts, respectively referring to the individual's cognitive and his behavioral response to the situation in which he finds himself. One of Levinson's conclusions is that "personal role-definition . . . becomes a linking concept between personality and social structure. It can be seen as a reflection of those aspects of a given personality that are activated and sustained in a given structural-ecological environment" (1959, p. 179).

A most extensive survey of concepts of role is found in *Explorations in Role Analysis* by Gross, Mason, and McEachern (1958), a book that also has contributed the most sophisticated and fruitful empirical study, so far as I know, of the expectations and behavior connected to a given role. (Another discerning study is contributed by Gouldner, 1957–58.) The role chosen for study by Gross et al. was that of school superintendent in the Commonwealth of Massachusetts, a role that carries a considerable amount of prestige and power, and whose incumbents tend to be highly articulate and self-confident persons. The authors chose to restrict their definition of "role" to *"a set of evaluative standards applied to an incumbent of a particular position"* (authors' italics). Perhaps the most important accomplishment of that study is the demonstration of how widely the degrees of agreement may differ, both among role incumbents and among members of the boards which hire the school superintendents and presumably determine their roles, with respect to the various aspects of their roles.

Quite apart from what Gross et al. have contributed of insights into the exigencies of being a school superintendent in Massachusetts, they have helped to sensitize the reader to the crying need for more precise terms and a more specific clarification of contexts in the analysis of social roles. Their work also raises the question in this reader's mind, however, of whether "role-expectation" is fully adequate as *the* key concept in the analysis of how individuals behave in social systems. Both this term and Levinson's "personal role-definition," while they no doubt are well suited to refer to essential variables in rational as well as institutional behavior, may well need to be supplemented by a term referring to more dynamic (and less purely perceptual-cognitive) variables in individual motivation. Also, in role theory and in most discussions of role concepts, including those just referred to, there seems to be too much of an assumption that the task of the individual is indeed to play his role; whether this implication is normative (saying in effect that this is the proper behavior, from society's or from the investigator's point of view) or merely descriptive (asserting that this is what people by and large do), it is an unfortunate one, in my judgment, because the individual's scope for challenging conventional expectations and for creative redefinitions of his role is either discounted or unduly de-emphasized. Different persons approach the same kinds of roles with very different degrees of independence, "willingness to play the game," loyalty to the various reference groups, personal involvement in objectives, and so on; moreover, the same person's attitude to his role may undergo considerable changes during a given time interval, and such changes may be due primarily to factors in his own private life or personality development, and not necessarily be responsive mainly to changes in the social environments of his role.

For a supplementary concept conducive to connect "role-expectation" and "role-definition" with the whole range of motives that account for the individual's attitude to a given role I shall here use the term *incentive*. This latter term shall refer to the relative prospects of motive satisfaction by way of a given role or a given effort, as these prospects are seen from the individual's point of view at a given time, when compared to roles or efforts which he sees as available alternatives. All the variables and components of measurement developed in the study of role-expectations by Gross et al. must be taken into account in the operational analysis of incentives, too; but in addition, we must develop variables such as the apparent instrumentality of role-conformance to larger aims, degrees of cultural integration or alienation, perhaps general optimism or pessimism, activism or passivism, and so on. The strength of a given incentive, generally speaking, depends in part on the relative strength of the relevant motive, in part on the degree to which the individual thinks or feels it can be satisfied in this way rather than by other means, and in part on the apparent probability that this approach will be successful by less expenditure of effort or incurring of risk than would be involved in alternate efforts or roles. Needless to say, incentives can be established by way of conscious deliberation, by way of preconscious "hunches," or by way of unconscious anxieties or wishes; most often, perhaps, elements from all three realms contribute to the total incentive situation from which a person acts.

If individual behavior normally is a succession of compromises between what the person would most want to do and what appears socially expected of him, then it may be said that an analysis of the relevant roles and incentives is the most hopeful approach toward clarifying the terms of those compromises.

Incentives are in a sense embedded in the social system, where they correspond to motives in the individual; as the individual perceives the various elements in his situation, those elements that he values or disvalues, and thinks or feels that he can do something about, are for him incentives. In a stable social system, institutions provide whatever incentives are minimally required, at least to keep enough persons motivated to behave properly in terms of the system's various role-requirements. In an organization deliberately established and charged with the task of solving given problems, incentives are artificially stimulated by way of rewards and punishments calculated to activate appropriate motives for persons in given roles or in all roles. The fact that no organization ever keeps functioning entirely in terms of its rational design and initial purposes can probably best be accounted for, generally speaking, in terms of the difficulty of designing a self-perpetuating system of over-riding incentives; that is, of incentives prone to keep activating motives that remain stronger than all possibly less appropriate (and relevant, that is, dysfunctional) motives combined, in all persons influentially involved in the organization.

It would be rash to assume that American colleges have in fact been established for men for whom the promotion of higher learning was the only or even the main purpose. Chapter 3† . . . ought to dispel any such notion and to impress on the reader the variety of social purposes that a college may serve. Among these purposes it may well happen that the task of intellectual development gets lost; we shall see in the next section what some of the odds may be, and on what social circumstances they may depend. But let me first define what, for the purposes of this inquiry, are the principal types of incentives: the social, the academic, and the intellectual incentives.

By *social incentives* is meant the relative attractiveness of prospects of social acceptance, of being admitted to membership in desired groups, and of being respected, liked, admired, or loved by relevant persons. Every human being appears to desire some kind of social acceptance, though there are great variations in the apparent intensity of this need and still greater variations in the categories of persons from whom acceptance is desired. Some persons appear to want everyone's approval, while others are satisfied by the approval, real or imagined, of very few. Perhaps it can be generalized that the better the individual is able to control his anxieties—be they unconscious, preconscious, or conscious— the less dependent he is on being approved by many. One application of this rule is that the more meaningful relationships a person can establish with a few (and this presumably depends in large part on his capacity to control his anxieties), the less dependent he is on social acceptance by greater numbers, and the more open he is to the development of other kinds of incentives. By "meaningful" relationships is here meant relationships between independent persons capable of forming other attachments as well,—not including the symbiotic type of relationship described by Erich Fromm.

Our concern with social incentives will have reference to the college community, and that means in particular, as we shall see, a concern with the student's incentives to seek acceptance among his peers.

By *academic incentives* is meant the value the student attaches to making a good academic record, in terms of conscientious fulfillment of course requirements and, above all, the achievement of good grades. This is something very different from *intellectual incentives;* the latter term here refers to the satisfaction the student perceives in the striving to broaden his understanding and sharpen his power of reflection.[2] Combinations are of course frequent, but this makes it not less but more important to distinguish the two concepts.

Purely intellectual incentives are tuned only to the development of the individual's intellectual development, or the growth of his rationality in tackling all of the problems of living, the problems of preservation that are pressed on him as well as the problems of progress that he and other intellectuals formulate. Purely academic incentives, on the other hand, are directed only toward solving the problems of preservation or of holding his own in relation to the immediate academic challenge; academic advancement in many disciplines requires only

---

† In Nevitt Sanford (ed.), *The American College* (New York: John Wiley & Sons, 1962).
[2] I am indebted to Christopher Jencks and David Riesman for having suggested this distinction.

the development of skills, not the broadening of the mind or the use of the mind toward formulating a meaning for the individual's existence. It is possible to become academically proficient and yet remain a child or an adolescent in the intellectual sense of lacking coherence of and independence of judgment on the basic issues of human existence.

Perhaps this conceptual distinction can be clarified by anticipating a proposition to be discussed in the next section: while one student's social anxieties may be of such nature that any development of intellectual incentives is barred by the predominance of his social incentives, another student's type of social anxieties may lead him to develop narrowly academic incentives to the exclusion of all others. The first type of student is concerned only with immediate acceptance, the other only with future acceptance in the larger society; both are barred from intellectual development by their social anxieties.

There are no doubt other types of incentives, too, of importance to various types of student. For one thing, I have made no allowance for students whose anxieties are not so much social as they are ego defensive; such students may be obsessed with desires for power, notoriety, defiance, conquests among the opposite sex, punishment, or much else. College teaching and college curricula are not designed to help in the mastery of severe neuroses, however; this task must be left to counselors and psychiatrists. My inquiry in this chapter assumes that most freshman students arrive in college with a certain amount of ego control and task-orientation, so that they are not barred from learning by personal circumstances beyond the reach of most professors.

Social anxieties can be almost equally constricting, however; but *they* can presumably be remedied by appropriate processes in the college, including proper teaching. And it seems important to ask why the college so often fails in giving its students the intellectual competence and mastery that would help them conquer their social anxieties and become task-oriented individuals. The urgency of this problem is underscored by the vast intellectual waste that this considerable degree of failure entails, in my judgment. Let me now turn, then, to a discussion of some probable social determinants, in the college community and in its larger environment, of intellectual development or its prevention in college students.

SOME SOCIAL DETERMINANTS OF STUDENT INCENTIVES

I have assumed that the university exists to promote the intellectual development of its students. Although there are many motives under the sun, a reading of almost any university or liberal arts college catalogue will confirm the impression that this is among the purposes most prominently claimed. It is on this or some very similar basis that students are invited to enter the hallowed grounds. And the students for their part, although they look forward to going to college with a variety of hopeful expectations, tend to stress as the most important one that they will get "a basic general education and appreciation of ideas." At any rate, this goal formulation has come out ahead of alternate goals, such as learning how to get along with people or acquiring skills applicable to one's career, in studies of attitudes and opinions of students from a broad variety of universities and liberal arts colleges in recent years (Goldsen et al., 1960, pp. 5–13 and 208). I do not know of any corresponding survey of what administrators and professors hope to achieve by their own efforts in the colleges.

It is open to doubt, of course, how much depth of intention is connected with the various goal formulations for higher education that one encounters, on either side of the ivied fence. College catalogues as well as young people's minds may thrive on clichés, as can happen to professors' minds, too. Yet clichés are not without consequences of their own, even though their primary function may be to hide more complex realities. One thing that distinguishes attempts at scientific inquiry from good common sense inquiry is a determination to try to unravel both these consequences and the underlying complexities, and by the use of appropriately abstract concepts try to make sense of what is discovered.

There is unquestionably a demand in our culture that at least some of the clichés of intellectual development as a main purpose must be approved by those who undertake to transform the money of taxpayers or private donors into organizations in the service of higher learning. And these clichés stimulate a variety of responses; for one thing, they are extensively communicated to students. Yet I am sure we can go much further than this, and assume that a great many administrators and professors, perhaps the great majority of both, sincerely and energetically try to determine what it takes to stimulate intellectual development in their students and to do what they can to provide whatever they believe it will take. The aim of the present inquiry is to contribute toward a fuller sociological understanding of circumstances that tend to defeat the labor of the many able and devoted educators; no sociological inquiry is needed to explain why those who fail to try are unlikely to succeed.

The sociologist's point of departure should be the concept of social system and the general empirical knowledge of social systems. As we have seen, the general dynamics of social systems characterize new organizations as well as the more traditional or institutional social systems; as new organizations, too, become institutionalized, their rational purposes may become dimmer, or even tend to evaporate within a pleasant mist of airy clichés. Colleges and universities, however intellectual in task-orientation and however rational in design, provide roles and careers for individuals who are rarely fully task-oriented and never fully rational in their choice of purposes. For one thing, even those teachers who are enthusiastically devoted to the cause of higher learning are likely to be interested also in their own and their families' social and economic welfare, and most of us also exhibit from time to time such human frailties as desires for comfort, or prestige, or personal influence or power.

While the ideal liberal arts college organizes the various staff roles according to an overall plan that seeks to promote a maximum intellectual development in a maximum proportion of the students, all the staff roles from the president's to the humblest teaching assistant's inevitably become reinterpreted in terms of the overall incentive situation of each person involved. The visibility of the various kinds of incentives may vary and, to some extent, so may the awareness people have of their own motivating incentives. Some relevant incentives are fairly obvious even without explicit recognition in print and may be widely recognized in the college community, especially if the people involved have power. Other incentives, important determinants of behavior though they may be, are more subtle and may be recognized only by acute observers or investigators. What needs to be stressed is that every college, ideal in design or not, soon becomes an institutionalized social system in which a fairly stable system of compromises is established. This latter system, with varying degrees of success, reconciles educational ideals with the variety of incentives and motives of the persons who occupy the significant roles inside and outside the college. (Some outside influences are discussed below.)

What practical conclusion should be drawn from these general observations? At least this one, that he who prepares plans for a new college should seek to emulate the intellectual techniques of the chess-player, even though he has hundreds of "opponents" instead of only one: He should so far as possible anticipate what incentives are likely to emerge in connection with each role, academic and nonacademic, of every person on the staff, given the kind of person who at a given salary is likely to occupy each kind of position; and he should deliberately seek to manipulate the design of the various roles, with their inter-relating obligations and rewards, so as to minimize sources of friction and to maximize the conditions for positive contributions to the purposes of the proposed college. Also, it may be concluded that those who head existing colleges should encourage experiments with separate subcolleges within the college, to provide new experience and new insights into how the discrepancies between ideals and performance can be reduced in the larger setting and in colleges generally.

I shall return to the idea of experimental colleges. First, however, an attempt will be made to analyze what happens now, as most colleges and universities operate at the present time. In succession, and without any claim to exhaustiveness, I shall review some of the social circumstances that appear to stimulate the principal categories of student incentives, — social, academic, and intellectual.

Each student who enters college is motivated by a variety of *social* incentives; the immediately obvious reference group, or group in which he aspires to be accepted, is normally that of his peers, or that of a section, at least, of the student community. Because all students on each campus will have many interests in common, a social system of all students will develop, along with a *student culture* influenced by and in turn contributing to the various norms and expectations that make up the variety of student subcultures. The norm-orientations embedded in the student culture and subcultures will also be influenced by various deliberate organizational enterprises, including a central student government as well as the various athletic, political, and social organizations that solicit memberships among all students. Also, there are other organizations seeking to recruit minorities only, including academic discipline-oriented associations as well as living groups such as fraternities, sororities, and student housing cooperatives (the latter usually recruit among all students, but can of course accept only limited numbers). By "student culture" is meant the profusion of beliefs and attitudes that emerges and endures for a while with an impact on the social system of all students; analogously, we speak of "subcultures" whose impact is limited to subsystems.

Is it inevitable that the student culture becomes rather antagonistic to the faculty culture or to the purposes of the administration? Conflicting interests always tend to create antagonisms; for example, workers and employers tend to develop mutual antagonism unless class differences are either alleviated or explained away. The role of the student is rather different from that of the worker, however; if the university is compared to an industrial corporation, the student's role is in important respects more similar to that of a stockholder: the university works for him, to provide benefits for him. He works, too, but supposedly for himself rather than for the university. The student is both the raw material and the end product of the university. Or, more precisely, the end product is a certain amount of change, either in the student's personality or in his social equipment, or both; the end product is either an unspecified amount of change in the student's intellectual habits and powers, or a specified number of course credits and an academic degree to his name, or both.

Depending on which of these types of end product is emphasized by each student, his orientation to the faculty will be primarily contractual or primarily collaborative. To the extent that the faculty is disposed to reward intellectual efforts more than mechanical efforts of memorizing, the intellectually bent students will tend to feel associated with professors in a joint enterprise while the more narrowly grade-oriented may become confused and antagonistic. If the professor, on the other hand, rewards primarily efficiency in memorization, the grade-seekers will tend to see him as a reasonable man with whom they have to bargain, while the intellectually bent will see him at best as an obstacle to be overcome in their own learning process, and at worst as a representative of an educational system toward which they feel alienated.

For the average entering student, then, his new social role as a student must appear a very complex one. There are, first of all, the role-expectations developed by his peers in the student culture; in the vast majority of the colleges these norms are primarily nonintellectual as well as nonacademic, and sometimes anti-intellectual though rarely anti-academic. One reason for this nonintellectualism may be that students with social skills almost inevitably acquire more influence on the shaping of peer-group culture than do those with intellectual skills, who by and large participate less persistently in social activities or at any rate tend to strive less hard for student leadership (at least when it comes to purely social leadership or leadership in organizations without independence and political influence). Since most entering students are at a developmental stage where social acceptance is very important to them, they will tend to model themselves after the social leaders, not the studious types. Furthermore, those who become social leaders will tend to be recruited in part from those with a self-assurance and relative lack of concern for academic achievement associated with an upper-class or wealthy upper-middle-class family background, and in part from the star athletes. In many colleges the system of fraternities and sororities serves to magnify even further the dominating influence of the less intellectually bent students in the continuous development of the student culture; very frequently these socially prominent nonintellectuals dominate as a matter of course the formal organs of student governments as well.

And from the point of view of university administrators the nonintellectual nature of this kind of student leadership, both formal and informal, has a considerable advantage, particularly from a public relations point of view: these students are never politically radical and rarely even relatively liberal; in fact, they tend to be externally submissive to symbols of authority and obedient to the deans as they are to their own fathers; they feel they have a head start and expect to remain in the upper strata in an unequal society by their ability to get along with and be accepted by influential people, not by intellectual effort. Occasionally, however, the leadership of the socially prominent nonintellectuals over the formal organs of student government will be challenged by more intellectual and more liberal students, particularly if the college has a considerable number of graduate students, who do tend to be more liberal than the undergraduates. The college administrators are in such situations likely to side with the nonintellectuals, as the more liberal students may be embarrassing campus critics and also tend to engage in wider political activities that may offend conservative legislators or donors to whom the college looks for financial support. Thus it happened on a large campus not long ago that the administration chose to separate the graduate students, the most mature part of the student body, from the general association of students, following the election of liberals to student leadership, as if to make sure that the less intellectual and more pliable students next time would recapture the positions of organizational leadership that had traditionally been theirs.

It goes without saying that a college administration cannot hope to create an even moderately intellectual college community unless it is prepared to guarantee complete freedom of political discussion and association within its walls. If a desire to placate outside interests leads the administration to discourage the expression of certain ideas, however misguided or even harmful these ideas may seem, then it is itself acting in a profoundly anti-intellectual manner, and is in a singularly weak position to encourage professors and students to apply their powers of rationality to the utmost in realms other than the political. The circumstance that most colleges today seem to practice a less than complete freedom of political controversy no doubt contributes significantly to the substantial degree of cynicism many students express concerning matters political *and* intellectual. In this way more often than not a gulf has come to separate intellectual faculty members from the "practical-minded" majority of their students, who have no use for idealism or indeed for any ideas whose practical utility for their own anticipated careers is dubious. These students are in college to earn the necessary grades with whatever minimum effort this will take; the reference group to which they look for recognition and approval remains during four years the student community or parts of it, not the faculty, except insofar as individual faculty members must be related to in order to provide grades.

The desire for reasonably good grades does provide certain kinds of powerful incentives, of course, which compete with and at times overshadow the purely social peer group-oriented incentives. And the college does have the power to strengthen these *academic* incentives by increasing course requirements or by instituting tougher grading policies. Also, the college can, aided by parents, impress on the students that they live in a competitive society and that success depends on diligent effort all the way, from now on.

Everyone must agree that efforts to do well on assignments benefit most students more than would the absence of all efforts of the mind. Yet it is regrettable, from an intellectual point of view, that grades receive as much emphasis as they do; they constitute by long odds the most plausible and widely accepted measuring rod for college performance, in nearly all colleges. The hunt for grades can be as much of an obstacle to intellectual growth as the striving for social popularity; both strivings are similar in that they aim at social acceptance instead of individual excellence of the mind. The social status seeker strives for acceptance in the student community, while the academic striver seeks acceptance later in the larger community by acquiring the grades and the skills that seem to be in demand; neither is primarily concerned with the broadening of his mind or the development of his rational powers in the service of his full range of needs as a human being or in the service of his society's genuine needs.

If academic incentives in this narrow sense tend to overshadow intellectual incentives for most students, this is in large measure because the system of teaching so frequently is tuned to the desires of the academic strivers rather than to those of the intellectuals in the class. This is so for many reasons. One is that academically oriented instructions are easier to communicate to students, who usually want to know specifically what is expected of them in each course; it is hard to be specific about how to meditate and become wiser. Another is that the proliferation of courses and the fragmentation of the student's time and the process by which he is given a daily spoonfeeding of reading assignments and lectures, all militate against opportunities for quiet reflection. Still another circumstance is the fact that the teacher's time is fragmented, too, by the variety of courses he teaches and by the extent to which he feels pressured to publish at frequent intervals; it is easier to throw the narrowly academic course requirements at one's students than it is to try to develop the frame of mind for embarking on a joint intellectual adventure. Also, the teacher has to give grades and it is far simpler to assess narrowly academic achievement than to evaluate intellectual effort or reflective achievement. In fact, sometimes owing to the sheer size of classes it may be a necessity to give objective exams that control only the ability to memorize data, and even when this is not a necessity it may be mighty convenient to the busy instructor. To make matters worse, many instructors determine grades quantitatively on the basis of a "curve" system, with predetermined proportions of good and poor grades. This further depersonalizes the grading process and also serves notice that students are in class together not so much for a joint intellectual enterprise as for a period of competition in memorizing, to be ended by that all-important contest, the final exam. This approach to learning may be appropriate in courses where the acquisition of skills or data is clearly the only purpose, but it should not be tolerated in any course that deals with problems of human or social significance.

A further circumstance that strengthens the academic at the expense of the intellectual incentives is the tendency for many teachers in uninspiring environments to lose whatever intellectual interests they may once have had, so that for them, too, the classroom experience may tend to become a primarily social experience with students, regulated only by the essential academic duties of teaching performance that are stipulated in the college employment contract. The problem of "deadwooditis" is not limited to second-rate colleges, of course. And among the younger teachers, less susceptible to this disease, the desire for financial security through academic tenure may well forestall the development of a strong interest in teaching. In the better colleges and universities they are given to understand that their promotion prospects depend almost entirely on the quantity or quality of their published research and other academic works. Most young professors are in effect told to publish or perish, and they by and large choose to publish at the expense of time and effort invested in teaching, in preference to becoming first-rate teachers who will perish for lack of published output, or at any rate will be relegated to less prestigeful and lower paying colleges. Tenure is normally granted only when the instructor is too old to take a renewed interest in his students and to improve his teaching. Moreover, the race to publish tends to be a life-long one, with both future pay-hikes and academic prestige, and sometimes even one's self-esteem, dependent on—as one college faculty employment form is alleged to have phrased the question—one's "current rate of publication."

Another circumstance of pervasive significance is that the horizons of most schools of education appear to have been limited by the far greater ease with which research can be done on academic as compared to intellectual achievement. The large literature on prediction of college achievement has invariably focused on narrowly academic achievement as the dependent variable. So has the vast literature on experiments in teaching techniques and classroom arrangements. The reason that much of this literature is so uninspiring is perhaps a feeling one gets that what is studied is not particularly important. In fact, this whole situation reminds one of the story of the man who was searching for his lost watch under the street lamp since it was light there, though he had lost it in the shadow nearby; we study grades because they are easy to measure, although the crucial task of the educator, most of us would agree under closer questioning, is to develop the minds of the students rather than equip them with masses of facts and the kinds of skills that make for good grades in the majority of college courses.

One of the crucial needs, I believe, if academic incentives are to allow more room for intellectual incentives, too, in the role perspective of the average college student, is a greater research inventiveness in the study of educational processes. It is obviously easier to count A's and B's than to make estimates of intellectual alertness and vigor; but this is not a good reason for continuing to count A's and B's to the exclusion of more meaningful inquiries. It is difficult but far from impossible to develop a variety of indices of such variables as reflectiveness, intellectual curiosity, depth of intention in interpersonal and political attitudes, universalism of moral judgment, psychological insight, and so on; qualities which in an intellectual college community would be promoted in preference to agility in memorizing.[3]

Even if most instructors had the incentives and the ability to make most courses stimulating, both the social pressures of the student community and the academic pressure toward competing for grades are, as we have seen, likely to discourage a concentration on intellectual pursuits in most students. Days or even weekends devoted to reflection, serious extracurricular readings, or participation in nonrequired task-oriented discussion groups are either unknown or are rare events in the lives of most students. Such activities are indulged in by a few, however, who are undaunted by or whose energies are not exhausted by demands for social acceptance and for grades. But those few appear to be primarily those who plan a life-long pursuit of learning inside the ivied walls, not those who aim at nonacademic careers.

And this brings us to a third source of pressures that militate against allowing intellectual incentives much scope in the educational experience in most colleges. I refer to the nature of the larger society of which the college is a small part, and in particular to the tenuous relationship in the larger society between intellectual quality and social mobility. What matters as one determinant of student incentives is the perceptions most students have concerning the instrumental value of their various kinds of efforts in college toward facilitating the performance of the roles they anticipate in their future careers. This is an area of inquiry where much more research is needed, but the following proposition may nevertheless be ventured: those students who believe that their future career prospects will depend heavily on skill in dealing with people, or influential people, are likely to be found exerting less academic effort as well as less intellectual effort than are those who believe that academic or intellectual effort is highly instrumental to their long-range purposes.

---

[3] The extensive researches sponsored by the Mary Conover Mellon Foundation at Vassar College have incorporated promising innovations in this area. . . .

To what extent and in what ways may *intellectual* effort seem *useful* for the long-range career purposes of most students? To a very limited extent, I suspect. From the perspective of certain academic career anticipations intellectual incentives are likely to become prevailing in a fair proportion among the hopefuls: in literature and the humanities, in liberal theology and philosophy, in art and music and psychology, and to a lesser extent in some of the other social sciences and in the more fundamental among the natural sciences. In these fields the more alert students may at some stage discover the enormous gains in understanding and motivation that can be won by way of cultivating broad extra-curricular interests and habits of speculation about deeper meanings and deeper connections; in a word, by developing a zest for "useless" enterprises in reflection. In most other fields there are few if any incentives for the average student to exert his mind for any purposes other than mastering the isolated fragments of human knowledge to which he is exposed. His mind becomes tailored to the anticipated needs of the type of job to which he aspires, not to the needs of his own person and to the fuller individuality that he might have developed.

It is probable that women students in most fields are in a somewhat better position than men students, on the average, to focus on intellectual incentives at the expense of the academic in their student role. They are not equally widely doomed to full-time participation in the kind of fierce competition for income and status that many male students anticipate; quite realistically, young women more often may come to believe that efforts toward a fuller understanding of men and of themselves may be highly useful; also, the anticipated role of wife and mother leaves more room for relaxed reflection than does the anticipated role of a socially up-and-coming young man in a business world. (On the other hand, the prettier coeds suffer the risk of not developing any capacity for effort of any kind; if they are placed on a pedestal of admiration too early they may be content to remain there, and spend a decade or two in shallow narcissism, until their mainly external attractiveness wanes.) Yet there are powerful incentives against the development and especially the display of intellectual excellence in women, as it is widely believed that the vast majority of young men would not marry women of superior intellect or intelligence (cf. Goldsen et al., p. 89; and for an intellectual woman's point of view on the ensuing dilemma, see Mannes, 1960).

The generalization may be ventured that a relatively low esteem for the intellect and for intellectual excellence prevails in contemporary American society; while "ability" in all jobs is admired, a display of articulate reflectiveness is widely considered "high brow," or something peculiar to a special breed of impractical people who are not to be imitated. The somewhat derisive term "egghead" tells more than volumes of analysis could about the orientation of the contemporary mass culture toward the more reflective and sophisticated minds. This general orientation is nobody's fault in particular if it indeed is a fault; the "mass" was not better but worse educated in earlier times, although what passes for mass opinion is taken more seriously today. This is so in part because the mythology and ideology of democracy require it, but also and more importantly because it is profitable to exploit most people's lack of discriminatory powers. In a commercially oriented "mass culture," phony and effortless ideas and other products easily hold their own when competing against more genuine and more carefully developed ideas and products; when the mass of judges are uninstructed, they will tend to favor not the best but the best advertised, most of the time. As Riesman has put it, the way to a fortune is no longer the proverbial invention of a better mousetrap—a genuine service, after all—but the placing of the same old mousetrap in a new wrapping (1954, p. 104). Because the schools and colleges by and large have done such a poor job, and this is not entirely the fault of the educators, most people in our modern society are not, so it appears, equipped to distinguish between the genuine and the phony, between excellence of character or mind and the superficial appearance of excellence of character or mind. From the vantage point of many a student hoping for future success in this kind of society, to develop skill in "selling his personality" may appear far more important than to develop any personality worth selling, or indeed worth having, in terms of his own long-range personal needs. A manipulative congeniality may appear more useful to the student than a contemplative genius, if he has acquired or held on to the conventionally supported goals of a suburban ranch home and the like. Students with this attitude to learning, whether they are conscious of the attitude or not, may acquire no more profit from college than a verbal glibness and the shallow smugness of half-learning; by a trained incapacity to serious reflection, they may become genuine bores and be doomed to bored lives.

Yet, such people may in terms of their careers become eminently "practical men" and become affluent and in the conventional sense of the term highly successful, and become models for succeeding generations of students. Not only for their own sons and nephews, who sometimes keenly perceive the personal costs that conventional success may require, but even more for people who rely on the mass media for their conceptions of success. Most of the mass media display the glories of economic success in second place only to the forbidden glories of sex. Not only do they convey the view that practical smartness and maybe a little luck is what it takes to succeed (and the explanatory function of the reference to luck is to account for failure and personal ruin as being nobody's fault, least of all the economic system's). The mass media frequently go much further, and urge that what the nation needs, too, even and indeed especially in the positions of highest leadership, is practical men, not men of intellectual excellence. Witness, for one example among numerous similar occurrences, a newspaper column by George Dixon who came to the defense of one candidate for the Presidency in 1960 who had been said to read few serious books; Mr. Dixon scornfully asks, "Since when has bookishness been a requisite for President (sic) of the United States?" And he concludes: "I don't think I would feel too easy about a President of the United States who prepared himself for the job by reading books, or even taking a correspondence course. I feel he should have some practical experience" (*San Francisco Examiner,* June 27, 1960).

It is possible that these cruder varieties of anti-intellectualism are on their way out. There is still a long way to go before candidates running for national office in this country would be likely even to *be* intellectuals, and longer still until candidates with intellectual erudition would want to emphasize this type of background—or even a habit of serious reading—as a qualification for important office.[4] But it does seem that more people are becoming aware of the need for better education and for less waste of intellectual resources, if American civilization is to hold its own in competition with other social systems in which ideas and their power have been taken more seriously for some time.

Another reason to anticipate a moderate reduction of anti-intellectualism in this country, including its college student population, is the apparently growing concern for liberal education and some of the liberal arts values among influential leaders of America's business world. Some large corporations even have made a practice of assigning a number of their junior and senior executives to participate in occasional liberal arts workshops. Whyte reports an increasing interest in people with liberal arts backgrounds for executive jobs in some of the corporations, though so far it seemed that it was the higher-ups rather than the actual recruiting agents who were so inclined; however, a significant trend may be in the making (Whyte, 1956, pp. 111–120). David Riesman has pointed out an increasing trend toward what he calls "conspicuous production," which may well come to include a greater attention to the "useless" adornments of the mind. More important, or at any rate more certainly, the business leaders as well as the population generally are becoming better educated and more literate, and competitiveness is becoming reduced as oligopolies and gentlemen's agreements on prices and marketing policies are established; more people of influence than before have some time and ability to think of their lives as something separate from their jobs, and I suspect that business leaders will become more and more prone to pay attention to admonitions such as John Ciardi's: "an ulcer, gentlemen, is an unwritten poem" (1960).[5]

It would be beyond the scope of this chapter to pursue an inquiry into the probable determinants of and the long range prospects for anti-intellectualism in the American society as a whole. Let it only be observed that every failure of rationality in a social system, as in a personality, surely is a symptom of insecurity; if those who rule the social order become more confident about the

---

[4] When a professor of my acquaintance recently decided to become a candidate for national office, he was strongly and convincingly advised against stressing his qualifications as an educator or a professor.

[5] F. Scott Fletcher, President of the Fund for Adult Education, argues in the Introduction to the same book that executives need "big" minds and that "the best way to cultivate the requisite 'bigness' of mind is through the liberal arts studies . . . which, at their highest levels, assist them to develop the capacity successfully to deal with these abstract ideas that illuminate and allow them more wisely to control the world in which they live."

legitimacy and the strength of their positions and programs, or if they are re-placed with people with more confidence in the future, a climate of greater hospitality to new ideas and to intellectual activity is likely to come about. The colleges could perform better, by and large, than they do now if a time comes when bold new ideas are communicated freely and intellectual excellence of all kinds is in heavy demand.

The interdependence of the colleges and the larger social system is both close and complex. If most of those college graduates who are now influential in government and business are disposed to tolerate or even support a considerable amount of anti-intellectualism, it is evident that these people never became intellectuals themselves; social or academic anxieties and incentives have domi-nated their college years, and they never developed their full powers of rational-ity. They probably never experienced as a personal matter the challenge of new ideas about man and society, for lack of intimacy with good books or with good intellectuals among faculty or students. This is a failure of the college first of all, whose crucial function, I have assumed, is to produce graduates capable of creative rationality in the service of their own needs and in the service of their society's stake in survival in a rapidly changing universe.

It seems clear enough that political changes could bring about a better college. Let us instead ask: given substantially the present political and economic system, what can be done most effectively to improve the American college? The prin-cipal answer is, I believe, in the small experimental college within the larger college. We cannot build the intellectual university community, much less the intellectual society, all at once; as Pinner concludes in the previous chapter, the builders of intellect and the men at the frontiers of new knowledge must first of all achieve protection against the consensus and the power of the multitude. Once academic freedom has been vindicated, to the extent that dissensual ideas compete freely for the minds of scholars and students, it is time to establish smaller enclaves within the larger college, in which new ideas and indeed all great issues can become the objects of vigorous cooperative inquiry. Ideas must be-come truly important to a few professors and students before they can excite most members of a college community; and a good beginning is made if we by way of organizational experimentation can learn how to create small groups within the college in which a vigorous exchange of intellectual stimuli is pursued.

Much of the discussion by Jencks and Riesman in Chapter 22 ‡ bears on this issue; a number of conclusions are drawn from the achievements as well as the failures of the Harvard experience with undergraduate houses of residence. Nevitt Sanford has in a discussion elsewhere (1960) addressed himself more directly to this issue, and I shall list some of the ground rules he proposes for the establishment of experimental colleges; his proposals overlap widely with those of Jencks and Riesman: Only a limited number of students, maybe around

‡ Sanford, *The American College* (New York: John Wiley & Sons, 1962), pp. 731–73.

a hundred, should be admitted to this organization; they should live together, have their meals together, and have all or most of their courses together; also, faculty members should share many of their meals. It is of vital importance that the learning processes and other social processes in the experimental college be studied carefully, and compared to what is achieved elsewhere in the larger college. For this reason, no attempt should be made to recruit outstanding freshmen to the experimental college; on the contrary, this student body should be as comparable as possible to the whole body of entering freshmen. If research comes to establish persuasively that far better results are achieved inside than outside the experimental college, then it is important that it should be easy to establish additional ones without substantial costs; consequently, the teacher-student ratio should be the same as in the college generally, and this also goes for the amount of time each teacher is expected to spend with his students. Since in the experimental college the teachers will be expected to be available frequently on an informal basis, the number of formal teaching hours must be cut, while efforts must be made to teach students how to study effectively by themselves and in small work-groups, and report to the professors in tutorial conferences.

What are the prospects that a rationally designed experimental college can remain maximally task-oriented, or as impervious as possible to the processes of institutional decay of purpose? I have been assuming that everything practically possible will be done to reduce the social and narrowly academic incentives of students in the new setting, for example by avoiding competitive grading and by encouraging practices of student-faculty as well as student-student cooperation in intellectual inquiry. What I am asking now is how it may be possible to discourage dysfunctional incentives also on the part of the faculty and the administration in the experimental college. Here, too, it would seem vital to establish roles of relative security; for one thing, only persons who like to teach, and who have tenure or are unworried about achieving tenure, should be employed in this context. There should be a regular turnover of faculty members, each of whom should serve for at least two and at most four years. The director, too, should be exchanged at intervals, to reduce incentives to empire-building; but he must be expected to stay long enough to allow an impact of his particular contribution to become discernible. To maximize the prospects for enduring rationality, the whole experimental college should be started all over again, as it were, though utilizing accumulated experience and existing facilities, every few years.

This is not the occasion for pursuing in greater detail the characteristics of the proposed experimental ventures. I have wished to say only enough here to make it clear that piecemeal innovations are possible within the present system of higher education, innovations which conceivably may lead to wider changes of educational processes even in the absence of any previous improvement of the intellectual climate of the larger social system. For the rest, I have tried in this section to contribute to explaining why the current turnout of truly educated minds from the colleges as they function today is so distressingly low.

THE ENDURING INTELLECT

For all that has been said about social circumstances inside and outside the college which at the present time appear to forestall intellectual learning and development, the fact remains that some students nevertheless do develop into full-grown intellectuals. At least so it appears, though if speaking strictly one should never assert that any man or woman is full-grown in the sense that he or she has become all of which he or she is capable. Potentialities are difficult to assess with exactitude, and it is conceivable that even a Socrates or a Gandhi might have been capable of living even more wisely and nobly than he did. Every mature and advanced intellectual mind might for all we know have been even more mature and advanced had his family or his college or his society given him a better chance to grow toward the fullest size, intellectually speaking, of which he was capable. And conversely, instead of saying of some young people that they are unable to learn, we should in all humility say that the sum total of the circumstances they have been up against, capped by a type of educational experience that we did not know how to tailor to their needs, has barred them from the use of faculties which are likely to remain undiscovered.

To account for the apparent successes as well as the far more frequent failures we need propositions on drives or pressures in both directions. I have in the previous section described social circumstances that seem destined to divert the developing student from intellectual incentives; it remains to be explained why some students not only refuse to be so diverted but go after intellectual stimuli and soak them in like sponges, and later report that the intellectual challenges in their college have transformed their lives.

Harry Stack Sullivan frequently spoke of a basic tendency toward health, both mental and physical: man has somewhere in himself a will to recuperate; the organism is not indifferent to the alternatives of illness or health. Educators need a similar assumption: there is embedded in every man and woman a will to grow, mentally as well as physically; the personality is not indifferent to the alternatives of unfolding or stymieing the rational faculties. The intellect is like a fragile plant. It requires the right kind of surroundings and nourishment, of soil and air and water; within the limits set by the surrounding social circumstances, the intellect will grow to whatever stature each individual is capable of achieving.

The social limits to intellectual growth appear primarily as anxieties from the individual's perspective; in addition, there is the kind of limit that is imposed by keeping information or knowledge or stimulation away from the individual. By virtue of the fact that the colleges in the Western democracies give students physical access to almost all varieties of books, the failure of most students to take advantage of this opportunity of broadening their rationality must be explained primarily in terms of the limits set by their various kinds of anxiety. Some anxieties, I have argued, are deeply rooted and subconscious; they drive the individual to acquire and hold on to beliefs and attitudes that serve ego-defense needs. These anxieties usually revolve around fundamentals such as guilt and shame and doubts about one's own worth as a human being, and they frequently emanate from experiences of having felt rejected by one's parents during infancy or early childhood. Other anxieties are preconscious or conscious and revolve around one's social relationships; some take the shape of worries about being accepted in the appropriate peer groups or by the appropriate reference groups, while others are concerned with the unknown future and are manifested as worries about adequate performance or rewards in future social roles. All varieties of personal and social anxiety presumably have one thing in common: while they may or may not stimulate mental effort, they invariably forestall a fully rational, fully task-oriented approach to the problems of the individual's life and of his society.

The beliefs we develop serve functions that are either ego defensive, social, or explanatory, as we have observed. And it is not a matter of chance to what extent an individual acquires beliefs that serve one or another of these functions. It depends on the nature and strength of the various anxieties in the individual's life: he is doomed to have his central beliefs serve ego-defensive functions at the expense of other functions until the ego anxieties become manageable; at the next step, he is doomed to concentrate on socially instrumental beliefs until his social or career anxieties are at bay; only from then on, or with what mental energies he has to spare, can he concentrate on the task of making sense of his life and his world and pursue intrinsically rewarding challenges to his mind at his leisure. As Rokeach observes toward the end of his important book, *The Open and Closed Mind* (1960, pp. 400–401):

> The beautiful thing about a belief system is that it seems to be constructed to serve both (purposes) at once; to understand the world insofar as possible, and to defend against it insofar as necessary. We do not agree with those who hold that people selectively distort their cognitive functioning so that they will see, remember, and think only what they want to. Instead, we hold to the view that people will do so only to the extent that they have to, and no more. For we are all motivated by the desire, which is sometimes strong and sometimes weak, to see reality as it actually is, even if it hurts.

The intellect endures as potential capital in every new human being. But few, unfortunately, get to see reality as it actually is, except in brief and fleeting fragments; our anxieties keep our gaze focused on the ground immediately or in a straight line ahead of us most of the time, and we fail to study the wider horizons, even though the wider vision might have eased our walk and certainly would have helped us decide more independently where to go. Like rats in the psychologist's maze, most of us are driven through our social labyrinths by our needs and anxieties; physically we walk erect but mentally we are too unsure of ourselves and our steps to stand upright and gain an overview of society and a perspective on life. Higher education exists, I assume, to give us this opportunity, both for our sake as individuals and for society's sake, on the assumption that a fuller view of reality produces a more responsible and a wiser, more foresightful citizenry. Students will take advantage of this opportunity to the extent that they can, as implied in Rokeach's argument; but the social odds against any spectacular unfolding of the fragile intellect are large, given the present type of college community and our present social order.

John Dewey's contributions toward a better understanding of educational processes are difficult to exaggerate; of particular importance in this context is his insistence that the child's impulse life must not only be tolerated in school but must be encouraged and utilized as a main motivational basis for his learning process. The child should not go to school to be asked questions by awe-inspiring teachers; on the contrary, the child should go to school to give vent to his natural curiosity and direct questions of his own to a friendly, permissive teacher in a relaxed atmosphere, and the only awe that belongs in the classroom concerns the infinite richness of nature and of potentialities in every human mind. Yet what Dewey and his successor took insufficiently into account is that while the removal of authoritarian teaching patterns eliminated some real obstacles to learning, other social anxieties tended to take the place of those that were removed; worries about social acceptance in a more democratic classroom may give the intellect no more of a chance than is given by worries about how to pacify an authoritarian teacher. Indeed, in moderate amounts the latter worry produces academic incentives, at least, which I have termed preferable to purely social incentives in that they activate some kind of mental effort rather than none at all.

Schools and universities are the products of their social order—of the politics and economics of the larger society—not only in the fairly obvious sense that they are expected to function in the service of general social needs as those are defined by those who rule the general social order. The incentives toward or against intellectual development in every school and university depend to a large extent on the types of anxieties that are most prominently institutionalized in each social order.

Perhaps it may be a helpful frame of reference to see every human life as a sort of handicap run toward the liberation of the full rational faculties. Few are able to come anywhere near the goal, for a combination of reasons: first, unloving parents may divert the individual into a life-long process of proving himself worthwhile; second, a precarious self-esteem may lead him to a constant quest for social approval and popularity, and the school and college become mainly an arena for developing social skills; third, the worries induced by a competitive society may make the individual acutely conscious of the hazards of an uncertain future, and the school and college experience is marked by a frantic striving for the improvement of his future prospects by hard work on assignments and striving for good grades; fourth, if his career ambitions become disappointed and the individual "goes down in the world," socially speaking (or if it so appears to him), then his social anxieties and the need to rationalize or to hate may occupy the front of his consciousness for the rest of his life; or, fifth, if his ambitions become gratified the chances are that he will come to see his own identity in terms of his role, in the sense that his vision will be limited by his status: he will reflect *as* a lawyer, doctor, man of wealth, executive, labor leader, or what have you; also, in many cases, *as* a professor.

Genuine curiosity belongs to the child, and to the child in man. In most lives the capacity to be curious keeps declining; every time a young person is induced to accept an answer for ego-defense reasons or on the ground that a belief is socially expected, his capacity to be curious is cut. On the other hand, every time a person is permitted to make an intellectual discovery on his own, to see a new connection, or make sense of a new idea, for example, his curiosity is nourished and expanded. This is how it happens that intellectual development tends to become either stymied at an early age or self-generating in a lifelong process. It becomes stymied in college or earlier if the student remains a prisoner of his immediate or anticipatory social anxieties; a person who has no intellectual curiosity at twenty is unlikely to develop it later, though there are exceptions to this rule. The intellect becomes liberated in college or earlier to the extent that the student has been helped to achieve a fair degree of mastery of his personal and social anxieties, and has developed the courage to define for himself what kind of life *he* wants to live. The chances are that he will want, if he in a real sense is able to choose for himself, a life of long-term humanitarian solidarity with his fellow men, in preference to a psychologically lonelier life in quest of more narrowly self-centered short-term goals.

REFERENCES

Ciardi, J.   An ulcer, gentlemen, is an unwritten poem. In Goldwin, R. A., and Nelson, C. A. (eds.). *Toward the liberally educated executive.* New York: Mentor Books, 1957.

Fromm, E.   *The fear of freedom.* London: Routledge and Kegan Paul, 1942.

Fromm, E.   *The sane society.* New York: Rinehart, 1955.

Goldsen, Rose K., Rosenberg, M., Williams, R. M., Jr., and Suchman, E. A. *What college students think.* Princeton: Van Nostrand, 1960.

Gouldner, A. W.   Cosmopolitans and locals: toward an analysis of latent social roles. *Administrative Science Quarterly,* 1957–58, **2**, 281–306, 444–480.

Gross, N., Mason, W. S., and McEachern, A. W.   *Explorations in role analysis.* New York: Wiley, 1958.

Katz, D.   The functional approach to the study of attitudes. *Public Opinion Quarterly,* 1960, **24**, 163–204.

Krech, D., and Crutchfield, R. S.   *Theory and problems of social psychology.* New York: McGraw-Hill, 1948.

Levinson, D. J.   Role, personality, and social structure in the organizational setting. *Journal of Abnormal and Social Psychology,* 1959, **58**, 170–180.

Mannes, Marya.   "Female intelligence: who wants it?" in *New York Times Magazine,* January 3, 1960.

Neiman, L. J., and Hughes, J. W. The problem of the concept of role—A re-survey of the literature. *Social Forces,* 1951, **30,** 141–149.

Parsons, T., and Shils, E. A. *Toward a general theory of action.* Cambridge, Mass.: Harvard University Press, 1953.

Riesman, D. *Individualism reconsidered.* Glencoe, Ill.: Free Press, 1954.

Rokeach, M. *The open and closed mind.* New York: Basic Books, 1960.

Sanford, N. (ed.). Personality development during the college years. *Journal of Social Issues,* 1956, **12**(4).

Sanford, N. Theories of higher education and the experimental college. In Harris, S. E. (ed.). *Higher education in the United States: the economic problems.* Cambridge, Mass.: Harvard University Press, 1960.

Sarbin, T. R. Role Theory. In Lindzey, G. (ed.). *Handbook of Social Psychology,* Vol. I. Cambridge, Mass.: Addison-Wesley, 1954.

Sarnoff, I., and Katz, D. The motivational bases of attitude change. *Journal of Abnormal and Social Psychology,* 1954, **49,** 115–124.

Sarnoff, I., Katz, D., and McClintock, C. Attitude-change procedures and motivating patterns. In Katz, D., Cartwright, D., Eldersveld, S., and Lee, A. McC. (eds.). *Public opinion and propaganda: a book of readings.* New York: Dryden Press, 1954.

Smith, M. B., Bruner, J. S., and White, R. W. *Opinions and personality.* New York: Wiley, 1956.

Whyte, W. H., Jr. *The organization man.* New York: Simon and Schuster, 1956.

22. The "cooling-out" function in higher education [1, *]

BURTON R. CLARK

A major problem of democratic society is inconsistency between encouragement to achieve and the realities of limited opportunity. Democracy asks individuals to act as if social mobility were universally possible; status is to be won by individual effort, and rewards are to accrue to those who try. But democratic societies also need selective training institutions, and hierarchical work organizations permit increasingly fewer persons to succeed at ascending levels. Situations of opportunity are also situations of denial and failure. Thus democratic societies need not only to motivate achievement but also to mollify those denied it in order to sustain motivation in the face of disappointment and to deflect resentment. In the modern mass democracy, with its large-scale organization, elaborated ideologies of equal access and participation, and minimal commitment to social origin as a basis for status, the task becomes critical.

The problem of blocked opportunity has been approached sociologically through means-ends analysis. Merton and others have called attention to the phenomenon of dissociation between culturally instilled goals and institutionally provided means of realization; discrepancy between ends and means is seen as a basic social source of individual frustration and recalcitrance.[2] We shall here extend means-ends analysis in another direction, to the responses of organized groups to means-ends disparities, in particular focusing attention on ameliorative processes that lessen the strains of dissociation. We shall do so by analyzing the

*From *The American Journal of Sociology,* Vol. 65 (May, 1960), pp. 569–76.
[1] Revised and extended version of paper read at the Fifty-fourth Annual Meeting of the American Sociological Association, Chicago, September 3–5, 1959. I am indebted to Erving Goffman and Martin A. Trow for criticism and to Sheldon Messinger for extended conceptual and editorial comment.

[2] "Aberrant behavior may be regarded sociologically as a symptom of dissociation between culturally prescribed aspirations and socially structured avenues for realizing these aspirations" (Robert K. Merton, "Social Structure and Anomie," in *Social Theory and Social Structure* [rev. ed.; Glencoe, Ill.: Free Press, 1957], p. 134). See also Herbert H. Hyman, "The Value Systems of Different Classes: A Social Psychological Contribution to the Analysis of Stratification," in Reinhard Bendix and Seymour M. Lipset (eds.), *Class, Status and Power: A Reader in Social Stratification* (Glencoe, Ill.: Free Press, 1953), pp. 426–42; and the papers by Robert Dubin, Richard A. Cloward, Robert K. Merton, and Dorothy L. Meier, and Wendell Bell, in *American Sociological Review,* Vol. 24 (April, 1959).

most prevalent type of dissociation between aspirations and avenues in American education, specifying the structure and processes that reduce the stress of structural disparity and individual denial. Certain components of American higher education perform what may be called the cooling-out function,[3] and it is to these that attention will be drawn.

THE ENDS-MEANS DISJUNCTURE

In American higher education the aspirations of the multitude are encouraged by "open-door" admission to public-supported colleges. The means of moving upward in status and of maintaining high status now include some years in college, and a college education is a prerequisite of the better positions in business and the professions. The trend is toward an ever tighter connection between higher education and higher occupations, as increased specialization and professionalization insure that more persons will need more preparation. The high-school graduate, seeing college as essential to success, will seek to enter some college, regardless of his record in high school.

A second and allied source of public interest in unlimited entry into college is the ideology of equal opportunity.[4] Strictly interpreted, equality of opportunity means selection according to ability, without regard to extraneous considerations. Popularly interpreted, however, equal opportunity in obtaining a college education is widely taken to mean unlimited access to some form of college: in California, for example, state educational authorities maintain that high-school graduates who cannot qualify for the state university or state college should still have the "opportunity of attending a publicly supported institution of higher education," this being "an essential part of the state's goal of guaranteeing equal educational opportunities to all its citizens."[5] To deny access to college is then to deny equal opportunity. Higher education should make a seat available without judgment on past performance.

Many other features of current American life encourage college-going. School officials are reluctant to establish early critical hurdles for the young, as is done in Europe. With little enforced screening in the pre-college years, vocational choice and educational selection are postponed to the college years or later. In

---

[3] I am indebted to Erving Goffman's original statement of the cooling-out conception. See his "Cooling the Mark Out: Some Aspects of Adaptation to Failure," *Psychiatry*, Vol. 15 (November, 1952), pp. 451–63. Sheldon Messinger called the relevance of this concept to my attention.

[4] Seymour Martin Lipset and Reinhard Bendix, *Social Mobility in Industrial Society* (Berkeley: University of California Press, 1959), pp. 78–101.

[5] *A Study of the Need for Additional Centers of Public Higher Education in California* (Sacramento: California State Department of Education, 1957), p. 128. For somewhat similar interpretations by educators and laymen nationally see Francis J. Brown (ed.), *Approaching Equality of Opportunity in Higher Education* (Washington, D.C.: American Council on Education, 1955), and the President's Committee on Education beyond the High School, *Second Report to the President* (Washington, D.C.: Government Printing Office, 1957).

addition, the United States, a wealthy country, is readily supporting a large complex of colleges, and its expanding economy requires more specialists. Recently, a national concern that manpower be fully utilized has encouraged the extending of college training to more and different kinds of students. Going to college is also in some segments of society the thing to do; as a last resort, it is more attractive than the army or a job. Thus ethical and practical urges together encourage the high-school graduate to believe that college is both a necessity and a right; similarly, parents and elected officials incline toward legislation and admission practices that insure entry for large numbers; and educational authorities find the need and justification for easy admission.

Even where pressures have been decisive in widening admission policy, however, the system of higher education has continued to be shaped partly by other interests. The practices of public colleges are influenced by the academic personnel, the organizational requirements of colleges, and external pressures other than those behind the open door. Standards of performance and graduation are maintained. A commitment to standards is encouraged by a set of values in which the status of a college, as defined by academicians and a large body of educated laymen, is closely linked to the perceived quality of faculty, student body, and curriculum. The raising of standards is supported by the faculty's desire to work with promising students and to enjoy membership in an enterprise of reputed quality—college authorities find low standards and poor students a handicap in competing with other colleges for such resources as able faculty as well as for academic status. The wish is widespread that college education be of the highest quality for the preparation of leaders in public affairs, business, and the professions. In brief, the institutional means of the students' progress toward college graduation and subsequent goals are shaped in large part by a commitment to quality embodied in college staffs, traditions, and images.

The conflict between open-door admission and performance of high quality often means a wide discrepancy between the hopes of entering students and the means of their realization. Students who pursue ends for which a college education is required but who have little academic ability gain admission into colleges only to encounter standards of performance they cannot meet. As a result, while some students of low promise are successful, for large numbers failure is inevitable and *structured*. The denial is delayed, taking place within the college instead of at the edge of the system. It requires that many colleges handle the student who intends to complete college and has been allowed to become involved but whose destiny is to fail.

RESPONSES TO DISJUNCTURE

What is done with the student whose destiny will normally be early termination? One answer is unequivocal dismissal. This "hard" response is found in the state university that bows to pressure for broad admission but then protects standards by heavy drop-out. In the first year it weeds out many of the incompetent, who may number a third or more of the entering class.[6] The response of the college is hard in that failure is clearly defined as such. Failure is public; the student often returns home. This abrupt change in status and in access to the means of achievement may occur simultaneously in a large college or university for hundreds, and sometimes thousands, of students after the first semester and at the end of the freshman year. The delayed denial is often viewed on the outside as heartless, a slaughter of the innocents.[7] This excites public pressure and anxiety, and apparently the practice cannot be extended indefinitely as the demand for admission to college increases.

A second answer is to sidetrack unpromising students rather than have them fail. This is the "soft" response: never to dismiss a student but to provide him with an alternative. One form of it in some state universities is the detour to an extension division or a general college, which has the advantage of appearing not very different from the main road. Sometimes "easy" fields of study, such as education, business administration, and social science, are used as alternatives to dismissal.[8] The major form of the soft response is not found in the four-year college or university, however, but in the college that specializes in handling students who will soon be leaving—typically, the two-year public junior college.

In most states where the two-year college is a part of higher education, the students likely to be caught in the means-ends disjuncture are assigned to it in large numbers. In California, where there are over sixty public two-year colleges in a diversified system that includes the state university and numerous four-year state colleges, the junior college is unselective in admissions and by law, custom, and self-conception accepts all who wish to enter.[9] It is tuition-free, local, and under local control. Most of its entering students want to try for the baccalaureate degree, transferring to a "senior" college after one or two years. About

---

[6] One national report showed that one out of eight entering students (12.5 per cent) in publicly controlled colleges does not remain beyond the first term or semester; one out of three (31 per cent) is out by the end of the first year; and about one out of two (46.6 per cent) leaves within the first two years. In state universities alone, about one out of four withdraws in the first year and 40 per cent in two years (Robert E. Iffert, *Retention and Withdrawal of College Students* [Washington, D.C.: Department of Health, Education, and Welfare, 1958], pp. 15-20). Students withdraw for many reasons, but scholastic aptitude is related to their staying power: "A sizeable number of students of medium ability enter college, but . . . few if any of them remain longer than two years" (*A Restudy of the Needs of California in Higher Education* [Sacramento: California State Department of Education, 1955], p. 120).

[7] Robert L. Kelly, *The American Colleges and the Social Order* (New York: Macmillan Co., 1940), pp. 220-21.

[8] One study has noted that on many campuses the business school serves "as a dumping ground for students who cannot make the grade in engineering or some branch of the liberal arts," this being a consequence of lower promotion standards than are found in most other branches of the university (Frank C. Pierson, *The Education of American Businessmen* [New York: McGraw-Hill Book Co., 1959], p. 63). Pierson also summarizes data on intelligence of students by field of study which indicate that education, business, and social science rank near the bottom in quality of students (*ibid.*, pp. 65-72).

[9] Burton R. Clark, *The Open Door College: A Case Study* (New York: McGraw-Hill Book Co., 1960), pp. 44-45.

two-thirds of the students in the junior colleges of the state are in programs that permit transferring; but, of these, only about one-third actually transfer to a four-year college.[10] The remainder, or two out of three of the professed transfer students, are "latent terminal students": their announced intention and program of study entails four years of college, but in reality their work terminates in the junior college. Constituting about half of all the students in the California junior colleges, and somewhere between one-third and one-half of junior college students nationally,[11] these students cannot be ignored by the colleges. Understanding their careers is important to understanding modern higher education.

THE REORIENTING PROCESS

This type of student in the junior college is handled by being moved out of a transfer major to a one- or two-year program of vocational, business, or semi-professional training. This calls for the relinquishing of his original intention, and he is induced to accept a substitute that has lower status in both the college and society in general.

In one junior college[12] the initial move in a cooling-out process is pre-entrance testing: low scores on achievement tests lead poorly qualified students into remedial classes. Assignment to remedial work casts doubt and slows the student's movement into bona fide transfer courses. The remedial courses are, in effect, a subcollege. The student's achievement scores are made part of a counseling folder that will become increasingly significant to him. An objective record of ability and performance begins to accumulate.

A second step is a counseling interview before the beginning of the first semester, and before all subsequent semesters for returning students. "At this interview the counselor assists the student to choose the proper courses in light of his objective, his test scores, the high school record and test records from his previous schools."[13] Assistance in choosing "the proper courses" is gentle at first. Of the common case of the student who wants to be an engineer but who is not a promising candidate, a counselor said: "I never openly countermand his choice, but edge him toward a terminal program by gradually laying out the facts of life." Counselors may become more severe later when grades provide a talking point and when the student knows that he is in trouble. In the earlier counseling the desire of the student has much weight; the counselor limits himself to giving advice and stating the probability of success. The advice is entered in the counseling record that shadows the student.

A third and major step in reorienting the latent terminal student is a special course entitled "Orientation to College," mandatory for entering students. All

---

[10] *Ibid.,* p. 116.

[11] Leland L. Medsker, *The Junior College: Progress and Prospect* (New York: McGraw-Hill Book Co., 1960), chap. iv.

[12] San Jose City College, San Jose, Calif. For the larger study see Clark, *op. cit.*

[13] San Jose Junior College, Handbook for Counselors, 1957–58, p. 2. Statements in quotation marks in the next few paragraphs are cited from this.

sections of it are taught by teacher-counselors who comprise the counseling staff, and one of its purposes is "to assist students in evaluating their own abilities, interests, and aptitudes; in assaying their vocational choices in light of this evaluation; and in making educational plans to implement their choices." A major section of it takes up vocational planning; vocational tests are given at a time when opportunities and requirements in various fields of work are discussed. The tests include the "Lee Thorpe Interest Inventory" ("given to all students for motivating a self-appraisal of vocational choice") and the "Strong Interest Inventory" ("for all who are undecided about choice or who show disparity between accomplishment and vocational choice"). Mechanical and clerical aptitude tests are taken by all. The aptitudes are directly related to the college's terminal programs, with special tests, such as a pre-engineering ability test, being given according to need. Then an "occupational paper is required of all students for their chosen occupation"; in it the student writes on the required training and education and makes a "self-appraisal of fitness."

Tests and papers are then used in class discussion and counseling interviews, in which the students themselves arrange and work with a counselor's folder and a student test profile and, in so doing, are repeatedly confronted by the accumulating evidence—the test scores, course grades, recommendations of teachers and counselors. This procedure is intended to heighten self-awareness of capacity in relation to choice and hence to strike particularly at the latent terminal student. The teacher-counselors are urged constantly to "be alert to the problem of unrealistic vocational goals" and to "help students to accept their limitations and strive for success in other worthwhile objectives that are within their grasp." The orientation class was considered a good place "to talk tough," to explain in an *impersonal* way the facts of life for the overambitious student. Talking tough to a whole group is part of a soft treatment of the individual.

Following the vocational counseling, the orientation course turns to "building an educational program," to study of the requirements for graduation of the college in transfer and terminal curriculum, and to planning of a four-semester program. The students also become acquainted with the requirements of the colleges to which they hope to transfer, here contemplating additional hurdles such as the entrance examinations of other colleges. Again, the hard facts of the road ahead are brought to bear on self-appraisal.

If he wishes, the latent terminal student may ignore the counselor's advice and the test scores. While in the counseling class, he is also in other courses, and he can wait to see what happens. Adverse counseling advice and poor test scores may not shut off his hope of completing college; when this is the case, the deterrent will be encountered in the regular classes. Here the student is divested of expectations, lingering from high school, that he will automatically pass and, hopefully, automatically be transferred. Then, receiving low grades, he is thrown back into the counseling orbit, a fourth step in his reorientation and a move justified by his actual accomplishment. The following indicates the nature of the referral system:

Need for Improvement Notices are issued by instructors to students who are doing unsatisfactory work. The carbon copy of the notice is given to the counselor who will be available for conference with the student. The responsibility lies with the student to see his counselor. However, experience shows that some counselees are unable to be sufficiently self-directive to seek aid. The counselor should, in such cases, send for the student, using the Request for Conference blank. If the student fails to respond to the Request for Conference slip, this may become a disciplinary matter and should be referred to the deans.

After a conference has been held, the Need for Improvement notices are filed in the student's folder. *This may be important* in case of a complaint concerning the fairness of a final grade.[14]

This directs the student to more advice and self-assessment, as soon and as often as he has classroom difficulty. The carbon-copy routine makes it certain that, if he does not seek advice, advice will seek him. The paper work and bureaucratic procedure have the purpose of recording referral and advice in black and white, where they may later be appealed to impersonally. As put in an unpublished report of the college, the overaspiring student and the one who seems to be in the wrong program require "skillful and delicate handling. An accumulation of pertinent factual information may serve to fortify the objectivity of the student-counselor relationship." While the counselor advises delicately and patiently, but persistently, the student is confronted with the record with increasing frequency.

A fifth step, one necessary for many in the throes of discouragement, is probation: "Students [whose] grade point averages fall below 2.0 [C] in any semester will, upon recommendation by the Scholarship Committee, be placed on probationary standing." A second failure places the student on second probation, and a third may mean that he will be advised to withdraw from the college altogether. The procedure is not designed to rid the college of a large number of students, for they may continue on probation for three consecutive semesters; its purpose is not to provide a status halfway out of the college but to "assist the student to seek an objective (major field) at a level on which he can succeed."[15] An important effect of probation is its slow killing-off of the lingering hopes of the most stubborn latent terminal students. A "transfer student" must have a C average to receive the Associate in Arts (a two-year degree) offered by the junior college, but no minimum average is set for terminal students. More important, four-year colleges require a C average or higher for the transfer student. Thus probationary status is the final blow to hopes of transferring and, indeed, even to graduating from the junior college under a transfer-student label. The point is reached where the student must permit himself to be reclassified or else drop out. In this college, 30 per cent of the students enrolled at the end of the

---

14 *Ibid.*, p. 20.
15 Statement taken from unpublished material.

spring semester, 1955–56, who returned the following fall were on probation; three out of four of these were transfer students in name.[16]

This sequence of procedures is a specific process of cooling-out;[17] its effect, at the best, is to let down hopes gently and unexplosively. Through it students who are failing or barely passing find their occupational and academic future being redefined. Along the way, teacher-counselors urge the latent terminal student to give up his plan of transferring and stand ready to console him in accepting a terminal curriculum. The drawn-out denial when it is effective is in place of a personal, hard "No"; instead, the student is brought to realize, finally, that it is best to ease himself out of the competition to transfer.

COOLING-OUT FEATURES

In the cooling-out process in the junior college are several features which are likely to be found in other settings where failure or denial is the effect of a structured discrepancy between ends and means, the responsible operatives or "coolers" cannot leave the scene or hide their identities, and the disappointment is threatening in some way to those responsible for it. At work and in training institutions this is common. The features are:

1. *Alternative Achievement.* Substitute avenues may be made to appear not too different from what is given up, particularly as to status. The person destined to be denied or who fails is invited to interpret the second effort as more appropriate to his particular talent and is made to see that it will be the less frustrating. Here one does not fail but rectifies a mistake. The substitute status reflects less unfavorably on personal capacity than does being dismissed and forced to leave the scene. The terminal student in the junior college may appear not very different from the transfer student—an "engineering aide," for example, instead of an "engineer"—and to be proceeding to something with a status of its own. Failure in college can be treated as if it did not happen; so, too, can poor performance in industry.[18]

2. *Gradual Disengagement.* By a gradual series of steps, movement to a goal may be stalled, self-assessment encouraged, and evidence produced of performance. This leads toward the available alternatives at little cost. It also keeps the person in a counseling milieu in which advice is furnished, whether actively

---

[16] San Jose Junior College, "Digest of Analysis of the Records of 468 Students Placed on Probation for the Fall Semester, 1956," September 3, 1956.

[17] Goffman's original statement of the concept of cooling-out referred to how the disappointing of expectations is handled by the disappointed person and especially by those responsible for the disappointment. Although his main illustration was the confidence game, where facts and potential achievement are deliberately misrepresented to the "mark" (the victim) by operators of the game, Goffman also applied the concept to failure in which those responsible act in good faith *(op. cit., passim)*. "Cooling-out" is a widely useful idea when used to refer to a function that may vary in deliberateness.

[18] *Ibid.*, p. 457; cf. Perrin Stryker, "How To Fire an Executive," *Fortune,* Vol. 50 (October, 1954), pp. 116–17 and 178–92.

sought or not. Compared with the original hopes, however, it is a deteriorating situation. If the individual does not give up peacefully, he will be in trouble.

3. *Objective Denial.*   Reorientation is, finally, confrontation by the facts. A record of poor performance helps to detach the organization and its agents from the emotional aspects of the cooling-out work. In a sense, the overaspiring student in the junior college confronts himself, as he lives with the accumulating evidence, instead of the organization. The college offers opportunity; it is the record that forces denial. Record-keeping and other bureaucratic procedures appeal to universal criteria and reduce the influence of personal ties, and the personnel are thereby protected. Modern personnel record-keeping, in general, has the function of documenting denial.

4. *Agents of Consolation.*   Counselors are available who are patient with the overambitious and who work to change their intentions. They believe in the value of the alternative careers, though of lower social status, and are practiced in consoling. In college and in other settings counseling is to reduce aspiration as well as to define and to help fulfil it. The teacher-counselor in the "soft" junior college is in contrast to the scholar in the "hard" college who simply gives a low grade to the failing student.

5. *Avoidance of Standards.*   A cooling-out process avoids appealing to standards that are ambiguous to begin with. While a "hard" attitude toward failure generally allows a single set of criteria, a "soft" treatment assumes that many kinds of ability are valuable, each in its place. Proper classification and placement are then paramount, while standards become relative.

IMPORTANCE OF CONCEALMENT

For an organization and its agents one dilemma of a cooling-out role is that it must be kept reasonably away from public scrutiny and not clearly perceived or understood by prospective clientele. Should it become obvious, the organization's ability to perform it would be impaired. If high-school seniors and their families were to define the junior college as place which diverts college-bound students, a probable consequence would be a turning-away from the junior college and increased pressure for admission to the four-year colleges and universities that are otherwise protected to some degree. This would, of course, render superfluous the part now played by the junior college in the division of labor among colleges.

The cooling-out function of the junior college is kept hidden, for one thing, as other functions are highlighted. The junior college stresses "the transfer function," "the terminal function," etc., not that of transforming transfer into terminal students; indeed, it is widely identified as principally a transfer station. The other side of cooling-out is the successful performance in junior college of students who did poorly in high school or who have overcome socioeconomic handicaps, for they are drawn into higher education rather than taken out of it. Advocates of the junior college point to this salvaging of talented manpower, otherwise lost to the community and nation. It is indeed a function of the open door to let hidden talent be uncovered.

Then, too, cooling-out itself is reinterpreted so as to appeal widely. The junior college may be viewed as a place where all high-school graduates have the opportunity to explore possible careers and find the type of education appropriate to their individual ability; in short, as a place where everyone is admitted and everyone succeeds. As described by the former president of the University of California:

> A prime virtue of the junior college, I think, is that most of its students succeed in what they set out to accomplish, and cross the finish line before they grow weary of the race. After two years in a course that they have chosen, they can go out prepared for activities that satisfy them, instead of being branded as failures. Thus the broadest possible opportunity may be provided for the largest number to make an honest try at further education with some possibility of success and with no route to a desired goal completely barred to them.[19]

The students themselves help to keep this function concealed by wishful unawareness. Those who cannot enter other colleges but still hope to complete four years will be motivated at first not to admit the cooling-out process to consciousness. Once exposed to it, they again will be led not to acknowledge it, and so they are saved insult to their self-image.

In summary, the cooling-out process in higher education is one whereby systematic discrepancy between aspiration and avenue is covered over and stress for the individual and the system is minimized. The provision of readily available alternative achievements in itself is an important device for alleviating the stress consequent on failure and so preventing anomic and deviant behavior. The general result of cooling-out processes is that society can continue to encourage maximum effort without major disturbance from unfulfilled promises and expectations.

---

[19] Robert Gordon Sproul, "Many Millions More," *Educational Record,* Vol. 39 (April, 1958), p. 102.

23. *Student culture and academic effort** *

EVERETT C. HUGHES, HOWARD S. BECKER, and
BLANCHE GEER

For the past several years, we have been engaged in a study of a large state medical school. We have centered our attention, primarily, on the problem of academic effort: how hard do students work? What do they work at? What determines the level and direction of their effort?

We present here two aspects of our continuing attack on these problems. First we present very briefly a general consideration of the range of actual situations one may expect to encounter in studying American schools and of the concepts most appropriate for use in such studies; then, a brief sketch of what we found in the medical school.

LEVEL, DIRECTION, AND STYLE OF EFFORT [1]

The difference between an American and an Englishman is that the American pretends to work harder than he does, while the Englishman works harder than he pretends. Thus runs one version—whether true or not—of a joke on an ancient theme, that of the relation between appearance and reality. Any difference that may exist between some typical British student and some typical American student as to either the appearance or the reality of his academic effort is nothing compared to the differences among American students and American educational institutions. In the amount of effort put forth by teachers and students, in the quality of their product, in the direction of their efforts toward one kind of learning or another, our country may well exhibit a larger variety in educational institutions than does any other country.

They also differ from one another in what one might call rhythm and style of effort. David Daiches (1957) has written some observations concerning the rhythm of academic effort in Britain and America. In Britain he observes that

---

*From Nevitt Sanford (ed.), *The American College* (New York: John Wiley & Sons, 1962), pp. 515–30.
[1] Most of the first part of this chapter appeared as "How Colleges Differ," *Planning College Policy for the Critical Decade Ahead* (New York: College Entrance Examination Board, 1958), pp. 16–22.

youngsters put on the great push in secondary school, achieving quite remarkable knowledge of some subjects; in university, they take it easier, and perhaps do not make equivalent progress. The American youngster comes to college not very learned, and probably unaccustomed to hard work, but may enter into college work with such verve and lively curiosity that he may come out ahead of the English graduate in some respects. That is what we mean by rhythm of effort. At Oxford, one must preserve the appearance of doing little but enjoy the intellectual and other amenities of the place during term, while also giving the impression of doing naught but "swat" between terms. That is a matter of both rhythm and style, since everyone there knows he really must work hard to survive. A man who teaches in the most gentlemanly of our state universities reports, without bitterness, that the students cannot be made to work except for a mad burning of midnight oil during the last ten days of term; only out-of-state "odd-balls" start work at the opening of the term and do all of the assignments. It may be that these gentlemanly students accomplish more than those of another, much larger, and more folksy state university at which the students are kept so busy at little daily-assigned chores that they have no time to develop or pursue a program of study (not that most of them had thought of such a thing). In the effort to get some reasonable level of accomplishment and effort in his own course, each instructor had resorted to the device of assigning a quota of daily chores. The student gives each teacher his due, claiming in return the right not to be held responsible several months from now for debts for which he already has a receipt. The rhythm is one of small, slight pulsations of effort. At McGill University, the young ladies from the upper-middle and upper slopes of Westmount seemed to have as their goal a good, solid *Second-Class* achieved by competent, unstrained effort. *First-Class* would have indicated eager competitiveness worthy only of those "pros" who were working for prizes and graduate scholarships; *Third-Class* would have betrayed either slackness or lack of ability to take things in one's stride.

There is an analogy in industry. Groups of skilled workmen will nearly always set, by informal understandings, the proper level of production. If they hate the rate-buster, they also despise the man who has to strain to make "bogey." How unlike those young ladies are the pious hard-working students in a certain sectarian college, who lack goals and style altogether, having no one to give them a model of either; how unlike also is the moderately bright, frightfully earnest young man who is rewarded with a teaching assistantship by a professor grateful to have at least one promising "major," and stays on for a dreary second-class M.A.; then, as an instructor at his home university or one of its satellites, he becomes that drone of American education, the premature pundit teaching too many subjects, and who is driven by his wife, the administration, and the accrediting boards to get a Ph.D. by applying what are known as tests of significance (sic) to what are indeed *data,* since they were handed him by his academic master. The poor fellow may have life made even worse by having to teach at a certain college where the students simply say, "Everybody has a right to go to college, even though they don't want to work hard"; or at another, a state teachers college that has had its name changed by law to "state university," where the students will not answer any examination question based on a book not on the list of those issued free (as a perquisite for being part of the public school system of the state).

Anyone who looks at all the concerns that go by the name of college and university in this country will see their great variety as to administrative and financial situation, historical concept of function, sensitivity to community forces, actual or potential numbers and kinds of students, and other character-istics. This variety is matched by one equally great in the amount, style, and directions of effort and accomplishment effectively expected of students by each other and by the people who teach them. Although we have a good many tests of the levels of accomplishment of students in various schools and colleges, we have less knowledge than we should have of the manner in which various levels of effort are set and maintained. From studies in industry we know that levels of production are set by many factors other than the wishes of management, ability of individuals to perform tasks at a certain rate, and by the formal re-wards of wages, promotion, and security. It is safe to say, as did Max Weber about fifty years ago, that any group of workingmen possessed of any solidarity whatsoever, and with some common image of themselves and their situation, will not easily yield to any authority full control over the amount of work they do or over the strenuousness of the effort they put forth (Weber, 1924). They will wrestle with management whenever a change is made in the conditions of their work and in the concept of normal effort. We have assumed that the individual goals of students are more compatible with those of the college than are the individual goals of workers with those of their employers, and that the main thing required to raise levels of accomplishment in the college is simply to raise standards required of individuals for entrance and graduation. We have not systematically studied the way in which students form their own cultures as we have studied the cultures of workers. By the term, student culture, we mean a whole body of conceptions and images of problems and situations and of proper and justifiable solutions of them arrived at by the students; in part passed along from one generation of students to another, in part apparently rediscovered—or at least re-enforced—by each succeeding generation as they pass through the same experiences. In the second part of this paper we shall discuss the student culture of the medical school in some detail. At this point, we need only note that the students in the school had a common goal—to become practicing physi-cians—and faced common problems: how to get through school without flunking out and how to prepare themselves to practice medicine. The resulting student culture is integral and homogeneous.

Ordinarily the students of a college or university will be less homogeneous as to goal and problems. That may make for a less distinctive and homogeneous student culture; it may be more difficult to discover just what it is in case of institutions with heterogeneous student bodies. But it does not mean that there is not a student culture, or that the understanding of it is not essential to the making and carrying out of educational policy.

A certain urban "underdog" college prides itself on providing education for those neglected by other institutions. Since the students work for a living many classes are held in the evening. The students, in spite of all the difficulties of their individual situations, have an exceedingly active collective life in the corridors and lounges. In their discussions, they—that is, some articulate group of them, at least—have come to the notion that since their education is so hard to come by, it is up to the professors to make it good, but good, and that allowance in assignments and in marking should be made for the fact that a student has to work long hours at some hard or tiresome task. It is not the attitude of passively accepting a hand-out from the professor, but of aggressively demanding it and of reserving the right to decide whether it is a good hand-out. These students work out their particular student-culture not so much in relation to a specific common goal (such as medicine), as in relation to a common set of difficulties in their immediate careers as students arising out of their life-situations. And note that their body of expectations includes some concerning what their professors owe them. When these students turn up in graduate school, as a good many of them do, they are at first resentful of the load of work given them and of what appears to them the indifferent attitude of the staff. Since, however, they are usually bright students and really eager, they often pick up the slack quickly. Their experience of life often makes them the good observers we prize in sociology and anthropology.

One solution offered for the problem of student cultures that are not what we would like is to pick the right young people to go to college, or, at any rate, to our own particular college. It should be pointed out that even in those cases where the college can and does pick its students from a national market, much of what is most prized is in the particular types of student culture achieved, and these emerge independently, for the most part, of the wishes of faculties. The issue is not presence or absence of a student culture, but its character. Most academic institutions, in any case, appear fated to offer several kinds of goods to several kinds of clients. And in colleges, as in hospitals for chronic ailments (which keep their patients around for a long time), the clients—or patients, as you wish—develop their own notions of what is wrong with them and of what to do with the medicines dispensed to them.

Although we all know it, it is well to remind ourselves of a certain great difference between the institutions called colleges and universities in this country and those of the same designations in Europe. There, these institutions provide for the later education of but a few young people in a very few lines of work. The great burden of vocational training is allocated to other institutions. In this country, a great and increasing part of vocational training is done in colleges and universities. The postponement of entry to work, in our era of automation, combined with the notion that he who does not yet work goes to school, and that college comes after high school, has brought about a huge increase in the number of things taught in American colleges, and in the number of vocational bachelor's degrees. The difference between this country and others is not that we or they do or don't support vocational training but that in this country a great and increasing part of the vocational training is done in the very institutions that also carry the burden of higher education. There is no way out of this, even if we wanted to find a way.

We all know that in many colleges and universities where the general level of aspiration and effort is miserably low, there are small nuclei of students of great intellectual verve. Such groups, in effect, create little subcultures all of their own, contrary in many respects to that of the prevailing mass student culture. We need to study such groups, so as to learn more of the circumstances in which they arise and disappear, and so as to learn how they may be planted, cultivated, and emulated. There are many experiments of this kind going on. We suspect that those experiments in quality will succeed best that make most use of knowledge of the propensities of groups of students for developing their own conceptions of their abilities, of setting their own group standards and goals. Encouragement of individual "rate-busting" will not succeed in more than a few cases (although all of us know of students who have wrung an education from an unwilling college). Nor will a general raising of minimum standards, or a purging of so-called extraneous matter, and unworthy material, create and increase the number of nuclei of students of superior effort and accomplishment. We would lay our bets on efforts to create or encourage groups of special quality within the bosom of the conglomerate institutions that go by the name of university or college.

American colleges and universities are, in a measure unknown in other countries, enterprises; it matters little whether they are private or public, they are still enterprises seeking formulas for survival or expansion in competition with others. A common formula for survival is retention of some measure of monopoly over an original function, while also entering into competition with other institutions for other functions and other kinds of students. Many of our colleges and universities are going concerns that have come to their present state through such processes and are still making adjustments of this kind to survive, consolidate their positions, or to expand. In each case, the students—usually several kinds of them—arrive with certain expectations and, in interaction with one another and with their faculties and with circumstances, gradually develop some culture of their own, including notions of how hard to work and what to work at. Our problem is to develop the means that will make it possible for experiments in excellence to be carried out in many of these wierd and interesting going-concerns; we waste our energies if we limit ourselves to thinking about the one ideal kind of institution with the one ideal kind of student. The problem is to develop, in real institutions, combinations of functions and of kinds of students in which the number who will seek higher achievement will be made greater; this is, in turn and in part, a matter of getting some students—and their teachers—to create new images of themselves and their possibilities.

STUDENT CULTURE IN MEDICAL SCHOOL: AN ILLUSTRATIVE CASE [2]

We turn now to a detailed consideration of one kind of student culture: the kind we found in an intensive examination of medical students. This is, clearly, an extreme type. One would not expect the students of any college to be so homogeneous in their goals, in their conceptions of the problems they face, or in the solutions they find to those problems. We have just begun a study of student culture in the undergraduate college of a medium-sized state university and hope that our findings there will enable us further to refine our present concepts and hypotheses.

Conditions for the development of subcultures

Subcultures (of which student cultures are one example) develop best where a number of people are faced with common problems and interact both intensively and extensively in the effort to find solutions for them, where people who face the same contingencies and exigencies in everyday life have an opportunity to deal with these communally (Sumner, 1907; Cohen, 1955). Medical school is an ideal hot-house for such a plant.

Medical students live with a number of pressing and chronic problems, the most important stemming from the fact that they are continuously presented with an enormous and, in any practical sense, unlimited amount of material to learn. Though students and faculty agree that the criterion for choosing what to learn should be relevance for medical practice, there is enough disagreement and uncertainty among the faculty as to what is relevant so that the student is never presented with a clear directive to guide him in his own studies. Students worry together over this problem, in one or another of its many transformations, during their four years of school.

Similarly, medical school provides extremely propitious conditions—intensive interaction and isolation from outside influences—for the development of common solutions to these problems. Students usually spend eight or more hours in school every weekday, working and studying together in the labs and on the wards, and are likely to spend many evenings and weekends together in similar activity as well. Much of their work is carried on in groups of four to twelve students, and these are arranged so differently from course to course that the students come to know many of their fellows with the intimacy that arises from close, continuous association at work. The students are insulated from contact

[2] This portion of the paper was originally read at the meetings of the American Sociological Society, August 28, 1957, Washington, D.C., and was later published in the *Harvard Educational Review*, Vol. 28 (Winter, 1958), pp. 70–80.

Our study of medical students was sponsored by Community Studies, Inc., of Kansas City, Missouri, and was further supported by grants from the Carnegie Corporation and the National Institutes of Health. Anselm Strauss has collaborated with us in both the field work and the preparation of the final report.

with other people, both by reason of their crowded schedules and because they find it difficult to talk with people who are not suffering under the same pressures as they are. Even those students who have friends or brothers only a year or two ahead of them in school report that they get little help with their immediate problems from these people. Each class of approximately one hundred students goes through school as a unit, meeting the problems they face together.

This intensive interaction in an isolated group produces a particularly meaningful and essential array of those understandings and agreements we call student culture. One set of understandings specifies goals and values, telling the students that they are in school to learn those things relevant to their prospective professional futures. In the school we studied, students came to believe that they were in school to acquire the knowledge and clinical experience one must have before he can assume the responsibility of the physician for the lives of his patients, a responsibility they intended and expected to have once they finished school. They based their interpretations of the worth of various school activities on the criterion of how well this function was served in each. Another set of understandings suggested modes of cooperation designed to meet examinations and other crises, and such recurrent problems as sharing loads of clinical work assigned to groups.

The student's interpretation of specific events and issues tends to be made in categories that are part of the student culture, because these events and issues are new and unfamiliar and do not fit easily into categories provided by his earlier experiences. These cultural understandings coerce his behavior though not, at least in medical school, by methods as crude as punishment by fellow-participants in the subculture (characteristic of subcultures in the underworld or industrial work groups). It is not that the student must abide by these informal and hardly conscious agreements, but rather that they constrain his thinking and perspective almost without his being aware of it (though an occasional student may be conscious of a degree of tension between what he might like to do and what the group norms specify as correct).

The academic years

Perhaps the most important factor in the development of student culture during the freshman year is the formation of a group in which all or nearly all members have opportunities for interaction with each other. When the freshmen arrive in medical school, although they come with the common intention of becoming physicians, they are not a group in any but the nominal sense that all are in the first year class. They begin to get to know some of their fellow students right away, but this takes place not in the class at large but within small groups. The small groups are of two types. First to form are friendship groups consisting of students similar in social status who have opportunities for leisure interaction because they live near or with each other. Fraternity members, for example, most of whom are unmarried, make friends in their own house, married students get to know other married students who live in the same neighborhood or trailer camp, and unmarried students who do not belong to a fraternity get together at the student center to eat and relax in their spare time. The second type of group forms in the anatomy laboratory. As the faculty assigns students in groups of four to a dissection tank, members of different friendship groups get to know each other under the intimate conditions that dissection of the same cadaver imposes. The intersection of work and friendship groups makes it possible for each student to learn the attitudes current in other groups toward student problems, and, at the same time, carry back to his own friends solutions he and his lab partners have tried out in the course of their work together.[3]

The spread of common understandings among the freshmen is also promoted by their isolation. Unlike most graduate students, all members of the medical school class are taught together. They spend an eight-to-five day in one building. Each morning and afternoon, lectures lasting as long as the instructors wish are followed immediately by laboratory periods. Review and preparation is done at night, usually at home (for there is little or no library work) or once again in the laboratory. On a schedule like this there is little opportunity for interaction with groups outside the class, nor do the students turn to the faculty with problems except about details of daily work. For as they begin to draw together and get a sense of themselves as a group, they think of the faculty as a group opposed to their own. To ask faculty advice is to break student ranks. Thus, the students come to an understanding among themselves of what the study of medicine is and how it should be accomplished. Their notions are derived from what the faculty says and does (which are sometimes quite different), from the future they envision for themselves as physicians, and from their past experience in getting through school and college.

The student concept of what medicine is develops first. They believe it is a great body of known facts, some of which will be imparted to them in the first year for eventual use when they become physicians. The idea that everything is important soon gets them into a dilemma, for there are more facts than they have time to learn. They are told this by the faculty, and prove it to themselves when, after studying four and five hours a night and on weekends as well, they have not mastered the material to their own satisfaction.

As they realize they can't learn everything, all but the most self-exacting students see that they must study only important things and let the rest go. But what is important? This question becomes the chief subject of discussion in student groups shortly before the first major examinations. Two points of view predominate. One group of students believes the most important facts are those they will use in medical practice. (Selection of these facts is a matter a student feels quite competent about even if he has only been in school a few weeks.) A second group of students, most of them fraternity members, takes into account the necessity of passing examinations to stay in school. On this basis, the impor-

---

[3] On intersecting groups, see Simmel (1955, pp. 149–50).

tant facts are those the faculty thinks important. Students who believe this develop various systems for finding out what the faculty wants them to know.

Although taking the examinations brings the issue of what to study to a head, it does not settle it. Rightly or wrongly, students consider some questions "impractical," unrelated, that is, to the practice of medicine. These questions lead students of the group that believes in studying things important for medical practice to begin thinking more about what the faculty thinks these are. In preparation for the next examinations these students pool their knowledge, make use of files of old tests, and consult members of the class who already study in this way. But the examinations also contain questions students consider "unfair"—points not emphasized in lectures or texts. Students who follow some system for learning what the faculty wants are unable to predict such questions. The faculty has not been "playing the game." As a result of their difficulties with the examinations, both groups of students begin to have doubts about the faculty. The practice-minded group wonders whether the faculty teaching first year subjects (most of whom are Ph.D.'s) knows much about practice. The system-minded group wonders whether the faculty is agreed about what is important; if not, perhaps it is impossible to predict what will show up on an examination. Both groups consider briefly whether the faculty is "out to get them." The significance of all this for the development of student culture is that in their bewilderment, students draw closer together and finally settle their problem in a way acceptable to all but a few.

They agreed that they ought to study the "basic medical facts." These are the only ones they have time for, as there is so much to learn. These are the facts important for practice, certain to be on examinations if the faculty is reasonable. To this central proposition the students add a number of other understandings which they apply to their daily activities.

1. Basic facts are most economically learned from textbooks. This means that lectures which do not follow the text are a waste of student time, and a faculty member who strays from the text is a poor lecturer who probably has some scientific axe to grind in connection with his own research which does not concern medical students.   2. Demonstrations and lab work which repeat classical experiments are a waste of time; the results are most easily learned in the text and students can't do them well enough to learn much anyway.   3. Theoretical material, concepts (except those which help to organize facts), and research findings, not yet in clinical use are not facts and are not useful to medical students.

These understandings of the student culture can be summed up in the student phrase "give it to us straight," which has its counterpart in the derogatory faculty phrase "spoon feeding." A student will say that he does not want to be spoon fed, but points out that there is so much to learn he hasn't time to think or worry about "minutiae" (details) and "all that academic crud" (nonfactual material). Once they have decided the question of what and how to study, the students settle down to hard work. They are no longer worried about how to select the important things to read because "you just go by the black type." In the same way, they learn to get through their lab work by various short-cuts which are both approved by student culture and not penalized in examinations by the faculty. The following incident shows how such a short-cut became widely used in the class.

Each anatomy student is given a dissecting guide with explicit directions on what to do, in what order, and what to look for during the lab session. Reflection of skin is the first step in dissection of each part of the cadaver. The laboratory guide calls for great care in reflecting so as not to pull off the underlying layer of fat which adheres to the skin. Embedded in this subcutaneous fat are tough, threadlike fibers—the peripheral nerves. These are to be traced to their origins and identified. It is a slow, exasperating task; virtually impossible if reflecting is not cleanly done.

When the class began dissection of the lower leg, we noticed one group had taken off skin and fat together leaving the nerves undissected. A student at the tank said, "You see, it's easier this way. I think it saves a lot of time because you really can't get those nerves anyway." His partner agreed, saying, "It's much better to get the nerves from the book." Another student, speaking for himself and his tank partners, said, "We knew we couldn't do the nerves because they are all different on every body. It doesn't make any difference if you do the nerves or a lot of other things." By the third week of dissection, most groups observed were stripping off skin and fat together; identification of the peripheral nerves was omitted.

Collective behavior of this sort does not mean students do not work hard. They continue to work very hard on the things they think important. One reason for their neglect of peripheral nerves, for instance, is their haste to get to the next layer down which contains the larger structures, muscles and blood vessels, that every doctor must know about. It does mean that where the faculty fails to "give it to them straight" in accordance with student concepts of why they are in school and what and how they ought to study, various short-cuts are devised in more or less open defiance of faculty instructions, and students who have deviant interests outside the student culture keep them increasingly to themselves (see Becker and Geer, 1958).

The clinical years

During the last two years of medical school—the clinical years—the student's work consists largely of taking medical histories from and performing physical examinations on patients, in order that he may develop these skills and use the information so gained in learning how to diagnose and treat various diseases. Although he continues to be tested on his knowledge through formal examinations, he is told in various ways and believes that the crucial decisions about his future in school—whether he passes or fails, for example—are based largely on the faculty's evaluation of his clinical work. Furthermore, he believes that, having got this far, it is very unlikely that he will be flunked out of school; few such cases are known to have occurred.

The major problems requiring collective solution no longer lie in the realm of examinations. Rather, students focus their attention on how to deal with the continuous pressure of a heavy load of clinical work and how to get the most out of that work in terms of the future one envisions for himself in medicine. Student culture develops as a set of perspectives on and solutions for these problems.

The view that the function of medical school is, among other things, to train students to recognize and deal with diseases that are commonly run across in a general medical practice constitutes one such perspective, shared by almost all students, even those who do not contemplate becoming general practitioners themselves. This basic proposition itself derives in part from statements by the school's faculty and administration and in part from the inability of most students to visualize anything but general practice for themselves before they have had clinical contact with other medical specialties. Once formed, the proposition continues as a more or less unquestioned premise even after the students know more about specialized kinds of practices.

The students draw several more specific conclusions about their school work from this proposition, in the course of conversations and discussions of specific incidents. These specific items of student culture may be summarized as follows. 1. The patients whom it is really important to study thoroughly are those who have common diseases—whether simple or complicated—for which there are available treatments a general practitioner could utilize. 2. All those kinds of clinical work that they cannot imagine themselves doing in a general practice are regarded as a waste of time. 3. Courses in which they are not given practice in techniques they regard as important for the practitioner to know tend to be disliked. Matters of this kind are widely discussed among the students and have important consequences for the way they interpret their experience in school and distribute their effort and time among their many competing interests.

The following incident, one among many observed, provides a nice example of the way students collectively draw inferences from the basic proposition stated above and use these to guide their behavior in school.

> In one of the third year courses students are required, at the end of the course, to turn in elaborate summaries of each case assigned to them during their time on the service. These summaries must include the important findings of their own examination, important laboratory findings, a discussion of all the possible causes for these findings, references to relevant literature, and a discussion of modes of possible treatment. They are long and require a great deal of time to prepare.
>
> The students in one group we observed established an informal norm specifying the number of such summaries they would turn in, although they were definitely directed to turn in one on every patient they had been assigned. Over a period of several days preceding the date the sum-

maries were due, the six students in this group discussed the matter at length and decided that they would all hand in no more than a certain number. Further, they agreed on the criteria for selecting those to be turned in, and on the premise that the real purpose for these summaries was to provide material for the faculty to quiz them on during oral exams, so that the actual number was unimportant (in spite of the definite order that all cases were to be so summarized).

The criteria for selection of cases discarded were those which it was agreed provided them with no knowledge they did not already have of treating common medical problems, or where the work involved in preparing the summary would not add to such knowledge. Thus, patients with fractures or simple infections, whose treatment was more or less standard and afforded the students no chance to participate were not summarized, and "crocks" were not summarized. ("Crocks" are patients who have no physical pathology, but only vague and untreatable psychosomatic complaints, thus patients from whom nothing can be learned that might prove of use in general medical practice.)

The decision that these criteria were the relevant ones was reached in a discussion between the students in the group and in discussions with students who had been through the course previously who confirmed this interpretation.

A similar set of attitudes has grown up around the routine laboratory work—blood counts and urinalyses—the students must do on incoming patients assigned to them. They greatly resent this work because, among other reasons, it wastes their time since they themselves will not do these procedures, they think, when they are in practice.

This general frame of mind, as we have said, coerces the students' thinking to a striking degree. The following excerpt from an interview, which also illustrates the way courses are judged with reference to the amount of training they provide for the exigencies of general practice, indicates this clearly.

I asked a third year student to compare his training in surgery at the University Hospital with that he had during the other half of the quarter at the Veterans Administration Hospital to which students are also sent. (This student had definite and realistic plans to specialize in internal medicine, having even made arrangements as to whom he would practice with and where; as an internist he would, of course, do no surgery at all.)

He said, "One thing about surgery over at the VA was that we really got to do quite a bit more. I mean, for example, they would let us sew up incisions over there, where you don't get to do that at the University. Another thing about surgery at the University is that they do a lot of very complicated operations. For example, they do a lot of heart surgery over there. Well, now, none of us are ever going to do any heart surgery. But every one of us will probably do some hernias and some appendectomies. And over at the VA you see a lot of these. So it is really a better experience for us in a lot of ways. We don't have the glamour of all that fancy surgery, but we do see the ordinary things that will be useful to us."

CONSEQUENCES OF STUDENT CULTURE

Student culture affects the larger social system in which it is embedded—the medical school—in two ways. On the one hand, it provides the basis for a modus vivendi between the students and their superiors, providing a perspective from which students can build consistent patterns of response enabling them to fit into the activities of the school and hospital. In this respect student culture is an accommodation on the part of the students to the facts of life of the school. On the other hand, student culture provides the students with the social support that allows them, in individual instances and as a group, independently to assess faculty statements and demands so that they can significantly reinterpret faculty emphasis and, in a meaningful sense, make what they will of their education. In this sense, student culture is a mechanism that creates the conditions for considerable deviance from formally stated institutional rules.

When students first enter school their emphasis on medical practice—their belief that they are in school to learn to save lives (Becker and Geer, 1958)—leads them to rebel against laboratory work, essentially nonmedical, and against the drudgery of studying for intensive academic examinations. Later, they must deal with the same problem of an overload of work in a clinical setting in which examinations are not so important although the possibility of being tested and found wanting is always present. The understandings and agreements that make up student culture, by solving these problems in one way or another, allow the students to fit into the system without being constantly so upset as to be unable to function. In this way, student culture is a mode of accommodation to what the students find expected of them in school.

At the same time student culture affects the level and direction of effort students expend while in school, by giving them a rationale for restricting the theoretically infinite amount of time and effort they might devote to their school work. More importantly, it provides them with sufficient collective support to allow them to direct their effort in quite different directions than those suggested by the faculty—considered as a unit or even considered with regard for the divisions of opinion within the faculty itself. Though members of a given department may feel that their course is really designed to put across such-and-such a brand of knowledge for this-and-that purpose, the students may remain relatively immune, drawing the strength to ignore the faculty's otherwise authoritative notions from the lore that makes up student culture. Student culture is thus the cornerstone of many faculty difficulties with students, one of the facts of life to which teachers must, in their turn, make some accommodation.

As we have said earlier, medical school represents an extreme case of the development and operation of student culture. We would not necessarily expect it to play so important a role in other educational institutions. But we do believe that it is likely to exist in such places and that it will likely be found to have at least the two functions we have discussed for the medical instance, that of providing a means of accommodation for the students to the difficulties of school life, and that of providing the basis for redirection of effort on the student's part, possibly in defiance of faculty standards and ideals.

REFERENCES

Becker, H. S., and Geer, B. The fate of idealism in medical school. *American Sociological Review,* 1958, **23**, 50–56.

Cohen, A. K. *Delinquent boys: the culture of the gang.* Glencoe, Ill.: Free Press, 1955.

Daiches, D. Education in democratic society. *Commentary,* 1957, **23**, 336–343.

Simmel, G. *The web of group affiliations.* Translated by Reinhard Bendix. Glencoe, Ill.: Free Press, 1955.

Sumner, W. G. *Folkways.* Boston: Ginn & Co., 1907.

Weber, M. Zur psychophysik der industriellen arbeit (1908–09). In *Gesammelte aufsaetze zur soziologie und sozialpolitik,* Tubingen, 1924, pp. 61–255.

INDEXES

Author index

A

Abegglen, James C., 233
Allensmith, W., 276
Amerman, Helen E., 261
Anderson, C. Arnold, 16, 145, 220
Arnstein, G. E., 275
Asheim, Lester, 39
Atkinson, John W., 263
Ausubel, David, 22, 23
Ausubel, Pearl, 22, 23

B

Bales, Robert F., 96, 97, 98, 100, 102, 210
Baltzell, E. Digby, 167
Banks, O., 229
Barnard, Chester I., 252, 262, 265, 289
Baron, G., 229
Barr, A. S., 264
Barton, Allen H., 23
Bateson, G., 103
Bay, Christian, 333
Beck, Walter H., 54
Becker, Howard, 221
Becker, Howard S., 16, 155, 156, 163, 193, 259, 293, 298, 299, 302, 309, 328, 372, 381, 385
Belisle, Eugene L., 237
Bell, Robert R., 105
Bell, Wendell, 362
Bendix, Reinhard, 47, 108, 130, 219, 233, 320, 362, 363
Benedict, Ruth, 46
Bensman, Joseph, 196, 254
Berelson, B. R., 212
Bernard, Jessie, 5, 222
Bernstein, Basil, 21
Bestor, Arthur, 277
Biddle, Bruce J., 26
Blau, Peter M., 233, 239
Bloom, Benjamin, 12
Bogue, Donald J., 28
Bond, Horace Mann, 23, 24, 25
Brodbeck, A. J., 212
Brogan, Dennis, 232
Brookover, Wilbur, 8, 251, 269
Brown, Bert, 23
Brown, Francis J., 363
Brown, K. E., 31
Brunner, J. S., 336

Buck, Roy C., 257
Burdick, E., 212
Burnstein, Eugene, 263

C

Caiger, George, 138
Callahan, Raymond E., 35
Campbell, Angus, 237
Campbell, Arthur A., 108
Cantril, Hadley, 232
Caplow, Theodore, 252, 322
Carlyle, Thomas, 274
Cartwright, D., 361
Chandler, B. J., 35, 261
Charters, W. W., 238
Chase, F. S., 367
Chase, Stuart, 327
Chauncy, Henry, 31
Child, Irvin L., 93, 95, 96, 237
Christenson, C. V., 108
Ciardi, John, 354, 360
Cicourel, Aaron U., 44
Clark, Burton R., 362, 365
Clark, Colin, 134
Clark, Kenneth B., 17
Clark, Russell A., 263
Clayton, A. Stafford, 260
Clews, Henry, 115
Cloward, Richard A., 362
Cohen, Albert K., 224, 385
Coleman, James S., 197
Conant, James B., 29, 139
Cooley, Charles H., 88, 90, 300
Corwin, Ronald G., 251, 253, 258, 259
Coser, Lewis, 255
Cottrell, Leonard S., Jr., 246
Cremin, Lawrence A., 13, 38
Crosland, Anthony, 11
Crutchfield, R. S., 335, 360
Cubberly, E. P., 278

D

Daiches, David, 372, 385
Davis, Allison, 95, 156, 157, 160
Davis, Hazel, 251
Davis, Kingsley, 45, 85
Dean, Stuart E., 276
de Carvalho, Alceu Vicente, 136
de Oliveira, Américo Barbosa, 136

Deutsch, Martin, 23
Dewey, John, 13, 187
Dickson, W. J., 327
Dipbrze, Wilbert, 263
Dixon, George, 353
Douglas, J. W. B., 23
Douvan, Elizabeth, 237
Drabick, L. W., 257
Dubin, Robert, 362
DuBois, Cora, 93
Durkheim, Émile, 221

E

Ebel, R. L., 240
Eckelberry, R. H., 230
Eells, K., 20
Eggleston, Frederic, 138
Eldersveld, S., 361
Elkins, Stanley M., 14
Elsbree, W. S., 324
Erickson, Erik H., 51
Etzioni, A., 259
Evans, L. H., 275

F

Fales, E., 92
Fauset, Charles E., 253
Fichter, Joseph H., 61, 64, 75
Flanigan, Jean, 257
Fletcher, F. Scott, 354
Flexner, Abraham, 279
Floud, J., 16, 145, 219, 220, 228, 234
Fox, William H., 253
Franklin, Benjamin, 167
Frazier, Benjamin W., 27
Frazier, E. F., 106, 108, 113
Freedman, Ronald, 108
Freeman, J. Leiper, 59
Freud, Anna, 102
Freud, Sigmund, 102
Friedenberg, Edgar Z., 38, 48, 51, 52, 186, 198
Fritz, John, 39
Fromm, Erich, 343, 360
Frymier, Jack R., 30

G

Gardner, Burleigh, 252
Gebhard, P. H., 108
Geer, Blanche, 193, 372, 381
Gerstl, Joel E., 254
Gerth, H. H., 309
Gerver, Israel, 254
Gesell, A., 94, 99, 101
Getzels, Jacob W., 188, 191, 193, 194, 255
Glaser, Barney, 263
Glass, D. V., 130, 133, 136, 140, 225
Goethals, G. W., 276

Goffman, Irving, 363, 369
Goldman, Richard F., 39
Goldsen, Ruth, 345, 352, 360
Goldwin, R. A., 360
Goodson, Max R., 266
Gordon, C. Wayne, 215, 288
Gordon, G. G., 251
Gorer, Geoffrey, 222, 225
Goslin, Willard E., 251
Goss, Mary E. W., 258
Gouldner, Alvin W., 246, 341, 342
Greenhoe, F., 324
Groff, Patrick J., 251
Gross, Edward, 259, 266, 319, 320, 321
Gross, Neal, 2, 326, 341, 360
Guba, E. G., 255
Guilford, J. P., 188
Gurin, Gerald, 237

H

Habakkuk, H. J., 40
Hagen, Elizabeth, 32, 262
Halsey, A. H., 16, 145, 228, 233
Hammond, S. B., 130, 133
Hansen, Donald, 254
Haubrick, Vernon F., 17
Havighurst, Robert J., 4, 5, 95, 129, 130, 135, 136, 140, 156, 165, 220, 288, 323
Hechinger, Fred, 30
Henderson, A. M., 257
Herder, B., 54
Herriot, Robert E., 261
Himmelweit, Hilde, 219
Hofstadter, Richard, 13, 38
Hogbin, H. I., 103
Hollenberg, E., 95
Hollingshead, August, 106, 156, 233, 234, 288, 291
Horton, John E., 236
Hughes, Everett S., 193, 298, 372
Hughes, J. W., 340
Hutchinson, B., 130, 133
Huxley, J., 84
Hyman, Herbert, 362

I

Iffert, Robert E., 365
Ilg, F. L., 94, 101

J

Jackson, Philip W., 188–91, 193, 194
Jenks, Christopher, 331, 343, 355
Johnson, Harry, 6, 79, 83, 97, 184
Johnston, Denis F., 28

K

Kahl, Joseph A., 80, 108, 109, 125, 150, 201, 213, 234, 324

Kardiner, A., 93
Katz, Daniel, 336, 360, 361
Keller, Suzanne, 22
Kelly, Father George A., 59, 61, 62, 66
Kelly, Robert L., 365
Keppel, Francis, 33, 34
Kershaw, J. A., 31
Kerr, Norman D., 256
Kitsuse, John I., 35, 44, 261
Kleiner, Robert J., 106, 109, 114
Kluckhohn, Florence R., 201
Koerner, James D., 29, 276
Kornhauser, Arthur, 260
Krech, D., 335, 360
Kuhler, Raymond, 263

L

Lazarsfeld, Paul F., 212
Lee, A. McC., 361
Lengyel, Emil, 280
Levinson, D. J., 340, 361
Liberty, Paul, Jr., 263
Lieberman, Myron, 251, 253, 263, 264, 279, 287, 322
Lindzey, G., 93, 237
Linton, R., 93
Lipset, Seymour, 47, 108, 130, 216, 219, 233, 320, 362, 363
Lipton, Lawrence, 224
Loeb, Martin B., 156, 165, 220, 288
Lortie, Dan C., 36, 37, 39
Lowell, Edgar L., 263
Lowenthal, L., 216
Lynd, Robert S., 260, 267

M

McClelland, David C., 59, 191, 205, 263
McClintock, C., 336, 361
McEachern, A. W., 326, 341, 360
McKean, Ronald M., 31
McLuhan, Marshall, 82
McMurrin, Sterling M., 34
McPhee, William N., 212
Malleson, Nicholas, 230
Mannes, Marya, 352, 360
Manor, Stella P., 32
Marburger, Carl, 17, 18–19
Marquand, J. P., 179
Marshall, T. H., 320
Martin, C. E., 108
Martin, F. M., 228
Martindale, Don, 222
Mason, Ward S., 288, 326, 341, 360
Mayer, Martin, 34, 36, 39, 194
Mead, George H., 89
Mead, Margaret, 45, 103
Medsker, Leland L., 366
Meir, Dorothy L., 362

Merrill, Francis E., 6
Merton, Robert K., 2, 246, 362
Messinger, Sheldon, 363
Miles, Matthew B., 23
Miller, H. P., 319
Miller, Van, 256
Miller, Warren E., 237
Mills, C. Wright, 309, 330
Mitchell, J. U., 285
Moeller, Gerald H., 236, 238, 258
Monachesi, Elio, 222
Moore, David G., 252
Moore, H. A., 257
Moore, M., 216
Morris, C. H., 89
Moulton, Robert, 263
Mowrer, O. H., 93, 101, 102, 104
Myers, Jerome K., 127

N

Neiman, L. J., 340, 361
Nelson, C. A., 360
Neugarten, Bernice L., 4, 5, 130, 135, 136, 140, 323
Newcomb, T., 85, 288
North, Robert D., 31, 281
Notestein, F., 108

O

Obourne, E. S., 31
Oeser, O. A., 130, 133
Olds, J., 87, 88, 92, 100, 288
Oppenheim, A. N., 234
Oxtoby, Toby, 31

P

Pareto, Vilfredo, 222
Parker, S., 106, 109, 114
Parry, L. J., 231
Parsons, Talcott, 87, 96, 97, 100, 102, 199, 210, 238, 257, 288, 291, 320, 338, 361
Passamanick, B., 251
Passow, A. Harry, 17, 23
Peck, R. V., 285
Pettigrew, Thomas F., 23
Piaget, J., 86, 87, 90
Pidgeon, D. A., 227
Pier, Arthur S., 180
Pierson, Frank C., 365
Pomeroy, W. B., 108
Popper, Hermine I., 261
Portis, Bernard, 59, 61-64

Q

Quattlebaum, C. A., 231

R

Ravitz, Mel, 17, 18, 20
Redlich, Frederick C., 106, 109, 233
Reiss, Albert, 253
Reissman, Leonard, 108
Remmheim, Madaline K., 257
Rennie, T. A. C., 285
Rettig, S., 251
Richy, Robert W., 253
Riesman, David, 48, 51, 331, 341, 353, 355, 361
Riessman, Frank, 18
Riley, J. W., Jr., 216, 239
Riley, M. W., 216, 239
Roberts, B., 127
Rodman, H., 105, 107, 109, 114
Roemer, Theodore, 54
Roethlisberger, F. J., 327
Rogoff, Natalie, 145
Rokeach, M., 358, 359, 361
Rose, Arnold M., 4, 79, 106, 108, 109
Rosenberg, M., 360
Rossi, Alice, 53, 67
Rossi, Peter, 15, 26, 53

S

St. John, Mary Hoyt, 261
Sanford, Nevitt, 331, 333, 341, 355, 361, 372
Sarbin, T. R., 361
Sarnoff, I., 336, 361
Scanlon, John, 34
Schachtel, Ernest G., 190
Schnepp, Father Gerald J., 67
Seeman, Melvin, 241
Sewell, William H., 150
Sexton, Patricia, 23
Shaeffer, Robert J., 19
Shaplin, Judson T., 35, 44, 261, 323
Shils, Edward A., 87, 238, 288, 338, 361
Shipton, James, 58, 67, 237
Simmel, Georg, 305, 385
Simpson, George, 106, 108, 109, 113
Slater, D. E., 98
Slotkin, J. S., 84
Smith, Adam, 40
Smith, M. B., 336, 361
Spalding, Willard B., 256
Sperry, M., 95
Spiro, A. G., 83
Spiro, M. E., 83
Sproul, Robert G., 371
Srole, Leo, 285
Stiles, Lindley J., 35, 44, 261, 323
Stoke, S. M., 104
Stouffer, Samuel A., 201
Strauss, Anselm L., 193

Strodtbeck, Fred L., 59, 62, 63, 64, 76, 191
Stryker, Perrin, 369
Stub, Holger R., 251
Suchman, E. A., 360
Sumner, W. G., 385

T

Terrien, Frederic W., 255
Thomas, L. G., 319
Thompson, Wayne E., 236
Thorndike, R. L., 32, 262
Toby, J., 239
Tolman, Edward C., 87
Trow, Martin, 8, 9, 26
Trump, J. Lloyd, 283
Turner, Ralph H., 219, 221, 228

U

Urick, Ronald, 30

V

Vaizey, John, 40
Valentine, E. C., 324
Vernon, P. E., 20, 227, 228
Vidich, Arthur J., 196
Vlick, Mary, 25, 258

W

Wagenschein, M., 161, 165, 327
Wagley, Charles, 221
Walkout, Donald, 251
Waller, Willard, 159, 251, 293
Ware, Martha L., 257
Warner, W. Lloyd, 156, 165, 220, 233, 288, 291
Washburn, Chandler, 253
Wattenberg, W., 323
Weber, Max, 221, 257, 309, 385
West, J., 93
Whelpton, P. K., 108
White, R. W., 85, 100, 102, 336, 361
White, Theodore H., 194
Whiting, J. W. M., 95, 96
Whyte, William F., 157, 252, 324
Whyte, William H., Jr., 115, 269, 354, 361
Wilder, David E., 23
William, R. M., Jr., 360
Wilson, Logan, 258
Wilson, Mary D., 228
Winterbottom, M. R., 92
Wolfe, Dael, 31
Wolff, Kurt, 305
Woodring, Paul, 27, 29, 34, 278
Worth, Walter H., 264
Woytinsky, E. S., 133
Woytinsky, W. S., 133
Wylie, L., 95

Y

Yarbrough, J., 328
Yates, Alfred, 227
Yinger, J. M., 106, 108, 109, 113

Z

Zelditch, M., Jr., 97

Subject index

A

Adolescent, status of, 51–52
Agnes Irwin School, 174
Alcott, A. Bronson, 171
Alcott, Louisa M., 171
Andover, 178, 179
Anti-intellectualism, 353, 354, 355
Australia
  differential birth rates, 135, 136
  industrialization, 132-34
  natural resources, 135
  productivity and income, 134-35
  social structure, 136, 137

B

Baldwin Locomotive Works, 172
Biddle, George, 180
Brazil
  differential birth rates, 135-36
  industrialization, 133-34
  natural resources, 135
  productivity and income, 134-35
  social structure, 136-37
British Education Act of 1944, 11
Brown University, 329
Buckingham, Walter, 271
Bunche, Ralph J., 274
Bureau of Applied Social Research of Columbia University, 148
Bureaucracy
  in schools, 237-50, 257, 258
  in search for talent, 49

C

Cambridge University, 178
Chestnut Hill, 170, 173, 174
Chestnut Hill Academy, 171, 174
Christ Church, 172
Clothier, Isaac H., 180
Colleges
  enrollments, 26-27, 28, 29
  expansion of, 27, 28
  experimental, 355, 356
  open door, 14
  planning, 150-53
    by community type, 151-53
    by scholastic ability, 152-53
Comenius, John Amos, 274
Commentary, 197

Committee on Education Beyond High School, 276
Conant, James, 274
Converse, John H., 172
Creativity, 188 ff.
Culturally deprived
  educational problem of, 8, 10, 11
  parents of, 10
Culture of defeat, 16, 19-25, 42
Curriculum
  change, college, 5
  strengthening, 29
  tracking, 14
  watering down of, 14
Cuyler, Thomas DeWitt, 172

D

Delancey School, 172
Dickens, Charles, 274
Disston, William, 180
Dixon, Fitz Eugene, 180
Drexel, George W. Childs, 170

E

Education
  college; see Colleges
  extension of
    college, 5
    high school, 5
    nursery school, 6
  history of, 26-27
  for mobility, 139-41, 142, 143; see also
    Social mobility
  quality, 34
  slum school, 9
Educational sociology, 2
Educational testing service, 31, 148
Eisenhower, Dwight, 276
Elementary school class
  achievement, 205, 206
  in relation to family and peer groups,
    206-10
  socialization and selection, 199, 210-14
  specialized teacher of, 283
  structure of, 202-4
  ungraded, 284
Elkins, William, 180
England
  differential birth rates, 135-36

England—*Cont.*
   industrialization, 132–34
   natural resources, 135
   productivity and income, 134–35
   social structure, 136–37
Episcopal Church, 170
Exeter, 178, 179

F

Fairleigh Dickinson University, 280
Fichte, Johann, 274
Fitzgerald, F. Scott, 178
Fortune Poll, 232
Frederick the Great, 277
Froebel, Friedrich, 274

G

Gallup Poll, 229
Garibaldi, Giuseppe, 274
Gates, Thomas S., III, 178
General Electric Company, 327
General Electric Program
   curriculum, 120–24
   trainees, 121–22
George Peabody College for Teachers, 276
Georgia Institute of Technology, 274
Germantown, Pa., 173
Germantown Friends School, 171
G.I. Bill of Rights, 329, 330
Girard Trust Company, 172
Gross, Calvin E., 280
Groton, 168, 178, 179

H

Handbook of Private Schools, 172
Hare, George Emlen, 172
Harris, Mark, 280
Harvard University, 54, 168, 175, 177, 178,
   179, 329
Haslam, Greville, 173
Haverford School, 171, 174
Herbart, Johann, 274
High school
   defining status, 47
   social structure of, 288
      teacher adaptation to, 296, 297
   socializing agency, 186–97
   as socializing agent, 48
   transformation of, 28
Hobart, John Henry, 172
Hopkinson, Francis, 172
Hughes, Emmet John, 274

I

Incentives
   academic, 343

Incentives—*Cont.*
   determinants of, 344–57
   intellectual, 343
   social, 343, 346
Instruction
   centralized, 40
   new modes, 9, 10, 29, 30, 35, 36, 38, 39
Intelligence tests, cultural bias, 20

J

Jayne, Horace Howard Furness, 172
Jefferson, Thomas, 167
Josephs, Devereux, 276

K

Kibbutz, 83
Kluckhohn, Florence, 168

L

Language, poverty of, 21–22
Lee, P. Blair, 180
Lewis, John Frederick, 172
Lippincott, Bertram, 172
Lippincott, Joseph Wharton, 178
Lish, Gordon, 280
Los Angeles *Times,* 195

M

McArthur, Charles, 168
McMurrin, Sterling M., 276
Madison, James, 177
Main Line, 171, 173, 174
Marriage
   and education, 6–7
   role change, 7
Marshall, Alfred, 287
Michelet, Jules, 274
Michigan State University, 337
Mitchell, S. Weir, 174
Morris, Effingham B., 172
Morris, Robert, 172
Motivational basis of opinion, 336, 337
Mount Desert, 174

N

National Council of Teachers of English,
   30
National Education Association, 30, 276,
   280, 282
National Opinion Research Center, 253
National Science Foundation, 29, 30, 282
Negroes
   children, 9, 14, 23, 24
   migrants, 14
   mothers
      and the American Dream, 112–13
      aspirations for children, 109
      education and occupation, 110

Negroes–*Cont.*
  mothers–*Cont.*
    lower class, 105–13
    marriage and parenthood of, 110, 111
    "revolution," 14
    scholarship, 23–25
    schools, 9
New York Teachers Association, 280
Nixon, Richard, 194, 195
Nonformal learning, 79–82
    family learning, 79–80; *see also* Sociali-
      zation
    mass media influence, 81–82
    peer group influence, 80–81
Nouveaux riches, 233
Nuclear family, 197

O

Organization
    formal structure of, 339
    informal structure of, 339–40

P

Parent-Teachers' Association, 276, 327
Parent-youth conflict, 44–45
Parochial education
    anti-Catholic movements, 56
    Catholic-Protestant relations, 75
    Evangelical Lutheran Church, 53, 55
    financial, 53
    France, 53–54
    German Lutheran, 55
    historical roots, 54–57
    pupils, number, 53
Parry, L. J., 231
Paul, J. Rodman, 172
Pemberton, Henry Rawle, 172
Penn, William, 171
Pennsylvania Gazette, 167
Pepper, George Wharton, 170
Pestalozzi, Johann, 274
Peter the Great, 277
Philadelphia Club, 170, 173
Poe, Edgar Allen, 180
Population change
    aging, 3–4
    birth rate, 3–4, 135, 136
    death rate, 3–4
    education, 4–5, 26, 28
    longevity, 3–5
    marriage rate, 6
    migration, 3–4
    sex ratio, 3–4
Potter, Alonzo, 172
President Kubitschek, 138
Princeton University, 175, 176, 177, 178,
    179

Problem defined, 333–35
Professional salaries
    and merit rating, 325–26
    power position of teachers, 321, 322, 323
    size of, 319–23
    of teachers, 319–28
Progressive teaching, 13, 42
Protestant Episcopal Academy, 171–74

R

Radcliffe College, 174
Rationality, defined, 333–34
Repplier, Agnes, 174
Rexroth, Kenneth, 280
Rittenhouse Club, 170, 173
Roberts, Isaac W., 180
Roles; *see* School *and* Socialization
Roman Catholic
    Bay City study, 60-62, 68, 70, 71, 72, 77
    community, 70–74
    contemporary attachment to Catholic
      leaders, 68–70
    Diocese of St. Augustine, Florida, 60–62
    doctrinal basis, 57–59
    effects on
      attachment to church, 67
      attachment to ethnic group, 67–68
      individual Catholics, 66
      religious behavior, 67
    elementary schools, 58
    parish, 57–59
    politics, 72–74
    public issues, 72–74
    pupils, number, 53
    secondary schools, 58–59
    social context, 59–66
    structure, 57–59
    success, 57
    Third Plenary Council, 55, 57, 58
Roosevelt, Franklin D., 179
Roosevelt, Theodore R., 176
Rosengarten, Adolph G., 178
Rosengarten, George D., 180
Rush, Benjamin, 172

S

Sargent, Porter, 172, 174
School
    community definition of, 271–72
    as female world, 270–71
    role
      concept of, 340, 341
      definition, 341, 342
      expectations, 341
      formal, 184
      informal, 185

School—*Cont.*
  secondary, differentiation and selection, 214–18
  status and authority structure, 260–63, 288 ff., 298, 299, 303–7
  superintendents, 256–57
  team teaching, 283
  ungraded, 284
  upper class rejection of, 187
School segregation, de facto, 9
Selective Service Qualification Test, 281
Sense-of-power scale, 241 ff.
Shippen, Edward, 168, 172
Slavery, 14–16, 23, 24
Slum school, 16–19, 41
Smith, Adam, 287
Social class
  and educational attainment, 145–54
    community setting, 147
    family relationships, 146
    rewards and punishment, 145–46
  lower class, 9, 14, 18, 47, 105, 126, 127, 156–59, 163–65
    value stretch, 105–7, 114, 269–70, 296
  middle class, 7, 16–18, 22, 47, 49, 57, 100, 127, 156–59, 196, 198, 269, 270, 296, 310–18, 330
  upper class, 18, 128, 158
Social mobility, 125–26
  Australia, 130
  Brazil, 130
  conditions for, 131–32
  contest, 220–35
  education and future, 137–43, 145, 148, 154
  England, 130
  group, 130–31
  individual, 130–31
  in relation to education, 143
  sponsored, 220–35
  United States of America, 130
Social problems
  aged, 44, 49–50
  defined, 8, 42
  youth, 44, 46, 52
Social Register, 169, 170, 173, 175, 176, 177, 180
Socialization, 79–83, 199
  of adolescents, 44–46
  biological potentialities, 84
  cognitive aspect, 88
  conditions of learning
    discrimination, 91–92
    frustration control, 94–96
    growth gradients, 95
    reinforcements, 92
    reward and punishment, 92–94
  identification, 103–4
  internalized objects, 86–89

Socialization—*Cont.*
  "looking-glass self," 90
  maturation, 85
  patterning of, 85
  plasticity of infant, 84–85
  roles, 90–91
  self, 89–90
    taking role of the other, 89–90
  social class; *see* Social class
  stages of, 96–105
    anal, 99
    latency, 101
    oedipal crisis, 101
    oral, 99
Sociology of education
  defined, 1
  history of, 2
Spender, Stephen, 280
Springside School, 174
St. Paul's School, 173, 178
Student culture
  in colleges, 346, 372
  consequences of, 384
  development of, 377, 378
  in medical school, 377 ff.
Students, classification of, 50–51
Superintendents; *see* School
Swarthmore College, 175, 176

T

Teacher
  authority of, 245, 258–63, 303–7
  career patterns of, 272, 280–82
  community status of, 252
  education, 26–27
  effectiveness, 37
  expectations, 310–18
    docility toward, 317, 318
  inadequacy of, 17, 30–31
  income, 32, 33
  master, 34
  mental health of, 285–86
  organizational status of, 252, 258–60
  and parents, 299–303
  and principal, 303–8
  problem of discipline, 159–63
  problem of moral acceptability, 163–66
  as a professional, 253–58, 263–67, 273
  recruitment, 284–87
  reeducation, 29
  role of, 288 ff.
    colleague relations, 307–8
    in the informal system, 294–95
    in relation to student organization, 295–96
    strain, 290–92
  selection, 31
  social distance, 254–55
  social origins of, 246–47

Teacher—*Cont.*
  social status of, 33, 263–67, 276–77
  social visibility of, 254–55
  training, 29
Thematic Apperception Test, 92, 169
Tocqueville, Alexis de, 195, 229
Trinity College, 173

U

United States of America
  differential birth rates, 135–36
  industrialization, 133–34
  natural resources, 135
  productivity and income, 134–35
  social structure, 136–37
United States Office of Education, 31
University of Bologna, 337
University College, London, 230
University of Paris, 237
University of Pennsylvania, 167, 173, 175, 176, 178

V

Van Rensselear, Alexander, 172
Vassar College, 274
Vick Chemical Company, 115
Vick School of Applied Merchandising, 115, 116, 117, 118

W

Wector, Dixon, 180
Weightman, William, 180
Who's Who, 168–70, 175, 176, 180
Widener, P. A. B., 180
William Penn Charter School, 171, 174
Willing, Thomas, 172
Wissahickon Inn, 171
Wister, L. Caspar, 180
Wolf, Elias, 173

Y

Yale University, 175–77, 179, 329
Youth culture, 44

This book has been set in 10 point Press Roman, leaded 2 points and 1 point. Part numbers and titles and article titles are in 24 point Univers Medium. Authors' names are in 12 or 10 point Univers Medium. The size of the type page is 27 by 45½ picas.

8-C